THE WILLIAM STALLINGS BOOKS ON COMPUTER AND DATA COMMUNICATIONS TECHNOLOGY

HANDBOOKS OF COMPUTER-COMMUNICATIONS STANDARDS

VOLUME 1
THE OPEN SYSTEMS INTERCONNECTION (OSI) MODEL AND OSI-RELATED STANDARDS

A description of the *master plan* for all computer-communications standards, the OSI model. The book also provides a detailed presentation of OSI-related standards at all 7 layers, including HDLC, X.25, ISO internet, ISO transport, ISO session, ISO presentation, Abstract Syntax One (ASN.1), and common application service elements (CASE).

VOLUME 2
LOCAL NETWORK STANDARDS

A detailed examination of all current local network standards, including logical link control (LLC, IEEE 802.2), CSMA/CD (IEEE 802.3), token bus (IEEE 802.4), token ring (IEEE 802.5), and fiber distributed data interface (FDDI, ANS X3T9.5).

VOLUME 3
DEPARTMENT OF DEFENSE (DOD) PROTOCOL STANDARDS

A description of the protocol standards that are mandated on all DOD computer procurements and are becoming increasingly popular on commercial local network prod including TCP, IP, FTP, SMTP, and TELNET.

All of these books provide a clear tu   f
the relevance and value of each st   s
within each standard, and an explanation of underlying technology.

2/11/93

DATE DUE

JUN 2 6 1995			
JUL 1 7 1995			
JUL 1 7 1995			
AUG 1 6 1995			
SEP 8 1995			
MAY 0 4 1996			

GAYLORD			PRINTED IN U.S.A.

ISDN

AN

INTRODUCTION

ISDN
AN
INTRODUCTION

WILLIAM STALLINGS

**MACMILLAN
PUBLISHING
COMPANY
NEW YORK**

**COLLIER
MACMILLAN
PUBLISHERS
LONDON**

Again, for my loving wife Tricia Antigone

Copyright © 1989, Macmillan Publishing Company, a division of Macmillan, Inc.

Printed in the United States of America

Macmillan Publishing Company
866 Third Avenue, New York, New York 10022

Collier Macmillan Canada, Inc.

Library of Congress Cataloging in Publication Data

Stallings, William.
    ISDN : an introduction / William Stallings.
      p.   cm.
    Bibliography: p.
    Includes index.
    ISBN 0-02-415471-7
    1. Integrated services digital networks.   I. Title.
TK5103.7.S73 1989
004.6--dc19   88-11083
                                                                        CIP

    Printing: 4 5 6 7 8   Year: 0 1 2 3 4 5 6 7

PREFACE

Perhaps the most important development in the computer-communications industry in the late 1980s and 1990s will be the evolution of the integrated services digital network (ISDN). The ISDN will have a dramatic effect on communications providers, component manufacturers, and both residential and business telecommunications users. Although the technology and standards for ISDN are still evolving, a clear picture of the architecture, design approaches, and services of ISDN is emerging.

OBJECTIVE

The objective of this book is to provide a comprehensive introduction to the underlying technology and user-visible architecture of ISDN. The book explores key topics related to ISDN in the following general categories:

- *Underlying technology:* The ISDN is based on the development of digital transmission and switching technologies and their use to construct an integrated digital network (IDN) for telecommunications. In addition, the technologies of packet-switching and common-channel signaling are essential ingredients of an IDN.
- *Architecture:* The architecture of the ISDN exploits the emerging application of digital technology to integrate

voice and data transmission and to provide structured interfaces and transmission services for the end user.
- *Standards:* A massive effort is underway to develop standards covering the broad spectrum of ISDN protocols, architecture, and services.
- *Services:* The ISDN supports a wide variety of current and new
digital services, including facsimile, Teletex, and videotex.

INTENDED AUDIENCE

This book is intended for a broad range of readers who will
benefit from an understanding of ISDN concepts. This includes students and professionals in the fields of data processing and data
communications, designers and implementers, and data communication and networking customers and managers. The book is intended to be self-contained. For the reader with little or no background in data communications, a number of basic topics are
covered in appendices.

PLAN OF THE TEXT

The book is organized in such a way that new material is seen to
fit into the context of the material already presented. The book divides into two major parts. Part I deals with the technology of the
integrated digital network (IDN), which is the essential foundation of
the integrated services digital network (ISDN). Part II is devoted to the
ISDN itself. The organization of the chapters is as follows:

1. *Introduction:* Introduces the concept of ISDN and discusses
   the evolution towards ISDN.
2. *Circuit switching:* Discusses circuit-switching mechanisms,
   network design, and common-channel signaling.
3. *Packet switching:* Examines the mechanisms of packet
   switched networking, including routing and congestion control. X.25 and fast packet switching are also examined.
4. *IDN technology:* Presents the technology of integrated digital networks, including digital subscriber loops. The role of
   signaling system number 7 (SS7) is also examined.
5. *ISDN overview:* Provides a general introduction to ISDN, plus a
   look at the structure of the ISDN standards.
6. *ISDN services:* presents the basic framework for specifying

services for ISDN. This is followed by a look at specific services (Teletex, facsimile, X.400) supported by ISDN.

7. *ISDN architecture:* looks at issues relating to the architecture of ISDN, including transmission structure, physical configuration, and the issues of addressing and interworking.

8. *ISDN protocols:* looks at the 3 layers of standards specifically designed for use in ISDN. The key protocols at each layer are examined. A portion of SS7 that is directly related to ISDN is also examined.

9. *Broadband ISDN:* Examines the latest development in ISDN technology and standards.

In addition, the book includes an extensive glossary, a list of frequently-used acronyms, and a bibliography. Each chapter includes problems and suggestions for further reading.

A final note: a considerable portion of Part II of this book is devoted to a set of standards for ISDN produced by CCITT. All ISDN development is being done with a view to the need for conformance to the CCITT standards. Thus, these standards are of central importance to any discussion of ISDN. These standards were initially published in 1984 and have been revised for the 1988 "second edition." This text reflects the 1988 edition of the standards.

RELATED MATERIALS

The author has produced other material that may be of interest to students and professionals. *Integrated Services Digital Networks, Second Edition* (1988, IEEE Computer Society Press, P.O. Box 80452, Worldway Postal Center, Los Angeles, CA 90080; telephone 800-272-6657) is a companion to this text. It contains reprints of many of the key references used herein.

A videotape course by the author on ISDN is available from the Instructional Television Department, College of Engineering, University of Maryland, College Park, MD 20742; telephone (301) 454-7451.

W.S.

CONTENTS

CHAPTER 1

INTRODUCTION

Ruth Jones was originally seen by Dr. Farnsworth at the Northern Virginia Hospital for an emergency ear trauma. She returned several times to his office at the hospital complex for follow-up. She is calling today to describe some new symptoms. Today, Dr. Farnsworth is at his suburban McLean office. The call that Mrs. Jones places to the hospital is automatically forwarded to Dr. Farnsworth's other office. The incoming call causes the phone of the physician's assistant in McLean to ring. At the same time, the name and phone number of the caller is displayed on a small screen that is part of the telephone. While the call is ringing, a message is automatically sent back to the hospital to search for any records associated with this call. A data base search reveals that the caller is a patient of Dr. Farnsworth. The medical record is transmitted to the McLean office, and the first page of that record is displayed on a terminal screen next to the phone by the time the receiver is picked up.

The technology for this type of service is available today. What is needed to make it available in a practical, affordable fashion is to integrate existing services and new technologies into a network that can handle telephone, data, and other services for residential and business users, both locally and around the world. This integration, with the tongue-twisting name of Integrated Services Digital Network (ISDN), is already being developed and will begin to appear by around 1990. It will truly be a supernetwork, providing universal, accessible, flexible telephone and information services.

This book is an introduction to ISDN. It will explore the technology, applications, and standards of ISDN. The technology underlying ISDN has been driven by market pressures to reduce the cost of voice and data telecommunications. This **technology** consists of the digital transmission and switching architecture being used to build a new all-digital telecommunications infrastructure. Although driven

1

by the need for low-cost voice and data transmission, this technology opens the way to a host of new information-related **applications.** Because a variety of providers will be involved in supplying both the underlying transmission and switching facilities as well as the applications, universal and flexible access can only be achieved with the imposition of **standards.** In this chapter, we give an overview of ISDN and some of the key factors driving the nature and pace of ISDN evolution. The remainder of the book explores these topics in depth.

1-1   THE ARRIVAL OF ISDN

Rapid advances in computer and communication technologies have resulted in the increasing merger of these two fields. The lines have blurred among computing, switching, and digital transmission equipment, and the same digital techniques are being used for data, voice, and image transmission. Merging and evolving technologies, coupled with increasing demands for efficient and timely collection, processing, and dissemination of information, are leading to the development of integrated systems that transmit and process all types of data. The ultimate goal of this evolution is something its proponents — some of the most powerful forces in the computing and telecommunications industries — call the integrated services digital network (ISDN).

The ISDN will be a worldwide public telecommunications network that will deliver a wide variety of services. The ISDN will be defined by the standardization of user interfaces, and will be implemented as a set of digital switches and paths supporting a broad range of traffic types and providing value-added processing services. In practice, there will be multiple networks, implemented within national boundaries, but from the user's point of view there will be a single, uniformly accessible worldwide network.

The impact of ISDN on both users and vendors will be profound. To control ISDN evolution and impact, a massive effort at standardization is underway. Although ISDN standards are still evolving, both the technology and the emerging implementation strategy are well understood.

There are two key aspects to ISDN: universal access and user services. By standardizing the interfaces to ISDN, all ISDN-compatible equipment (e.g., telephones, computer terminals, personal computers) will be able to attach to the network anywhere in the world and connect to any other attached system. This can lead to extraordinary flexibility. For example, telephone numbers could be assigned in the same fashion as U.S. social security numbers, good for a lifetime. No matter where you lived, or how often you moved, dialing the number permanently assigned to you would always ring your telephone. Or, it would be possible to assign names that connect to the nearest user of that name. Wherever you were, you could reach, say, the nearest Holiday Inn by tapping the telephone buttons marked H-O-L-I-D-A-Y-I-N-N.

The other aspect of ISDN is services. We have already mentioned one example, the medical record retrieval associated with a patient. As another example, consider the banking industry. Bank-by-phone services will depend on automatic identification of the calling party. Transaction privacy and security must be guaranteed. Other features that ISDN will support are increased and increasingly easy-to-use electronic funds transfer facilities and rapid check clearing.

A sample of the trends that are driving ISDN and that will be accelerated by ISDN:

- *Computers are joining together instead of standing alone.* An estimated 30 percent of today's personal computers have communications capability, and the percentage is rising. While yesterday's corporate computer was a stand-alone device, businesses today rely on a mix of small, medium, and large computers that can share resources (e.g., printers), share data, and exchange messages. Our analytical tools have sprouted wires; more and better wires are coming, and the wires will extend everywhere.

- *Cellular radio is making communications mobile.* Automobiles, taxis, and boats are becoming workstations. People can not only talk via cellular radio phones; they can also transmit data by linking up their portable computers. Look for the development of cellular phone/computer combinations. In time, automobiles will provide communication/computer systems as options. Any vehicle, then, will be a unit that can link up to the global information network.

- *Computers for personal use will be ubiquitous.* This will be especially so for students (from elementary school on up) and "knowledge workers," who deal primarily with paper — documents, reports, numbers. Soon many office workers will have at least one workstation at the office and one at home. In fact, many people already have such work stations. Furthermore, most people will own a powerful portable and possibly a wearable model — a very personal computer (VPC). The hotels you stay at in the future may have personal computers in their rooms as amenities; some hotels already do. Computing power will be at every hand; and, most important, each computer will tap into the network.

- *The volume and richness of data are increasing dramatically.* The first-generation personal computers have given way to the latest IBM PSs and MAC-IIs with color and high-quality graphics. New applications in the office environment are being developed which require much higher networking capacity, and desktop image processors will soon increase network data flow by an unprecedented rate. Examples of these applications include digital fax machines, document image processors, and graphics programs on personal computers. Resolutions as high as 400×400 per page are typical for these applications. Even with compression techniques, this will generate a tremendous data communications load. Table 1-1 compares the load generated by image processing and some other office applications. In addition, optical disks are beginning to reach technical maturity and are being developed toward realistic desktop capacities exceeding 1 Gbyte.

- *Voice recognition and natural language processing technology will increase the intelligence of systems and networks.* These have been two of the most difficult applications to develop, but are now gradually emerging from artificial-intelligence laboratories. Voice recognition is the ability to recognize spoken words. Natural language processing is the ability to extract the meaning of words and sentences. As these two applications develop, access to information banks and data bases will becoming increasingly easier and therefore will create a greater demand. A user will be able to perform a transaction or access information with simple spoken or keyed commands. Interfacing with the worldwide network will be like talking with a very knowledgeable telephone operator, librarian, and universal expert rolled into one.

- *Government use of computer systems will become more efficient.* The government is the most prodigious producer and user of information in our society. ISDN will improve and disperse access and help to remove incompatibilities between different systems so that more can be done with less effort.

- *National and global business activities will become easier to promote.* The brokerage business has become almost a computer network in itself, depending upon instant transmission of information and automated buy-sell orders. Banking today relies upon more than automatic tellers and computerized accounting; money itself is becoming akin to information as fund transfers take place over growing data networks. And banks are beginning to sell online information services as adjuncts to electronic banking. Companies of all sizes are coming to depend upon telecommunications for their daily business activities. Remote data entry, electronic mail, facsimile transmission, and decision support systems are just some of the operations that rely upon communications. Multinational corporations and joint ventures between American and

TABLE 1-1 NETWORK LOAD COMPONENT COMPARISON

Traffic Type	Size in Bits
Compressed Page Image (400 × 400)	600,000
Compressed Page Image (200 × 200)	250,000
Word-processing page	20,000
Typical memo	3,500
Data Processing Transaction	500

Source: [BEVA86]

foreign firms depend upon quick interchange of information. Communication networks are absolutely essential for the continued globalization of trade and industry.

- *Office buildings are being wired for intelligence.* The so-called "smart building" is beginning to appear. Such a building contains a network for voice, data, environmental control (heat, humidity, air conditioning), and security (burglar, fire), and closed-circuit TV. Many of these services generate out-of-building transmission requirements.

- *Person-to-person interaction will increase.* Business is responding to the need for employees to interact and to avoid "telephone tag" with electronic mail, voice mail, file transfer, document exchange, and video teleconferencing facilities. All of these generate large data communications requirements.

- *The fiber revolution will bring enormous capacity that will generate its own demand.* In developed countries, fiber is rapidly replacing microwave and coaxial cable transmission paths. Fiber, together with satellite, is appearing more gradually elsewhere. The resulting quantum jump in capacity has permitted the planning and deployment of new applications on public and private networks.

These trends, and others, are part of the evolution to ISDN. In this book, we will relate these trends and the requirements they generate to the solution that ISDN represents.

1-2   THE COMPUTER – COMMUNICATIONS REVOLUTION

Ours has been called the postindustrial era. By that is meant that industrialization, which was the dominating factor and engine of change for over a century, no longer fulfills that role. To those societies that have experienced the industrial revolution, the social and economic changes have been profound. The postindustrial era is producing even greater and more rapid changes. Many trends are visible as threads making up the rope that is dragging mankind into a life and life-style dictated not by politicians and economists, but by the technologists. All of these threads, at bottom, depend on two major technologies: computers and communications.

Consider one example: biotechnology. One of the youngest technologies, biotechnology has already brought with it a number of firms in the business of producing commercially-available products and some of the hottest action in the stock market in the 1980s. Biotechnology firms are doing research on substances that can combat cancer, eat oil spills, and solve many other problems facing society. It has been repeatedly alleged that biotechnology is also being applied in the Soviet Union to the development of biological weapons of immense potency. All of the goods, and ills, of this technology are impossible without sophisticated use of computers. Computers are used to monitor and control the fabrication of new biological entities, and to model the process of creating new substances so that the most likely direction of research can be followed. Extremely fast and powerful computer systems are needed for this purpose.

Another example is what is known as factory automation. General Motors, in particular, is convinced that the only way to compete with Japanese automakers is to drastically reduce the labor cost of producing cars. To do this, the factory environment must increasingly include microcomputers, programmable controllers, and robots. Computer technology must replace human labor on the assembly line. For the automated factory to work, sophisticated computer-controlled devices are required. Equally important, all of these devices must be interconnected with a local area network (LAN). The LAN ties together all of the equipment in the factory so that control signals can be sent to the automated devices on the assembly line, and data and alarm signals can be sent by these devices to computers that act in the role of foreman and supervisor.

As a final example, consider office automation, which can be defined as the incorporation of appropriate technology in the office to help people manage information. The key motivation for the move to office automation is, again, productivity. As the percentage of white-collar workers has increased, the information and paperwork volume has grown. In most installations, secretarial and other support functions are heavily labor intensive. Increased labor costs combined with low productivity and increasing work load have caused employers to seek effective ways of increasing their rather low capital investment in office-related work. At the same time principals (managers, skilled information workers) are faced with their own productivity bind. Work needs to be done faster with less wait time and less waste time between segments of a job. This requires better access to information and better communication and coordination with others. As in the factory environment, the solution is a collection of computer-based equipment interconnected with a LAN.

It has become commonplace to talk about the dramatic pace of change in these two technologies, computers and communications. Rapid technological change has been characteristic of these two areas since the 1960s. What is new is that there has been a merger of these two technologies. This merger has been called the computer–communications revolution. It has had a profound impact on the providing industries, and on the users—businesses and individuals. That merger, or revolution, was substantially accomplished by the late 1970s and early 1980s. We are now on the threshold of the aftermath and logical conclusion of that revolution: ISDN.

1-3   FROM COMMUNICATIONS TO COMPUTERS

The communications facilities that provide voice, data, and video transmission services are increasingly relying on digital technology and computerized systems. The two driving forces here are the changing economics and regulatory focus of telephone networks and the increasing demand for terminal user services.

The Evolving Telephone Network

The U.S. public telephone network, once the almost-exclusive property of AT&T, and now fragmented among a number of companies, was originally an analog network. It is now in the slow process of evolving to what is being referred to as the integrated digital network (IDN), which is the subject of Part I of this book.

Increasingly, the choice of network designers is to use digital technology for transmission and switching. Despite its massive investment in analog equipment, AT&T is gradually converting to an all-digital network. Other long-distance transmission providers, such as MCI, are doing the same. The major reasons for this trend:

- *Component cost:* While the cost of analog components has remained fairly stable, the cost of digital components continues to drop. The use of large-scale integration (LSI) and very-large-scale integration (VLSI) decreases not only the size, but also the cost of virtually all equipment used to process digital signals.
- *Line sharing:* Over long distance, the signals from many telephone calls will share common transmission paths by means of multiplexing. Time–division multiplexing, using digital techniques, is more efficient than the analog-based frequency–division multiplexing. Thus, the voice input from the telephone is converted to digital for the long-distance links.
- *Network control:* Control signals that monitor the status and control the operation of networks are inherently digital. They can be more easily incorporated into an all-digital network.

Thus, more and more, digital technology is being applied to the telephone network. The techniques used are the same as those used in computer systems. So, increasingly, the major components of the telephone network are either computers themselves or computer-controlled.

Teleprocessing and Telematics

Historically, and still today, telephone traffic has been the major reason for, and the major user of, long-distance communications facilities. Over the past 25 years, however, there has been a growing use of these facilities to transmit digital data. By far, the major component of this digital data requirement has been for communication between a user at a terminal and a computer remote from that user. The communications function that provides this remote terminal access is known as teleprocessing. More recently, additional services built on the basic teleprocessing function, known as telematics, have appeared.

To understand these trends, we need to say something about the way in which computer usage has evolved (see [STAL87a] for a lengthier discussion). In the 1950s, the typical computer was large and expensive. It was a limited resource that needed to be used efficiently. For this purpose, operating systems were developed. The original operating systems were batch, which controlled the execution of a sequence of user programs, called jobs. A user could submit a job, and that job would be queued up waiting for the use of the computer. As soon as one job finished, the operating system would fetch the next job in line for execution.

As computers became more powerful and the demand for their use grew, batch operating systems became obsolete. The problem was that if only one program is executing, many of the system's resources are idle at any given time. For example, while data to be processed are being read in, those portions of the system that can perform arithmetic and logical functions are unused. To overcome this inefficiency, the time-sharing operating system was developed. With time-sharing, many jobs can be active at any one time. The operating system orchestrates matters so that various resources are applied to particular jobs at any given time. And, whereas the user of a batch-oriented system would typically submit a job to a computer operator and come back some time later for the results, the time-sharing user interacts directly with the operating system from a terminal.

The first time-sharing users used terminals that were in close proximity to the computer. But soon the demand for remote terminal access, known as **teleprocessing**, developed. A large organization (e.g., a bank or an insurance company) might have a central data processing facility but potential users in a number of satellite offices. Time-sharing services sprang up. Such a service "rented time" on its computer to users who could not afford their own system. More recently, transaction-processing systems have appeared. Point-of-sale systems, airline reservation systems, and so forth involve many terminal users who perform transactions that are recorded in a data base on a remote computer.

Remote terminal access can be and is handled by the public telephone network. The digital data are converted to analog signals and transmitted just as the voice signals in an ordinary telephone call. But this is inefficient. When a call is placed, resources within the network are dedicated to setting up and maintaining the call. In effect, a circuit through the network is dedicated for the duration. Now, with a telephone call, generally one party or the other is talking most of the time, and good use is made of the circuit. But with a terminal-to-computer connection, much of the time the circuit is idle, when neither side is transmitting.

To improve efficiency, packet switching was developed. Terminal and computer data are sent out in small blocks, known as packets. These packets are routed through the network using paths and resources that are shared among a number of users sending packets. Thus the network must know how to handle and process packets—another example of the computerization of communications.

The demand for data communications and the use of packet switching continue to grow. In addition to the more traditional teleprocessing services, new **telematic** services are appearing. Telematic facilities provide a user at a terminal with access to a specific application or data base. An example is a catalog-ordering service. The user is connected to the service and may select various items for viewing. Each catalog item is described on the user's terminal screen, and the user may place an order.

U.S. Regulatory Implications

Thus we see the increasing incorporation of computer technology into the public telecommunications networks, due to two driving forces. First, it has become more economical to use digital transmission and switching techniques in the network, and these require the use of computer technology. Second, there is an increased use of data communications services (teleprocessing and telematics), and the provision of these services by communication providers blurs the distinction between computer and communication technologies. This incorporation of computer technology into communications is reflected clearly by the history of communications regulation in the United States, the highlights of which are now recounted.

With the Communications Act of 1934, Congress established universal and affordable telephone service as a national goal. The Federal Communications Commission (FCC) was created to regulate and promote telecommunications. The FCC had primary responsibility for regulating the rates and conditions of interstate telephone service. Soon after its formation, the FCC began an investigation of the Bell Telephone System which resulted in the development of a major antitrust suit against AT&T by the Department of Justice. Delayed by World War II, the suit was filed in 1949 and was settled by the **1956 Consent Decree.** For the present discussion, the key element of the Consent Decree was that Bell confine its activities to providing telecommunications services under regulation and refrain from providing commercial data-processing services.

The Consent Decree proved inadequate in the face of advances in data communications and data processing. In the late 1960s, there was an increasing use of centralized mainframe computers with distributed terminals and increasing use of the telecommunications network for data transmission. This prompted the FCC to begin the first of three "computer inquiries": The first, known as **Computer Inquiry I,** asked for public and industry comments on the impact of data processing on communications. Two key issues:

1. The nature and extent of FCC regulation that should be applied along the continuum from pure data processing to pure data communications.
2. Whether and, if so, under what circumstances and subject to what conditions and safeguards should common carriers be allowed to provide data processing services.

The inquiry, completed in 1971, distinguished between telecommunications and data processing service, with the former to be regulated and the latter unregulated and open to competition. Hybrid services were to be dealt with on an ad hoc basis.

The 1971 definitions also proved to be inadequate as technology marched on. With the increased use of digital transmission and switching technology, and the development of packet switching, the distinctions between data processing and communications blurred. Data processing became increasingly distributed, with the attendant reliance on data communications and networks. Computer hardware and software were increasingly incorporated into telephone network equipment and private branch exchanges (PBXs). The FCC tried again in 1980 with the final report of **Computer Inquiry II.** The decision distinguished between basic and enhanced services. Basic services were the offering of transmission capacity for the transport of data. Enhanced services were defined as:

> . . . services offered over common carrier facilities used in interstate communications, which employ computer processing applications that act on format, content, code, protocol or similar aspects of the subscriber's transmitted information; provide the subscriber additional, different, or restructured information; or involve subscriber interaction with stored information.

Again, the basic services were to be subject to regulation, while enhanced services were to be deregulated. Computer Inquiry II also specified that basic services would be provided to enhanced service providers with a fair rate structure. In addition, the Bell System was required to set up a separate corporate entity to offer enhanced services and customer premises equipment so that cross subsidization would be avoided.

A final noteworthy event is **Computer Inquiry III,** the latest chapter in the FCC's 20-year struggle to deal with the increasing integration of computers and transmission systems in telecommunications. The inquiry was begun in 1985 and a first Report and Order was issued in 1986. The most important part of the report is the decision to rest the future regulation of integrated telecommunication and information networks upon a new mandate for an **Open Network Architecture (ONA)** for equal access to basic telecommunication services:

> We consider Open Network Architecture to be the overall design of a carrier's basic network facilities and services to permit all users, including the enhanced service operations of the carrier and its competitors, to interconnect to specific basic network functions and interfaces on an unbundled and "equal access" basis. A carrier providing enhanced services through Open Network Architecture must unbundle key components of its basic service and offer them to the public under tarriff, regardless of whether its enhanced services utilize the unbundled components. These components, such as trunking interconnections, may utilize subcomponents that themselves are offered on an unbundled basis, such as separate channel signaling and called or calling signal identification. Such unbundling will ensure that competitors for the carrier's enhanced services operations can develop enhanced services that utilize the carrier's network on an economical basis.

The commission has so far not described in any significant detail what is meant by open network architecture. Indeed, with the increasing software component of telecommunication networks, which makes them increasingly virtual and "soft" and the evolution toward ISDN, any technical definition is working against a moving target. What can be said is that the concept of ONA is in the spirit of both deregulation and reliance on standardized interfaces, and that it reflects the essential unity of data communications and computing.

1-4   FROM COMPUTERS TO COMMUNICATIONS

While communications facilities have increasingly made use of computer technology, the opposite is also true. The hardware and software within a computer specifically devoted to the communications function have grown in size and importance. The reason for this is that, increasingly, data processing facilities are being implemented as a collection of cooperating computers rather than a single large computer. This is known as distributed processing, since the processing function is distributed among a number of computers. To follow what has happened, we need to look at three aspects:

- the economic forces that have made distributed processing possible;
- the potential benefits of distributed processing that have encouraged its development;
- the implications in terms of the communications function.

Economic Forces and Potential Benefits

Two trends have combined to change the economic equation for distributed processing: the dramatic and continuing decrease in computer hardware costs, accompanied by an increase in computer hardware capability.

Today's microprocessors have speeds, instruction sets, and memory capacities comparable to those of minicomputers and even mainframes of just a few years ago. In general terms, this phenomenon is illustrated in Figure 1-1. By almost any

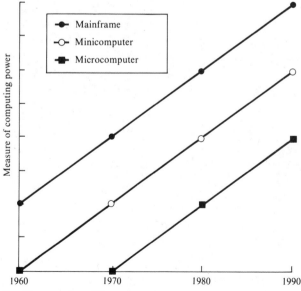

FIGURE 1-1   Computer Classes

measure of computer power, each class has grown in power over time. Going up the chart diagonally, one sees that a class of computers becomes more powerful as time goes on. Going across the chart horizontally, one sees that, over time, the same computing power can be provided by smaller, cheaper computers. This trend has spawned a number of changes in the way information is collected, processed, and used in organizations. There is an increasing use of small, single-function systems, such as word processors and small business computers, and of general-purpose microcomputers, such as personal computers and Unix workstations. These small, dispersed systems are more accessible to the user, more responsive, and easier to use than large central time-sharing systems. This explosion of small systems is shown in Figures 1-2 and 1-3. Note especially that, while large and medium-size systems continue to represent the majority of shipments in terms of installed value, the sheer number of microcomputers is overwhelming.

As the number of systems increases, there is likely to be a desire to interconnect these systems for a variety of reasons, including:

- sharing expensive resources, and
- exchanging data between systems.

Sharing expensive resources, such as bulk storage and laser printers, is an important measure of cost containment. Although the cost of data processing hardware has dropped, the cost of such essential electromechanical equipment remains

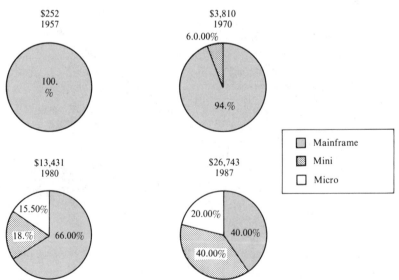

FIGURE 1-2 U.S. Consumption of Micros, Minis, and Mainframes (value in millions of 1986 dollars) (HODG87)

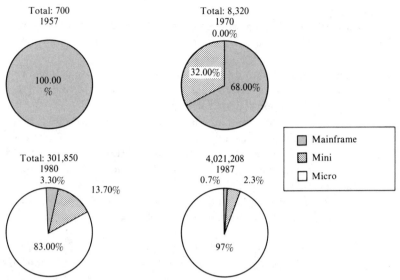

FIGURE 1-3 U.S. Shipments of Micros, Minis, and Mainframes (HODG87)

high. Even in the case of data that can be uniquely associated with a small system, economies of scale encourage the storage of those data on some sort of centralized server system. The cost per bit for storage on a microcomputer's floppy disk is orders of magnitude higher than that for a large disk or tape.

The ability to exchange data is an equally compelling reason for interconnection. Individual users of computer systems do not work in isolation and will want to retain some of the benefits provided by a central system, including the ability to exchange messages with other users, and the ability to access data and programs from several sources in the preparation of a document or the analysis of data.

In addition to these benefits, several others are worth mentioning. A distributed system can be more reliable, more available to the user, and more able to survive failures. The loss of any one component should have minimal impact, and key components can be made redundant so that other systems can quickly take up the load after a failure. Finally, a distributed system provides the potential to connect devices from multiple vendors, which gives the customer greater flexibility and bargaining power.

The Computer's Communication Function

Distributed processing relies upon a communications facility for interconnecting the computers that make up the distributed processing system. But more is involved. In order to achieve cooperative action, the computers themselves must incorporate functions traditionally thought of as communications functions.

Consider, for example, the transfer of a file between two computers. There must be a data path between the two computers, either directly or via a communication network. In addition, a number of functions must be provided, such as:

1. The source system must either activate the direct data communication path, or inform the communication network of the identity of the desired destination system.
2. The source system must ascertain that the destination system is prepared to receive data.
3. The file transfer application in the source system must ascertain that the file management program in the destination system is prepared to accept and store the file.
4. If the file formats used on the two systems are incompatible, one or the other system must perform a format translation function.

It is clear that there must be a high degree of cooperation between the two computer systems. The exchange of information between computers for the purpose of cooperative action is generally referred to as computer communications. Similarly, when two or more computers are interconnected via a communication network, the set of computers is referred to as a computer network. Since a similar level of cooperation is required between a user at a terminal and a computer, these terms are often used when some of the communicating entities are terminals.

These functions, which deal with control and cooperation, have been developed for use within the telephone network, and are now finding application in the computers that make up a distributed processing system. Thus, just as the communications providers are increasingly using computer technology, the opposite is also occurring.

1-5 OUTLINE OF THE BOOK

This chapter, of course, serves as an introduction to the entire book. A brief synopsis of the remaining chapters follows.

Circuit Switching

The first part of the book, after the introductory chapter, deals with the concept of the integrated digital network (IDN). The key technology of today's telecommunications, and the dominant technology of the evolving IDN, is circuit switching. Chapter 2 looks at the principles of circuit switching. In the digital realm, circuit switching is based on the use of time-division techniques, and these are examined. The chapter then looks at the way in which wide-area circuit-switched networks are constructed, examining multiplexing, routing, and signaling.

Packet Switching

The other key technology in wide-area networking is packet switching. In Chapter 3, the operational principles of packet switching are examined. The key technical issues of routing and congestion control are also discussed. The common standard for interfacing to packet-switched networks, X.25, is also examined. Finally, the new technology of fast packet switching, which is expected to play an important role in ISDN, is introduced.

Integrated Digital Networks

The evolution of the existing telecommunication networks, specialized carrier facilities, and value-added data communication networks to an ISDN is based on two technological developments: digital transmission and digital switching. One outcome of the migration to digital techniques is that it allows the functions of transmission and switching to be integrated in a way that reduces cost, enhances reliability, and provides a base for ISDN. This integration of transmission and switching is referred to as an integrated digital network (IDN). Chapter 4 examines the key technologies and features of the IDN, including the use of Signaling System Number 7 for common channel signaling, thus setting the stage for the discussion in Part II.

ISDN Overview

With many of the technical underpinnings dealt with in Part I, Part II turns to a discussion of ISDN. Chapter 5 serves as an overview. The relationship between IDN and ISDN is examined, and key issues, such as standards, applications, ISDN-specific technology, and status are introduced.

ISDN Services

The reason for the existence of ISDN is the set of services that it will provide. These services define the requirements for ISDN. In Chapter 6, we look first at the general specification of services found in the ISDN standards. In these standards, services are defined in terms of a set of attributes that can take on a range of values. The chapter then examines three services that will be used extensively over ISDN: teletex, facsimile, and X.400 electronic mail.

ISDN Architecture

Chapter 7 describes the architecture of ISDN. ISDN includes a small set of standardized interfaces for users that support a wide variety of services. These services are available through a transmission structure that provides various data rates over a multiplexed line. Two related issues are the addressing of subscribers over

ISDN and the need for interworking between ISDNs and between an ISDN and a non-ISDN network.

ISDN Protocols

CCITT has developed standards for protocols to be used in accessing ISDN. These protocols include a specification of the physical layer of the interface from subscriber to network, a data link control protocol known as LAP-D, and a call control protocol. In addition, standards have been developed for the common-channel signaling facility that is used internal to ISDN. Chapter 8 provides a description of each of these protocols.

Broadband ISDN

Although the original version of ISDN, defined in a preliminary way in 1984 and more fully in 1988, is still in the early stages of implementation, attention in the standards community is already beginning to shift to a "second-generation" ISDN, known as broadband ISDN. A broadband ISDN will have significantly greater capacity than the current "narrowband" ISDN. Chapter 9 examines some of the key technical developments that are driving the broadband ISDN effort.

Flow Control, Error Detection, and Error Control

A number of the protocols discussed in this book make use of some basic techniques for flow control, error detection, and error control. These include X.25 level 3, LAP-B, the Signaling Link layer of Signaling System Number 7, and LAP-D. For the reader unfamiliar with these widely-used techniques, Appendix A provides a brief description.

The OSI Model

Throughout this book, repeated reference is made to the open systems interconnection (OSI) model, and the structure of ISDN protocols is often compared to this model. The OSI model is of fundamental importance in the study of data and computer communications. It provides an architecture within which protocol standards can be developed. Furthermore, because of its universal acceptance, it provides a terminology and frame of reference that are commonly used in networking discourses. For the reader unfamiliar with this model, Appendix B provides a brief description.

PART I

INTEGRATED DIGITAL NETWORKS

The evolution of existing public tele communications networks, specialized carrier facilities, and value-added telecommunication networks to an ISDN is based on the development and integration of digital transmission and switching technologies. The integration of these technologies has been termed the **integrated digital network** (IDN). The term integrated in IDN has been used to refer to:

- The integration of transmission and switching equipment;
- The integration of voice and data communications;
- The integration of circuit-switching and packet-switching facilities.

The IDN is the foundation and prerequisite for ISDN. Accordingly, the first part of this book is devoted to the study of IDN. The two major technologies underlying the development of IDN, circuit switching and packet switching, are examined in separate chapters. Integrated digital networks are evolving from today's circuit-switching networks, and this technology is examined in Chapter 2. The chapter examines the basic mechanism used in digital circuit switches, time-division switching. The chapter also looks at a number of issues related to the operation and control of circuit-switching networks, including multiplexing strategies, routing, and control signaling. Then, packet switching is examined in Chapter 3. Although the increasing availability of digital circuit-switched networks in some sense offers competition to packet-switched networks, the latter will continue to play a key role in both IDN and ISDN. The technology and operation of such networks is examined, together with the standard interface to such networks, X.25.

Finally, Chapter 4 looks at other aspects of IDN beyond the basic technologies of circuit switching and packet switching. Following an overview of the IDN concept, the essential issue of bringing digital service to the end subscriber is examined. Next, a key standard in the implementation and operation of IDN, Signaling System Number 7, is described. We will see that SS7 embodies the integration of circuit-switching and packet-switching technologies. Finally, software defined networks, which may be viewed as a precursor to ISDN, are introduced.

CHAPTER 2
CIRCUIT SWITCHING

2-1 OVERVIEW

Circuit switching is the dominant technology for both voice and data communications today, and will remain so into the ISDN era. Communication via circuit switching implies that there is a dedicated communication path between two stations. That path is a connected sequence of links between network nodes. On each physical link, a channel is dedicated to the connection. Communication via circuit switching involves three phases, which can be explained with reference to Figure 2-1.

1. Circuit establishment. Before any signals can be transmitted, an end-to-end (station-to-station) circuit must be established. For example, station A sends a request to node 4 requesting a connection to station E. Typically, the link from A to 4 is a dedicated line, so that part of the connection already exists. Node 4 must find the next leg in a route leading to node 6. Based on routing information and measures of availability and perhaps cost, node 4 selects the link to node 5, allocates a free channel (using frequency-division multiplexing, FDM, or time-division multiplexing, TDM) on that link and sends a message requesting connection to E. So far, a dedicated path has been established from A through 4 to 5. Since a number of stations may attach to 4, it must be able to establish internal paths from multiple stations to multiple nodes. How this is done is the main topic of this chapter. The remainder of the process proceeds similarly. Node 5 dedicates a channel to node 6 and internally ties that channel to the channel from

19

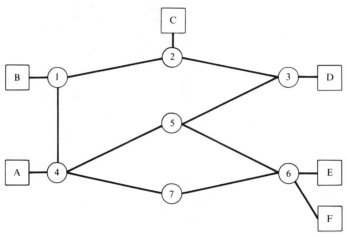

FIGURE 2-1 Generic Switching Network

    node 4. Node 6 completes the connection to E. In completing the connection, a test is made to determine if E is busy or is prepared to accept the connection.

2. Signal transfer. Signals can now be transmitted from A through the network to E. The transmitted signals may be analog voice, digitized voice, or binary data, depending on the nature of the network. As the carriers evolve to fully integrated digital networks, the use of digital (binary) transmission for both voice and data is becoming the dominant method. The path is: A-4 link, internal switching through 4, 4-5 channel, internal switching through 5, 5-6 channel, internal switching through 6, 6-E link. Generally, the connection is full duplex, and data may be transmitted in both directions simultaneously.

3. Circuit disconnect. After some period of data transfer, the connection is terminated, usually by the action of one of the two stations. Signals must be propagated to nodes 4, 5, and 6 to deallocate the dedicated resources.

    Note that the connection path is established before data transmission begins. Thus channel capacity must be reserved between each pair of nodes in the path and each node must have available internal switching capacity to handle the requested connection. The switches must have the intelligence to make these allocations and to devise a route through the network.

    Circuit switching can be rather inefficient. Channel capacity is dedicated for the duration of a connection, even if no data are being transferred. For a voice connection, utilization may be rather high, but it still does not approach 100 percent. For a terminal-to-computer connection, the capacity may be idle during most of the time of the connection. In terms of performance, there is a delay prior to data transfer for call establishment. However, once the circuit is established, the network is effectively transparent to the users. Data are transmitted at a fixed data rate with no delay other than the propagation delay through the transmission links. The delay at each node is negligible.

Some of the key characteristics of circuit switching are summarized in Box 2-1. In terms of applications, circuit switching was developed to handle voice traffic but is now also used for data traffic. The best-known example of a circuit-switching network is the public telephone network. This is actually a collection of national networks interconnected to form the international service. Although originally designed and implemented to service analog telephone subscribers, it handles substantial data traffic via modem, and is gradually being converted to a digital network. Within the United States, the network is primarily provided by AT&T and the Bell Operating Companies (BOCs) that split off from AT&T in 1984. Another well-known application of circuit switching is the private branch exchange (PBX), used to interconnect telephones within a building or office. Circuit switching is also used in private networks. Typically, such a network is set up by a corporation or other large organization to interconnect its various sites. Such a network usually consists of PBX systems at each site interconnected by dedicated, leased lines obtained from one of the carriers, such as AT&T. A final common example of the application of circuit switching is the data switch. The data switch is similar to the PBX, but is designed to interconnect digital data processing devices, such as terminals and computers. The more recent generations of the PBX, known as digital PBXs, are able to easily handle both voice and data attachments.

Circuit-switching technology has been driven by those applications that handle voice traffic. This is reflected in the list of key requirements listed in Box 2-1. Voice signals must be transmitted with virtually no delay and certainly with no variation in delay. A constant signal transmission rate must be maintained since transmission and reception occur at the same signal rate. These requirements are necessary to allow normal human conversation. Further, the quality of the received signal must be sufficiently high to provide, at a minimum, intelligibility. The last requirement, on blocking probability, refers to the capacity of a switch and is defined below.

Circuit switching achieved its widespread, dominant position because it is well-suited to the analog transmission of voice signals. In today's digital world, its inefficiencies are more apparent. However, despite the inefficiency, circuit switching is and will remain an attractive choice for both local area and wide area networking. One of its key strengths is that it is transparent. Once a circuit is established, it appears like a direct connection to the two attached stations; no special networking logic is needed at the station. In addition, circuit switching avoids the complex routing, flow control, and error control requirements that we will see for packet-switched networks.

Circuit switching provides a transparent, relatively inexpensive, and highly reliable form of transmission service. It is the basis on which ISDN services will be built.

BOX 2-1

CIRCUIT SWITCHING

APPLICATIONS

Voice

Public Telephone Network

Provide interconnection for two-way voice signal exchange between attached telephones. Calls can be placed between any two subscribers on a national and international basis. This network is evolving to handle an increasing amount of data traffic.

Private Branch Exchange (PBX)

Provide a telephone exchange capability within a single building or cluster of buildings. Calls can be placed between any two subscribers within the local site; interconnection is also provided to public or private wide-area circuit-switched networks.

Private Wide-Area Network

Provide interconnection among a number of sites. Generally used to interconnect PBXs that are part of the same organization.

Data

Data Switch

Provide for the interconnection of terminals and computers within a local site.

REQUIREMENTS

1. Establish, maintain, and terminate call on subscriber request.
2. Provide transparent, full-duplex signal transmission.
3. Limit delay to that acceptable for voice connection (≤ 0.5 s).
4. Provide quality adequate for voice connection.
5. Limit blocking probability.

TECHNOLOGY

Switching Techniques

Space-division
Time-division
TDM Bus

Time-slot Interchange (TSI)
Time-multiplexed switching (TMS)

Transmission

Multiplexed carrier
Routing algorithm
Control signals

In the remainder of this chapter, we examine the basic technology of circuit-switching. As we shall see, any treatment of the technology and architecture of circuit-switched networks must of necessity focus on the internal operation of a single switch. This is in contrast to packet switching, discussed in the next chapter, which is best explained by the collective behavior of the set of switches that make up the network.

2-2   ONE-NODE NETWORKS

A network built around a single circuit-switching node consists of a collection of devices or stations attached to a central switching unit. The central switch established a dedicated path between any two devices that wish to communicate. Figure 2-2 depicts the major elements of such a one-node network.

The heart of a modern system is a **digital switch.** The function of the digital switch is to provide a transparent signal path between any pair of attached devices. The path is transparent in the sense that it appears to the attached pair of devices that there is a direct connection between them. Typically, the connection must allow full-duplex transmission. Figure 2-3 depicts a switch with 20 attached lines. The dotted lines inside the switch symbolize the connections that are currently active. Later in this chapter, we will discuss various techniques that may be used to establish and maintain such connections.

The advent of digital switching technology has dramatically improved the cost, performance, and capability of circuit-switched networks. Key to the operation of such a system are that (1) all signals are represented digitally, and (2) synchronous time-division multiplexing (TDM) techniques are used.

The **network interface** element represents the functions and hardware needed to connect digital devices, such as data processing devices and digital telephones, to the network. Analog telephones can also be attached if the network interface contains the logic for converting to digital signals. Trunks to other digital switches carry TDM signals and provide the links for constructing multiple-node networks.

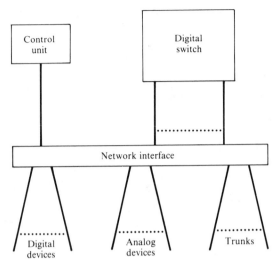

FIGURE 2-2 Elements of a Circuit-switching Node

The **control unit** performs three general tasks. First, it establishes connections. This is generally done on demand, that is, at the request of an attached device. To establish the connection, the control unit must handle and acknowledge the request, determine if the intended destination is free, and construct a path through the switch. Second, the control unit must maintain the connection. Since the digital switch uses time-division principles, this may require ongoing manipulation of the switching elements. However, the bits of the communication are transferred transparently (from the point of view of the attached devices). Third, the control unit must tear down the connection, either in response to a request from one of the parties or for its own reasons.

An important characteristic of a circuit-switching device is whether it is blocking or nonblocking. Blocking occurs when the network is unable to connect two stations because all possible paths between them are already in use. A blocking network is one in which such blocking is possible. Hence a nonblocking network permits all stations to be connected (in pairs) at once and grants all possible connection requests as long as the called party is free. When a network is supporting only voice traffic, a blocking configuration is generally acceptable, since it is expected that most phone calls are of short duration and that therefore only a fraction of the telephones will be engaged at any time. However, when data-processing devices are involved, these assumptions may be invalid. For example, for a data entry application, a terminal may be continuously connected to a computer for hours at a time. [BHUS85] reports that typical voice connections on a private branch exchange (PBX) have a duration of 120 to 180 seconds, whereas data calls have a range of from 8 seconds to 15 hours. Hence, for data applications, there is a requirement for a

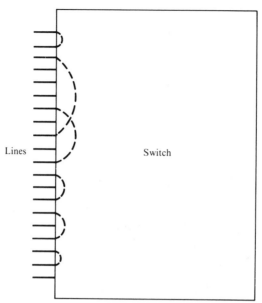

FIGURE 2-3   Abstract Representation of Circuits

nonblocking or "nearly nonblocking" (very low probability of blocking) configuration.

We turn now to an examination of the switching techniques internal to a single
circuit-switching node.

2-3   SPACE-DIVISION SWITCHING

Space-division switching was originally developed for the analog environment
and has been carried over into digital technology. The fundamental principles are
the same, whether the switch is used to carry analog or digital signals. As its name
implies, a space-division switch is one in which the signal paths that are set up are
physically separate from one another (divided in space). Each connection requires
the establishment of a physical path through the switch that is dedicated solely to the
transfer of signals between the two endpoints. The basic building block of the switch
is a metallic crosspoint or semiconductor gate [ABBO84] that can be enabled and
disabled by a control unit.

Figure 2-4 shows a simple crossbar matrix with N full-duplex I/O lines. The
matrix has N inputs and N outputs; each device attaches to the matrix via one input
and one output line. Interconnection is possible between any two lines by enabling
the appropriate crosspoint. Note that a total of N^2 crosspoints is required. The
crossbar switch has a number of limitations:

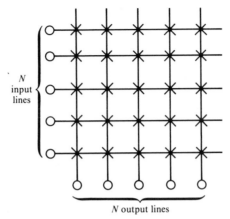

N input lines

N output lines

FIGURE 2-4   Single-stage Space-Division Switch

- The number of crosspoints grows with N^2. This is costly for large N, and results in high capacitive loading on any message path.
- The loss of a crosspoint prevents connection between the two devices involved.
- The crosspoints are inefficiently utilized (at most N out of N^2).

To overcome these limitations, multiple-stage switches are employed. N input lines are broken up into N/n groups of n lines. Each group of lines goes into a first-stage matrix. The outputs of the first-stage matrices become inputs to a group of second-stage matrices, and so on. The last stage has N outputs; thus, each device attaches its input line to the first stage and its output line to the last stage. Figure 2-5 depicts a three-stage network of switches. There are k second-stage matrices, each with N/n inputs and N/n outputs. The exact number of second-stage matrices is a design decision, as discussed below. Each first-stage matrix has k outlets so that it connects to all second-stage matrices. Each second-stage matrix has N/n outputs so that it connects to all third-stage matrices.

This type of arrangement has several advantages over a single-stage crossbar matrix:

- The number of crosspoints is reduced (see below), increasing crossbar utilization.
- There is more than one path through the network to connect two endpoints, increasing reliability.

Of course, a multistage network requires a more complex control scheme. To establish a path in a single-stage network, it is only necessary to enable a single gate. In a multistage network, a free path through the stages must be determined and the appropriate gates enabled.

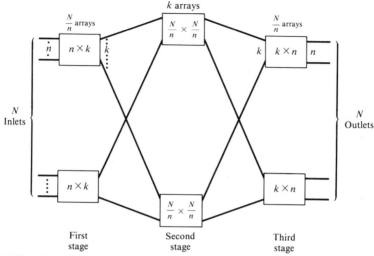

FIGURE 2-5 Three-stage Space-Division Switch

A consideration with a multistage space-division switch is that it may be blocking. It should be clear from Figure 2-4 that a crossbar matrix is nonblocking; that is, a path is always available to connect an input to an output. That this may not be the case with a multiple-stage switch can be seen in Figure 2-6. The figure shows a three-stage switch with $N = 9$, $n = 3$, and $k = 3$. The heavier lines indicate lines that are already in use. In this state, input line 9 cannot be connected to either output line 4 or 6, even though both of these output lines are available.

It should also be clear that by increasing the value of k (the number of outputs from each first-stage switch and the number of second-stage switches), the probabil-

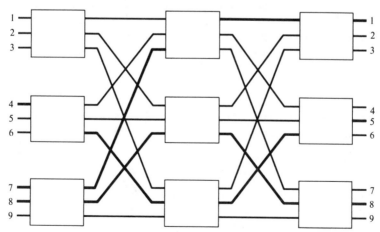

FIGURE 2-6 Example of Blocking in a Three-stage Switch

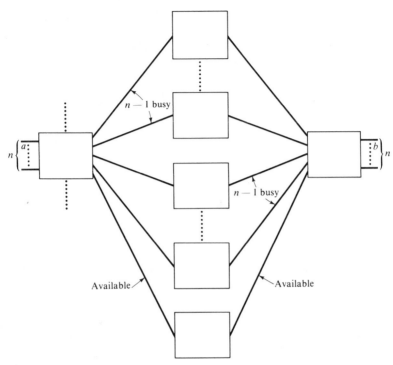

FIGURE 2-7 Nonblocking Three-stage Switch

ity of blocking is reduced. Figure 2-7 illustrates the value of k required to eliminate blocking. Consider that we wish to establish a path from input line a to output line b. The worst case situation for blocking occurs if all of the remaining $n - 1$ input lines and $n - 1$ output lines are busy and are connected to different center-stage switches. Thus a total of $(n - 1) + (n - 1) = 2n - 2$ center switches are unavailable for creating a path from a to b. However, if one more center-stage switch exists, the appropriate links must be available for the connection. Thus, a three-stage network will be nonblocking if

$$k = 2n - 1$$

We now return to the claim that a multiple-stage switch requires fewer crosspoints than a single-stage switch. From Figure 2-5, the total number of crosspoints N, in a three-stage switch is

$$Nx = 2Nk + k(N/n)^2$$

Substituting the first equation above into the second:

$$Nx = 2N(2n - 1) + (2n - 1)(N/n)^2$$

for a nonblocking switch. The actual value as a function of N depends on the number

TABLE 2-1   NUMBER OF CROSSPOINTS IN A NONBLOCKING SWITCH

Number of Lines	Number of Crosspoints for Three-Stage Switch	Number of Crosspoints for Single-Stage Switch
128	7,680	16,384
512	63,488	262,144
3,048	516,096	4.2×10^6
8,192	4.2×10^6	6.7×10^7
32,768	3.3×10^7	1×10^9
131,072	2.6×10^8	1.7×10^{10}

of switches (N/n) in the first and third stages. To optimize, differentiate Nx with respect to n and set the result to zero. For large N, the result converges to $n = (N/2)^{1/2}$. Substituting into the last equation above:

$$Nx = 4N(\sqrt{2N} - 1)$$

Table 2-1 compares this value with the number of crosspoints in a single-stage switch. As can be seen, there is a savings that grows with the number of lines.

2-4   TIME-DIVISION SWITCHING

The technology of switching has a long history, most of it covering an era when analog signal switching predominated. With the advent of digitized voice and synchronous time-division multiplexing techniques, both voice and data can be transmitted via digital signals. This has led to a fundamental change in the design and technology of switching systems. Instead of relatively dumb space-division systems, modern digital systems rely on intelligent control of space- and time-division elements.

Virtually all modern circuit switches use digital time-division techniques for establishing and maintaining "circuits." Time-division switching involves the partitioning of a lower-speed bit stream into pieces that share a higher-speed stream with other bit streams. The individual pieces, or slots, are manipulated by control logic to route data from input to output. Three concepts comprise the technique of time-division switching:

- TDM bus switching
- Time-slot interchange (TSI)
- Time-multiplex switching (TMS)

Table 2-2 briefly describes these forms of switching, as well as space-division switching.

TABLE 2-2 CIRCUIT-SWITCHING TECHNIQUES

Technique	Description	Comments
Space-Division	Uses an interconnection matrix. Each connection through the switch takes a physically distinct path.	Inefficient use of crosspoints. Can be used for either analog or digital switching. Less complex than time-division switching.
TDM Bus	All lines are connected to a bus. Time on the bus is divided into slots. A circuit is created between two lines by assigning repetitive time slots, as in synchronous TDM.	Simplest form of time-division switching. Size of switch is limited by the data rate on the bus. This architecture is common for small and medium-sized data switches and PBXs.
Time-Slot Interchange	All lines are connected to a synchronous TDM multiplexer and a synchronous TDM demultiplexer. A circuit is created by the interchange of time slots within a time-division multiplexed frame.	Size of switch is limited by the speed of the control memory. Can be used as a building block in multistage switches.
Time-Multiplexed	A form of space-division switching in which each input line is a TDM stream. The switching configuration may change for each time slot.	Used in conjunction with TSI units to form multistage switches. There is a small increase in delay by the use of multiple stages, but this allows much larger capacity.

TDM Bus Switching

TDM bus switching, and indeed all digital switching techniques, are based on the use of synchronous time-division multiplexing (TDM). As shown in Figure 2-8, synchronous TDM permits multiple low-speed bit streams to share a high-speed line. A set of inputs is sampled in turn. The samples are organized serially into slots (channels) to form a recurring frame of N slots. A slot may be a bit, a byte, or some longer block. An important point to note is that with synchronous TDM, the source and destination of the data in each time slot are known. Hence there is no need for address bits in each slot.

The mechanism for synchronous TDM may be quite simple. For example, each input line deposits data in a buffer; the multiplexer scans these buffers sequentially, taking fixed size chunks of data from each buffer and sending them out on the line. One complete scan produces one frame of data. For output to the lines, the reverse operation is performed, with the multiplexer filling the output line buffers one by one. The I/O lines attached to the multiplexer may be synchronous or asynchronous; the multiplexed line between the two multiplexers is synchronous and must have a data rate equal to the sum of the data rates of the attached lines.

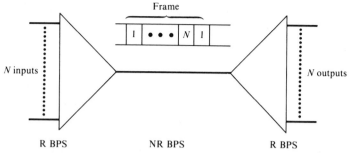

FIGURE 2-8 Synchronous Time-Division Multiplexing (TDM)

Actually, the multiplexed line must have a slightly higher data rate, since each frame will include some overhead bits for synchronization. The time slots in a frame are assigned to the I/O lines on a fixed, predetermined basis. If a device has no data to send, the multiplexer must send empty slots. Thus the actual data transfer rate may be less than the capacity of the system.

Figure 2-9 shows a simple way in which this technique can be adapted to achieve switching. Each device attaches to the switch through two buffered lines, one for input and one for output. These lines are connected through controlled gates to a high-speed digital bus. Each input line is assigned a time slot. For the duration of the slot, that line's gate is enabled, allowing a small burst of data onto the bus. For that same time slot, one of the output line gates is also enabled. Thus, during that time slot, data are switched from the enabled input line to the enabled output line. During successive time slots, different input/output pairings are enabled, allowing a number of connections to be carried over the shared bus. An attached device achieves

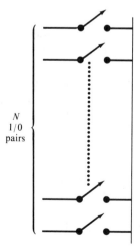

FIGURE 2-9 TDM Bus Switching

full-duplex operation by transmitting during one assigned time slot and receiving during another. The other end of the connection is an I/O pair for which these time slots have the opposite meanings. We will refer to this technique as **TDM bus switching**.

Let us look at the timing involved more closely. First, consider a nonblocking implementation of Figure 2-9. For a switch that supports N devices, there must be N repetitively occurring time slots, each one assigned to an input and an output line. One iteration for all time slots is referred to as a *frame*. The input assignment may be fixed; the output assignments vary to allow various connections. When a time slot begins, the designated (enabled) input line may insert a burst of data onto the line, where it will propagate to both ends past all other lines. The designated (enabled) output line, during that time, copies the data, if present, as they go by. The time slot, therefore, must equal the transmission time of the input plus the propagation delay between input and output across the bus. In order to keep successive time slots uniform, time slot length is defined as transmission time plus the end-to-end bus propagation delay. For efficiency, the propagation delay must be much less than the transmission time.

To keep up with the input lines, the data rate on the bus must be high enough that the slots recur sufficiently frequently. For example, consider a system connecting 100 full-duplex lines at 19.2 kbps. Input data on each line are buffered at the gate. Each buffer must be cleared, by enabling the gate, fast enough to avoid overrun. Thus the data rate on the bus in this example must be greater than 1.92 Mbps. The actual data rate must be high enough to also account for the wasted time due to propagation delay.

These considerations determine the traffic-carrying capacity of a blocking switch as well. For a blocking switch, there is no fixed assignment of input lines to time slots; they are allocated on demand. The data rate on the bus dictates how many connections can be made at a time. For a system with 200 devices at 19.2 kbps and a bus at 2 Mbps, about half of the devices can be connected at any one time.

The TDM bus switching scheme can accommodate lines of varying data rates. For example, if a 9600-bps line gets one slot per frame, a 19.2-kbps line would get two slots per frame. Of course, only lines of the same data rate can be connected.

Figure 2-10 is an example that suggests how the control for a TDM bus switch can be implemented. Let us assume that the propagation time on the bus is 0.01 μsec. Time on the bus is organized into 30.06-μsec frames of six 5.01-μsec time slots each. A control memory indicates which gates are to be enabled during each time slot. In this example, 6 words of memory are needed. A controller cycles through the memory at a rate of one cycle every 30.06 μsec. During the first time slot of each cycle, the input gate from device 1 and the output gate to device 3 are enabled, allowing data to pass from device 1 to device 3 over the bus. The remaining words are accessed in succeeding time slots and treated accordingly. As long as the control memory contains the contents depicted in Figure 2-10, connections are maintained between 1 and 3, 2 and 5, and 4 and 6.

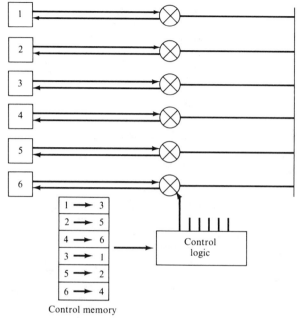

FIGURE 2-10   Control of a TDM Bus Switch

Time-Slot Interchange

The basic building block of many time-division switches is the **time-slot interchange** (TSI) mechanism. A TSI unit operates on a synchronous TDM stream of time slots, or channels, by interchanging pairs of slots to achieve full-duplex operation. Figure 2-11a shows how the input line of a device I is connected to the output line of device J, and vice versa. In this figure, the input lines of N devices are passed through a synchronous time-division multiplexer to produce a TDM stream with N slots. To achieve the interconnection of two devices, the slots corresponding to the two inputs are interchanged; the resulting stream is demultiplexed to the outputs of the N devices. This results in a full-duplex connection between pairs of lines.

Figure 2-11b depicts a mechanism for TSI. Individual I/O lines are multiplexed and demultiplexed. A random-access data store whose width equals one time slot of data and whose length equals the number of slots in a frame is used. An incoming TDM frame is written sequentially, slot by slot, into the data store. An outgoing TDM frame is created by reading slots from memory in an order dictated by an address store that reflect the existing connections. In the figure, the data in channels I and J are interchanged, creating a full-duplex connection between the corresponding stations.

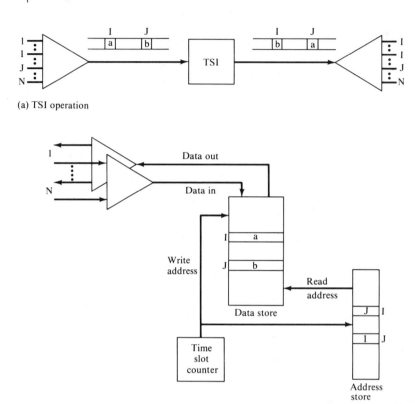

(a) TSI operation

(b) TSI mechanism

FIGURE 2-11   Time-Slot Interchange (TSI)

We can see that, to allow the interchange of any two slots, the incoming data in a slot must be stored until they can be sent out on the right channel in the next frame cycle. Hence, the TSI introduces a delay and produces output slots in the desired order. Since each channel is provided a time slot in the frame, whether or not it transmits data, the size of the TSI unit must be chosen for the capacity of the TDM line, not the actual data transfer rate at any given time.

Let us look more closely at the operation of the data store; in particular, we need to view it as a function of time. As an example [DAVI73], consider a system with eight I/O lines, in which the following connections exist: 1-2, 3-7, and 5-8; the other two stations are not in use. Figure 2-12 depicts the contents of the data store over the course of one frame (eight slots). During the first time slot, data are stored in location 1 and read from location 2. During the second time slot, data are stored in location 2 and read from location 1, and so on.

As can be seen, the write accesses to the data store are cyclic, that is, accessing successive locations in sequential order, whereas the read accesses are acyclic, requiring the use of an address store. The figure also depicts two frames of the input

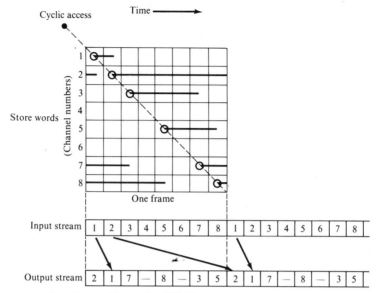

FIGURE 2-12   Operation of a TSI Store

and output sequences and indicates the transfer of data between channels 1 and 2. Note that in half the cases, data slots move into the next frame.

As with the TDM bus switch, the TSI unit can handle inputs of various data rates. Figure 2-13 suggests a way in which this may be done. Instead of presenting the input lines to a synchronous multiplexer, they are presented to a selector device. This device will select an input line based on a channel assignment provided from a store controlled by the time slot counter. Instead of sampling equally from each input, it may gather more slots from some channels than others.

Time-Multiplexed Switching

TSI is a simple, effective way of switching TDM data. However, the size of such a switch, in terms of number of connections, is limited by the memory access speed. It is clear that, in order to keep pace with the input, data must be read into and out of memory as fast as they arrive. So, for example, if we have 24 sources operating at 64 kbps each, and a slot size of 8 bits, we would have an arrival rate of 192,000 slots per second. For each time slot, both a read and a write are required. In this example, memory access time would need to be $1/(192,000 \times 2)$, or about 2.6 μsec.

We can see, then, that a TSI unit can support only a limited number of connections. Further, as the size of the unit grows, for a fixed access speed, the delay at the TSI unit grows. To overcome both of these problems, multiple TSI units are used. Now, to connect two channels entering a single TSI unit, their time slots can be interchanged. However, to connect a channel on one TDM stream (going into

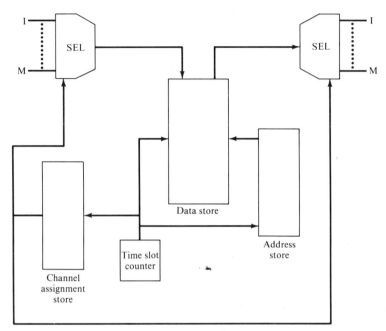

FIGURE 2-13 TSI Operation with a Variable-rate Input

one TSI) to a channel on another TDM stream (going into another TSI), some form of interconnection of the TSI units is needed. This interconnection must allow a slot in one TDM stream to be interchanged with a slot in another TDM stream. Naturally, we do not wish to switch all of the time slots from one stream to another; we would like to do it one slot at a time. This technique is known as **time-multiplexed switching** (TMS).

Multiple-stage networks can be built up by concatenating TMS and TSI stages. TMS stages, which move slots from one stream to another, are referred to as S (space), and TSI stages are referred to as T (time). Systems are generally described by an enumeration of their stages from input to output, using the symbols T and S. Figure 2-14 shows examples of both STS and TST three-stage architectures. In both cases, the TMS stages are implemented by digital selectors (SEL), which select one input at time on a time-slot basis. These SEL devices provide the same function as those described in the preceding section, except that here each of their inputs is a TDM stream rather than a single line.

In an STS architecture, the path between an incoming and an outgoing channel has multiple possible physical routes equal to the number of TSI units, but only one time route. For a fully nonblocking switch, the number of TSI units must be double the number of incoming and outgoing TDM streams. On the other hand, the multiple routes between two channels in a TST network are all in the time domain; there is only one physical path possible. Here, too, blocking can occur. One

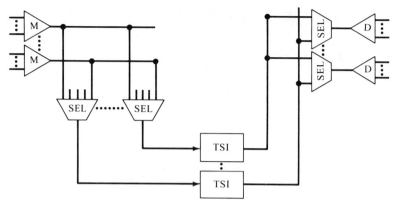

(a) Space-time-space network

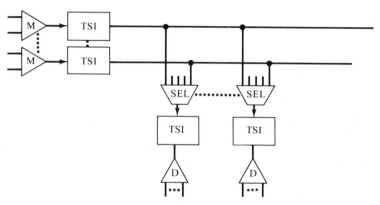

(b) Time-Space-Time network

FIGURE 2-14 Three-stage TDM Switches

way to avoid blocking is by expanding the number of time slots in the space stage. In all multistage switches, a path-search algorithm is needed to determine the route from input to output.

2-5 DIGITAL CARRIER SYSTEMS

In the preceding section, we examined the internal switching mechanisms of a circuit-switched node. Of course, a wide-area circuit-switched network will involve a number of interconnected nodes. A link between a pair of nodes, referred to as a *trunk*, uses multiplexing to carry the traffic on a number of channels, or circuits. This multiplexing may be in the form of frequency-division multiplexing (FDM) or synchronous time-division multiplexing (TDM). Table 2-3 briefly compares the

TABLE 2-3 MULTIPLEXING TECHNIQUES FOR CARRIER SYSTEMS

Technique	Description	Comments
Frequency-division multiplexing	The division of a transmission facility into two or more channels by splitting the transmitted frequency band into narrower bands, each of which is used to carry a separate channel.	Traditional scheme used in telephone networks. Each analog voice signal is assigned its own channel. This technique requires considerable signal processing which reduces signal quality and increases cost compared to TDM.
Synchronous time-division multiplexing	The division of a transmission facility into two or more channels by dividing the transmission capacity into time slots and assigning time slots on a fixed, predetermined basis to various attached devices. The repetitive sequence of time slots allocated to a device constitutes the channel for that device.	This technique is preferred to FDM for digital signals, including digital data and digitized voice. It is more efficient and results in higher-quality received signals than FDM.

two techniques. As wide-area telecommunication networks evolve toward an integrated digital network, synchronous TDM techniques are becoming dominant. We will explore this evolution in Chapter 4. In this section, we look at the transmission structure of the TDM traffic.

The long-distance carrier system provided in the United States and throughout the world was designed to transmit voice signals over high-capacity transmission links, such as optical fiber, coaxial cable, and microwave. Part of the evolution of these telecommunications networks to digital technology has been the adoption of synchronous TDM transmission structures. In the United States, AT&T developed a hierarchy of TDM structures of various capacities; this structure is used in Canada and Japan, as well as the United States. A similar, but unfortunately not identical, hierarchy has been adopted internationally under the auspices of CCITT (Table 2-4). As we shall see, this dichotomy remains unresolved in the ISDN standards.

The basis of the TDM hierarchy is the DS-1 transmission format (Figure 2-15), which multiplexes 24 channels [RUFF87]. Each frame contains eight bits per channel plus a framing bit for $24 \times 8 + 1 = 193$ bits. For voice transmission, the following rules apply. Each channel contains one word of digitized voice data. The original analog voice signal is digitized using pulse code modulation (PCM) at a rate of 8000 samples per second. Therefore each channel slot and hence each frame must repeat 8000 times per second. With a frame length of 193 bits, we have a data rate of $8000 \times 193 = 1.544$ Mbps. For five of every six frames, 8-bit PCM samples are used. For every sixth frame, each channel contains a 7-bit PCM word plus a

TABLE 2-4 NORTH AMERICAN AND INTERNATIONAL TDM CARRIER STANDARDS

(a) North American			(b) International (CCITT)		
Digital Signal Number	Number of Voice Channels	Data Rate (Mbps)	Level Number	Number of Voice Channels	Data Rate (Mbps)
DS-1	24	1.544	1	30	2.048
DS-1C	48	3.152	2	120	8.448
DS-2	96	6.312	3	480	34.368
DS-3	672	44.736	4	1920	139.264
DS-4	4032	274.176	5	7680	565.148

signaling bit. The eighth bits form a stream for each voice channel which contains network control and routing information. For example, control signals are used to establish a connection or terminate a call.

The same DS-1 format is used to provide digital data service. For compatibility with voice, the same 1.544-Mbps data rate is used. In this case, 23 channels of data are provided. The twenty-fourth channel position is reserved for a special sync byte which allows faster and more reliable reframing following a framing error. Within each channel, seven bits per frame are used for data, with the eighth bit used to indicate whether the channel, for that frame, contains user data or system control data. With seven bits per channel, and since each frame is repeated 8000 times per second, a data rate of 56 kbps can be provided per channel. Lower data rates are provided using a technique known as subrate multiplexing. For this technique, an additional bit is robbed from each channel to indicate which subrate multiplexing rate is being provided. This leaves a total capacity per channel of 6 × 8000 = 48 kbps. This capacity is used to multiplex five 9.6-kbps channels, ten 4.8-kbps channels, or twenty 2.4-kbps channels. For example, if channel 2 is used to provide

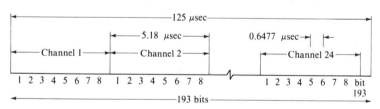

Notes:
1. Bit 193 is a framing bit, used for synchronization.
2. Voice channels:
   . 8-bit PCM used on five of six frames.
   . 7-bit PCM used on every sixth frame, bit 8 of each channel is a signalling bit.
3. Data channels:
   . Channel 24 used for signaling only in some schemes.
   . Bit 8 is a control bit.
   . Bits 1-7 used for 56 kbps service.
   . Bits 2-7 used for 9.6 kbps, 4.8 kbps, and 2.4 kbps service.

FIGURE 2-15 DS-1 Transmission Frame

9.6-kbps service, then up to five data subchannels share this channel. The data for each subchannel appear as six bits in channel 2 every fifth frame.

Finally, the DS-1format can be used to carry a mixture of voice and data channels. In this case, all 24 channels are utilized; no sync byte is provided.

Above this basic data rate of 1.544 Mbps, higher-level multiplexing is achieved by interleaving bits from DS-1 inputs. For example, the DS-2 transmission system combines four DS-1 inputs into a 6.312-Mbps stream. Data from the four sources are interleaved 12 bits at a time. Note that $1.544 \times 4 = 6.176$ Mbps. The remaining capacity is used for framing and control bits. The reader interested in the details of this and other digital carrier TDM formats should consult [BELL82a].

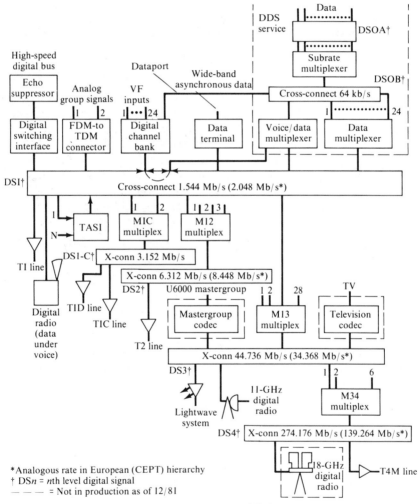

FIGURE 2-16   AT&T TDM Hierarchy (BELL82a)

TABLE 2-5 CAPACITY OF SOME COMMUNICATION CARRIERS

Carrier Designation	Number of Voice Channels	Data Rate (Mbps)	Combinations		
T-1	24	1.544	—	—	—
T-1C	48	3.152	2 T-1	—	—
T-2	96	6.312	4 T-1	2 T1-C	—
T-3	672	44.736	28 T-1	14 T1-C	7 T-2
T-4	4032	274.176	168 T-1	84 T-1C	42 T-2

Each higher level of the TDM hierarchy is formed by multiplexing signals from the next lower level or by combination of those signals plus input at the appropriate data rate from other sources. Figure 2-16 illustrates this hierarchy. First, the DS-1 transmission rate is used to provide both a voice and data service. The data service is known as the Dataphone Digital Service (DDS). The DDS provides digital transmission service between customer data devices at data rates of from 2.4 to 56 kbps [KELC83, ERIK86]. The service is available at customer premises over two twisted-pair lines.

The mastergroup codec performs a function known as transmultiplexing. It converts a 600-channel analog FDM signal into a digital TDM signal. This provides an interface between high-speed analog and digital systems.

Figure 2-16 also specifies a number of transmission lines at the various data rates. These refer to AT&T-provided carrier facilities (Table 2-5). These facilities provide high-capacity transmission for today's long-distance telecommunications systems.

2-6 ROUTING

In a large circuit-switched network, such as the AT&T long-distance telephone network, many of the circuit connections will require a path through more than one switch. When a call is placed, the network must devise a route through the network from calling subscriber to called subscriber that passes through some number of switches and trunks. As Box 2-2 indicates, there are two main requirements for the network's architecture that bear on the routing strategy. First, it is desirable to minimize the amount of equipment (switches and trunks) in the network, subject to the ability to handle the expected load. The load requirement is usually expressed in terms of a *busy hour traffic load*. This is simply the average load expected over the course of the busiest hour of use during the course of a day. From a functional point of view, it is necessary to handle that amount of load. From a cost point of view, we would like to handle that load with minimum equipment. However, there is another requirement, namely resilience. Although the network may be sized for the busy hour load, it is possible for the traffic to temporarily surge above that level (e.g.,

---

BOX 2-2

ROUTING FOR CIRCUIT-SWITCHED NETWORKS

FUNCTION

Define a path from calling subscriber to called subscriber through a series of switches and trunks.

REQUIREMENTS

Efficiency

The measure of how few facilities are required to carry the steady busy hour traffic load of the network.

Resilience

The measure of the level of service maintained when either a traffic surge or equipment failure is experienced by the network.

APPROACHES

Direct

A fixed preestablished route is followed for any pair of subscribers.

Alternate Hierarchical

Switches are arranged in a hierarchy with additional trunks beyond those required for the tree structure. The additional trunks provide alternate routes that may be taken to compensate for load or unavailability.

Dynamic Nonhierarchical

A more complex, peer network architecture is used. The route between subscribers is dynamically chosen at call setup time based on traffic load and availability.

---

during a major storm). It will also be the case that, from time to time, switches and trunks will fail and be temporarily unavailable (unfortunately, maybe during the same storm). We would like the network to provide a reasonable level of service under such conditions.

In the past, the two requirements of efficiency and resilience have been competing. That is, there has been a trade-off between the two. Network efficiency is achieved by minimizing switching and transmission capacity, whereas resilience was achieved by increasing that capacity, in the form of small trunk sections and high inter-exchange connectivity. This situation is rapidly changing with the availability of high-bandwidth fiber trunks and high-capacity digital switches capable of handling tens of thousands of trunks. As we will see, all of this is tied to the routing strategy. Traditional routing strategies that have been common in telephone networks are unable to adapt to major network perturbations. Newer, dynamic routing strategies can take advantage of evolving technology to simultaneously improve both network efficiency and network resilience [HURL87].

These concepts are best explained with an example. In the remainder of this section, we look at the evolution of the AT&T network.

Architecture of a Public Telephone Network

The public telecommunications network in the United States consists primarily of the local service offered by the Bell Operating Companies (BOCs) that used to be part of AT&T and the long-distance service still offered by AT&T. There are, of course, a growing number of other providers, particularly of long-distance service. In this section, we look at the architecture of the BOC/AT&T network, which still handles the bulk of telephone traffic in the United States. Although both the routing and the architecture of this network have and are evolving since divestiture, the overall architecture can still be described as follows.

As with any network, the public telephone network can be described using four generic architectural components:

- *Stations*: generally denoted as *subscribers*, these are the devices that attach to the network.
- *Interfaces*: the interface between the stations and the network, referred to in the phone system as the *local loop*.
- *Nodes*: the *switching centers* in the network.
- *Links*: the branches between nodes, referred to as *trunks*.

Most of the **subscribers** on the network are telephones. The telephone contains a transmitter and receiver for converting back and forth between analog voice (sound waves) and analog (voice frequency) electrical signals. Some subscribers that transmit digital signals are being incorporated into the network.

The **local loop** is a pair of wires, generally twisted pair, that connects a subscriber to one of the nodes in the network. It is a direct-current (dc) loop that supplies a metallic path for the following [FREE80]:

- Voltage potential for the telephone transmitter. This is supplied over the line from the switching center and is used to convert acoustic energy into electric energy.

- An ac ringing voltage for the bell on the telephone instrument supplied from the switching center.
- Current to flow through the loop when the telephone instrument is taken out of its cradle (off hook), telling the serving switch that it requires access.
- Signals generated by the telephone dial or keypad used to communicate to the switch the number of the called subscriber.

The local loop generally covers a distance of a few kilometers to a few tens of kilometers at most. More detail on telephone transmission over the local loop can be found in [ATT61].

Each subscriber connects via local loop to a **switching center,** known as an end office. Typically, an end office will support many thousands of subscribers in a localized area. There are over 19,000 end offices in the United States, so it is clearly impractical for each end office to have a direct link to each of the other end offices; this would require on the order of 2×10^8 links. Rather, intermediate switching nodes are used. The function of these intermediate nodes and the manner in which they are interconnected determine the routing mechanism that is used.

The switching centers are linked together by **trunks.** These trunks are designed to carry multiple voice-frequency circuits using either FDM or synchronous TDM. Earlier, these were referred to as carrier systems.

Alternate Hierarchical Routing

Until recently, the organization of the end offices into a network has involved the use of a hierarchical or tree structure (Figure 2-17), consisting of five classes of switching centers or nodes [REY83]:

- *Class 1*: regional center
- *Class 2*: sectional center
- *Class 3*: primary center
- *Class 4*: toll center
- *Class 5*: end office

Subscribers connect directly to an end office, which must perform the same functions listed earlier for a one-node network. The remaining centers simply serve the function of concentrating traffic so as to reduce transmission facility equipment. This distinction is shown in Figure 2-18. To connect two subscribers attached to the same end office, a circuit is set up between them in the same fashion as described before. If two subscribers connect to different end offices, a circuit between them consists of a concatenation of circuits through one or more intermediate offices. In the figure, a connection is established between lines *a* and *b* by simply setting up the connection through the end office. The connection between *c* and *d* is more complex. In *c*'s end office, a connection is established between line *c* and one

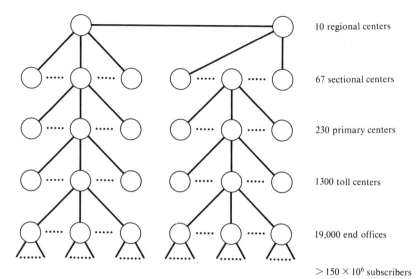

10 regional centers

67 sectional centers

230 primary centers

1300 toll centers

19,000 end offices

$> 150 \times 10^6$ subscribers

FIGURE 2-17 U.S. Public Circuit-Switched Network Organization

channel on a TDM or FDM trunk to the intermediate switch. In the intermediate switch, that channel is connected to a channel on a trunk to a's end office. In that end office, the channel is connected to line d.

The hierarchical structure depicted in Figure 2-17 is actually a set of 10 trees, each rooted in a regional center. The 10 regional centers are meshed together (45 full-duplex links) to provide full connectivity. In the early days of the telephone network, this was the extent of the architecture, and a very simple form or routing, known as **direct routing**, was used. With direct routing, connection establishment follows these rules:

1. If both subscribers attach to the same end office, that end office makes the connection.
2. If the two subscribers attach to different end offices that are attached to the same toll center, a connection is established between the end offices via that toll center.

And so on. The search continues up the hierarchy until a common node is reached. If the two subscribers are under the aegis of different regional centers, the circuit will involve a trunk between regional centers, for a total of nine trunks in the path between the two subscribers.

This architecture and routing strategy has several drawbacks. First, during peak hours, a tremendous amount of traffic must be carried at the upper levels of the hierarchy; accordingly, the facilities at these levels will be inefficiently used most of the time. Second, the loss or saturation of a single switching center decouples the

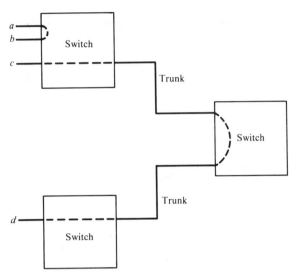

FIGURE 2-18   Circuit Establishment in a Multiple-Switch Network

network into isolated subnetworks. Finally, signal quality degrades as the number of switches and trunks increases (for analog transmission).

To compensate for these problems, two additional elements are added to the basic architecture. In addition to the five classes of switching centers, the network is augmented with additional switching nodes called *tandem switches*. These are used to interconnect adjacent end offices. Also, a large number of *high-usage trunks* are used for direct connection between switching centers with high volumes of inter-node traffic.

With these additions, an **alternate hierarchical routing** algorithm can be used. Traffic is always routed through the lowest available level of the network. Figure 2-19 shows the basic order of selection for alternate routes. The high-usage trunks are depicted as dashed lines, and the backbone hierarchical network is shown with solid lines. With alternate hierarchical routing, connection establishment is as follows. The basic rule is to complete the connection at the lowest possible level of the hierarchy, thus using the fewest trunks in sequence. In the figure, a call placed from telephone 1 to telephone 2 is first handled by the end office of telephone 1. Since telephone 2 is not served by the same end office and is not reachable via a tandem office, the call is routed to toll center A. Toll center A searches for an available high-usage (HU) trunk, first in the HU1 group and then in the HU2 group. If all trunks in these groups are busy, the call overflows to the final trunk group, which moves the call up one level in the hierarchy to primary center B. The primary center again searches for an available HU trunk in the order indicated. This process is dynamic and depends on the availability of high-usage trunks at the time the call is placed. Thus calls between two subscribers might follow different routes at different

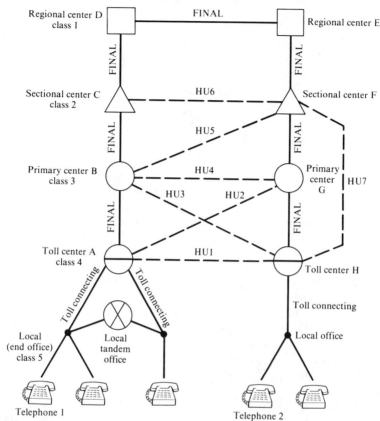

FIGURE 2-19 Alternate Hierarchical Routing (REY83)

times. The routing algorithm is driven by the seven- or ten-digit telephone number, which uniquely identifies a subscriber and the centers in its direct hierarchy [FREE80, REY83].

Beginning in the 1940s, when it became possible for an exchange to choose a route based on trunk loading status, alternate hierarchical routing was gradually introduced until it reached the level of complexity just described. The high-usage trunks are sized based on cost in the following way. The requirement to be satisfied is that the probability of blocking during the average busy hour on any of the final paths (see Figure 2-19) is no more than 0.01 [REY83]. For any given high-usage trunk, the capacity of that trunk is optimized by increasing its capacity until the incremental cost of adding further capacity on the high usage trunk would exceed the cost of carrying the incremental traffic on the final route. Figure 2-20 suggests the analysis involved. For a particular high-usage trunk, the cost of that trunk is a linearly-increasing function of capacity. As the capacity of the high-usage trunk increases, the capacity of the final trunks needed to guarantee the 0.01 blocking measure decreases

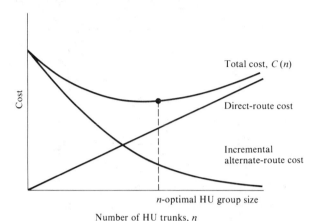

FIGURE 2-20   Cost Function for Alternate Routing (REY83)

and accordingly the cost of the final trunks decrease. As shown, there is a unique minimum which dictates the size of the high-usage trunk.

The alternate hierarchical routing approach provided significant gains in efficiency over the direct routing approach. More of the traffic is carried at lower levels of the hierarchy. Thus the average length of a connection (number of exchanges and trunks) is decreased for a given level of traffic. Furthermore, the way in which high-usage capacity is determined means that all trunk groups except the final ones are virtually fully loaded.

There are, however, remaining limitations. These limitations are in both the area of efficiency and of resilience. The single measure of an average busy hour is not powerful enough to permit a design that is optimum from the point of view of efficiency. For example, the busy hours for east/west traffic and north/south traffic do not coincide. It is difficult to analyze the effects of this, which leads to oversizing. In terms of resilience, the shortcoming of alternate hierarchical routing is that it is rigid, and assumes no equipment or trunk failure. A major failure will cause a major local congestion near the site of the failure. Over time, various automatic and manual network control procedures have been added to the network, but the basic problem of a rigid hierarchical structure remained. What is required is a more flexible scheme that allows more dynamic routing with a greater ability to adapt to changing conditions in the network. To achieve this, it is necessary to move away from a hierarchical architecture.

Dynamic Nonhierarchical Routing

A nonhierarchical architecture is one in which the circuit-switching nodes have a peer relationship with each other. All nodes are capable of performing the same functions. In such an architecture, routing is both more complex and more flexible. It is more complex because the architecture does not provide a "natural" path or set of paths based on hierarchical structure. But it is also more flexible since more alternative routes are available.

In general terms, the objective for moving from a hierarchical to a nonhierarchical structure is to exploit both regular (time of day, seasonal) and random traffic variations in choosing a route to improve efficiency and resiliency. Routes are chosen dynamically. With a peer network with a relatively large number of interconnections, very effective load sharing is possible. For example, if a direct path between two switches is fully loaded, blocking new calls, alternate paths may be taken for additional calls, reducing the blocking probability. On the other hand, at times when the load on this direct path is lighter, it may be used as an alternate path or part of an alternate path for other calls to help reduce blocking. Therefore, calls with different source/destination pairs share a larger pool of transmission and switching capacity for connection.

In order to employ dynamic routing of a peer architecture, three capabilities must be added to the network [HURL87]:

- Switches must be enhanced to include the capability to make dynamic routing decisions and to be able to communicate traffic status information to other parts of the network.
- One or more network management centers are needed to determine routes and disseminate routing information.
- A control signaling technique, or protocol, is needed to enable switches to pass traffic status information to the network management centers and for the centers to return routing information to the switches.

The details of the routing capability are, of course, dependent on the architecture. The capability developed by AT&T, referred to as dynamic nonhierarchical routing (DNHR), is an evolution of the existing network. AT&T began the changeover to this capability in 1984, and has substantially completed the initial effort. With DNHR, the network contains a large number (about 100) of regional centers. These centers are peer to each other, and make up the DNHR part of the total network. Any call that makes use of the DNHR switches will pass through no more than three switches and two trunks. Routing is based on known historical traffic patterns and on current traffic status.

Figure 2-21 illustrates the DNHR scheme [GLEN86]. There are two or three switches involved in each route. The originating switch is responsible for making the routing decision. The terminating switch is the intended destination. Finally, in some cases, there is an intermediate switch that is part of the route. Each switch is given a set of preplanned routes for each destination, in order of preference. Usually, the first preference is a direct trunk connection from the originating switch to the terminating switch. These routing sequences reflect the optimal routes for a particular call, based on extensive operational measurement data which is periodically

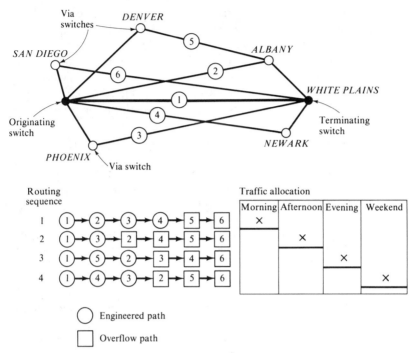

FIGURE 2-21 DNHR Routing

provided by each participating switch to the central network planning system. To take advantage of the differing traffic patterns in different time zones and at different times of day, the day is divided into ten time periods, with a different set of pre-planned routes for each time period. In addition to the preplanned routes, additional overflow paths may be assigned. These paths are assigned by a network management center, but the ability to use them depends on the current load. For example, if utilization on a given trunk group is high, no overflow traffic will be allowed on that trunk so that its limited remaining capacity stays available for preplanned routes.

In Figure 2-21, the originating switch has six possible routes to the terminating switch. The direct route (1) will always be tried first. If this trunk is unavailable (busy or out of service), the other routes will be tried in a particular order depending on the time of day. For example, during the morning, route (2) is tried next. If the intermediate switch on a route is unable to complete a requested call, it sends a control message back to the originating switch so that it may try another route. After all preplanned routes have been tried, additional routes (overflow routes), which are not engineered to handle the specific origination-termination traffic, may be used if sufficient capacity is available. The distinction between the preplanned and overflow routes is that the capacity of the network (switch and trunk size) is engineered to handle the preplanned traffic at a particular probability of blocking (1 percent).

Control signaling is used to allow the switches to provide traffic information to a network management center. If the network management center determines that an overflow condition exists, it may dynamically change the route sets of any of the switches. The routing updates are communicated back to the switches by control signals.

Below the DNHR network, the remainder of the network is still hierarchical, much as in Figure 2-17. Calls within a particular hierarchy are still handled by alternate hierarchical routing. Each hierarchy attaches to a single regional switch, by which it enters the DNHR network to reach a switch in another hierarchy. This somewhat awkward arrangement is dictated by the need to migrate gradually and with minimum cost and network impact from a hierarchical to a nonhierarchical structure.

The DNHR approach does provide for increased efficiency and resiliency. Because there is more potential for sharing temporarily unused resources in the DNHR network, and because it lends itself to more elaborate, time-dependent routing, fewer trunks are required in the DNHR network than in an equivalent hierarchical network. Because the interconnection structure and routing alternatives are richer, DNHR is more resilient than an equivalent nonhierarchical network. As we move toward ISDN, which will place a greatly increased burden on public circuit-switched networks, the nonhierarchical approach will become more prevalent.

2-7   CONTROL SIGNALING

In a circuit-switched network, control signals are the means by which the network is managed and by which calls are established, maintained, and terminated. Both call management and overall network management require that information be exchanged between subscriber and switch, among switches, and between switch and network management center. For a large public telecommunications network, a relatively complex control signaling scheme is required. In this section, we provide a brief overview of control signal functionality and then look at the technique that is the basis of modern integrated digital networks: common channel signaling.

Signaling Functions

Control signals are necessary for the operation of a circuit-switched network, and involve every aspect of network behavior, including both network services visible to the subscriber and internal mechanisms. As networks become more complex, the number of functions performed by control signaling necessarily grows. The following functions, listed in [MART76], are among the most important:

1.   Audible communication with the subscriber, including dial tone, ringing tone, busy signal, and so on.

2. Transmission of the number dialed to switching offices that will attempt to complete a connection.
3. Transmission of information between switches indicating that a call cannot be completed.
4. A signal to make a telephone ring.
5. Transmission of information used for billing purposes.
6. Transmission of information giving the status of equipment or trunks in the network. This information may be used for routing and maintenance purposes.
7. Transmission of information used in diagnosing and isolating system failures.
8. Control of special equipment such as satellite channel equipment.

An example of the use of control signaling is shown in Figure 2-22 [REY83], which illustrates a typical telephone connection sequence from one line to another in the same central office. The steps involved appear as circled numbers in the figure:

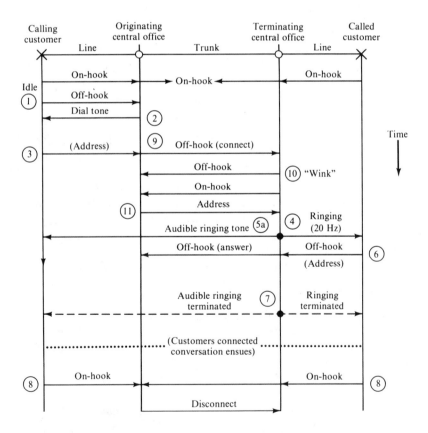

FIGURE 2-22   Signaling on a Typical Completed Call (REY83)

1. Prior to the call, both telephones are not in use (on-hook). The call begins when one subscriber lifts the receiver (off-hook), which is automatically signaled to switch.

2. The switch responds with an audible dial tone, signaling the subscriber that the number may be dialed.

3. The caller dials the number, which is communicated as a destination address to the switch.

4. If the called subscriber is not busy, the switch alerts that subscriber to an incoming call by sending a ringing signal, which causes the telephone to ring.

5. Feedback is provided to the calling subscriber by the switch:
   a) If the called subscriber is not busy, the switch returns an audible ringing tone to the caller while the ringing signal is being sent to the called subscriber.
   b) If the called subscriber is busy, the switch sends an audible busy signal to the caller (not shown in the figure).
   c) If the call cannot be completed through the switch, the switch sends an audible "reorder" message to the caller (not shown in the figure).

6. The called party accepts the call by lifting the receiver (off-hook), which is automatically signaled to the switch.

7. The switch terminates the ringing signal and the audible ringing tone, and establishes a connection between the two subscribers.

8. The connection is released when either subscriber hangs up.

When the called subscriber is attached to a different switch than the calling subscriber, the following switch-to-switch trunk signaling functions are required:

9. The originating switch seizes an idle interswitch trunk, sends an off-hook indication on the trunk, and requests a digit register at the far end, so that the address may be communicated.

10. The terminating switch sends an off-hook followed by an on-hook signal, known as a "wink." This indicates a register-ready status.

11. The originating switch sends the address digits to the terminating switch.

This example gives some idea of the functions that are performed using control signals. A somewhat more detailed overview is given in Box 2-3. The functions performed by control signals can be roughly grouped into the categories of supervisory, address, call information, and network management.

The term **supervisory** is generally used to refer to control functions that have a binary character (true/false; on/off), such as request for service, answer, alerting, and return to idle. They deal with the availability of the called subscriber and of the needed network resources. Supervisory control signals are used to determine if a needed resource is available and, if so, to seize it. They are also used to communicate the status of requested resources.

BOX 2-3
SIGNALING FUNCTIONS

SUPERVISORY

Supervisory signaling provides the mechanism for obtaining the resources to establish a call. It is used to initiate a call request, to hold or release an established connection, to initiate or terminate charging, to recall an operator on an established connection, to alert a subscriber, and to initiate custom calling. It involves the recognition of busy or idle states on subscriber lines and interoffice trunks, and the transmission of that information to the caller and switching system. This form of signaling involves both control and status functions.

Control

Supervisory signaling is used to control the use of resources. Switch and trunk capacity is assigned to a connection with supervisory signals. These resources, once seized, are held for the duration of the call and released upon call termination.

Status

Supervisory signaling also encompasses information concerning the status of a call or attempted call. This information is sent back through the network to the subscriber's switch.

ADDRESS

Address signaling provides the mechanism for identifying the subscribers participating in a call or call attempt. It conveys such information as the calling or called subscriber's telephone number and an area or country code or PBX trunk access code. It involves the transmission of digits of a called telephone number to a switching system from a subscriber or by one switching system to another. Address signaling includes both station-related and routing-related signals.

Station-Related

Address signaling originates with the calling subscriber. From a telephone the signal is generated as a sequence of pulses (rotary dial) or a sequence of two-frequency tones (push button). For digital subscribers, a digital control signal may be used.

Routing-Related

If more than one switch is involved in the call setup, signaling is required between switches. This includes address signaling that supports the routing function, and supervisory signaling that is involved in allocating resources.

CALL INFORMATION

Call information signals are transmitted to a caller to provide information to callers and operators relative to the establishment of a connection through a telephone network. A variety of audible tones are used for this purpose. These signals can be categorized as alerting and progress.

Alerting

Alerting signals are provided to a subscriber who is not placing a call. These include ringing a called telephone and alerting the subscriber that the phone is off the hook.

Progress

Call progress signals indicate the status of the call to the calling subscriber.

NETWORK MANAGEMENT

Network management signals include all those signals related to the ongoing operation and management of the network. They include signals that cause control to be exerted and signals that provide status.

Control

Network management control signals are used to control the overall routing selection process (e.g., to change the preplanned routes of a switch) and to modify the operating characteristics of the network in response to overload and failure conditions.

Status

Network management status signals are used by a switch to provide status information to network management centers and to other switches. Status information includes traffic volume, overload conditions, persistent error conditions, and failures.

Address signals identify a subscriber. Initially, an address signal is generated by a calling subscriber when dialing a telephone number. The resulting address may be propagated through the network to support the routing function and to locate and ring the called subscriber's phone.

The term **call information** refers to those signals that provide information to the subscriber about the status of a call. This is in contrast to internal control signals between switches used in call establishment and termination. Such internal signals are analog or digital electrical messages. In contrast, call information signals are audible tones that can be heard by the caller or an operator with the proper phone set.

Supervisory, address, and call information control signals are directly involved in the establishment and termination of a call. In contrast, **network management** signals are used for the maintenance, troubleshooting, and overall operation of the network. Such signals may be in the form of messages, such as a list of preplanned routes being sent to a station to update its routing tables. These signals cover a broad scope and it is this category that will expand most with the increasing complexity of switched networks.

Common Channel Signaling

Traditional control signaling in circuit-switched networks has been on a per-trunk or inchannel basis. With **inchannel signaling,** the same channel is used to carry control signals as is used to carry the call to which the control signals relate. Such signaling begins at the originating subscriber and follows the same path as the call itself. This has the merit that no additional transmission facilities are needed for signaling; the facilities for voice transmission are shared with control signaling.

Two forms of inchannel signaling are in use: inband and out-of-band. **Inband signaling** uses not only the same physical path as the call it serves, it also uses the same frequency band as the voice signals that are carried. This form of signaling has several advantages. Because the control signals have the same electromagnetic properties as the voice signals, they can go anywhere that the voice signals go. Thus there are no limits on the use of inband signaling anywhere in the network, including places where analog-to-digital or digital-to-analog conversion takes place. In addition, it is impossible to set up a call on a faulty speech path, since the control signals that are used to set up that path would have to follow the same path.

Out-of-band signaling takes advantage of the fact that voice signals do not use the full 4 kHz bandwidth allotted to them. A separate narrow signaling band, within the 4 kHZ, is used to send control signals. The major advantage of this approach is that the control signals can be sent whether or not voice signals are on the line, thus allowing continuous supervision and control of a call. However, an out-of-band scheme needs extra electronics to handle the signaling band.

The information transfer rate is quite limited with inchannel signaling. With inband signals, the channel is only available for control signals when there are no voice signals on the circuit. With out-of-band signals, a very narrow bandwidth is available. With such limits, it is difficult to accommodate, in a timely fashion, any but the simplest form of control messages. However, to take advantage of the potential services and to cope with the increasing complexity of evolving network technology, a richer and more powerful control signal repertoire is needed.

A second drawback of inchannel signaling is the amount of delay from the time a subscriber enters an address (dials a number) and the connection is established. The requirement to reduce this delay is becoming more important as the network is used in new ways. For example, computer-controlled calls, such as with transaction

TABLE 2-6 SIGNALING TECHNIQUES FOR CIRCUIT-SWITCHED NETWORKS

Technique	Description	Comment
Inchannel		
Inband	Transmit control signals in the same band of frequencies used by the voice signals.	The simplest technique. It is necessary for call information signals, and may be used for other control signals. Inband can used over any type of line plant.
Out-of-band	Transmit control signals using the same facilities as the voice signal but a different part of the frequency band.	In contrast to inband, provides continuous supervision during the life of a connection.
Common Channel	Transmit control signals over signaling links that are dedicated to control signals and are common to a number of voice channels.	Reduces call-setup time compared to inchannel methods. It is also more adaptable to evolving functional needs.

processing, use relatively short messages; therefore, the call setup time represents an appreciable part of the total transaction time.

Both of these problems can be addressed with **common channel signaling,** in which control signals are carried over paths completely independent of the voice channels (Table 2-6). One independent control signal path can carry the signals for a

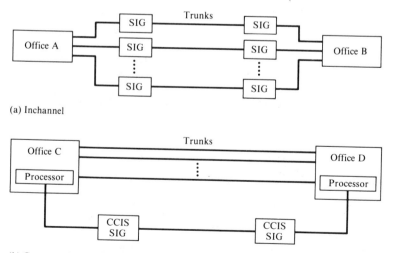

(a) Inchannel

(b) Common channel

CCIS SIG: common-channel interoffice signaling equipment
SIG: per-trunk signaling equipment

FIGURE 2-23 Inchannel and Common Channel Signaling

BOX 2-4

COMMON CHANNEL SIGNALING

REQUIREMENTS [REY83]

- Transfer of network management signals.
- Combining different types of traffic on one trunk group but retaining their identity at the far end.
- Far-end make-busy of trunks for maintenance purposes.
- Return of busy signal from originating rather than terminating station, so that the intermediate trunk(s) can immediately be made available to other calls.
- Increased transparency for the network (such as removal of constraints imposed on customer data transmissions to prevent harmful interaction with inband signaling equipment).
- Call tracing.
- Elimination or improved handling of simultaneous seizure of both ends of 2-way trunks.
- Reduction of fraud.

MODES OF OPERATION

Associated

A separate voice channel or channels carry signaling information, and the channel or channels are routed with the speech channels being served.

Nonassociated

Signaling information traverses a completely separate route from the the voice paths that it controls. Signals are routed through signal transfer points.

COMPARISON WITH INCHANNEL SIGNALING [BELL82b]

Advantages

- Only one set of signaling facilities is needed for each trunk group instead of separate facilities for each individual circuit.
- Control information is transferred directly between control elements of switches without

Disadvantages

- Control information pertaining to an established circuit (e.g., disconnect) must be relayed from one switch to the next. An inchannel signal automatically propagates through the network on the route of the circuit.

going through the voice-channel processing equipment.

- There is no chance of interference between voice and control signals.
- The control channel is inaccessible to users, eliminating a potential means of fraud.
- Connections involving multiple switches can be set up more rapidly, since the control signals do not need to wait for circuit setup.
- The signaling channel does not have to be associated with any particular trunk group, allowing centralized control.

- If one node fails to relay the control signal, facilities downstream from the failure will not receive the control information. Thus reliability is more critical with common-channel signaling.
- There is no automatic test of the voice circuit.

number of subscriber channels, and hence is a common control channel for these subscriber channels.

The principle of common channel signaling is illustrated and contrasted with inchannel signaling in Figure 2-23. As can be seen, the signal path for common channel signaling is physically separate from the path for voice or other subscriber signals. The common channel can be configured with the bandwidth required to carry control signals for a rich variety of functions. Thus, both the signaling protocol and the network architecture to support that protocol are more complex than inchannel signaling. However, the continuing drop in computer hardware costs makes common channel signaling increasingly attractive. The control signals are messages that are passed between switches and between a switch and the network management center. Thus, the control signaling portion of the network is in effect a distributed computer network carrying short messages.

Box 2-4 lists some of the requirements that common channel signaling is intended to address. These and other functions require that the control signals be independent of the subscriber signals, and that quite elaborate control messages be used in some instances.

Two modes of operation are used in common channel signaling (Figure 2-24). In the **associated mode,** the common channel closely tracks along its entire length the interswitch trunk groups that are served between endpoints. The control signals are on different channels from the subscriber signals, and inside the switch, the control signals are routed directly to a control signal processor. A more complex, but more powerful, mode is the **nonassociated mode.** With this mode, the network is augmented by additional nodes, known as signal transfer points. There is now no close or simple assignment of control channels to trunk groups. In effect, there are now two separate networks, with links between them so that the control portion of the network can exercise control over the switching nodes that are servicing the subscriber calls. Network management is more easily exerted in the nonassociated mode since control channels can be assigned to tasks in a more flexible manner. The nonassociated mode is likely to be the mode used in ISDN.

Box 2-4 also summarizes the merits of common channel signaling relative to inchannel signaling. Some of the points listed bear elaboration. With inchannel signaling, control signals from one switch are originated by a control processor and switched onto the outgoing channel. On the receiving end, the control signals must be switched from the voice channel into the control processor. With common channel signaling, the control signals are transferred directly from one control processor to another, without being tied to a voice signal. This is a simpler procedure, and one that is less susceptible to accidental or intentional interference between subscriber and control signals. This is one of the main motivations for common channel signaling. Another key motivation for common channel signaling is that call setup time is reduced. Consider the sequence of events for call setup with inchannel signaling when more than one switch is involved. A control signal will be sent from one switch to the next in the intended path. At each switch, the control signal cannot be transferred through the switch to the next leg of the route until the associated circuit is established through that switch. With common channel signaling, forwarding of control information can overlap the circuit-setup process.

With nonassociated signaling, a further advantage emerges: One or more central control points can be established. All control information can be routed to a network control center where requests are processed and from which control signals are sent to switches that handle subscriber traffic. In this way, requests can be processed with a more global view of network conditions.

Of course, there are disadvantages to common channel signaling, as suggested in Box 2-4. These primarily have to do with the complexity of the technique. However, the dropping cost of digital hardware and the increasingly digital nature of telecommunication networks make common channel signaling the appropriate technology.

All of the discussion in this section has dealt with the use of common channel signaling inside the network, that is, to control switches. Even in a network that is completely controlled by common channel signaling, inchannel signaling is needed for at least some of the communication with the subscriber. For example, dial tone, ringback, and busy signals must be inchannel to reach the user. In general, the subscriber does not have access to the common channel signaling portion of the network and does not employ the common channel signaling protocol. However, we will see in Part II, that this statement will not be true for ISDN.

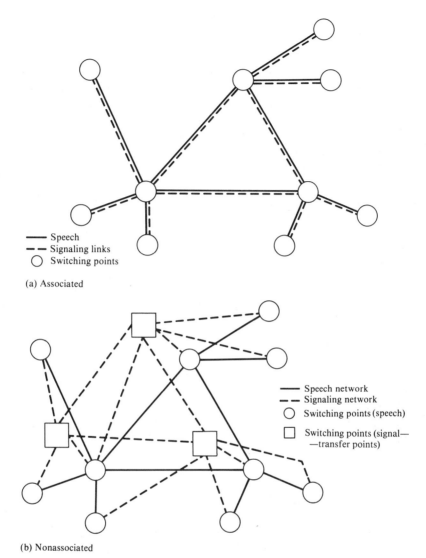

Speech
Signaling links
Switching points

(a) Associated

Speech network
Signaling network
Switching points (speech)
Switching points (signal—
—transfer points)

(b) Nonassociated

FIGURE 2-24   Common Channel Signaling Modes

2-8   SUMMARY

Circuit switching was primarily designed to provide an efficient and high-quality facility for voice traffic. Key distinguishing features of circuit switching are that a
circuit, once established, is transparent to the subscribers (equivalent to a direct

connection) and that the delay across the circuit is nonvariable and small (the propagation delay of the transmission path).

Increasingly, digital switching and transmission techniques are being used. Digital switching involves the manipulation of time-division multiplexed streams of bits, representing either data or digitized voice. Several time-division switching techniques are in common use. Synchronous time-division multiplexing techniques are now preferred to analog frequency-division multiplexing techniques for carrier systems, both because of reduced cost and improved signal quality. The increasing use of both digital switching and digital transmission has paved the way for integrated digital networks, which are described in Chapter 4.

Several important aspects of circuit-switched networks are changing dramatically in the wake of the increasing complexity and digitalization of public telecommunication networks. Simple hierarchical routing schemes are being replaced with more flexible and powerful nonhierarchical schemes. This reflects a corresponding change in the underlying architecture, which leads to increased efficiency and resilience. Simple inchannel control signaling methods are being replaced with more complex and higher-speed common channel signaling. Again, this has implications for the architecture of the network.

2-9 RECOMMENDED READING

As befits its age, circuit switching has inspired a voluminous literature. Two good books on the subject are [BELL82b] and [KEIS85]. The first of these is particularly lucid and comprehensive. Worthwhile accounts may also be found in [FREE80] and [DAVI73]. [BROO83] discusses alternative internal organizations for a switch. The subject of routing is covered in [HURL87] and [YUM87]. Discussions of control signaling can be found in [FREE80], [REY83], and [KEIS85].

2-10 PROBLEMS

2-1 Consider a nonblocking three-stage space-division switch with 2048 inputs and 2048 outputs (2048 full-duplex ports). For an optimum design, what is the total number of crosspoints required? How many arrays are needed for each stage and how many input and output lines are there per stage?

2-2 How many crosspoints would be required for a three-stage space division switch to serve 500 ports:
(a) in a nonblocking configuration?
(b) in a blocking configuration which has 20 ports in each concentration and expansion array with 15 center-stage arrays?

2-3 For the system of problem 2-1, how many switch points would be needed if a TDM bus were used?

2-4 What is the magnitude of delay through a TSI stage?

2-5 Consider a simple TSI switch whose memory has a 50-nsec cycle time. The memory is organized into 16-bit words. Frames are 1024 bits. What is the maximum data rate per channel? What is the data rate of the trunk lines to and from the switch?

2-6 For STS, give an example of blocking when the number of TSI units equals the number of incoming channels. What is the minimum number of TSI units for proper functioning (even in blocking mode)?

2-7 Assume that the velocity of propagation on a TDM bus is 0.7 c, its length is 10 m, and the data rate is 500 Mbps. How many bits should be transmitted in a time slot to achieve a bus efficiency of 99 percent?

2-8 Demonstrate that in a TSI store at most only half of the memory is usefully occupied at any one time. Devise a means of reducing the TSI memory requirement while maintaining its nonblocking property.

2-9 Consider the use of a 500-ns memory in a TSI device. Assume that voice signals are digitized for transmission at 64 kbps. How many full-duplex voice channels can be supported by a TSI switch?

2-10 Justify the assertion in Section 2-4 that, for an STS network, the number of TSI units must be double the number of incoming and outgoing lines for nonblocking.

2-11 Determine the number of crosspoints and the total number of memory bits required for a TST switch defined as follows:

- Number of voice lines = 32
- Single-stage space switch
- Number of channels per frame = 30
- Time expansion = 2

2-12 How many bits of memory are needed in a TSI unit for a 60-channel signal with nine bits per time slot?

2-13 Consider a simple telephone network consisting of two end offices and one toll center with a 1-Mhz full-duplex trunk between each end office and the toll center. Each full-duplex voice channel on the trunk occupies a bandwidth of 4 kHz. Assume that the average telephone is used to make four calls per 8-hour workday, with a mean call duration of six minutes. Ten percent of the calls are long distance. What is the maximum number of telephones an end office can support?

2-14 If one examines the rate structure of the long distance telephone services, it would appear that distance, while important, is not the major factor in determining cost. Speculate on the reason for this.

CHAPTER 3

PACKET SWITCHING

Around 1970, research began on a new form of architecture for long-distance digital data communications: packet switching. Although the technology of packet switching has evolved substantially since that time, it is remarkable that: (1) the basic technology of packet switching is fundamentally the same today as it was in the early-1970s networks, and (2) packet switching remains one of the few effective technologies for long-distance data communications. Even with the continuing evolution and increasing digital capability of long-haul circuit-switched networks, packet switching will continue to play an important role in integrated digital networks (IDNs).

This chapter provides an overview of packet switching technology. We will see that many of the advantages of packet switching (flexibility, resource sharing, robustness, responsiveness) come with a cost. The packet-switched network is a distributed collection of packet-switched nodes. In the ideal, all packet-switched nodes would always know the state of the entire network. Unfortunately, because the nodes are distributed, there is always a time delay between a change in status in one portion of the network and the knowledge of that change elsewhere. Furthermore, there is overhead involved in communicating status information. As a result, a packet-switched network can never perform "perfectly," and elaborate algorithms are used to cope with the time delay and overhead penalties of network operation.

The chapter begins with an introduction to packet-switched network operation. Next, we look at the internal operation of these networks, introducing the concepts of virtual circuits and datagrams. Following this, the key technologies of routing and flow control are examined. The chapter concludes with an introduction to fast packet switching, which is one of the few genuine recent advances in packet-switching technology and will be important in the evolution of the IDN and ISDN networks.

3-1 OVERVIEW

The long-haul circuit-switched telecommunications network was originally designed to handle voice traffic, and the majority of traffic on these networks continues to be voice. A key characteristic of circuit-switched networks is that resources within the network are dedicated to a particular call. For voice connections, the resulting circuit will enjoy a high percentage of utilization since, most of the time, one party or the other is talking. However, as the circuit-switched network began to be used increasingly for data connections, two shortcomings became apparent:

- In a typical terminal-to-host data connection, much of the time the line is idle. Thus, with data connections, a circuit-switched approach is inefficient.
- In a circuit-switched network, the connection provides for transmission at constant data rate. Thus both devices that are connected must transmit and receive at the same data rate. This limits the utility of the network in interconnecting a variety of host computers and terminals.

To understand how packet switching addresses these problems, let us briefly summarize packet-switching operation. Data are transmitted in short packets. A typical upper bound on packet length is 1000 octets (bytes). If a source has a longer message to send, the message is broken up into a series of packets (Figure 3-1). Each packet contains a portion (or all for a short message) of the user's data plus some control information. The control information, at a minimum, includes the information that the network requires in order to be able to route the packet through the network and deliver it to the intended destination. At each node en route, the packet is received, stored briefly, and passed on to the next node.

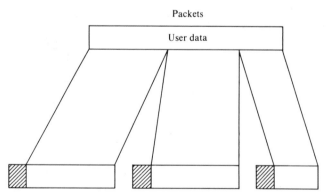

Packets

User data

FIGURE 3-1   Packets

Let us return to Figure 2-1, but now consider that this is a simple packet-switched network. Consider a packet to be sent from station A to station E. The packet will include control information that indicates that the intended destination is E. The packet is sent from A to node 4. Node 4 stores the packet, determines the next leg of the route (say 5), and queues the packet to go out on that link (the 4-5 link). When the link is available, the packet is transmitted to node 5, which will forward the packet to node 6, and finally to E. This approach has a number of advantages over circuit switching:

- Line efficiency is greater, since a single node-to-node link can be dynamically shared by many packets over time. The packets are queued up and transmitted as rapidly as possible over the link. By contrast, with circuit switching, time on a node-to-node link is preallocated using synchronous time-division multiplexing. Much of the time, such a link may be idle because a portion of its time is dedicated to a connection which is idle.
- A packet-switched network can carry out data-rate conversion. Two stations of different data rates can exchange packets since each connects to its node at its proper data rate.
- When traffic becomes heavy on a circuit-switched network, some calls are blocked; that is, the network refuses to accept additional connection requests until the load on the network decreases. On a packet-switched network, packets are still accepted, but delivery delay increases.
- Priorities can be used. Thus, if a node has a number of packets queued for transmission, it can transmit the higher-priority packets first. These packets will therefore experience less delay than lower-priority packets.

3-2 INTERNAL OPERATION

Switching Technique

A station has a message to send through a packet-switched network that is of length greater than the maximum packet size. It therefore breaks the message up into packets and sends these packets, one at a time, to the network. A question arises as to how the network will handle this stream of packets as it attempts to route them through the network and deliver them to the intended destination. There are two approaches that are used in contemporary networks: datagram and virtual circuit.

In the **datagram** approach, each packet is treated independently, with no reference to packets that have gone before. Let us consider the implication of this approach. Suppose that station A in Figure 2-1 has a three-packet message to send to E. It transmits the packets, 1-2-3, to node 4. On *each* packet, node 4 must make a routing decision. Packet 1 arrives for delivery to *E*. Node 4 could plausibly forward this packet to either node 5 or node 7 as the next step in the route. In this case, node 4 determines that its queue of packets for node 5 is shorter than for node 7, so it queues the packet for node 5. Ditto for packet 2. But for packet 3, node 4 finds that its queue for node 7 is now shorter and so queues packet 3 for that node. So the packets, each with the same destination address, do not all follow the same route. Because of this, it is just possible that packet 3 will beat packet 2 to node 6. Thus it is possible that the packets will be delivered to *E* in a different sequence from the one in which they were sent. It is up to *E* to figure out how to reorder them. Also, it is possible for a packet to be destroyed in the network. For example, if a packet-switched node crashes momentarily, all of its queued packets may be lost. If this were to happen to one of the packets in our example, node 6 has no way of knowing that one of the packets in the sequence of packets has been lost. Again, it is up to *E* to detect the loss of a packet and figure out how to recover it. In this technique, each packet, treated independently, is referred to as a datagram.

In the **virtual circuit** approach, a preplanned route is established before any packets are sent. For example, suppose that *A* has one or more messages to send to *E*. It first sends a special control packet, referred to as a Call Request packet, to 4, requesting a logical connection to *E*. Node 4 decides to route the request and all subsequent packets to 5, which decides to route the request and all subsequent packets to 6, which finally delivers the Call Request packet to *E*. If *E* is prepared to accept the connection, it sends a Call Accept packet to 6. This packet is passed back through nodes 5 and 4 to *A*. Stations *A* and *E* may now exchange data over the route that has been established. Because the route is fixed for the duration of the logical connection, it is somewhat similar to a circuit in a circuit-switching network, and is referred to as a virtual circuit. Each packet now contains a virtual circuit identifier as well as data. Each node on the preestablished route knows where to direct such packets; no routing decisions are required. Thus every data packet from *A* intended for *E* traverses nodes 4, 5, and 6; every data packet from *E* intended for *A* traverses nodes 6, 5, and 4. Eventually, one of the stations terminates the connection with a Clear Request packet. At any time, each station can have more than one virtual circuit to any other station and can have virtual circuits to more than one station.

So, the main characteristic of the virtual-circuit technique is that a route between stations is set up prior to data transfer. Note that this does not mean that this is a dedicated path, as in circuit switching. A packet is still buffered at each node, and queued for output over a line. The difference from the datagram approach is that, with virtual circuits, the node need not make a routing decision for each packet. It is made only once for all packets using that virtual circuit.

If two stations wish to exchange data over an extended period of time, there are certain advantages to virtual circuits. First, the network may provide services related to the virtual circuit, including sequencing and error control. *Sequencing* refers to the fact that, since all packets follow the same route, they arrive in the original order. *Error control* is a service that assures not only that packets arrive in proper sequence,

---

BOX 3-1

COMPARISON OF VIRTUAL CIRCUITS AND DATAGRAMS

INTERNAL OPERATION

Virtual Circuit Advantages

- Connection-oriented services, such as sequencing, and error control may be provided.
- Routing decisions are not required for each packet for each node, but only once at setup time. Thus packet transmission and delivery may take less time.

Datagram Advantages

- Call setup time is avoided. This is an advantage for short transactions.
- Network congestion can be bypassed, improving delivery performance.
- Network failures can be bypassed, improving reliability.

EXTERNAL SERVICE

Virtual Circuit Advantages

- Provides the user with connection-oriented services, such as sequencing and error control.

Datagram Advantages

- Supports connectionless applications.
- Avoids call setup time.

---

but that all packets arrive correctly. For example, if a packet in a sequence from node 4 to node 6 fails to arrive at node 6, or arrives with an error, node 6 can request a retransmission of that packet from node 4. Another advantage is that packets should transit the network more rapidly with a virtual circuit; it is not necessary to make a routing decision for each packet at each node.

One advantage of the datagram approach is that the call setup phase is avoided. Thus, if a station wishes to send only one or a few packets, datagram delivery will be quicker. Another advantage of the datagram service is that, because it is more primitive, it is more flexible. For example, if congestion develops in one part of the network, incoming datagrams can be routed away from the congestion. With the use of virtual circuits, packets follow a predefined route, and thus it is more difficult for the network to adapt to congestion. A third advantage is that datagram delivery is inherently more reliable. With the use of virtual circuits, if a node fails, all virtual circuits that pass through that node are lost. With datagram delivery, if a node fails, subsequent packets may find an alternate route that bypasses that node.

Box 3-1 summarizes the relative merits of the two approaches. Most currently-available packet-switched networks make use of virtual circuits for their internal operation. To some degree, this reflect a historical motivation to provide a network that presents a service as reliable (in terms of sequencing) as a circuit-switched network. There are, however, several providers of private packet-switched

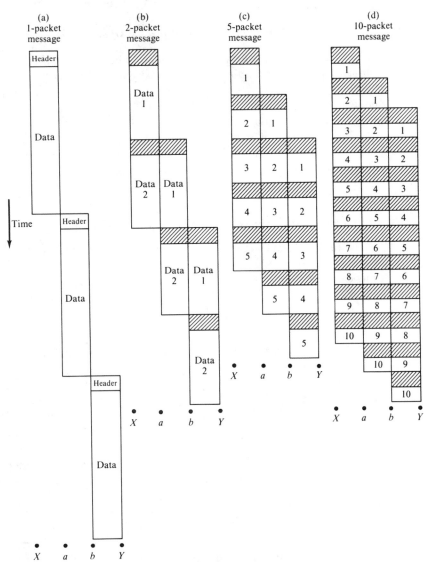

FIGURE 3-2 Effect of Packet Size on Transmission Time

networks that make use of datagrams operation. From the user's point of view, there should be very little difference in the external behavior based on the use of datagrams or virtual circuits. If a manager is faced with a choice, other factors such as cost and performance should probably take precedence over whether the internal network operation is datagram or virtual circuit.

Packet Size

One important design issue is the packet size to be used in the network. There is a significant relationship between packet size and transmission time, as shown in Figure 3-2. In this example, it is assumed that there is a virtual circuit from station X through nodes a and b to station Y. The message to be sent comprises 30 octets, and each packet contains 3 octets of control information, which is placed at the beginning of each packet and is referred to as a *header*. If the entire message is sent as a single packet of 33 octets (3 octets of header plus 30 octets of data), then the packet is first transmitted from station X to node a (Figure 3-2a). When the entire packet is received, it can then be transmitted from a to b. When the entire packet is received at node b, it is then transferred to station Y. The total transmission time is 99 octet-times (33 octets $\times$ 3 packet transmissions).

Suppose now that we break the message up into two packets, each containing 15 octets of the message and, of course, 3 octets each of header or control information. In this case, node a can begin transmitting the first packet as soon as it has arrived from X, without waiting for the second packet. Because of this overlap in transmission, the total transmission time drops to 72 octet-times. By breaking the message up into 5 packets, each intermediate node can begin transmission even sooner and the savings in time is greater, with a total of 63 octet-times. However, this process of using more and smaller packets eventually results in increased, rather than reduced delay, as illustrated in Figure 3-2d. This is because each packet contains a fixed amount of header, and more packets mean more of these headers. Furthermore, the example does not show the processing and queuing delays at each node. These delays are also greater when more packets are handled for a single message. Thus, packet-switched network designers must consider these factors in attempting to find an optimum packet size.

3-3   COMPARISON OF CIRCUIT SWITCHING AND PACKET SWITCHING

Having looked at the internal operation of packet switching, we can now return to a comparison of this technique with circuit switching. We first look at the important issue of performance, and then examine other characteristics.

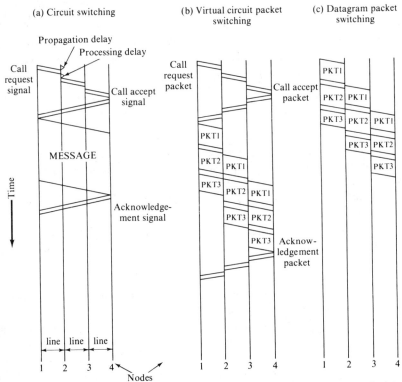

FIGURE 3-3 Event Timing for Various Communication Switching Techniques

Performance

A simple comparison of circuit switching and the two forms of packet switching is provided in Figure 3-3. The figure depicts the transmission of a message across four nodes, from a source station attached to node 1 to a destination station attached to node 4.

For circuit switching, there is a certain amount of delay before the message can be sent. First, a call request signal is sent through the network, to set up a connection to the destination. If the destination station is not busy, a call accepted signal returns. Note that a processing delay is incurred at each node during the call request; this time is spent at each node setting up the route of the connection. On the return, this processing is not needed since the connection is already set up. After the connection is set up, the message is sent as a single block, with no noticeable delay at the switching nodes.

Virtual-circuit packet switching appears quite similar to circuit switching. A virtual circuit is requested using a call request packet, which incurs a delay at each node. The virtual circuit is accepted with a call accept packet. In contrast to the circuit-switching case, the call acceptance also experiences node delays, even though the virtual circuit route is now established. The reason is that this packet is queued at each node and must wait its turn for retransmission. Once the virtual circuit is established, the message is transmitted in packets. It should be clear that this phase of the operation can be no faster than circuit switching, for comparable networks. This is because circuit switching is an essentially transparent process, providing a constant data rate across the network. Packet switching requires some node delay at each node in the path. Worse, this delay is variable and will increase with increased load.

Datagram packet switching does not require a call setup. Thus, for short messages, it will be faster than virtual circuit packet switching and perhaps circuit switching. However, since each individual datagram is routed independently, the processing for each datagram at each node may be longer than for virtual-circuit packets. Thus, for long messages, the virtual circuit technique may be superior.

Figure 3-4 is intended only to suggest what the relative performance of the techniques might be; however, actual performance depends on a host of factors, including the size of the network, its topology, the pattern of load, and the characteristics of typical exchanges. The interested reader may pursue these topics in [KLEI76], [ROSN82], [SAND80], [KUMM80], [MIYA75], and [STUC85].

Other Characteristics

Besides performance, there are a number of other characteristics that may be considered in comparing the techniques we have been discussing. Table 3-1 summarizes the most important of these. Box 3-2 attempts to summarize some of the key relative merits of circuit switching and packet switching.

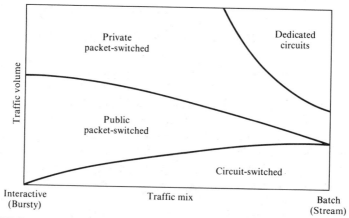

FIGURE 3-4 Alternatives for Data Communications (BLAC87)

TABLE 3-1   COMPARISON OF COMMUNICATION SWITCHING TECHNIQUES

Circuit Switching	Datagram Packet Switching	Virtual-Circuit Packet Switching
Dedicated transmission path	No dedicated path	No dedicated path
Continuous transmission of data	Transmission of packets	Transmission of packets
Fast enough for interactive	Fast enough for interactive	Fast enough for interactive
Messages are not stored	Packets may be stored until delivered	Packets stored until delivered
The path is established for entire conversation	Route established for each packet	Route established for entire conversation
Call setup delay. Negligible transmission delay	Packet transmission delay	Call setup delay. Packet transmission delay
Busy signal if called party busy	Sender may be notified if packet not delivered	Sender notified of connection denial
Overload may block call setup; no delay for established calls	Overload increases packet delay	Overload may block call setup; increases packet delay
Electromechanical or computerized switching nodes	Small switching nodes	Small switching nodes
User responsible for message loss protection	Network may be responsible for individual packets	Network may be responsible for packet sequences
Usually no speed or code conversion	Speed and code conversion	Speed and code conversion
Fixed bandwidth transmission	Dynamic use of bandwidth	Dynamic use of bandwidth
No overhead bits after call setup	Overhead bits in each packet	Overhead bits in each packet

3-4   APPLICATION OF PACKET SWITCHING

Although we will later in this chapter explore some of the details of packet-switching technology, we are already in a position to comment on the applicability of this networking approach (Box 3-3). Recall that we said that packet switching held certain advantages over circuit switching for data communications. In particular, packet switching may make more efficient use of internal (to the network) communications resources and allow devices of differing data rates to interconnect. However, in order to be more specific about the applicability of packet switching, we need to examine in more detail the nature of the data communications traffic.

Data communications traffic can be roughly classified into two categories: stream and bursty. **Stream traffic** is characterized by lengthy and fairly continuous transmission. Examples are file transfer, telemetry, other sorts of batch data process-

BOX 3-2

RELATIVE MERITS OF CIRCUIT SWITCHING AND PACKET SWITCHING OF DATA

CIRCUIT SWITCHING

Advantages

- Compatible with voice. Economies of scale can be realized by using the same network for voice and data.
- Commonality of calling procedures for voice and data. No special user training or communication protocols are needed to handle data traffic.

Disadvantages

- Subject to blocking. This makes it difficult to size the network properly. The problem is less severe with the use of dynamic nonhierarchical routing techniques.
- Requires subscriber compatibility. The devices at each end of a circuit must be compatible in terms of protocol and data rate, since the circuit is a transparent connection. Furthermore, for each terminal connected to a host, a separate physical line into the host is required.
- Large processing and signal burden. For transaction-type applications, data calls are of short duration and need to be set up rapidly. This proportionally increases the overhead burden on the network.

PACKET SWITCHING

Advantages

- Provides speed conversion. Two attached devices with different data rates may exchange data; the network buffers the data and delivers it at the appropriate data rate.

Disadvantages

- Complex routing and control. To achieve efficiency and resilience, a packet-switched network must employ a complex set of routing and control algorithms.

BOX 3-2 continued

Advantages	*Disadvantages*
• Appears nonblocking. As the network load increases, the delay increases, but new exchanges are usually permitted.	• Delay. Delay is a function of load. It can be long and it is variable.
• Efficient utilization. Switches and trunks are used on demand rather than dedicating capacity to a particular call.	
• Logical multiplexing. A host system can have simultaneous conversations with a number of terminals over a single line.	

ing applications, and digitized voice communication. **Bursty traffic** is characterized by short, sporadic transmissions. Interactive terminal-host traffic, such as transaction processing, data entry, and time-sharing, fits this description.

Figure 3-4 shows the relative applicability of four alternative networking approaches. The **circuit-switched network** approach makes use of dial-up lines. The cost is based on data rate, connection time, and distance. As we have said, this is quite inefficient for bursty traffic. However, for occasional stream-oriented requirements, this may be the most appropriate choice. For example, a corporation may have distributed offices. At the close of the day, each office transfers a file to headquarters summarizing the activities for that day. A dial-up line used for the single transfer from each office appears to be the most cost-effective solution. When there is a high volume of stream traffic between a few sites, the most economical solution is to obtain **dedicated circuits** between sites. These circuits, also known as leased lines or semipermanent circuits, may be leased from a telecommunications provider, such as a telephone company, or from a satellite provider. The dedicated circuit carries a constant fixed cost based on data rate and, in some cases, distance. If the traffic volume is high enough, then the utilization will be high enough to make this approach the most attractive.

On the other hand, if the traffic is primarily bursty, then packet switching has the advantage. Furthermore, packet switching permits terminals and computer ports of various data rates to be interconnected. If the traffic is primarily bursty, but is of relatively modest volume for an organization, then a **public packet-switched network** provides the best solution. A public packet-switched network works much like a public telephone network. In this case, the network provides a packet transmission service to a variety of subscribers, each of which has moderate traffic requirements. If there are a number of different subscribers, then the total traffic should be great enough to result in high utilization. Hence, the public network is cost-effective

---

BOX 3-3
PACKET SWITCHING

APPLICATIONS
Data

Public Data Network (PDN)/Value-Added Network (VAN)

Provide a wide-area data communications facility for computers and terminals. The network is a shared resource, owned by a provider who sells the capacity to others. Thus it functions as a utility service for a number of subscriber communities.

Private Packet-Switched Network

Provide a shared resource for one organization's computers and terminals. A private packet-switched network is justified if there are a substantial number of devices with a substantial amount of traffic in one organization.

Voice

Packetized Voice Network

Provide a communications facility for real-time voice traffic. This application requires the capability to transmit voice signals with very low delay and with virtually no delay variability.

TECHNOLOGY

Internal Operation

Datagram
Virtual Circuit

External Interface

Connection-oriented (Virtual Circuit)
Connectionless (Datagram)

---

from the provider's point of view. The subscriber gets the advantages of packet switching without the fixed cost of implementing and maintaining the network. The cost to the subscriber is based on both connection time and traffic volume, but not distance. Such a network is called a value-added network (VAN), reflecting the fact that the network adds value to the underlying transmission facilities. In most countries other than the United States, there is a single public network owned or controlled by the government, and referred to as a public data network (PDN).

If the volume of an organization's bursty traffic is high, and concentrated among a small number of sites, then a **private packet-switched network** is the best solution. This is a network in which the organization that owns the data communicating equipment (terminals, hosts) also owns the packet-switching nodes. The nodes are interconnected by dedicated circuits. With a lot of bursty traffic between sites, the private network provides much better utilization and hence lower cost than using circuit switching or simple dedicated lines. The cost of a private network (other than the initial fixed cost of the packet switching nodes) is based solely on distance. Thus, it combines the efficiencies of public packet switching with the time and volume independence of dedicated circuits.

3-5 ROUTING

Requirements

The primary function of a packet-switched network is to accept packets from a source station and deliver them to a destination station. To accomplish this, a path or route through the network must be determined. To provide good performance and robustness, packet-switched networks typically have many interconnected nodes. Between any pair of stations, there will be a number of possible routes and a routing function must be performed. The requirements for this function include:

- Correctness
- Simplicity
- Robustness
- Stability
- Fairness
- Optimality

The first two items on the list are self-explanatory. Robustness has to do with the ability of the network to deliver packets via some route in the face of localized failures and overloads. Ideally, the network can react to such contingencies without loss of packets or the breaking of virtual circuits. The designer who seeks robustness must cope with the competing requirement for stability. Techniques that react to changing conditions have an unfortunate tendency to either react too slowly to events or to experience unstable swings from one extreme to another. For example, the network may react to congestion in one area by shifting most of the load to a second area. Now the second area is overloaded and the first is underutilized, causing a second shift. During these shifts, packets may travel in loops through the network.

A trade-off also exists between fairness and optimality. Some performance criteria may give higher priority to the exchange of packets between nearby stations compared to an exchange between distant stations. This policy may maximize average throughput but will appear unfair to the station which primarily needs to communicate with distant stations. Finally, any routing technique involves some processing overhead at each node and often a transmission overhead as well. The penalty of such overhead needs to be less than the benefit accrued based on some reasonable metric, such as increased robustness or fairness.

Routing Techniques

In this section, our objective is to give the reader a feel for the complexity of the routing function and for some of the trade-offs involved in assessing alternate approaches. For a more complete treatment, the reader is referred to [STAL88a] or to one of the many survey articles on the subject, including [HSIE84a], [BELL86], [GERL84}, [GERL81], and [SCHW80].

Before examining some typical routing algorithms, we need to specify the design criterion that is to be used. The selection of a route is generally based on some performance criterion. The simplest criterion is to choose the minimum-hop route (one that passes through the least number of nodes) through the network. This is an easily measured criterion, and should minimize the consumption of network resources. A generalization of the minimum-hop criterion is least-cost routing. In this case, a cost is associated with each link, and, for any pair of attached stations, the route through the network that accumulates the least cost is sought. For example, the costs in the network of Figure 3-5 are shown as numeric labels on the links. The shortest path (fewest hops) from node 1 to node 6 is 1-3-6 (cost $= 5 + 5 = 10$), but the least-cost path is 1-4-5-6 (cost $= 1 + 1 + 2 = 4$). Costs are assigned to links to support one or more design objectives. For example, the cost could be inversely related to the data rate (i.e., the higher the data rate on a link, the lower the assigned cost of the link), or the current queuing delay on the link. In the first case, the least-cost route should provide the highest throughput, since higher-rate links are

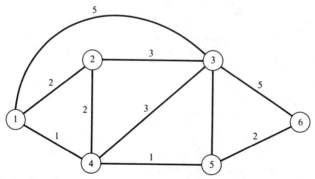

FIGURE 3-5 Packet-Switched Network

preferred to lower-rate links. In the second case, the least-cost route should minimize delay, since less busy links are preferred to more busy links.

In either the minimum-hop or least-cost approach, the algorithm for determining the optimum route for any pair of stations is relatively straightforward [STAL88a], and the processing time would be about the same for either computation. Because the least-cost criterion is more flexible, this is more common than the minimum-hop criterion.

With this background, we now look at some of the important alternative routing techniques (Table 3-2).

Fixed Routing.   One of the simplest routing strategies is fixed routing. In this case, a route is selected for each source-destination pair of nodes in the network. The

TABLE 3-2   ROUTING FOR PACKET-SWITCHED NETWORKS

Technique	Description	Comment
Fixed	All routes through the network are preplanned and do not change with changing conditions.	A simple algorithm that might be useful in a very stable network
Flooding	A packet to be sent from one station to another is replicated as required so that all possible routes through the network are followed. A hop-count limit is used to terminate the process.	An extremely wasteful procedure and not useful for general-purpose routing. Because it is highly reliable, this technique could be used for occasional, important network control packets.
Adaptive Isolated	Each node makes a routing decision based only on some predefined preferences and the current state of queuing delays on outgoing links.	The simplest form of adaptive routing. In a small and relatively stable network, this technique might be attractive.
Distributed	Routing decisions are based on knowledge of network topology and delay conditions. This information is shared among the packet-switching nodes, and each node makes its own routing decisions.	A flexible and robust approach. There is a trade-off between the amount of information provided to the nodes and the need to minimize overhead so as to avoid degrading performance.
Centralized	Routing decisions are based on knowledge of network topology and delay conditions. This information is provided to a central controller by all the nodes. The central controller then issues routing instructions back to the nodes.	A relatively efficient adaptive approach. There is a risk that the controller will become a bottleneck. Also, failure of the controller disables the routing mechanism.

routes are fixed, or at least only changed when there is a change in the topology of the network. Thus the link costs used in designing routes cannot be based on any dynamic variable, such as traffic. They could, however, be based on actual transmission cost or expected traffic.

Figure 3-6 suggests how fixed routing might be implemented. A central routing directory is created, to be stored perhaps at a network control center. Note that it is not necessary to store the route for each possible pair of nodes. Rather, it is sufficient to know, for each pair of nodes, the identity of the first node on the route. To see that this is sufficient, consider the least-cost route between a pair of nodes i and n. Suppose that the least-cost route begins with the link from node i to node k. Let us use the label R_1 to refer to the remainder of the route, which is the part from k to n. Now, define the least-cost route from k to n to be R_2. If the cost of R_1 is greater than the cost of R_2, then the i-n route can be improved by using R_2 instead. If the cost of R_1 is less than the cost of R_2, then R_2 is not the least-cost route from k to n. Therefore, R_1 and R_2 are the same route. This line of reasoning demonstrates that, at each point along a route, it is only necessary to know the identity of the next node, not the entire route. Because of this, each node need only store a single row of the routing directory; the node's directory shows the next node to take for each destination.

With fixed routing, there is no difference between routing for datagrams and virtual circuits. All packets from a given source to a given destination follow the same route. The advantage of fixed routing is its simplicity, and it should work well in a reliable network with a steady load. Its disadvantage is its lack of flexibility. It does not react to network congestion or failures. Thus, fixed routing is typically not used in large networks. However, the method is worth presenting, since the use of a next-node directory is to be found in many more-sophisticated routing techniques.

		To node					
		1	2	3	4	5	6
From node	1	—	2	4	4	4	4
	2	1	—	3	4	4	4
	3	5	2	—	5	5	5
	4	1	2	5	—	5	5
	5	4	4	3	4	—	6
	6	5	5	5	5	5	—

FIGURE 3-6 Fixed Routing

Flooding.   Another simple routing technique is flooding. This technique requires no network information whatsoever, and works as follows. A packet is sent by a source node to every one of its neighbors. At each node, an incoming packet is retransmitted on all outgoing links except for the link upon which it arrived. This technique is illustrated in Figure 3-7, which shows a packet transmission from node 1 to node 6. If node 1 has a packet to send to node 6, it sends a copy of that packet to nodes 2, 3, and 4. Node 2 will send a copy to nodes 3 and 4. Node 4 will send a copy to nodes 2, 3, and 5. And so it goes. Eventually, a number of copies of the packet will arrive at node 6. The packet must have some unique identifier (e.g., sequence number) so that node 6 knows to discard all but the first copy.

It is clear that unless something is done to stop the incessant retransmission of packets, the number of packets in circulation just from a single source packet grows without bound. A simple solution is to limit the number of hops, or times, that a packet can be forwarded, by the inclusion of a *hop count* field in each packet. The count is initially set by the source node to some positive integer value. Each time a node receives a packet to be passed on, it decreases the hop count by one. If the count reaches zero, the packet is discarded.

One interesting property of the flooding technique is that all possible routes between source and destination are tried. Thus, no matter what link or node outages have occurred, a packet will always get through so long as at least one path between source and destination exists. As a result, the technique is highly robust and could be used to send high-priority messages. An example application is for a military network that is subject to extensive damage. Flooding could also be used to broadcast a message to all nodes. Broadcasting is sometimes used in adaptive routing, which is described next.

Adaptive Routing.   The routing strategies discussed so far do not react to changing conditions within the network, or at most react infrequently as the result of some system operator action. This characteristic is not necessarily a bad one. Consider these drawbacks of an adaptive strategy, one in which the routing decision depends on the changing conditions of the network:

- The routing decision is more complex; therefore, the processing burden on the network increases.
- In most cases, adaptive strategies depend on status information that is collected at one place but used at another; therefore, the traffic burden on the network increases.
- An adaptive strategy may react too quickly, causing congestion-producing oscillation, or too slowly, being irrelevant.

Despite these real dangers, adaptive routing strategies are by far the most prevalent, for two reasons:

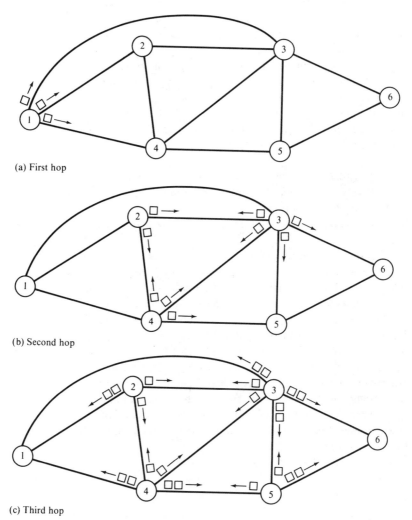

(a) First hop

(b) Second hop

(c) Third hop

FIGURE 3-7 Flooding Example

- From the user's point of view, an adaptive routing strategy can improve performance, since packets are routed by the best route available at the time of the routing decision.
- From the network's point of view, an adaptive strategy aids in congestion control by smoothing out the network load. That is, when some areas of the network experience relatively heavy load, subsequent traffic will favor the lightly-loaded portions of the network.

These benefits may or may not be realized, depending on the soundness of design and the nature of the load. By and large, it is an extraordinarily complex task to perform properly.

All adaptive routing strategies, by definition, produce routing decisions that adapt to changing conditions in the network. Two parameters that serve to differentiate adaptive routing strategies are the place at which the routing decision is made and the amount of information used to make the decision. Based on these two parameters, virtually all strategies are in one or a hybrid combination of the following categories:

- *Isolated adaptive*: local information, distributed control.
- *Distributed adaptive*: information from adjacent nodes or all nodes, distributed control.
- *Centralized adaptive*: information from all nodes, centralized control.

A simple **isolated adaptive** scheme is for a node to route each packet to the outgoing link with the shortest queue length, Q, regardless of destination. This would have the effect of balancing the load on outgoing links. However, some outgoing links may not be headed in the correct general direction. An improvement can be obtained by also taking into account preferred directions. Each link emanating from a node can be assigned a bias $B_{i,j}$ for each neighbor node i and each destination node j. For each incoming packet headed for node j, the node would choose the link that has the minimum $Q_i + B_{i,j}$ for all neighbors i, where Q_i is the current queue length for the link to node i. Thus a node would tend to send packets in the right direction with concession made to current traffic delays.

As an example, Figure 3-8 shows the status of node 4 of Figure 3-5 at a certain point in time. Node 4 has links to four other nodes. A fair number of packets have

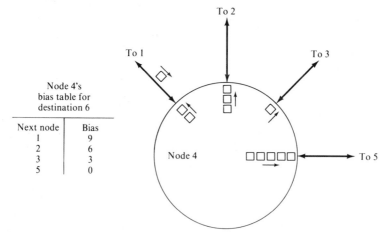

Next node	Bias
1	9
2	6
3	3
5	0

Node 4's bias table for destination 6

FIGURE 3-8 Example of Isolated Adaptive Routing

been arriving and a backlog has built up, with a queue of packets waiting for each of the outgoing links. A packet arrives from node 1 destined for node 6. Based on current queue lengths and the values of the biases $(B_{i,6})$ for each outgoing link, the minimum value of $Q + B$ is four, on the link to node 3. Thus the packet is routed through node 3.

Isolated adaptive schemes are not in general use. Since they make little use of available information, they do not adapt well to changing conditions. The other two adaptive (distributed, centralized) strategies are more commonly found. Both take advantage of the information that other nodes have about the link delays and outages that they experience.

An example of a **distributed adaptive** algorithm is that used in the Defense Data Network (DDN). This algorithm was developed on ARPANET, which is one of the components of DDN [MCQU80]. For this algorithm, each node maintains two data structures. First, there is a delay matrix which shows, for each directly connected pair of nodes, this node's current estimate of the delay on the intervening link in both directions (for a pair of nodes not directly connected, the corresponding matrix entry has the value infinity). With this information, the node can calculate a least-cost route to each of the other nodes, and develop a routing matrix, such as was seen in Figure 3-6. The vector shows, for each possible destination node, the identity of the next node on the route.

The key design issue for this algorithm is the manner in which the values for the delay matrix are obtained. Every 10 seconds, each node computes the average delay on each of its outgoing links. If there are any significant changes in any of the delay values since the last computation, or if there is any change in connectivity, the information is sent to all other nodes using flooding. Each node updates its delay matrix every time one of these flooded packets arrives. Experience with this algorithm indicates that it is responsive and stable. The overhead induced by flooding is moderate since each node does this at most once every 10 seconds.

An example of a **centralized adaptive** algorithm is that used in TYMNET [TYME81]. In TYMNET, one node is designated as supervisor (with a backup for reliability). The supervisor performs the routing function on a virtual-circuit basis. When a virtual circuit is requested, the supervisor determines the least-cost route and passes the necessary routing information for this virtual circuit to each node on the route. When the virtual circuit terminates, the supervisor informs each node on the route.

There are two key design issues with this algorithm: how costs are assigned to each link, and how the route is communicated to the nodes that will form a virtual circuit. Link cost is based on data rate, satellite versus land-based link, traffic type, and load condition. For example, if a virtual circuit is requested by a low-speed interactive terminal, a 9600-bps land link is assigned a lower cost than a 56-kbps satellite, because of the longer delay of the satellite. If the virtual circuit is to be used for host-to-host file transfer, the satellite link has the lower cost; throughput is more important than response time. The load component of cost also depends on the traffic type. For stream-oriented traffic, a link is assigned additional cost if it has reached "high-speed overload." This condition occurs when the link cannot support all of its current virtual circuits at the desired data rates. For interactive traffic, a link is assigned additional cost if it has reached "low-speed overload." This condition occurs when the average delay on a link exceeds 0.5 seconds several times in a 4-minute period. When either form of overload occurs or ceases to occur, the affected node reports this to the supervisor.

When a virtual circuit is requested, the request is sent to the supervisor, which computes the least-cost route based on the costs appropriate for the traffic type. The supervisor then sends a "needle" to the source node, containing the route as an ordered list of nodes. The needle threads its way along the designated route, depositing routing information as it goes. If an outage is encountered, the needle retraces to the origin and the supervisor is informed.

There are several problems with a centralized adaptive routing strategy compared to a distributed one. Most important is a problem of reliability. The loss of the supervisor disables the entire network with respect to new virtual circuits. This problem can be fixed at the cost of redundant supervisors. Also related to reliability is that the centralized approach is only practical for virtual-circuit operation, and as we have mentioned, a datagram network is inherently more robust. Finally, there is a potential congestion problem in the proximity of the supervisor, since it receives all routing requests and link status information, and transmits all routing information.

There are also some advantages of centralized compared to distributed routing. The computation requirements at individual nodes are reduced. Centralized routing permits a more accurate optimization of the routes, eliminating loops and oscillations that may occur when routing decisions are made collectively by nodes acting independently. Finally, with centralized routing, the supervisor has a reasonably accurate and reasonably current picture of the network load distribution. This permits the supervisor to limit new virtual circuits in an effort to control congestion.

3-6   CONGESTION CONTROL

The Need for Congestion Control

In addition to routing, the other main function of a packet-switched network is congestion control. The objective of congestion control is to maintain the number of packets within the network or a region of the network below the level at which queuing delays become excessive. In essence, a packet-switched network is a network of queues. At each node, there is a queue of packets for each outgoing link. If the rate at which packets arrive and queue up exceeds the rate at which packets are transmitted, the queue size grows without bounds and the delay experienced by a packet goes to infinity. Even if the packet arrival rate is less than the packet transmission rate, queue length will grow dramatically as the arrival rate approaches the transmission rate. As a rule of thumb, when the line for which packets are queuing becomes more than 80 percent utilized, the queue length grows at an alarming rate.

Figure 3-9 shows the effects of congestion in general terms. Figure 3-9a plots the throughput of a network (number of packets delivered to destination stations) versus the offered load (number of packets transmitted by source stations). Both axes are normalized to the theoretical capacity of the network, which can be expressed as the rate at which the network is theoretically capable of handling packets, based on the data rates of the network links. In the ideal case, throughput and hence network utilization increases to accommodate an offered load up to the capacity of the network. Utilization then remains at 100 percent if the load is increased further. The ideal case, of course, requires that all stations somehow know the timing and rate of packets that can be presented to the network with no overhead and no time delay in

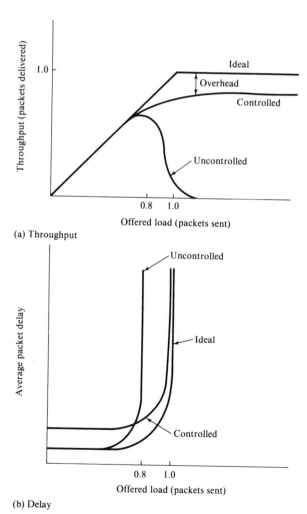

(a) Throughput

(b) Delay

FIGURE 3-9 The Effects of Congestion

acquiring this information, which is impossible. If no congestion control is exercised, we have the curve labeled "uncontrolled." For this case, as the load increases, utilization increases for a while. Then as the queue lengths at the various nodes begin to grow, throughput actually drops. The reason for this is that the buffers at each node are of finite size. When a node's buffers are full, it must discard additional incoming packets. Thus the source stations must retransmit the discarded packets in addition to new packets. This only exacerbates the situation: As more and more packets are retransmitted, the load on the system grows, and more buffers become saturated. While the system is trying desperately to clear the backlog, stations are pumping old (retransmitted) and new packets into the system. Even a successfully-delivered packet may be retransmitted, because it takes so long for the receiver to acknowledge it that the sender assumes the packet was lost and tries again. Under these circumstances, the effective capacity of the system is virtually zero.

It is clear that these catastrophic events must be avoided, which is the task of congestion control. The object of all congestion control techniques is to limit queue lengths at the nodes so as to avoid throughput collapse. This control involves some unavoidable overhead. Thus a congestion control technique cannot perform as well as the theoretical ideal. However, a good congestion control strategy will avoid throughput collapse and maintain a throughput that differs from the ideal by an amount roughly equal to the overhead of the control (Figure 3-9a).

Figure 3-9b points out that no matter what technique is used, the average delay experienced by packets grows without bounds as the load approaches the capacity of the system. Note that initially the uncontrolled policy results in less delay than a controlled policy, because of its lack of overhead. However, the uncontrolled policy will saturate at a lower load.

Techniques

A key tool in most congestion control techniques is flow control. **Flow control** is used to regulate the flow of data between two points. The receiver limits the rate at which data can be transmitted by the sender. This technique is used on point-to-point configurations in data link control protocols, such as HDLC and LAP-D (see Chapter 8). Flow control can also be used between indirectly connected points, such as two stations that are attached to a packet-switched network and are the endpoints of a virtual circuit. One application of this latter technique is in the X.25 standard discussed later in this chapter.

As with routing, the techniques used for congestion control will be addressed only briefly. For a more complete treatment, the reader is referred to [STAL88a], or one of the survey articles on the subject, including [GERL84], [GERL81], [HSIE84b], [GERL80], and [POUZ81].

Congestion control techniques can be categorized along two dimensions:

- Datagram versus virtual circuit
- Hop versus entry-to-exit versus network access

Box 3-4 defines these terms, and Figure 3-10 [GERL84] illustrates the distinction between hop, entry-to-exit, and network access control. These various techniques are used alone or in combination on different packet-switched networks. As with routing, congestion control involves a trade-off between the power of the congestion control capability and the need to minimize overhead.

ARPANET, which is a datagram network, provides an example of an entry-to-exit technique. The network enforces a limit of eight messages in transit between any pair of hosts. Each message may in turn consist of up to eight packets per message. The source node is required to reserve buffer space at the destination node for each message to be sent, up to the limit of eight. If the destination node is experiencing buffer congestion, it may withhold allocation in order to limit the flow of incoming packets. In addition, ARPANET uses hop-level flow control to prevent buffer congestion in individual nodes.

Another interesting example is afforded by TYMNET, which operates on a virtual-circuit basis and includes both network access and hop-level mechanisms [RIND79, TYME81]. The route for an individual virtual circuit is, of course, defined as a series of hops from node to node. On each node-to-node hop, each current virtual circuit that uses that hop is assigned a quota by the receiving node to the sending node. As a node becomes congested, it reduces the quota for the incoming hops. This controls congestion at the node. Furthermore, this hop-level technique produces a backpressure phenomenon: When one node reduces quotas, adjacent nodes are unable to transmit as fast, and must therefore exert flow control on their incoming traffic. For each virtual circuit, these restrictions work their way backward to the node to which the source station is attached. This node then restricts the flow of traffic coming from the source station by means of the X.25 network access protocol, described next.

3-7   X.25

Perhaps the best-known and most widely used protocol standard is X.25, which was originally approved in 1976, and subsequently revised in 1980, 1984, and 1988. The standard specifies an interface between a host system and a packet-switched network. This standard is almost universally used for interfacing to packet-switched networks and will be employed for packet switching in ISDN. In this section, a brief overview of the standard is provided. Greater detail can be found in [STAL87b], and in a number of survey articles, including [DHAS86], [SIRB85], and [ERDE86].

The standard specifically calls out three levels of protocols:

- Physical level
- Link level
- Packet level

BOX 3-4

CONGESTION CONTROL FOR PACKET-SWITCHED NETWORKS

FUNCTION

Control the number and distribution of packets within the network in order to minimize delays in the network as a whole and in regions of the network.

REQUIREMENT

Limit the length of queues of packets at each node, so that the queuing delay is limited. Specifically, this requires that overall and local traffic loads should be limited to no more than 80 percent of theoretical capacity.

TECHNIQUES

Scope of Control

Packet

Concerned with the movement of individual packets at various points in the network. Such techniques are localized and primarily concerned with the loading on a single node. These techniques are used in datagram networks, but may also find application in a virtual-circuit network.

Virtual Circuit

Concerned with controlling the flow of packets through a virtual circuit. By controlling activity on all the virtual circuits that are currently active in a network, the packets moving through that network are controlled.

Level of Control

Hop

Deals with controls exerted between adjacent nodes. These controls can be used to avoid local buffer congestion.

Entry-to-Exit

Concerned with the flow of packets between two endpoints. These controls are generally exerted on a virtual-circuit basis, and prevent buffer congestion at the exit switch.

Network Access

Limit the number of packets transmitted by a particular attached station. These controls limit external inputs based on internal congestion.

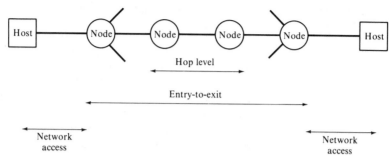

FIGURE 3-10   Flow Control Levels

These three levels correspond to the lowest three layers of the OSI model (see Appendix B). The physical level deals with the physical interface between an attached station (computer, terminal) and the link that attaches that station to the packet-switching node. It makes use of the physical-level specification in a standard known as X.21, but in many cases other standards, such as RS-232-C, are substituted. The link level provides for the reliable transfer of data across the physical link, by transmitting the data as a sequence of frames. The link level standard is referred to as LAP-B (Link Access Protocol - Balanced). LAP-B is a subset of a well-known data link control protocol, HDLC (high-level data link control). LAP-B is very similar to the more recent LAP-D, which is described in Chapter 8. The packet level provides a virtual-circuit service, and is described briefly in this section.

Figure 3-11 illustrates the relationship between the levels of X.25. User data are passed down to X.25 level 3, which appends control information as a header, creating a packet. This control information is used in the operation of the protocol, as we shall see. The entire X.25 packet is then passed down to the LAP-B entity, which appends control information at the front and back of the packet, forming a LAP-B frame. Again, the control information in the frame is needed for the operation of the LAP-B protocol.

Before examining the details of the packet level of X.25, it would be well to distinguish the concepts of internal operation and external service.

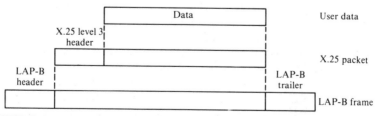

FIGURE 3-11   User Data and X.25 Protocol Control Information

Internal Operation and External Service

One of the most important characteristics of a packet-switched network is whether it uses datagrams or virtual circuits. Actually, there are two dimensions of this characteristic, as illustrated in Figure 3-12. At the interface between a station and a network node, a network may provide either a connection-oriented or connectionless service. With a connection-oriented service, a station performs a call request to set up a logical connection to another station. All packets presented to the network are identified as belonging to a particular logical connection and are numbered sequentially. The network undertakes to deliver packets in sequence-number order. The logical connection is usually referred to as a virtual circuit, and the connection-oriented service is referred to as an **external virtual-circuit service;** unfortunately, this external service is distinct from the concept of **internal virtual-circuit operation,** as we shall see. With connectionless service, the network only agrees to handle packets independently, and may not deliver them in order or reliably. This type of service is sometimes known as an **external datagram service;** again, this is a distinct concept from that of **internal datagram operation.** Internally, the network may actually construct a fixed route between endpoints (virtual circuit) or not (datagram). These internal and external design decisions need not coincide:

- *External virtual circuit, internal virtual circuit:* When the user requests a virtual circuit, a dedicated route through the network is constructed. All packets follow that same route.
- *External virtual circuit, internal datagram:* The network handles each packet separately. Thus, different packets for the same external virtual circuit may take different routes. However, the network buffers packets at the destination node, if necessary, so that they are delivered to the destination station in the proper order.
- *External datagram, internal datagram:* Each packet is treated independently from both the user's and the network's point of view.
- *External datagram, internal virtual circuit:* This combination makes little sense, since one incurs the cost of a virtual-circuit implementation but gets none of the benefits.

The question arises as to the choice of virtual circuits or datagrams, both internally and externally. This will depend on the specific design objectives for the communication network and the cost factors that prevail. We have already made some comments concerning the relative merits of internal-datagram versus virtual-circuit operation. With respect to external service (Box 3-1), we can make the following observations. The datagram service, coupled with internal datagram operation, allows for efficient use of the network; no call setup and no need to hold up packets while a packet in error is retransmitted. This latter feature is desirable in some real-time applications. The virtual-circuit service can provide end-to-end sequencing and error control. This service is attractive for supporting connection-oriented

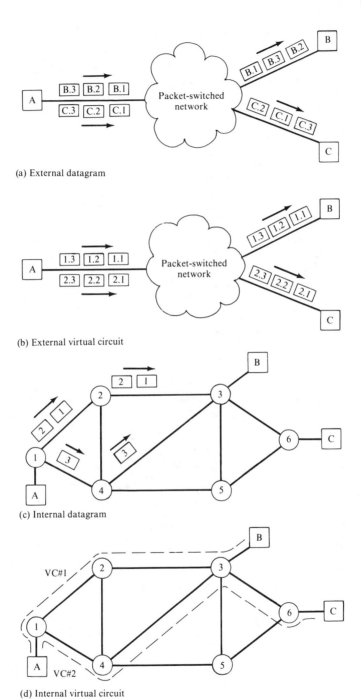

(a) External datagram

(b) External virtual circuit

(c) Internal datagram

(d) Internal virtual circuit

FIGURE 3-12 External and Internal Virtual Circuits and Datagrams

applications, such as file transfer and remote terminal access. In practice, the virtual-circuit service is much more common than the datagram service, and will remain so for ISDN-related packet-switched networks. The reliability and convenience of a connection-oriented service is seen as more attractive than the benefits of the datagram service.

X.25 Packet Level

With the X.25 packet level, data are transmitted in packets over external virtual circuits. A variety of packet types are used (Table 3-3), all using the same basic format, with variations (Figure 3-13). The standard refers to user machines as Data Terminal Equipment (DTE) and to a packet-switching node to which a DTE is attached as Data Circuit-Terminating Equipment (DCE).

The virtual-circuit service of X.25 provides for two types of virtual circuit: virtual call and permanent virtual circuit. A *virtual call* is a dynamically-established virtual circuit using a call setup and call clearing procedure explained below. A

TABLE 3-3   X.25 PACKET TYPES

Packet Type		Service	
From DCE to DTE	*From DTE to DCE*	VC	PVC
Call Setup and Clearing			
Incoming call	Call request	X	
Call connected	Call accepted	X	
Clear indication	Clear request	X	
DCE clear confirmation	DTE clear confirmation	X	
Data and Interrupt			
DCE data	DTE data	X	X
DCE interrupt	DTE interrupt	X	X
DCE interrupt confirmation	DTE interrupt confirmation	X	X
Flow Control and Reset			
DCE RR	DTE RR	X	X
DCE RNR	DTE RNR	X	X
	DTE REJ	X	X
Reset indication	Reset request	X	X
DCE reset confirmation	DTE reset confirmation	X	X
Restart			
Restart indication	Restart request	X	X
DCE restart confirmation	DTE restart confirmation	X	X
Diagnostic			
Diagnostic		X	X
Registration			
Registration confirmation	Registration request	X	X

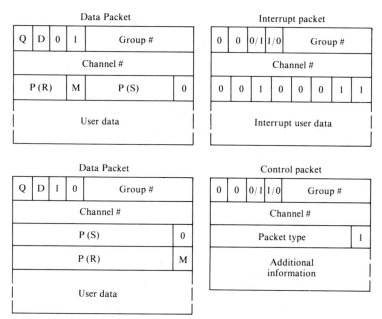

FIGURE 3-13   X.25 Packet Formats

permanent virtual circuit is a permanent, network-assigned virtual circuit. Data transfer occurs as with virtual calls, but no call setup or clearing is required.

Virtual Calls.   Figure 3-14 shows a typical sequence of events in a virtual call. The left-hand part of the figure shows the packets exchanged between user machine A and the packet-switching node to which it attaches; the right-hand part shows the packets exchanged between user machine B and its node. The routing of packets inside the network is not visible to the user.

The sequence of events is as follows:

1. A requests a virtual circuit to B by sending a Call Request packet to A's DCE. The packet includes the source and destination addresses, as well as the virtual circuit number to be used for this new virtual circuit. Future incoming and outgoing transfers will be identified by this virtual-circuit number.
2. The network routes this call request to B's DCE.
3. B's DCE receives the call request and sends a Call Indication packet to B. This packet has the same format as the Call Request packet but a different virtual-circuit number, selected by B's DCE from the set of locally unused numbers.
4. B indicates acceptance of the call by sending a Call Accepted packet specifying the same virtual circuit number as that of the Call Indication packet.

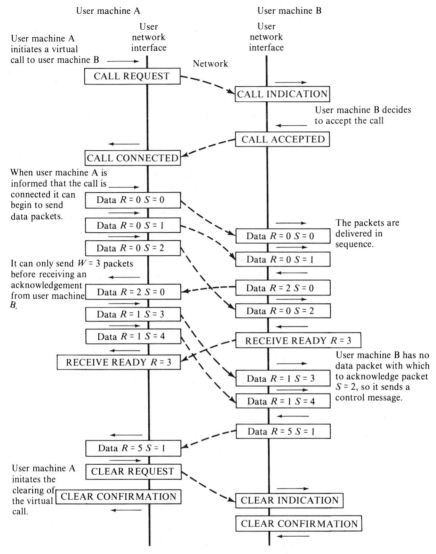

FIGURE 3-14 Sequence of Events: X.25 Protocol (MART81)

5. A receives a Call Connected packet with the same virtual circuit number as that of the Call Request packet.

6. A and B send data and control packets to each other using their respective virtual circuit-numbers.

7. A (or B) sends a Clear Request packet to terminate the virtual circuit and receives a Clear Confirmation packet.

8.   *B* (or A) receives a Clear indication packet and transmits a Clear
     Confirmation packet.

We now turn to some of the details of the standard.

Packet Format.   Figure 3-13 shows the packet formats used in the standard. For
user data, the data are broken up into blocks of some maximum size, and a 24-bit
header is appended to each block to form a **data packet.** The header includes a
12-bit virtual-circuit number (expressed as a 4-bit group number and an 8-bit
channel number). The P(S) and P(R) fields support the functions of flow control and
error control on a virtual circuit basis, as explained below. The M, D, and Q bits
support specialized functions, which will not be explored here (see [STAL87b]) or
one of the other references cited earlier.
     In addition to transmitting user data, X.25 must transmit control information
related to the establishment, maintenance, and termination of virtual circuits. Control information is transmitted in a **control packet.** Each control packet includes the
virtual-circuit number, the packet type, which identifies the particular control function, and additional control information related to that function. For example, a Call
Request packet includes the following additional fields:

- Calling DTE address length (4 bits): Length of the corresponding
  address field in 4-bit units.
- Called DTE address length (4 bits): Length of the corresponding
  address field in 4-bit units.
- DTE addresses (variable): The calling and called DTE addresses.
- Facility length: Length of the facility field in octets.
- Facilities: A sequence of facility specifications. Each specification
  consists of an 8-bit facility code and zero or more parameter codes.
  Facilities are discussed below.

The way in which user data is encapsulated is as follows. The transmitting
DTE must break its data up into units of some maximum length. X.25 specifies that
the network must support a maximum user field length of at least 128 octets (i.e., the
user data field may be some number of bits up to the maximum). In addition, the
network may allow selection of some other maximum field length in the range 16 to
4096 octets. The DTE constructs control packets and encapsulates user data in data
packets. These are then transmitted to the DCE via LAP-B. Thus the packet is
encapsulated in a layer 2 frame (one packet per frame). The DCE strips off the layer
2 control fields and may encapsulate the packet according to some internal network
protocol. The reader unfamiliar with the concept of encapsulation should consult
Appendix B.

Flow and Error Control.   Flow control and error control in X.25 are implemented using sequence numbers. The flow control is the sliding-window mecha-

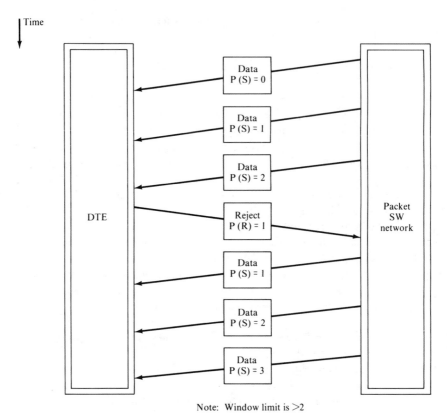

Note: Window limit is >2

FIGURE 3-15   X.25 Packet Exchange

nism, and error control is the go-back-N automatic-repeat-request (ARQ) mechanism. The basic operation of these mechanisms is explained in Appendix A. The **send sequence number,** P(S), is used to uniquely number packets. As a default, 3-bit sequence numbers are used, and P(S) of each new packet on a virtual circuit is one more than that of the preceding packet, modulo 8. Optionally, a DTE may request, via the user facility mechanism described below, the use of extended 7-bit sequence numbers.

The **receive sequence number,** P(R), contains the number of the next packet expected from the other side of a virtual circuit; this is known as piggybacked acknowledgment. If one side has no data to send, it may acknowledge incoming packets with the Receive Ready (RR) control packet, which contains the number of the next packet expected from the other side.

Flow control is provided by means of the Receive Not Ready (RNR) control packet; this packet acknowledges receipt of previous packets but indicates that the issuer is unable to receive additional packets. When such an indication is received, all transmission of data packets must cease; the busy side will notify the other side that it can resume transmission by means of an RR packet.

The basic form of **error control** is go-back-N ARQ (see Appendix A). Negative acknowledgment is in the form of a Reject (REJ) control packet. If a node receives a negative acknowledgment, it will retransmit the specified packet and all subsequent packets. Figure 3-15 illustrates this algorithm.

Reset and Restart.   X.25 provides two facilities for recovering from errors. The reset facility is used to reinitialize a virtual circuit. This means that the sequence numbers on both ends are set to zero. Any data or interrupt packets in transit are lost. It is up to a higher-level protocol to recover from the loss of packets. A reset can be triggered by a number of error conditions including loss of a packet, sequence number error, congestion, or loss of the network's internal virtual circuit. In this latter case, the two DCEs must rebuild the internal virtual circuit to support the still-existing X.25 DTE-DTE external virtual circuit. Either a DTE or DCE can initiate a reset, with a Reset Request or Reset Indication. The recipient responds with a Reset Confirmation. Regardless of who initiates the reset, the DCE involved is responsible for informing the other end.

A more serious error condition calls for a restart. The issuance of a Restart Request packet is equivalent to sending a Clear Request on all virtual calls and a Reset Request on all permanent virtual circuits. Again, either a DTE or DCE may initiate the action. An example of a condition warranting restart is temporary loss of access to the network.

Interrupt Packets.   A DTE may send an interrupt packet that bypasses the flow control procedures used for data packets. The packet does not contain send and receive sequence numbers and is not blocked by an RNR or a closed window. The interrupt packet carries up to 32 octets of user data, and is to be delivered to the destination DTE by the network at a higher priority than data packets in transit. A DTE may not send another interrupt packet on any virtual circuit until delivery of the outstanding interrupt packet is confirmed. This prevents flooding the network with packets that are not flow controlled. An example of the use of this service is to transmit a terminal break character.

Call Progress Signals.   X.25 includes provision for call progress signals, and these are defined by X.96 (Table 3-4). These signals fall into two overlapping categories. **Clearing call progress signals** are used to indicate the reason why a Call Request is denied; they are also used to indicate the reason for a Clear Request. In both cases the signal is carried in a Clear Indication Packet. **Resetting call progress signals** are used to indicate the reason why a virtual circuit is being reset or why a restart takes place. The appropriate code is contained in a Reset Request, Reset Indication, Restart Request, or Restart Indication packet.

TABLE 3-4 PACKET-SWITCHED CALL PROGRESS SIGNALS (X.96)

Signal	Applicable to[a] VC	PVC	Usage[b]	Description
Local Procedure Error	X	X	C, R	Procedure error caused by local DTE
Network Congestion	X	X	C, R	Temporary network congestion or fault
Invalid Facility Request	X		C	Requested user facility not valid
RPOA Out of Order	X		C	Recognized private operating agency unable to forward call
Not Obtainable	X		C	Called DTE address unassigned or unknown
Access Barred	X			
Reverse Charging Acceptance Not Subscribed	X		C	Called DTE will not accept charges on collect call
Fast Select Acceptance Not Subscribed	X		C	Called DTE does not support fast select
Incompatible Destination	X		C, R	The remote DTE does not have a function used or a facility requested
Out of Order	X	X	C, R	Remote DTE out of order
Number Busy	X		C	Called DTE is busy
Remote Procedure Error	X	X	C, R	Procedure error caused by remote DTE
Network Operational	X	X	R	Network ready to resume after temporary failure or congestion
Remote DTE Operational		X	R	Remote DTE ready after temporary failure
DTE Originated	X	X	C, R	Remote DTE has refused call or requested reset
Ship Absent	X		C	Called ship absent (used with mobile maritime service)
Network Out of Order		X	R	Network temporarily unable to handle data traffic
Registration/Cancellation Confirmed	X	X	R	Facility request confirmed

[a] VC, virtual call; PVC, permanent virtual circuit.
[b] C, clearing call progress signal; R, resetting or restarting call progress signal.

User Facilities. X.25 provides for the use of optional user facilities. These are facilities that may be provided by the network and that may be employed at the user's option. Some facilities are selectable for use for an agreed period of time, and are arranged ahead of time between subscriber and network provider. Other facilities are requested on a per-virtual-call basis, as part of the Call Request packet; with these facilities, the capability or value applies only to the one virtual call.

The facilities that may be provided are defined in X.2, which contains a rather long list. Some of these are termed "essential." Essential facilities must be offered by the network, although their use is optional (Table 3-5). The remaining facilities are termed "additional" and need not be offered by the network.

TABLE 3-5 ESSENTIAL OPTIONAL PACKET-SWITCHED USER FACILITIES (X.2)

Assigned for an Agreed Contractual Period

Flow Control Parameter Negotiation

This facility permits negotiation on a per call basis of the window size and maximum user data field length to be used on that call in each direction.

Throughput Class Negotiation

This facility permits negotiation on a per call basis of the number of bits of data that can be transferred on a virtual circuit. The range of values is 75 bps to 48 Kbps.

Closed User Group

This enables the DTE to belong to one or more closed user groups. A closed user group permits the DTEs belonging to the group to communicate with each other but precludes communication with all other DTEs. Thus members are protected by the network from unauthorized access. A DTE may belong to one or more closed user groups.

Fast Select Acceptance

This facility authorizes the DCE to transmit to the DTE incoming Fast Select calls. Without such authorization, the DCE blocks such incoming calls. This is useful to prevent the enlarged Fast Select packets from being delivered to a DTE that has not implemented Fast Select.

Incoming Calls Barred

This facility prevents incoming calls from being presented to the DTE.

Outgoing Calls Barred

This facility prevents the DCE from accepting outgoing virtual calls.

One-way Logical Channel Outgoing

This facility reserves a block of virtual circuit numbers for outgoing calls. A subscriber reserves a number of logical channels in this fashion to match an expected or desired pattern of calls.

Requested on a Per-Virtual-Call Basis

Flow Control Parameter Negotiation

When a DTE has subscribed to this facility, it may, in a CALL REQUEST packet, separately request user data field sizes and window sizes. The DCE indicates its acceptance or modification of these values in the CALL CONNECTED packet. The DCE may modify window size requests in the direction of $W = 2$, and may modify user data field size requests in the direction of 128 octets.

Throughput Class Negotiation

Operates in a manner similar to Flow Control Parameter Negotiation. The DCE may revise the proposed values in either direction to values smaller than those requested.

Closed User Group Selection

When a DTE has subscribed to this facility, it may, in a CALL REQUEST packet, indicate the closed user group applicable to this call. Similarly, the DCE can indicate the closed user group applicable to an incoming call in a INCOMING CALL packet.

Fast Select

The DTE may employ the fast select facility.

Transit Delay Selection and Identification

The DTE may request a particular transit delay that the network will attempt to meet.

3-8 FAST PACKET SWITCHING

Packet switching was developed to operate in an environment characterized primarily by relatively low-speed transmission facilities (≤ 64 kbps) and relatively high bit error rates. In today's era of integrated digital networks, high-speed transmission facilities (> 1 Mbps) with very low error rates are becoming increasingly important. This evolution has led to the development of the concept of *fast packet switching*, which refers to the exploitation of packet switching in a high-speed technology environment [RAHN88, BAUW87, GREE87, NOJI86, TURN86, HOBE83]. Fast packet switching is an attractive technology for incorporation in an ISDN facility. In this section, we begin by looking at the requirements that have driven the development of this technology, and then briefly introduce the technology itself.

Requirements

The technology of packet switching was developed to provide an efficient data-rate-independent facility for wide-area data communication. Figure 3-4 illustrates its area of applicability. A broader area of application is that of providing a wide-area facility that can support both voice and data communication. For this application, the following requirements can be identified:

- Availability
- Message integrity
- End-to-end delay limit
- Voice connections
- Trunk utilization
- Data-rate independence
- Fast connect/disconnect

There are two aspects to the requirement for **availability:** call setup and call maintenance. The first can be expressed as the probability that the network can support a connection request. This simply requires that the capacity of the network be sufficiently great to handle the anticipated peak load. With the use of high-speed trunks, the key design issues here are ensuring that there is sufficient connectivity in the network and ensuring that the packet-switching nodes are sufficiently numerous and of sufficient capacity. Once the call is set up, the second aspect of availability has to do with maintaining the virtual circuit. If a node or trunk failure occurs after a call is established, then the network must be able to switch to an alternate route quickly enough so that the two end users are unaffected. For a data connection, this means that there should be no loss of packets or only the loss of a few packets. If there is a long delay in route switching, and/or if a large number of packets are lost, it is likely that a higher layer of software will break the connection, requiring the user to set up a new connection. In the case of packetized voice, the loss of voice packets should be so small that there is no serious disruption of the voice signal.

The requirement for **message integrity** places a limit on the number of packets that may be lost. In the case of data packets and a virtual-circuit service, we would like to guarantee that no data are lost. This requires, at a minimum, that there be end-to-end error control within the network. For packetized voice, voice users can tolerate occasional short dropouts of the speech signal as long as the probability of such loss stays within prescribed limits.

The requirement for an **end-to-end delay limit** is dependent on the application. In the case of data connections, it will depend on whether the connection is for stream or interactive traffic. For interactive traffic, there is evidence that productivity is greatly enhanced if the response time is less than one second [THAD81, SHNE84]. Since part of this delay is host software and part is network delay, a delay budget of 0.5 seconds for the network might be reasonable. This implies a one-way delay of less than a quarter of a second. Thus, satellite links, which involve a one-way delay of a quarter of a second, become questionable for interactive traffic. In the case of a voice connection, there are two aspects. First, the overall delay should be small. Again, this suggests that satellite links may be inappropriate. A second aspect is that the delay should not be variable. The speech signal must emerge at a smooth rate matching the rate at which it is generated. This implies that voice packets cannot be buffered waiting for the retransmission of a packet that suffers an error.

Trunk utilization remains a requirement, as in an ordinary packet-switching network. With the tremendous capacities of the fiber systems now installed and in the pipeline, there is some question of the degree of importance of this requirement. However, past experience indicates that workload always expands to fill the available capacity. Consequently, utilization should remain an important issue and the potential efficiency gains of packet switching compared to circuit switching remain attractive in a high-capacity environment.

Data-rate independence will also remain a requirement. Terminals and compressed voice digitizers of varying data rates will continue to compete in the marketplace, and full interoperability requires that the network be able to cope with a variety of data rates.

Finally, **fast connect/disconnect** will be expected by customers who are paying for the use of a high-speed network. If internal virtual circuits are used, which seems likely in a high-speed environment, then the techniques for setting up virtual circuits must be designed to provide for rapid route selection.

Characteristics of Fast Packet-Switching Networks

In reviewing the requirements for high-speed wide-area networks listed above, traditional packet-switching technology has a number of strengths. Its key strengths include:

- *Data rate independence*: Because of the dynamic allocation of trunk capacity and the use of buffering, it is not necessary that source and destination systems operate at the same data rate.
- *Accommodation of bursty traffic*: As was discussed, packet switching is more efficient than circuit switching for bursty traffic.
- *Flexibility*: Packet switching can handle devices of a variety of data rates, can respond easily to load changes, and lends itself to dynamic route reconfiguration.

However, traditional packet switching has some weaknesses in the context of high-speed networking:

- *Large delay*: This is because of packet processing and queuing time at each node and packet retransmissions due to errors.
- *Variable delay*: Because capacity is not dedicated to a given call, the queuing time experienced through the various hops from source to destination may vary from packet to packet, even on the same internal virtual circuit.
- *Throughput bottlenecks*: Despite the use of sophisticated adaptive routing and congestion control algorithms, bottlenecks can develop in a large, complex network.

An attempt to retain the advantages of packet switching while overcoming its weaknesses has led to ongoing research in fast packet switching. The key characteristics of this approach are:

- No link-by-link error control.
- No link-by-link flow control.
- End-to-end error control if necessary.
- The use of internal virtual circuits.
- Hardware switching.

The first two points have to do with the nature of the processing on each packet hop through the network. In a traditional packet-switched network, a packet is passed from one node to the next using a data link control protocol such as HDLC, which provides both error control and flow control (see Appendix A). As each packet is transmitted on each hop from one node to the next, the packet is encapsulated with a link-level header and trailer. The trailer includes a frame check sequence (FCS) used for error detection. If an error is detected, then the frame is discarded by the receiver and must be retransmitted over the link. Each header includes a sequence number, and the receiving node can regulate the rate at which frames are received from adjacent nodes. These techniques are useful in an environment in which errors are reasonably common and in which the hop-by-hop delay introduced by such processing is tolerable.

With fast packet switching, this hop-by-hop processing is eliminated. Figure 3-16 gives an example of the kind of format that is used in fast packet switching for hop-level transmission, compared to the X.25-HDLC combination. In traditional packet switching, there are two levels of processing at each node: the packet level and the data link level. In fast packet switching, there is only one level of processing. The use of flags for delimiting and the use of an FCS for error detection are retained from HDLC. However, if an error is detected, the packet is simply discarded; there is no attempt to provide for hop-level retransmission. Flow control and error control are dispensed with; hence there is no need for sequence numbers. The only other field required (other than the data field) is for the virtual circuit number, which is used for routing.

The high quality and speed of modern digital transmission trunks, such as optical fiber links, eliminate the need for error control on a per-link basis. Services that require completely error-free transmission and that do not employ some higher-level error-recovery protocol can use a network-provided end-to-end error recovery mechanism. Thus, end-to-end error control can be incorporated within the network, but its use will be decided on a virtual-circuit basis. For example, it will not be provided for a packetized voice connection.

To complete the picture, a fast packet-switching facility requires that there be little or no time spent on routing decision once an external virtual circuit is set up. To accomplish this, internal virtual circuits are used, and the packet-switch nodes implement the routing function in hardware or firmware. Thus, the information required to map from a virtual circuit number to a next-node decision must be organized in some sort of simple table format.

Application

We have outlined the major features of a fast packet-switched network. To conclude, let us briefly describe the application of such an architecture to both voice and data communication.

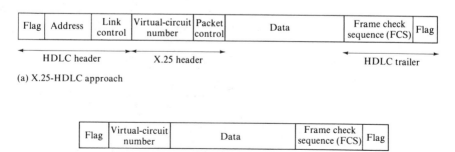

| Flag | Address | Link control | Virtual-circuit number | Packet control | Data | Frame check sequence (FCS) | Flag |

⟵ HDLC header ⟶⟵ X.25 header ⟶   ⟵ HDLC trailer ⟶

(a) X.25-HDLC approach

| Flag | Virtual-circuit number | Data | Frame check sequence (FCS) | Flag |

(b) FPS approach

FIGURE 3-16   Packet Switching Formats

Voice Communication.   Voice signals can be digitized and transmitted as a stream of small packets. The key requirements, recall, are that the delay be short and that the rate of delivery be constant. The architecture that has just been discussed assures that the delay will be short. Nevertheless, even with very fast packet-switching nodes and high-speed trunks, there is a queuing delay at each node, which is variable and which is cumulative across a virtual-circuit route. Several measures can be taken. First, voice packets can be given higher priority than data packets. This will cut down on the queuing delay and hence its variability. Second, end-to-end error control is not employed. If an error is detected, the packet is discarded. Finally, corrective means must be employed to ensure that the packet delivery rate is constant.

One procedure for achieving near-constant data rate is illustrated in Figure 3-17. Each voice packet includes an additional field in the header that is used to measure the accumulated queuing and node processing delay along a route.. The field in the ith packet, $D(i)$, is initialized to zero. At each node en route, the node measures, with a local clock, the intranode delay and adds this to $D(i)$. At the destination node, an amount C is added to the accumulated $D(i)$. C is an estimate of the transmission delay contributed by all of the trunks along the route. Since the route for a given virtual circuit is fixed, this will not vary during the call and can be estimated from the topology of the network. Finally, at the destination node, prior to delivery of each packet, the packet is delayed a variable amount $V(i)$ so that:

$$D(i) + C + V(i) = T$$

The observed accumulated delay is increased to produce a constant total delay of T, so that the delay experienced by voice packets is constant. If a packet arrives for which $D(i) + C$ already exceeds T, then that packet is discarded. Periodically, based on the observed performance of a given virtual circuit, T is adjusted. The competing

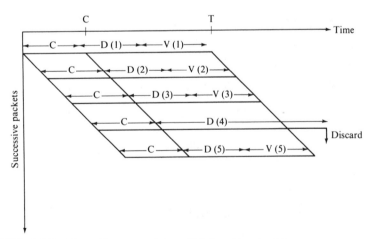

FIGURE 3-17   Time Reassembly of Voice Packets

objectives are to minimize end-to-end delay (make T smaller) and to minimize packet discard (make T bigger).

Data Communication. With voice packets, a detected error results in packet discard. In general, the user expects a reliable service for data packets, and so a discard strategy is not acceptable. However, hop-by-hop flow and error control are likely to lead to unacceptable delays. Accordingly, an end-to-end strategy is used both for congestion control and error control. On each virtual circuit, incoming packets are numbered, and the destination node maintains a buffer that allows it to retain packets while requesting a retransmission of a damaged packet.

Data packets are of lower priority than voice packets. In addition, several levels of priority may be used for data packets. For example, interactive traffic may be given higher priority than batch traffic.

3-9 SUMMARY

Packet switching was designed to provide a more efficient facility than circuit switching for bursty data traffic. Key distinguishing elements of packet-switched networks are whether the internal operation is datagram or virtual circuit and whether the external service is datagram or virtual circuit. The virtual-circuit service, using the X.25 network access protocol, is by far the most common, but this may be supported by either a datagram or virtual circuit operation.

With traditional packet switching, the key technical problems are routing and congestion control. Adaptive routing techniques are typically employed. These allow the network to continue to function in the face of lost nodes or trunks and also provide a degree of load leveling. Congestion control is intended to avoid the buildup of excessive queuing delays.

Current research in packet switching is focused on the development of fast packet switching. This technology adapts the techniques of packet switching to the high-speed digital environment of the IDN, and appears to offer considerable promise as a component service for ISDN.

3-10 RECOMMENDED READING

The literature on packet switching is enormous. Only a few of the worthwhile references are mentioned here. A number of survey articles were written in the early days of packet switching; among the most interesting are [KIMB75], [GREE77], and [KLEI78]. Surveys of specific networks include [WOOD85], [ROBE78], [QUAR86], and [AMAN86]. Books with good treatments of this subject include [BERT87], [ROSN82], and [DAVI79]. There is also a large body of literature on performance. Good summaries are to be found in [KLEI76] and [SCHW77]. [AHUJ83] provides a mathematical analysis of performance and reliability aspects of traffic control and routing. [MARU83] is an exhaustive analysis of the performance of virtual-circuit-based routing algorithms.

There is a large literature on X.25. [DHAS86], [SIRB85], and [ERDE86] are recommended. [BURG83] is a discussion of the practical application of X.25.

3-11 PROBLEMS

3-1 Consider a packet-switched network of N nodes, connected by the following topologies:
   a.   Star: one central node with no attached station; all other nodes attach to the central node.
   b.   Loop: each node connects to two other nodes to form a closed loop.
   c.   Fully connected: each node is directly connected to all other nodes.
   For each case, give the average number of hops between stations.

3-2 Consider a binary tree topology for a packet-switched network. The root node connects to two other nodes. All intermediate nodes connect to one node in the direction toward the root, and two in the direction away from the root. At the bottom are nodes with just one link back toward the root. If there are $2^N - 1$ nodes, derive an expression for the mean number of hops per packet for large N, assuming that trips between all node pairs are equally likely.

3-3 In Figure 3-5, node 1 sends a packet to node 6 using flooding. Counting the transmission of one packet across one link as a load of one, what is the total load generated if:
   a.   Each node discards duplicate incoming packets?
   b.   A hop count field is used and is initially set to 5?

3-4 With the flooding technique, because all routes are followed, at least one copy of the packet follows the minimum-hop route; therefore flooding could be used to initially determine all minimum-hop routes. Can flooding be used to determine the minimum delay route?

3-5 How does the inclusion of a second criterion, bias, improve an isolated adaptive routing strategy based on queue length? What is the basis for the bias? Is bias static or dynamic?

3-6 Another adaptive routing technique is known as *backward learning*. As a packet is routed through the network, it carries not only the destination address, but the source address plus a running hop count that is incremented for each hop. Each node builds a routing table that gives the next node and hop count for each destination. How is the packet information used to build the table? What are the advantages and disadvantages of this technique?

3-7 A proposed congestion control measure is known as *isarithmic control*. In this method, the total number of packets in transit is fixed by inserting a fixed number of permits into the network. These permits circulate through the network at random. Whenever a node wants to send a packet just given to it by an attached station, it must first capture and destroy a permit. When a packet reaches the destination node, that node reissues the permit. List three potential problems with this technique.

3-8 Assuming no malfunction in any of the stations or nodes of a network, is it possible for a packet to be delivered to the wrong destination?

3-9 Define the following parameters for a switching network:

- N: number of hops between two given stations.
- L: message length in bits
- B: data rate, in bps, on all links
- P: packet size in bits
- H: overhead (header) bits per packet
- S: call setup time (circuit-switched or virtual circuit) in seconds
- D: propagation delay per hop, in seconds

a. For $N = 4$, $L = 3200$, $B = 9600$, $P = 1024$, $H = 16$, $S = 0.2$, $D = 0.001$, compute the end-to-end delay for circuit switching, virtual circuit packet switching, and datagram packet switching. Assume that there is no node delay.

b. Derive general expressions for the three techniques, taken two at a time (three expressions in all) showing the conditions under which delays are equal.

3-10 What value of P, as a function of N, B, and H results in minimum end-to-end delay in a datagram network? Assume that L is much larger than P, and that D is zero.

3-11 Flow control mechanisms are used at both levels 2 and 3 of X.25. Are both necessary or is this redundant? Explain.

3-12 There is no error detection mechanism (frame check sequence) in X.25. Isn't this needed to assure that all of the packets are delivered properly?

3-13 When an X.25 DTE and the DCE to which it attaches both decide to put a call through at the same time, a call collision occurs and the incoming call is canceled. When both sides try to clear the same virtual circuit simultaneously, the clear collision is resolved without canceling either request; the virtual circuit in question is cleared. Do you think that simultaneous resets are handled like call collisions or clear collisions? Why?

3-14 In X.25, why is the virtual circuit number used by one station of two communicating stations different from the virtual circuit number used by the other station? After all, it is the same full-duplex virtual circuit.

CHAPTER 4
IDN
TECHNOLOGY

Public telephone and telecommunications networks are rapidly evolving to the exclusive use of digital technology. The ways in which these networks employ digital technology are listed in Box 4-1.

The movement toward digital technology has been "pushed" by the competitive desire to lower cost and improve quality of voice transmission and networking services. As the use of distributed processing and data communications has grown, this evolution of an all-digital network has been "pulled" by the need to provide a framework for ISDN.

This chapter focuses on the technology of IDN. We begin with an overview of the evolution of integrated digital networks. The remainder of the chapter looks at some of the most important elements of IDN technology:

- *Digital subscriber loops*: the most difficult technical requirement for IDN is the provision of a digital interface to the subscriber.
- *Signaling System Number 7*: this standard defines the common channel signaling necessary to manage and control a complex digital network.
- *Software-defined networks*: this technology provides a preview of the type of services that will be available to users with fully digital networks.

4-1 THE EVOLUTION OF IDN

The evolution of the existing telecommunications networks and specialized carrier facilities to integrated digital networks is based on two technological developments: digital switching and digital transmission. The technology of digital switching

---

BOX 4-1

USE OF DIGITAL TECHNOLOGY IN PUBLIC TELECOMMUNICATIONS NETWORKS

SWITCHING

The circuit-switching nodes of the network make use of digital time-division switching techniques rather than analog space-division switching techniques.

TRUNK (CARRIER) TRANSMISSION

Digital transmission technology is used on the multiplexed trunks between switches, although either analog or digital signaling may be used. Each trunk carries multiple voice and/or data channels using synchronous time division multiplexing.

SUBSCRIBER LOOP

Digital transmission technology may also be used between the subscriber and the switch to which the subscriber attaches over the "subscriber loop." This implies that digitized voice is employed and that full-duplex digital transmission over the subscriber loop is used.

CONTROL SIGNALING

Common channel signaling over a packet-switched network embedded into the public telecommunications network is used. Packets contain messages used for routing, monitoring, and control.

---

was discussed in Chapter 2. Digital transmission, in essence, means that the signals being transmitted are interpreted as a stream of binary digits. At each switching or relay point, the binary data are recovered from the signal and a new signal is generated. Such handling results in higher-quality (lower error) transmission compared to analog transmission.*

Both digital switching and digital transmission are, of course, well established. The first T-carrier system was introduced into commercial service by AT&T in

---

* The concept of digital transmission is distinct from that of digital signal. Digital transmission techniques can be applied to both digital and analog signals. This topic is explored in Appendix 4A. For voice traffic, both digital transmission and digital switching require the use of digitized voice input. This topic is briefly summarized in Appendix 4B.

1962, and the first large-scale time-division digital switch, the Western Electric 4ESS, was introduced in 1976. More important than the benefits of either of these two technologies, however, was the revolutionary idea that the functions of transmission and switching could be integrated to form an **integrated digital network** (IDN). The idea was proposed as early as 1959 [VAUG59] and is in the process of being implemented worldwide [DORR83, COOK84].

To understand the implications of an IDN, consider Figure 4-1. Traditionally, the transmission and switching systems of an analog telephone network have been designed and administered by functionally separate organizations. The two systems are referred to by the operating telephone companies as outside plant and inside plant, respectively. In an analog network, incoming voice lines are modulated and multiplexed at the end office and sent out over a frequency-division multiplexed (FDM) line. As you know, the constituent signals may pass through one or more intermediate switching centers before reaching the destination end office (Figure 2-17). At each switching center, the incoming FDM carrier has to be demultiplexed and demodulated by an *FDM channel bank*, before being switched by a space-division switch (Figure 4-1a). After switching, the signals have to be multiplexed and modulated again to be transmitted. This repeated process results in an accumulation of noise, as well as cost.

When both the transmission and switching systems are digital, integration as in Figure 4-1b can be achieved. Incoming voice signals are digitized using pulse-code modulation (PCM) and multiplexed using time-division multiplexing (TDM). Time-division digital switches along the way can switch the individual signals without decoding them. Furthermore, separate multiplex/demultiplex channel banks are not needed at the intermediate offices, since that function is incorporated into the switching system.

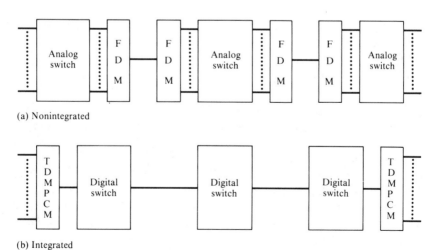

(a) Nonintegrated

(b) Integrated

FIGURE 4-1   The Integration of Transmission and Switching

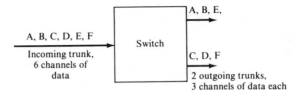

A, B, E,

A, B, C, D, E, F

Switch

Incoming trunk,
6 channels of
data

C, D, F

2 outgoing trunks,
3 channels of data each

(a) General block diagram

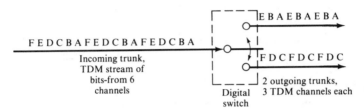

E B A E B A E B A

F E D C B A F E D C B A F E D C B A

Incoming trunk,
TDM stream of
bits-from 6
channels

F D C F D C F D C

2 outgoing trunks,
3 TDM channels each

Digital
switch

(b) Digital time division switch

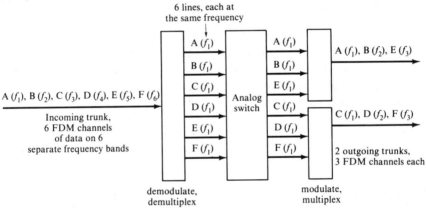

6 lines, each at
the same frequency

A (f_1)   A (f_1)

B (f_1)   B (f_1)   A (f_1), B (f_2), E (f_3)

C (f_1)   E (f_1)

A (f_1), B (f_2), C (f_3), D (f_4), E (f_5), F (f_6)   Analog
switch

D (f_1)   C (f_1)   C (f_1), D (f_2), F (f_3)

Incoming trunk,
6 FDM channels
of data on 6
separate frequency bands

E (f_1)   D (f_1)

F (f_1)   F (f_1)

2 outgoing trunks,
3 FDM channels each

demodulate,
demultiplex

modulate,
multiplex

(c) Analog space-division switch

FIGURE 4-2   Example of Digital Versus Analog Switching

Figure 4-2 gives a simple example which suggests the architectures that are involved in the two approaches. Consider an intermediate switch in a circuit-switched network that has six voice channels (labeled A, B, C, D, E, F) of data coming in on one trunk (Figure 4-2a). Based on the calls that are currently established, three of the channels are to be switched out on one trunk (A, B, E) and three channels on another trunk (C, D, F). All three trunks link to other switches and are multiplexed to carry multiple channels of data. In the case of a digital system (Figure 4-2b), the voice signals are digitized and transmitted as a stream of bits. On a multiplexed trunk, bits from various voice signals are interleaved using time-division multiplexing (TDM). Thus, the incoming trunk has bits from six different voice channels interleaved in time. Inside the digital switch, one or more of the techniques discussed in Chapter 2 are employed to extract the slots of data from the incoming stream and route them to the appropriate outgoing stream.

The architecture for the equivalent analog system is considerably more complex. Each voice signal occupies a frequency band of about 4 kHz. The incoming trunk requires a bandwidth of at least 24 kHz, and each voice signal occupies one channel centered on a unique frequency (f_1 for channel A, f_2 for channel B, etc.). These channels must be fed into a space-division analog switch. However, such a switch is only capable of switching signals from a collection of input lines to a collection of output lines. For general operation, any input line must be connectable to any output line; therefore all inputs and outputs must be at the same frequency. Thus, the frequency-division multiplexed (FDM) input must be demultiplexed and each signal must be returned to the base voice frequency (f_1) to provide input to the switch. The switch routes the incoming data to the appropriate output lines, with each output line dedicated to a particular output trunk. For each trunk, the associated lines must pass through a modulator/multiplexer to produce an FDM signal for transmission over the outgoing trunk.

The conversion of telecommunications networks to digital transmission and digital switching is well under way. Much less well developed is the extension of digital service to the end user. Telephones are still sending analog voice signals to the end office where they must be digitized. Lower-speed (< 56 kbps) end-user digital service is commonly available via leased lines at present, and higher-speed leased services are being introduced [HOLM83]. The provision of switched digital service over the local loop [KELC83, HARR86, ERIK86] will eventually lead to an end-to-end switched digital telecommunications network.

A number of advantages to the use of digital rather than analog techniques in wide-area circuit-switched networks can be cited (Box 4-2). However, the evolution from analog to digital has been driven primarily by the need to provide economic voice communications. The resulting network is also well suited to meet the growing variety of digital data service needs. Thus, the IDN will combine the coverage of the geographically extensive telephone network with the data-carrying capacity of digital data networks in a structure called the **integrated services digital network** (ISDN). In this latter context, the "integrated" of ISDN refers to the simultaneous carrying of digitized voice and a variety of data traffic on the same digital transmission links and by the same digital exchanges. The key to ISDN is the small marginal cost for offering data services on the digital telephone network, with no cost or performance penalty for voice services already carried on the IDN.

4-2   DIGITAL SUBSCRIBER LOOPS

The extension of the digital links to network subscribers is an essential part of IDN evolution. It is not sufficient that the internal transmission and switching facilities of the network be digital. To provide the wide range of digital services

---

BOX 4-2
ADVANTAGES OF DIGITAL NETWORKING

COST

The advent of large-scale integration (LSI) and very-large-scale integration (VLSI) has caused a continuing drop in the cost and size of digital circuitry. Analog equipment has not shown a similar drop. Further, maintenance costs for digital circuitry are a fraction of those for analog circuitry.

DATA INTEGRITY

With the use of digital repeaters rather than analog amplifiers, the effects of noise and other signal impairments are not cumulative. Thus it is possible to transmit data longer distances and over lesser-quality lines by digital means while maintaining the integrity of the data.

CAPACITY UTILIZATION

It has become economical to build transmission links of very high bandwidth, including satellite channels and optical fiber. A high degree of multiplexing is needed to effectively utilize such capacity, and this is more easily and cheaply achieved with digital (time-division) rather than analog (frequency-division) techniques.

SECURITY AND PRIVACY

Encryption techniques can be readily applied to digital data and to analog data that have been digitized.

INTEGRATION

By treating both analog and digital data digitally, all signals have the same form and can be treated similarly. Thus economies of scale and convenience can be achieved by integrating voice, video, and digital data.

---

planned for IDN and ISDN, the link between the network subscriber and the network switch, known as the subscriber loop or local loop, must be digital.

The simplest approach to providing digital service is the use of two twisted-pair wires between each subscriber and the local office or switch to which the subscriber attaches. One twisted-pair link would be used for transmission in each direction. However, the existing telephone network plant installed worldwide is based on the use of a single twisted-pair link between each subscriber and the local office. Thus, this approach would require the installation of a tremendous amount of new cable. Because of the economic impractibility of this approach, interest has focused on schemes that would allow full-duplex digital transmission over a single twisted-pair connection.

Figure 4-3 illustrates two techniques for providing digital service over a single twisted pair: time-compression multiplexing and echo cancellation. Both techniques have been seriously considered for use in IDNs. At present, the consensus is that echo cancellation is the superior system. For example, there is currently a draft American National Standard* for the local loop which uses echo cancellation; this should become an approved standard. Nevertheless, it is instructive to examine both approaches.

Time-Compression Multiplexing

In the technique of time-compression multiplexing, also known as the ping-pong method, data are transmitted in one direction at a time, with transmission alternating between the two directions. To achieve the desired subscriber data rate, the subscriber's bit stream is divided into equal segments, compressed in time to a higher transmission rate, and transmitted in bursts which are expanded at the other

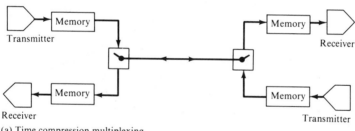

(a) Time compression multiplexing

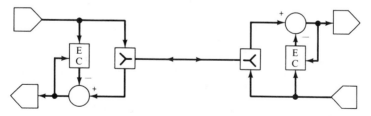

(b) Echo cancellation

FIGURE 4-3 Techniques for Full-Duplex Transmission Over the Subscriber Loop

---

* American National Standards are issued by the American National Standards Institute (ANSI) and are widely used in the United States. Many ANSI standards subsequently become international standards.

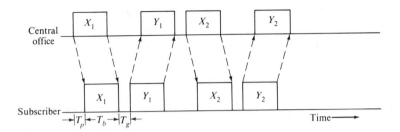

T_p = Propagation delay
T_b = Burst transmission time
T_g = Guard time

FIGURE 4-4 Transmission Using Time Compression Multiplexing

end to the original rate. A short quiescent period is used between bursts going in opposite directions to allow the line to settle down. Thus the actual data rate on the line must be greater than twice the data rate required by the subscriber and local office.

The timing implications are shown in Figure 4-4. The two sides alternate in the transmission of data. Each side sends blocks of some fixed length, which takes a time T_b to transmit; this time is a linear function of the number of bits in a block. In addition, a time T_p is required for the propagation of a signal from one end to the other; this time is a linear function of the length of the subscriber loop. Finally, a guard time T_g is introduced to turn the line around. Thus we can see that the time to send one block is $(T_p + T_b + T_g)$. However, since the two sides must alternate transmissions, the rate at which blocks can be transmitted is only $1/2(T_p + T_b + T_g)$. We can relate this to the effective data rate, R, as seen by the two endpoints as follows. Let B be the size of a block in bits, and R be the desired data rate in bits per second. Then the effective number of bits transmitted per second is

$$R = \frac{B}{2(T_p + T_b + T_g)}$$

The actual data rate, A, on the medium can easily be seen to be

$$A = \frac{B}{T_b}.$$

Combining the two, we have

$$A = 2R\left(1 + \frac{T_p + T_g}{T_b}\right)$$

Thus, the actual data rate on the link is more than double the effective data rate seen by the two sides. We will see that one of the basic data rates offered by ISDN is 144 kbps. To achieve this, it is necessary to transmit at over twice this rate, which would be something greater than 288 kbps. The actual value is in the neighborhood of 350 kbps. This is quite difficult to achieve on an ordinary twisted pair.

The choice of block size, B, is a compromise between competing requirements. If B is increased, there is a decrease in the actual data rate, A. This makes the task of implementation easier. On the other hand, this is accompanied by an increase in the signal delay due to buffering which is undesirable for voice traffic. A block size of 16 to 24 bits seems reasonable [KADE81].

Figure 4-5 depicts the internal structure of a TCM unit. In both directions (transmit and receive) a buffer is needed that is equal to the block size, B. Data to be transmitted are entered into the buffer at a data rate of $R = B/2(T_p + T_b + T_g)$. The data are subsequently transmitted at a rate $A = B/T_b$. The reverse process occurs for reception. Transmission and reception alternate under a central timing control.

Echo Cancellation

With the echo cancellation method, digital transmission is allowed to proceed in both directions within the same bandwidth simultaneously. Both transmitter and receiver are connected to the subscriber line through a hybrid, which is a device that allows signals to pass in both directions simultaneously. This procedure introduces a technical difficulty known as echo. An echo is a reflection of the transmitted signal back to the sender, either from the sender's hybrid and the cable (near-end echo) or from the receiver's hybrid (far-end echo). The relative magnitude of the echo, compared to the true signal arriving from the other side, may be significant. This is because of the considerable difference in amplitude between transmitted and received signals at the ends of the wire pair, which may be as much as three orders of magnitude.

The technique used to overcome this problem is echo cancellation [MESS84a, MESS86]. An estimate of the echo signal is generated at the transmitting end and is subtracted from the incoming signal. This effectively cancels the echo. Because the transmitted signal is known, the echo canceller can estimate the echo characteristics and produce an approximation. However, the exact behavior of

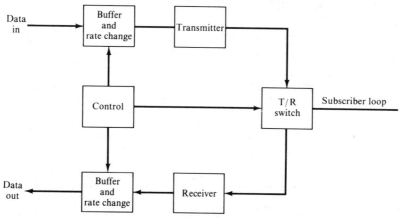

FIGURE 4-5   Internal Structure of TCM Unit

the echo will depend on the physical characteristics and configuration of the copper wire. Not only is it difficult to measure these characteristics precisely, but they will vary over time. To enable more accurate approximation, a feedback circuit is included.

A typical approach to echo cancellation is illustrated in Figure 4-6 [BELL82a, TAO84]. Because the transmitted signal will be reflected at various points in the system, a number of signal elements, each delayed by a different amount, will contribute to the echo at any point in time. Furthermore, since the different contributing signal elements have traveled different distances, they will suffer different amounts of attenuation. This can be expressed in discrete time notation as follows:

$$e(k) = \sum_{n=1}^{\infty} h_n x(k - n)$$

where

$$e(k) = \text{echo signal sampled at time } k$$
$$x(k - n) = \text{transmitted signal transmitted at time } k - n$$
$$h_n = \text{weighting factor for signal delayed by a time } n$$

This echo signal can be estimated with:

$$\hat{e}(k) = \sum_{n=1}^{N} \hat{h}_n(k) x(k - n)$$

where

$$\hat{h}_n(k) = \text{estimate of } h_n \text{ at time } k$$

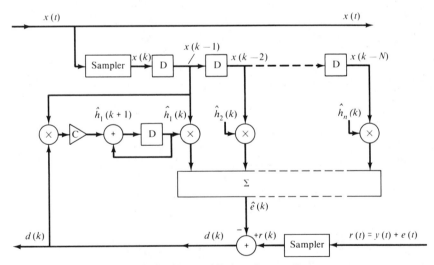

FIGURE 4-6   Internal Structure of Echo Canceller

If signal elements delayed longer than a time N make no measurable contribution to the echo, and if the $\hat{h}_n$ are exactly equal to the h_n, then the estimate will be equal to the actual echo. Of course, the $\hat{h}_n$ can only be approximations. In any case, this approximation is subtracted from the received signal to attempt to cancel the echo:

$$d(k) = r(k) - \hat{e}(k) = y(k) + e(k) - \hat{e}(k)$$

where

> $d(k) =$ signal resulting after cancellation
> $r(k) =$ received signal
> $y(k) =$ component of received signal due to transmission from other side.

Again, assuming that only the first N components of the transmitted signal are significant, we can rewrite this as:

$$d(k) = y(k) + \sum_{n=1}^{N} (h_n - \hat{h}_n(k))\, x(k - n)$$

As Figure 4-6 illustrates, the outgoing signal, $x(t)$, is sampled periodically to produce $x(k)$ for various sampling times $k(k = 1,2,3, \ldots)$. This sample is passed through a series of delays to retain delayed versions of the signal, $x(k - n)$. These delayed samples are then available at time k to produce the estimate $\hat{e}(k)$. The weighting factors, $\hat{h}_n(k)$, are updated at each sampling time by means of feedback:

$$\hat{h}_n(k + 1) = \hat{h}_n(k) + Cx(k - n)d(k)$$

where C is a scaling factor. This equation is somewhat easier to appreciate if we consider the case when there is no signal from the other side. In that case, we have:

$$d(k) = \Sigma(h_n - \hat{h}_n(k))x(k - n)$$

In this case, the value of $d(k)$ would be zero if the echo estimate were exact. If the estimate is not exact, then each weighting factor $\hat{h}_n(k)$ is adjusted by an amount proportional to $x(k - n)d(k)$. This procedure will result in a convergence of the weighting factors to the true values. Even in the presence of an actual signal, $y(t)$, the weighting factors converge, although more slowly [GERW84, FALC82].

The technique of echo cancellation avoids the necessity, found in TCM, of transmitting at more than double the subscriber rate. At the 144-kbps rate recommended by CCITT for ISDN, this gives echo cancellation a distinct advantage over TCM. A careful analysis of the two systems indicates that for typical twisted-pair installations at a subscriber data rate of 144 kbps, a range of 2 km is practical for TCM, compared to a range of 4 km for echo cancellation [SZEC86]. Thus, the introduction of TCM into the subscriber loop would require the extensive use of equipment such as concentrators and repeaters to overcome the poor range of the technique. Echo cancellation systems would require such equipment in far fewer cases.

Echo cancellation has the disadvantage of requiring complex digital signal processing circuitry. However, with the continuing advances in VLSI technology, the cost of echo cancellation is dropping, and it has become the preferred technique to achieve digital subscriber loops [MESS86, LECH86].

4-3   Signaling System Number 7

In Chapter 2, we discussed the transition of network control signaling from an inchannel to a common channel approach. Common channel signaling is more flexible and powerful than inchannel signaling, and is well suited to support the requirements of integrated digital networks. The culmination of this transition is Signaling System Number 7 (SS7), first issued by CCITT in 1980, with revisions in 1984 and 1988. SS7 is designed to be an open-ended common channel signaling standard that can be used over a variety of digital circuit-switched networks. Furthermore, SS7 is specifically designed to be used in ISDNs. SS7 is the mechanism that provides the internal control and network intelligence essential to an ISDN.

The overall purpose of SS7 is to provide an internationally standardized general-purpose common channel signaling system with five primary characteristics:

- It is optimized for use in digital telecommunication networks in conjunction with digital stored program control exchanges utilizing 64-kbps digital channels.
- It is designed to meet present and future information transfer requirements for call control, remote network management, and maintenance.
- It provides a reliable means for the transfer of information in the correct sequence without loss or duplication.
- It is suitable for operation over analog channels and at speeds below 64 kbps.
- It is suitable for use on point-to-point terrestrial and satellite links.

The scope of SS7 is immense, since it must cover all aspects of control signaling for complex digital networks, including the reliable routing and delivery of control messages, and the application-oriented content of those messages. Box 4-3, which lists the CCITT Recommendations that comprise SS7, should give the reader some feel for the complexity of the standard. In this section, we provide an overview of SS7 and highlight key aspects of it. More detail can be found in [SCHL86], [FREE85], and [ROEH85].

Architecture

With common channel signaling, control messages are routed through the network to perform call management (setup, maintenance, termination) and network management functions. These messages are short blocks or packets that must be routed through the network. Thus, although the network being controlled is a circuit-switched network, the control signaling is implemented using packet-

BOX 4-3

THE 1988 CCITT SIGNALING SYSTEM NUMBER 7 RECOMMENDATIONS

MESSAGE TRANSFER PART (Q.701-Q.710)

The Message Transfer Part (MTP) provides a connectionless transport system for the reliable transfer of signaling messages between the locations of communicating user functions. MTP provides a service similar to that of X.25 for packet-switched networks.

Q.701 Functional Description of the Signaling System (Message Transfer Part)

An overall description of the signaling system and the division of functions and the interaction between the Message Transfer Part (MTP) and the other parts.

Q.702 Signaling Data Link

Covers the physical layer characteristics of links used to convey MTP messages. Digital and analog channels operating between 4.8 and 64 kbps are specified. The design is optimized for use over 64-kbps connections.

Q.703 Signaling Link

Covers the layer 2 (data link control) characteristics of links used to convey MTP messages. Includes specification of frame format and technique for error detection and control.

Q.704 Signaling Network Functions and Messages

Covers the layer 3 characteristics of MTP. Relates to the transfer of messages between signaling points

Q.705 Signaling Network Structure

Presents network architecture considerations and discusses aspects pertinent to the design of international signaling networks.

Q.706 Message Transfer Part Signaling Performance

Performance-related requirements are presented, including availability, errors, delays, and capacities.

Q.707 Testing and Maintenance

A limited capability for testing the signaling links and the network routing is provided. Covers testing, fault location, signaling network monitoring, and testing and maintenance messages.

BOX 4-3 *continued*

Q.708 Numbering of International Signaling Point Codes

Describes the 14-bit code and allocations of signaling point codes in the international SS7 network. Networks may use larger codes nationally.

Q.709 Hypothetical Signaling Reference Connection

Based on information from Q.706 and Q.725, defines a hypothetical connection in terms of mean and 95 percentile delays in message processing. Networks are defined in terms of distance from subscriber to signaling point and total subscribers as large or average sized.

Q.710 Use of Signaling System No. 7 for PABX Application

Defines the method for connecting digital PBXs to SS7-MTP while using the layer 3 (Recommendation I.450) message structure of ISDN. This is intended to provide the richer network interface capabilities of the SS7-MTP with the call control functions of ISDN for those PBXs requiring the additional functionality.

SIGNALING CONNECTION CONTROL PART (Q.71X)

The Signaling Connection Control Part (SCCP) provides the full OSI Network Layer functions not included in the original message transfer part, such as full global addressing and connection control.

Q.711 Function Description of the Signaling Connection Control Part (SCCP) of Signaling System Number 7

Contains a general description of the functions within the SCCP and the services provided to users.

Q.712 Definition and Functions of Signaling Connection Control Part Messages

Defines the meaning of each SCCP message and of the information elements contained in each message.

Q.713 Signaling Connection Control Part (SCCP) Functions and Codes

Defines the messages and codes used in the SCCP.

Q.714 Signaling Connection Control Part Procedures

Details the procedures for connectionless transport services, connection-oriented transport service, specialized addressing, routing, and multinode management.

TELEPHONE USER PART (Q.72X)

The telephone user part (TUP) utilizes the transport capabilities of the MTP to provide circuit-related signaling for telephone call control. This includes the control of both digital and analog circuits.

Q.721 Functional Description of the Signaling System Telephone User Part (TUP)

A brief description of the TUP.

Q.722 General Function of Telephone Messages and Signals

Provides a description of TUP message types and nomenclature, plus a general description of the function of TUP messages.

Q.723 Formats and Codes

Specifies the encoding of TUP signaling information elements and the format of messages in which they are conveyed.

Q.724 Signaling Procedures

Details the procedures for basic call control.

Q.725 Signaling Performance in the Telephone Application

Provides performance criteria for TUP message transfer over Signaling System No. 7 networks. Objectives for availability, dependability, and cross-exchange delay are presented.

ISDN USER PART (Q.76X)

The ISDN user part (ISUP) utilizes the transport capabilities of the MTP and SCCP to provide call-related services for ISDN. Because of the overall role of Signaling System No. 7 in providing interexchange signaling for ISDN, there is a correspondence between many of the capabilities of the ISUP and the I.44x/I.45x series of control signal specifications for ISDN.

Q.761 Functional Description of the ISDN User Part of Signaling System No. 7

A brief description of the ISUP.

Q.762 General Function of Messages and Signals

Provides a description of ISUP message types and nomenclature, plus a general description of the function of ISUP messages.

BOX 4-3 *continued*

Q.763 Formats and Codes

Specifies the encoding of ISUP signaling information elements and the format of messages in which they are conveyed.

Q.764 Signaling Procedures

Details the procedures for basic call control, and for providing a variety of other services with the ISUP.

Q.766 Performance Objectives in the Integrated Services Digital Network Application

Provides performance criteria for ISUP message transfer over Signaling System No. 7. Objectives for availability, dependability, and cross-exchange delay are presented.

OPERATIONS, ADMINISTRATION, AND MAINTENANCE (Q.79X)

Currently, this portion of the specification is limited. It is intended to cover all aspects of Operations, Administration, and Maintenance (OA&M) that are amenable to standardization.

Q.791 Monitoring and Measurements for the MTP

Describes methods for monitoring and measuring performance of the MTP. It specifies the set of parameters and the timing of measurements.

Q.795 Operations and Maintenance Application Part

Intended to provide application-layer procedures and protocols related to accomplishing OA&M functions at signaling points. Much in this area is for further study.

switching technology. In effect, a packet-switched network is overlaid on a circuit-switched network in order to operate and control the circuit-switched network.

SS7 defines the functions that are performed in the packet-switched network but does not dictate any particular hardware implementation. For example, all of the SS7 functions could be implemented in the circuit-switching nodes as additional functions; this approach is the associated signaling mode depicted in Figure 2-24a. Alternatively, separate switching points that carry only the control packets and are not used for carrying circuits can be used, as depicted in Figure 2-24b. Even in this case, the circuit-switching nodes would need to implement portions of SS7 so that they could receive control signals.

SS7 defines two functional entities: signaling points and signal transfer points. A **signaling point** (SP) is any point in the signaling network capable of handling control messages. It may be an endpoint for control messages and incapable of processing messages not directly addressed to itself. The circuit-switching nodes of the network, for example, could be endpoints. Another example is a network control center. A **signal transfer point** (STP) is a signaling point that is capable of routing control messages; that is, a message received on one signaling link is transferred to another link. An STP could be a pure routing node or could also include the functions of an endpoint.

One possible realization of an SS7 architecture is depicted in Figure 4-7, which shows the approach taken by AT&T [PHEL86, DONO86]. SPs and STPs are connected by links that are defined by function (Table 4-1). STPs are configured in pairs for redundancy and linked by cross (C) links. Circuit-switching nodes hook into the SS7 packet-switching network by means of access (A) links to paired STPs. Bridge (B) links are provided between STP pairs in different regions and D links between STP pairs at different hierarchical levels. The remaining link types (E and F) provide additional paths to and from circuit-switching nodes to reflect particular high traffic demands.

So far, we have been discussing SS7 architecture in terms of the way in which functions are organized to create a packet-switching control network. The term architecture can also be used to refer to the structure of protocols that specify SS7. As with the OSI model, the SS7 standard is a layered architecture. The SS7 standard was not initially developed with OSI in mind but, as it evolves, it is increasingly reflecting the functional organization of OSI. Figure 4-8 shows the current structure of SS7 and attempts to relate it to OSI.

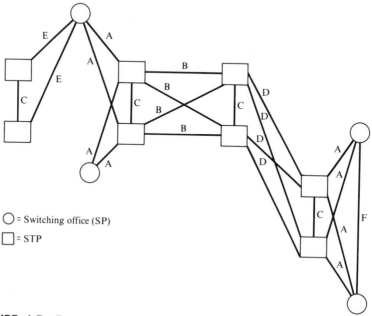

FIGURE 4-7 Examples of Links Used in an SS7 Network

TABLE 4-1 SIGNALING LINKS

Designation	Connection	Use
A	SP to STP	Provides access to the signaling network from a switching office.
B	STP to STP at same level of a hierarchy	Primary routing of messages from one SP to another via multiple STPs.
C	STP to mated STP	Communication between paired STPs; also provides alternate route around failed B links.
D	STP to STP at different levels of a hierarchy	Routing of messages up or down in a hierarchy.
E	SP to STP	Provides direct connection to non-home STP from a switching office.
F	SP to SP	Provides direct access between switching offices with a high community of interest.

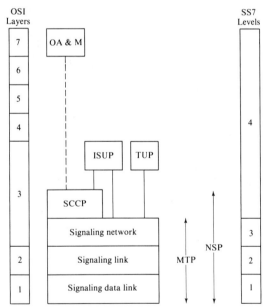

ISUP = ISDN user part
TUP = Telephone user part
OA & M = Operations administration, and maintenance
MTP = Message transfer part
NSP = Network service part
SCCP = Signaling connection control part

FIGURE 4-8 Signaling System No. 7 Protocol Architecture

The SS7 architecture consists of four levels. The lower three levels, referred to as the **message transfer part** (MTP) provide a reliable but connectionless (datagram style) service for routing messages through the SS7 network. The lowest level, **signaling data link,** corresponds to the physical layer of the OSI model, and is concerned with the physical and electrical characteristics of the signaling links. These include links between STPs, between an STP and an SP, and control links between SPs. The **signaling link** level is a data link control protocol that provides for the reliable sequenced delivery of data across a signaling data link; it corresponds to layer 2 of the OSI model. The top level of the MTP, referred to as the **signaling network** level or function, provides for routing data across multiple STPs from control source to control destination. These three levels together do not provide the complete set of functions and services specified in the OSI layers 1 – 3, most notably in the areas of addressing and connection-oriented service. In the 1984 version of SS7, an additional module was added that resides in level 4, known as **signaling connection control part** (SCCP). The SCCP and MTP together are referred to as the **network service part** (NSP). A variety of different network-layer services are defined in SCCP, to meet the needs of various users of NSP. The remainder of the modules of SS7 are at level 4 and comprise the various users of NSP. NSP is simply a message delivery system; the remaining parts deal with the actual contents of the messages. The **telephone user part** (TUP) is invoked in response to actions by a subscriber at a telephone. TUP control signals deal with the establishment, maintenance, and termination of telephone calls. The **ISDN User Part** (ISUP) provides for the control signaling needed in an ISDN to deal with ISDN subscriber calls and related functions. Finally the **Operations and Maintenance Application Part** (OA&M) specifies network management functions and messages related to operations and maintenance. This final area is in a preliminary state and will be expanded in future versions of the Recommendations.

In the remainder of this section, we examine each of the modules in the network service part. The ISDN user part will be examined in Part II.

Signaling Data Link Level

The signaling data link is a full-duplex physical link dedicated to SS7 traffic. SS7 is optimized for use over 64-kbps digital links. However, the recommendations allow for the use of circuit-switched connections to the data link, lower speeds, and for the use of analog links with modems. The link can be routed via a satellite.

Signaling Link Level

The signaling link level corresponds to the data link control layer of the OSI model. Thus, its purpose is to turn a potentially unreliable physical link into a reliable data link. Reliability implies:

- All transmitted blocks of data are delivered with no losses or duplications.
- Blocks of data are delivered in the same order that they were transmitted.
- The receiver is capable of exercising flow control over the sender.

The last point assures that blocks of data are not lost after delivery because of buffer overflow.

The reader familiar with the better-known data link control protocol, HDLC, and its variants such as LAP-B, will see that many of the same principles are used in the SS7 signaling link level. However, the formats and some of the procedures are different.

Signal Unit Formats.   We begin our discussion of the signaling link protocol with a description of the formats of the basic elements of the protocol. The blocks of data transmitted at the signaling link level are referred to as signal units. As Figure 4-9 illustrates, there are three types of signal units:

- *Message Signal Unit (MSU):* Carries user data from level 4.
- *Link Status Signal Unit (LSSU):* Carries control information needed at the signaling link level.
- *Fill-in Signal Unit (FISU):* Transmitted when no other signal units are available.

Let us begin by examining the fields of the MSU. The MSU begins and ends with a **flag** field, which delimits the signal unit at both ends with the unique pattern 01111110. A single flag may be used as the closing flag for one signal unit and the opening flag for the next. Each of the two receivers attached to a link looks for the flag sequence to synchronize on the start of a signal unit. While receiving a signal unit, the receiver continues to hunt for that sequence to determine the end of the frame. Since the signal unit allows the presence of arbitrary bit patterns (i.e., there are no restrictions on the content of the various fields imposed by the link protocol), there is no assurance that the pattern 01111110 will not appear somewhere inside the signal unit, thus destroying synchronization. To avoid this problem, a procedure known as *bit stuffing* is used. Between the transmission of the starting and ending flags, the transmitter will always insert an extra 0 bit after each occurrence of five 1s in the signal unit. After detecting a starting flag, the receiver monitors the bit stream. When a pattern of five 1s appears, the sixth bit is examined. If this bit is 0, it is deleted. If the sixth bit is a 1 and the seventh bit is a 0, the combination is accepted as a flag. If the sixth and seventh bits are both 1, the sender is indicating an abort condition.

Figure 4-10 shows an example of bit stuffing. Note that in the first two cases, the extra 0 is not strictly necessary for avoiding a flag pattern, but is necessary for the operation of the algorithm. The pitfalls of bit stuffing are also illustrated in this figure. When a flag is used as both an ending and starting flag, a 1-bit error merges two signal units into one. Conversely, a 1-bit error inside the signal unit could split it in two.

The next four fields are used to implement the typical flow control and error control mechanisms found in many layer 2 and layer 3 protocols. The flow control is

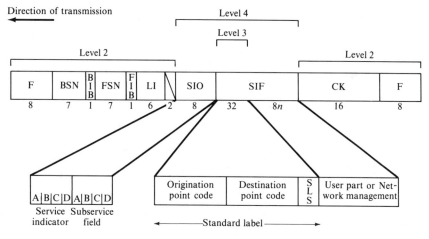

FIGURE 4-9   Signal Unit Formats

the sliding-window mechanism, and error control is the go-back-N automatic-re-peat-request (ARQ) mechanism. The basic operation of these mechanisms is ex-plained in Appendix A. The **backward sequence number** (BSN) contains the number of the last MSU successfully received from the other side; this provides for piggybacked acknowledgment. Negative acknowledgment associated with this BSN is indicated by inverting the **backward indicator bit** (BIB). The new value of the BIB will be maintained in all subsequent signal units to indicate positive acknowledg-ment until another error is detected. When this occurs, the BIB is again inverted on the next outgoing signal unit. The **forward sequence number** (FSN) is used to

Original pattern

1 1 1 1 1 1 1 1 1 1 1 1 0 1 1 1 1 1 1 0 1 1 1 1 1 1 0

After bit-stuffing

1 1 1 1 1 0 1 1 1 1 1 0 1 1 0 1 1 1 1 0 1 0 1 1 1 1 1 0 1 0

(a) Example

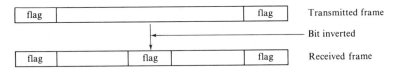

Transmitted frame

Bit inverted

Received frame

(b) An inverted bit splits a frame in two.

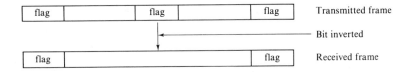

Transmitted frame

Bit inverted

Received frame

(c) An inverted bit merges two frames.

FIGURE 4-10   Bit Stuffing

uniquely number MSUs, modulo 128. The FSN of each new MSU is one more than the preceding MSU. The **forward indicator bit** (FIB) is used to indicate whether the MSU containing it is a new MSU or a retransmission due to receipt of a negative acknowledgment. For a retransmission, the FIB is inverted; all succeeding signal units maintain the same value of FIB until another negative acknowledgment is received.

The **length indicator** (LI) field specifies the length in octets of the following upper-level fields. This provides a cross-check on the closing flag. It also serves as a signal unit type indicator, since the three types of signal units carry upper-level data of different lengths. The FISU has no user data field; the LSSU has a single user data field of one octet; and the MSU has a data portion that is longer than 2 octets. Thus a value of 0 indicates an FISU; a value of 1 indicates an LSSU; and a value of 3 to 63 provides for various lengths of the MSU.

The next two fields contain information of use to higher levels and are simply treated as data to be transferred across the link. The **service information octet** (SIO) indicates the nature of the MSU. This octet consists of two subfields, the service indicator and the subservice field (Table 4-2). The service indicator specifies the user of the MTP: what type of message is being carried. The subservice field indicates whether the message relates to a national or international network. Some of the bits in the subservice field are either unused, reserved for future use, or available for national use. The **signaling information field** (SIF) contains information of interest to both levels 3 and 4 of SS7. This field consists of two subfields, the standard label and user data. The standard label is a 32-bit address field, containing 14-bit source and destination node addresses and a 4-bit signaling link selection field that is used to distribute the traffic among alternative routes. The second part of the SIF contains user data from some SS7 application or network management data. For example, an ISDN user part or a telephone user part would be contained here.

TABLE 4-2   SERVICE INFORMATION OCTET AND STATUS FIELD CODES

(a) Service Information Octet

Service Indicator

DCBA	Indication
0000	Signaling Network Management Messages
0001	Signaling Network Testing and Maintenance Messages
0010	Spare
0011	Signaling Connection Control Part (SCCP)
0100	Telephone User Part
0101	ISDN User Part
0110	Data User Part (call and circuit-related messages)
0111	Data User Part (facility registration and cancellation)
1000 to 1111	Spare

Subservice Field

DCBA	Meaning
00XX	International Network
01XX	Spare
10XX	National Network
11XX	Reserved for National Use

(b) Status Field

CBA	Indication
000	Out of Alignment
001	Normal Alignment
010	Emergency Alignment
011	Out of Service
100	Processor Outage
101	Busy

The **check bits** (CK) field contains an error-detecting code used to enable the receiver to determine if there have been any transmission errors. The check bits are calculated from the remainder of the bits in the signal unit exclusive of flags, using a cyclic redundancy check (CRC). The CRC is calculated by the transmitter and inserted into the signal unit. The same calculation is performed by the receiver. If there is a discrepancy between the received CRC and the CRC calculated by the receiver, then an error is assumed. The 16-bit CRC-CCITT formula is used. This formula and the error detection process are examined in Appendix A.

The link status signal unit (LSSU) shares many of the same fields as the MSU. The only difference is that instead of the two user fields (SIO and SIF) in the MSU, there is a single **status field** (SF) that is carried as user data in the LSSU. Again, this field is simply treated as data to be transferred across the link. The field is used to indicate the sender's view of the actual status of the link. This information may be used for network management purposes.

Finally, the fill-in signal unit (FISU) contains no new fields. It has the same structure as the MSU and the LSSU, but with no user fields.

Operation. The key functions performed by the signaling link protocol are flow control and error control. Both functions employ a sliding-window technique (see Appendix A), in which each message signal unit (MSU) is numbered sequentially. Each new MSU is given a new forward sequence number (FSN) that is one more (modulo 128) than the preceding sequence number. Link status signal units (LSSU) and fill-in signal units (FISU) are not numbered separately but carry the FSN of the last transmitted MSU. All three types of signal units carry piggybacked acknowledgments and negative acknowledgments, in the form of backward sequence numbers (BSN). Figure 4-11 provides an example of an error-free exchange of signal units.

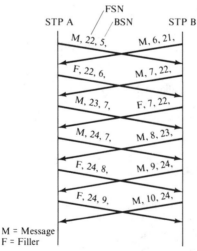

FSN
STP A BSN STP B
M, 22, 5, M, 6, 21,
F, 22, 6, M, 7, 22,
M, 23, 7, F, 7, 22,
M, 24, 7, M, 8, 23,
F, 24, 8, M, 9, 24,
F, 24, 9, M, 10, 24,

M = Message
F = Filler

FIGURE 4-11 Error-Free Signal Unit Exchange

Note that when both sides have data to send, via the MSU, then the MSU is used to provide a piggybacked acknowledgment. When one side has no data to send, it transmits FISUs, which provide acknowledgment.

Flow control is provided by the LSSU. When one side is unable to keep up with the flow of data from the other side, it transmits an LSSU with a busy indication in the status field. When such an indication is received, all transmission of MSUs must cease; the busy side will notify the other side that it can resume transmission by means of another LSSU. This activity is generally invisible to the next higher level (signaling network level), which may simply notice that throughput has declined. However, if a congestion condition persists and is not reported to the signaling network level, then the performance of the entire signaling network may be degraded. If the network level is aware of a congestion problem, then control packets can be routed around the point of congestion. For this purpose, tight timer control on the allowable duration of the busy condition is imposed. Two rules specify the time constraints:

1. If a receiver becomes overloaded, it must send a busy signal to stop transmission from the other side. If the busy condition persists, the node must repeatedly send a busy indication every 200 milliseconds while in the overloaded state. If the other side receives neither a busy indication or a normal indication for a period of 200 milliseconds, it reports to the network level that the link is *out-of-service*.
2. Even if repeated busy indications are received every 200 milliseconds, a node will report a link to be *out-of-service* after 10 seconds.

The basic form of **error control** is go-back-N ARQ (see Appendix A). If a node receives a negative acknowledgment in an MSU, LSSU, or FISU, it will retransmit the specified signal unit and all subsequent signal units. Figure 4-12 illustrates this algorithm. As an alternative to go-back-N, a technique known as *preventive cyclic retransmission* is used on all satellite links and on intercontinental links with a one-way propagation delay of 15 msec or more. For a link with a relatively long propagation delay, each message unit is comparatively short, and the link may be idle most of the time. In such a circumstance, it is not efficient to wait for a negative acknowledgment before retransmitting. Instead, whenever a node has no MSUs to send, it automatically retransmits unacknowledged MSUs, without waiting for a positive or negative acknowledgment. Only positive acknowledgments are sent by the other side.

Signaling Network Level

As Figure 4-13 illustrates, the signaling network level includes functions related to message handling and functions related to network management. The **message handling functions** fall into three categories:

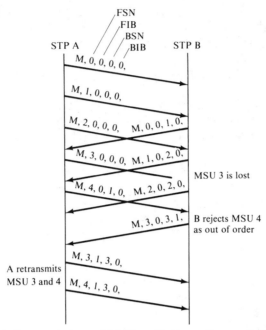

FIGURE 4-12   Transmission of MSUs with Error Correction

- *Discrimination:* Determines if a message is at its destination or is to be relayed to another node. This decision is based on analysis of the destination code in the standard label of the message. If this is the destination, the signal unit is delivered to the distribution function; otherwise, it is delivered to the routing function. The discrimination function is only needed in signal transfer points (STP).
- *Routing:* Determines the signaling link to be used in forwarding a message. The message may have been received from the discrimination function or from a local level 4 entity.
- *Distribution:* Determines the user part to which a message should be delivered. The decision is based on analysis of the service indicator.

The routing decision is based on the value of the signaling link selection (SLS) field, which is assigned by a user part in level 4. For a given source/destination pair, several alternate routes may be possible; the value of the SLS field specifies which particular route is to be followed. With a 4-bit field, a total of 16 different routes through the network may be defined. These different routes are, in effect, different internal virtual circuits. In general, all of the control signals associated with a single call will follow the same route; this guarantees that they will arrive in sequence. However, the MTP needs to distribute traffic uniformly. This requirement can be satisfied if the user part varies the route selection from one call to the next.

The other function of the signaling network level is the **signaling network management function.** The main objective of this function is to overcome link degradations (failures or congestion). To meet this objective, the signaling management function is concerned with monitoring the status of each link, with dictating alternate routes to overcome link degradation and communicating the alternate routes to the affected nodes, and with recovering from the loss of messages due to link failure. The goal for SS7 is no more than 10 minutes of unavailability per year for any route. This goal is achieved through redundancy of links and dynamic re-routing.

This emphasis on the internal management of the network is rare; virtually all other network protocols make no mention of network management. In most cases, it is preferable to leave network management details to the provider, so that the provider can pursue the most-cost effective approach and be responsive to changes both in customer expectations and advances in technology. However, in the case of SS7, there are strong reasons for the emphasis on network management:

1.   The function being specified is critical. The performance of a network's control signaling architecture affects all subscribers to the network.
2.   The various networks involved must support international traffic. Degradations in one nation's signaling system will have repercussions beyond that nation's borders. Thus, some international agreement on the degree of reliability of national networks is indicated.
3.   Recovery and restoration actions may involve multiple networks (e.g., in the case of international calls). If SS7 did not include failure and congestion recovery procedures, it would be necessary for the administration of each public network to enter into bilateral agreements with a number of other networks.

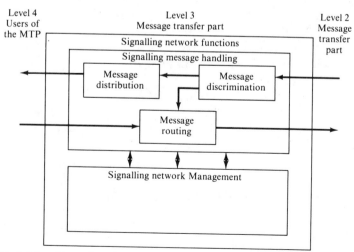

FIGURE 4-13   Signaling Network Function

Signaling Connection Control Part

The signaling network level does not provide all of the routing and addressing capabilities that the OSI model dictates for the network layer. As an example, the message distribution function provides only a limited addressing capability. For newer user part applications, a more complex specification of the user of a message at a node is necessary; this can be provided by the signaling connection control part (SCCP). The SCCP enhances the connectionless sequenced transmission service provided by the MTP, to meet the needs of those user parts requiring enriched connectionless or connection-oriented service to transfer signaling information between nodes. For those user parts for which MTP suffices, the extra overhead of SCCP can be avoided.

Five classes of network service are defined for SCCP:

0. Basic unsequenced connectionless
1. Sequenced (fixed signaling link selection number) connectionless class
2. Basic connection-oriented
3. Flow control connection-oriented
4. Error recovery and flow control connection-oriented

To date, only classes 0 and 1 have been fully specified.

Comparison with X.25

Both the X.25 and SS7 standards deal with packet-switched networks. The applications, however, are very different. X.25 defines an interface between a subscriber device and a packet-switched network and contains both control signaling (call setup and termination) and subscriber data transfer functions. X.25 is not concerned at all with the internal structure of the network. SS7 is primarily for the use of applications residing in the combined circuit-switched/packet-switched network, although the ISDN user part relates to subscriber devices. SS7 contains only control signal functions, with no subscriber data transfer capability. Finally, SS7 is concerned with internal details of the network and addresses issues such as routing, reliability, and performance.

Despite these differences in function, it is instructive to look at the similarities between the two sets of protocols. Table 4-3, based on [BHUS83], lists some of the main points of comparison. The significant differences pertain to packet length, number of outstanding packets, and signal transfer delay.

4-4   SOFTWARE DEFINED NETWORKS

A relatively recent offering from a number of telecommunications providers is a capability referred to as a software defined network (SDN), or a virtual private network [GILH87, GAWD86, COCH85]. A number of providers are offering

TABLE 4-3 COMPARISON OF X.25 AND CCITT SIGNALING SYSTEM NO. 7

Basis of Comparison	CCITT X.25	CCITT No. 7	Comments
1) Function	Procedure for connecting data equipment to packet network	Procedure for Common Channel Signaling for establishing circuit switched telephone and data calls. Includes: Call Control, Management and Maintenance Signaling	
2) Functional Division	One: Data Communications	Two: (1) Message Transfer Part (Specifies the data communication function and its performance) (2) Specific User Parts	
3) Protocol Structure	Three Levels	Four Levels	The three lower levels of No. 7 are equivalent to the three levels of X.25
4) Modes of Operation	Switched Virtual Circuit (SVC) or Autoconnect (AC)	Preestablished path equivalent to X.25 Autoconnect (AC).	
5) Level I	Bit Rate Independent Network Links (2.4 to 56 KBPS)	Optimized for 64 KBPS. Applicable down to 4.8 KBPS.	
6) Level II	HDLC	No. 7 Level 2	Comparison follows.
7) Flag	01111110	01111110	
8) Zero Insertions Deletion	Yes	Yes	
9) Block Formats	a. Information Frame b. Supervisory Frame c. Unnumbered Frame Identified by 4 Bits	a. Message Signal Unit (MSU) b. Link Status Signal Unit (LSSU) c. Fill-in Signal Unit (FISU) Identified by 6 Bits	
10) Block Sequence Number	4 or 8 bit field	Not required in No. 7	

Cont.

TABLE 4-3   COMPARISON OF X.25 AND CCITT SIGNALING SYSTEM NO. 7 (continued)

Basis of Comparison	CCITT X.25	CCITT No. 7	Comments
11) Outstanding Blocks	8	128	
12) Address Field	8 bits	Not required	
13) Error Control	CRC	CRC	
14) Polynomial	$X^{16} + X^{12} + X^5 + 1$	$X^{16} + X^{12} + X^5 + 1$	
15) Error Correction	a. Timeouts and/or b. Negative acknowledgment	a. Positive and negative acknowledgment or b. Length threshold or unacknowledged messages	
16) Level III	Does not require full interconnection	Requires full interconnection	
17) Connection Establishment	By packet interchange or Autoconnect	Route preestablished	
18) Routing	By packet header	By routing label	
19) Level IV	None	User Parts	

services that fit into this category. In general terms, an SDN is a facility based on a public circuit-switched network that gives the user the appearance of a private network. The network is "software defined" in the sense that the user provides the service supplier with entries to a data base used by the supplier to configure, manage, monitor, and report on the operation of the network.

SDNs are the first offering of a new wave of networking services characterized by flexibility, a rich set of features, a high degree of user control, and an ability to be changed quickly based on user needs. In this respect, they may be viewed as precursors to ISDNs. Thus, a brief review of the SDN will give us some idea of the kinds of capabilities that will become available with ISDN.

Private Networks

The use of private networks by subscribers with large traffic demands has been commonplace for decades. A typical example is a private voice network. Such a network supports telephone connections in a number of sites belonging to the same organization, and consists of the following ingredients:

- Subscriber telephones.
- PBX.
- Network trunks.
- Access lines to a public switched telecommunications network.

Typically, the network trunks are lines leased from a telecommunications provider. Each subscriber is provided with a unique on-network telephone number. One user may dial another user anywhere on the network simply by dialing the on-net number. In addition, each PBX is equipped with an access line to a public telecommunications network so that off-network calls can be sent and received.

These private networks have evolved both in scope and sophistication. With the use of digital technology, a private network can support both data devices and telephones. This requires the use of digital PBXs and digital trunks, typically T1 (1.544 Mbps) trunks in the United States. Such a private network supports a number of features, including:

- Uniform numbering plans for all users, regardless of specific location.
- Alternate routing of calls around the network based on load factors, resulting in fewer on-net calls being blocked.
- End user authorization codes and charge-back mechanisms
- Call detail reporting and traffic reports.

In general, this sort of private network allows an organization to reduce costs by concentrating traffic from a number of corporate locations and funneling it onto a limited number of long distance circuits.

Although a private network, particularly a private digital network, can afford the user cost savings plus a greater degree of network control, there are a number of shortcomings:

- The network may not be economically extendible to all the remote points the user might want. For example, the user may have one or more small offices with only a limited number of telephones that generate a small amount of traffic to the remainder of the organization. This may not be sufficient to justify a leased network line to the nearest network switch. Such offices must be reached by ordinary dial service. Thus, there is a nonuniform numbering scheme and advanced network services are limited to on-net subscribers.
- Changes are often difficult to implement when requirements change. The acquisition of a new PBX or additional leased line is a significant rather than a small incremental step.
- Similarly, the economic viability of any network configuration may depend on idiosyncratic tariffs that, when changed, may drastically alter the configuration's cost-effectiveness.

With the increasing use of common-channel signaling, and the increasingly digital nature of the public circuit-switched networks, an alternative to the private network becomes possible. That alternative is to provide the types of services and user control available on a private network by means of public-network services tailored to a particular user by means of software.

SDN Architecture

The SDN concept involves substituting a long-distance circuit-switched network for the leased trunks customarily used in private networks, while giving the user a special set of interfaces to that network that make it seem to the user as if it is an actual private network. For the most part, these special interfaces have to do with the ways calls are processed, and with the monitoring and reporting functions involved.

A simple example of an SDN is the Advanced 800 Service that has been available from AT&T since 1982 [RAAC84], which is illustrated in Figure 4-14. The figure illustrates a customer with two locations, one on the West Coast and one on the East Coast. A single toll-free number is used by customers. A data base is maintained at a network control point (NCP) that shows the destination for each call based on the area code of the originating call. A portion of that data base is shown. Thus, calls originating in area code 717 (Pennsylvania) are always routed to the East Coast location, with the terminating number of 919-567-7000. Calls coming in from the 602 area (Arizona) are routed to the West Coast during business hours and to the East Coast at other times. These events are illustrated in parts b through d of the figure. A call is placed by dialing the 800 number. This triggers a query from a switch in the network to the NCP, which directs the call to the appropriate destina-

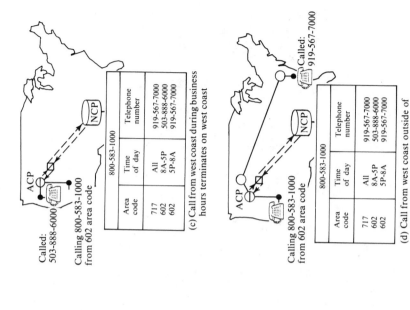

(a) AT & T advanced 800 service: the terminating numbers are determined by originating NPA and time of day

800-583-1000		
Area code	Time of day	Telephone number
717	All	919-567-7000
602	8A-5P	503-888-6000
602	5P-8A	919-567-7000

Called: 503-888-6000

Called: 919-567-7000

(b) Call from east coast terminates on east coast

800-583-1000		
Area code	Time of day	Telephone number
717	All	919-567-7000
602	8A-5P	503-888-6000
602	5P-8A	919-567-7000

Calling 800-583-1000 from 717 area code

Called: 919-567-7000

(c) Call from west coast during business hours terminates on west coast

800-583-1000		
Area code	Time of day	Telephone number
717	All	919-567-7000
602	8A-5P	503-888-6000
602	5P-8A	919-567-7000

Called: 503-888-6000

Calling 800-583-1000 from 602 area code

(d) Call from west coast outside of business hours terminates on east coast

800-583-1000		
Area code	Time of day	Telephone number
717	All	919-567-7000
602	8A-5P	503-888-6000
602	5P-8A	919-567-7000

Called: 919-567-7000

Calling 800-583-1000 from 602 area code

FIGURE 4-14 Example Use of AT&T Advanced 800 Service

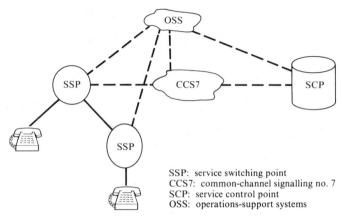

SSP: service switching point
CCS7: common-channel signalling no. 7
SCP: service control point
OSS: operations-support systems

FIGURE 4-15   SDN Architecture

tion number. These control messages are communicated using common channel signaling. The switches, which are part of the AT&T network, are referred to as Action Points (ACP) to reflect the fact that the switches now have sufficient intelligence to work with the NCP to provide tailored customer service.

The Advanced 800 Service allows incoming 800 calls to be routed based on:

- Originating area code.
- Time of day.
- Day of week.
- Caller-entered digits: Callers hear a recorded message that will help them route their calls to the department or service of their choice by dialing additional digits.
- Percent allocation: A customer can apportion calls to two or more call-answering locations by specifying the percentage of calls each location should receive.
- Customer-preplanned special situations: Allows customers to respond to spontaneous needs, such as emergencies by pre-establishing alternate routes for handling incoming calls.

This service is a relatively primitive form of software-defined network, but gives an indication of the kinds of things that can be done with digital networks controlled by a common channel signaling protocol such as Signaling System Number 7.

Figure 4-15 illustrates, in general terms, the key ingredients of a software-defined network [GILH87]. These are:

- A set of switches (service switching points) interconnected to provide both a public dial-up circuit-switched capability, and the intelligence to provide software-defined private network capability.

- A central network management location (service control point) that maintains a centralized data base with algorithms and customer instructions for routing the information to be transported.
- An operations-support center that provides features such as planning, engineering, ordering, provisioning, maintenance, and repair, offering greatly enhanced network management and increased customer control.
- An SS7 packet-switched network that interconnects the service control point, the operations-support center, and the service switching points.

Box 4-4 lists the types of services that can be provided by a software-defined network. The advantages of such networks, compared to a private network, are [COOL87]:

- The use of the public telecommunications facilities means that the circuits may be shared among many users providing for greater efficiency at lower cost.
- The overall flexibility is greater and its reliability is enhanced, since the user is no longer constrained to a particular physical private line.
- Because the network is implemented in software, it is able to support network-based services not normally provided by dedicated special-service circuits.
- The software that supports such a network allows enhanced user management and control of the communications facility.

Of course, as with any technology, there are disadvantages to SDN, and it is not the right solution for every organization [MCQU85]. In particular, if the traffic patterns of an organization are relatively stable and not subject to significant fluctuations, the extra expense of implementing the interfaces to an SDN may not be justified. Also, for smaller networking needs, the expense of incorporating the new SDN interfaces may be too much.

4-5 RECOMMENDED READING

Books that provide good overall coverage of IDN concepts are [KEIS85], [BELL82b], and [INOS79].

There is not a great deal of literature on the digital subscriber loop. [WYND82] is a special issue devoted to the topic; however, this issue predates recent advances in echo cancellation and concentrates on time compression multiplexing. Significant portions of [MESS84b] and [DECI86a] are devoted to echo cancellation. [LIN88] is a good recent reference; it focuses on echo cancellation.

[ROEH85] and [SCHL86] are good overviews of Signaling System Number 7; [DONO86] describes a practical implementation of this standard. [GILH87], [GAWD86], [BROW86], and [COOL87] present aspects of the software defined network.

BOX 4-4

TYPICAL FEATURES OF A SOFTWARE DEFINED NETWORK

CALL PROCESSING

Uniform Numbering Plan

Each subscriber in the network has a unique number.

Access to Switched Network

Call may be placed from an on-net subscriber to a number off-net, and off-net callers can directly dial on-net subscribers. Frequently-called off-net numbers can be incorporated into the uniform numbering plan.

Off-Net Overflow

SDN calls automatically overflow off-net for completion when all dedicated SDN direct lines are busy.

Private Network Interface

A uniform numbering plan can be provided to encompass an SDN and a private network. Callers need not know whether the called subscriber is an SDN location or a private network location. The resulting hybrid network is beneficial to an organization that is migrating from private to SDN and to an organization for which the private network is the most economical for part of its needs.

Routing

Routing incoming off-net calls to different locations specified by the customer based on location of the calling party, time of day, day of week, additional digits dialed by caller in response to prompt, and busy-idle status of customer's destination numbers.

CALL MANAGEMENT

Originating Screening

Allows the SDN customer to define a list of numbers that may not be called from a given number or group of numbers (caller group). Individual numbers may be assigned to one or more caller groups. The list of numbers that may not be called can vary by time of day or day of week. Also, authorization codes may be required to call particular numbers. The requirement to enter an authorization code may also vary by time and day.

Location Screening

Allows the SDN customer to define a list of numbers that may not be called from a given location

Queuing

Calls may be queued to a particular number or called group (rotary group).

MANAGEMENT AND CONTROL

Update

Customers can update their own data base on-line. This includes changes to routing, authorization codes, and group membership.

Reports

Detailed reports on network activity are provided, including data base definition reports, summary traffic, and call detail.

4-6   PROBLEMS

4-1   Assume that a digital subscriber line, using TCM, carries 64-kbps PCM voice plus 8-kbps data in each direction plus one additional bit for every nine to be used for framing and synchronization. Let each burst in each direction have a length of 20 bits. For a typical cable, the propagation delay is 5 μs/km. Assume a guard time of 25 μs. What is the maximum length of cable that can be accommodated?

4-2   It is clear that bit stuffing is needed for user data fields in SS7 signal units, since we wish to accommodate arbitrary user data. Is it needed for the other fields? Specify which ones.

4-3   Suggest improvements to the bit-stuffing algorithm to overcome the problems of a single-bit error.

4-4   It was pointed out that some of the stuffed bits in Figure 4-10 were not strictly necessary. Consider the following rule: a 0 is stuffed by the transmitter only after the appearance of 011111.
a. Describe the destuffing rule.
b. Apply the rules to the bit stream in Figure 4-10.

4-5   Would it be possible to provide a circuit-switched rather than a packet-switched implementation of SS7? What would be the relative merits of such an approach?

4-6   Is something like SS7 needed to provide control signaling in a packet-switched network? If so, why not use SS7?

4-7 Are the modem and the codec functional inverses (i.e., could an inverted modem function as a codec, and vice versa)?

APPENDIX 4A: ANALOG AND DIGITAL DATA TRANSMISSION

The terms **analog** and **digital** correspond, roughly, to continuous and discrete, respectively. These two terms are used frequently in data communications in at least three contexts:

- Data
- Signaling
- Transmission

Very briefly, we define data as entities that convey meaning. A useful distinction is that data have to do with the form of something; information has to do with the content or interpretation of those data. Signals are electric or electromagnetic encoding of data. Signaling is the act of propagating the signal along some suitable medium. Finally, transmission is the communication of data by the propagation and processing of signals. In what follows, we try to make these abstract concepts clear, by discussing the terms "analog" and "digital" in these three contexts.

The concepts of analog and digital data are simple enough. **Analog data** take on continuous values on some interval. For example, voice and video are continuously varying patterns of intensity. Most data collected by sensors, such as temperature and pressure, are continuous-valued. **Digital data** take on discrete values; examples are text and integers.

In a communications system, data are propagated from one point to another by means of electric signals. An **analog signal** is a continuously-varying electromagnetic wave that may be propagated over a variety of media, depending on frequency; examples are wire media, such as twisted pair and coaxial cable, fiber optic cable, and atmosphere or space propagation. A **digital signal** is a sequence of voltage pulses that may be transmitted over a wire medium; for example, a constant positive voltage level may represent binary 1 and a constant negative voltage level may represent binary 0.

The principal advantages of digital signaling are that it is generally cheaper than analog signaling and is less susceptible to noise interference. The principal disadvantage is that digital signals suffer more from attenuation than do analog signals. Figure 4-16 shows a sequence of voltage pulses, generated by a source using two voltage levels, and the received voltage some distance down a conducting medium. Because of the attenuation or reduction of signal strength at higher frequencies, the pulses become rounded and smaller. It should be clear that this attenuation can rather quickly lead to the loss of the information contained in the propagated signal.

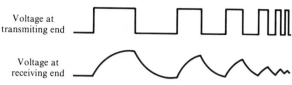

Voltage at transmiting end

Voltage at receiving end

FIGURE 4-16 Attenuation of Digital Signals

Both analog and digital data can be represented, and hence propagated, by either analog or digital signals. This is illustrated in Figure 4-17. Generally, analog data are a function of time and occupy a limited frequency spectrum. Such data can be directly represented by an electromagnetic signal occupying the same spectrum. The best example of this is voice data. As sound waves, voice data have frequency components in the range 20 Hz to 20 kHz. However, most of the speech energy is in a much narrower range. The standard spectrum of voice signals is 300 to 3400 Hz, and this is quite adequate to propagate speech intelligibly and clearly. The telephone instrument does just that. For all sound input in the range of 300 to 3400 Hz, an electromagnetic signal with the same frequency-amplitude pattern is produced. The process is performed in reverse to convert the electromagnetic energy back into sound.

Digital data can also be represented by analog signals by use of a *modem* (modulator-demodulator). The modem converts a series of binary (two-valued) voltage pulses into an analog signal by modulating a *carrier frequency*. The resulting signal occupies a certain spectrum of frequency centered about the carrier and may be propagated across a medium suitable for that carrier. The most common modems represent digital data in the voice spectrum and hence allow those data to be propagated over ordinary voice-grade telephone lines. At the other end of the line, a modem demodulates the signal to recover the original data.

In an operation very similar to that performed by a modem, analog data can be represented by digital signals. The device that performs this function for voice data is a *codec* (coder-decoder). In essence, the codec takes an analog signal that directly represents the voice data and approximates that signal by a bit stream. At the other end of the line, the bit stream is used to reconstruct the analog data. This topic is explored in Appendix 4B.

Finally, digital data can be represented directly, in binary form, by two voltage levels. To improve propagation characteristics, however, the binary data are often encoded into a more complex form of digital signal [STAL88a].

A final distinction remains to be made. Analog and digital signals may be transmitted on suitable transmission media. The way these signals are treated is a function of the transmission system. Table 4-4 summarizes the methods of data transmission. **Analog transmission** is a means of transmitting analog signals without regard to their content; the signals may represent analog data (e.g., voice) or digital data (e.g. data that pass through a modem). In either case, the analog signal will suffer attenuation which limits the length of the transmission link. To achieve

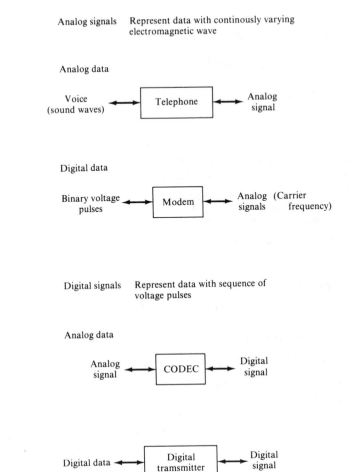

Analog signals   Represent data with continously varying
                  electromagnetic wave

Analog data

Voice   Telephone   Analog
(sound waves)   signal

Digital data

Binary voltage   Modem   Analog (Carrier
pulses   signals   frequency)

Digital signals   Represent data with sequence of
                  voltage pulses

Analog data

Analog   CODEC   Digital
signal   signal

Digital data   Digital   Digital
                tramsmitter signal

FIGURE 4-17   Analog and Digital Signaling of Analog and Digital
Data

longer distances, the analog transmission system includes amplifiers that boost the
energy in the signal. Unfortunately, the amplifier also boosts the noise components.
With amplifiers cascaded to achieve long distance, the signal becomes more and
more distorted. For analog data, such as voice, quite a bit of distortion can be
tolerated and the data remain intelligible. However, for digital data transmitted as
analog signals, cascaded amplifiers will introduce errors.

Digital transmission, in contrast, is concerned with the content of the signal.
We have mentioned that a digital signal can be propagated only a limited distance
before attenuation endangers the integrity of the data. To achieve greater distances,
repeaters are used. A repeater receives the digital signal, recovers the pattern of ones
and zeros, and retransmits a new signal. Thus the attenuation is overcome.

TABLE 4-4 ANALOG AND DIGITAL TRANSMISSION

(a) Treatment of Signals

	Analog Transmission	Digital Transmission
Analog Signal	Is propagated through amplifiers; same treatment for both analog and digital data	Assumes digital data; at propagation points, data in signal are recovered and new analog signal is generated
Digital Signal	Not used	Repeaters retransmit new signal; same treatment for both analog and digital data

(b) Possible Combinations

	Analog Transmission	Digital Transmission
Analog Data	Analog signal	Digital signal
Digital Data	Analog signal	Digital signal
		Analog signal

The same technique may be used with an analog signal if it is assumed that the signal carries digital data. At appropriately-spaced points, the transmission system has retransmission devices rather than amplifiers. The retransmission device recovers the digital data from the analog signal and generates a new, clean analog signal. Thus noise is not cumulative.

For long-haul communications, digital signaling is not as versatile and practical as analog signaling. For example, digital signaling is impossible for satellite, microwave, and optical fiber systems. However, digital transmission is superior to analog, both in terms of cost and quality (see Box 4-2), and the long-haul communications systems are gradually converting to digital transmission for both voice and digital data.

APPENDIX 4B: DIGITAL ENCODING OF ANALOG DATA

The evolution of public telecommunications networks to digital transmission requires that voice data be represented in digital form. It is important to note that this does not necessarily imply that the voice data be transmitted using digital signals. Figure 4-18 illustrates a common situation. Analog voice signals are digitized to produce a pattern of ones and zeros. As a digital signal, this pattern of ones and zeros may be fed into a modem so that an analog signal may be transmitted. However, this new analog signal differs significantly from the original voice signal, in that it represents an encoding of a binary stream. Hence, the digital transmission techniques discussed in Appendix 4A can be applied. In particular, retransmission devices rather than amplifiers are used to extend the length of a transmission link. Ultimately, of course, the new analog signal must be converted back to analog data

FIGURE 4-18 Digitizing Analog Data

that approximates the original voice input. For the remainder of this appendix, we can safely ignore the step of converting the digital data back into analog form and concentrate on the voice digitization process.

The best-known technique for voice digitization is **pulse-code modulation** (PCM). PCM is based on the sampling theorem, which states:

> If a signal $f(t)$ is sampled at regular intervals of time and at a rate higher than twice the highest significant signal frequency, then the samples contain all the information of the original signal. The function $f(t)$ may be reconstructed from these samples by the use of a low-pass filter.

A proof of this theorem can be found in [STAL88a].

If voice data are limited to frequencies below 4000 Hz, a conservative procedure for intelligibility, then 8000 samples per second would be sufficient to completely characterize the voice signal. Note, however, that these are analog samples. To convert to digital, each of these analog samples must be assigned a binary code. Figure 4-19 shows an example in which each sample is approximated by being "quantized" into one of 16 different levels. Each sample can then be represented by four bits. Of course, it is now impossible to recover the original signal exactly. By using an 8-bit sample, which allows 256 quantizing levels, the quality of the recovered voice signal is comparable to that achieved via analog transmission. Note that this implies that a data rate of 8000 sample per second $\times$ 8 bits per sample $= 64$ kbps is needed for a single voice signal.

Typically, the PCM scheme is refined using a technique known as *nonlinear encoding*, which means, in effect, that the 256 quantization levels are not equally spaced. The problem with equal spacing is that the mean absolute error for each sample is the same, regardless of signal level. Consequently, lower-amplitude values are relatively more distorted. By using a greater number of quantizing steps for signals of low amplitude, and a smaller number of quantizing steps for signals of large amplitude, a marked reduction in overall signal distortion is achieved.

PCM can, of course, be used for other than voice signals. For example, a color TV signal has a useful bandwidth of 4.6 MHz, and reasonable quality can be achieved with 10-bit samples, for a data rate of 92 Mbps.

In recent times, variations on the PCM technique, as well as other encoding techniques, have been used to reduce the digital data rate required to carry voice [AOYA88]. Good-quality voice transmission can be achieved with data rates of 32 kbps and 16 kbps [MULL87]. A reasonable long-term goal appears to be in the

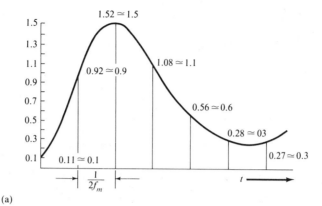

(a)

Digit	Binary equivalent	Pulse-code waveform
0	0000	
1	0001	
2	0010	
3	0011	
4	0100	
5	0101	
6	0110	
7	0111	
8	1000	
9	1001	
10	1010	
11	1011	
12	1100	
13	1101	
14	1110	
15	1111	

(b)

FIGURE 4-19 Pulse Code Modulation

neighborhood of 4 kbps [ROBI86, JAYA86, HASK81]. With video, advantage can be taken of the fact that from frame to frame most picture elements will not change. Interframe coding techniques should allow the video requirement to be reduced to about 15 Mpbs [MURA87], and for slowly-changing scenes, such as found in a video teleconference, down to 1.5 Mbps or less [SABR84, NETR80, KANE80]. Indeed, recent advances have resulted in commercial videoconference products with data rates as low as 64 kbps [HASK87].

PART II

INTEGRATED SERVICES DIGITAL NETWORKS

In Part I of this book, we looked at the underlying technology that supports the ISDN, that is, the technology of integrated digital networks (IDN). We are now in a position to turn to the ISDN itself. We begin, in Chapter 5, with an overview that provides a general description of the architecture of ISDN and looks at the standards that define ISDN.

Chapter 6 examines the services to be provided by ISDN. These services, in effect, are the requirements that ISDN must satisfy. This chapter looks at the general service capabilities defined for ISDN, and then examines three specific applications: Teletex, facsimile, and electronic mail.

The next two chapters focus on the detailed standards that specify ISDN. Chapter 7 looks at the architecture of ISDN. This includes a consideration of the multiplexed transmission structure, the possible configurations of ISDN, and issues relating to addressing and interworking. Chapter 8 examines the protocols for ISDN. Most of these are user-to-network protocols, which allow the ISDN subscriber to access ISDN, set up connections, and request particular network facilities and services. The chapter also looks at the ISDN User Part of Signaling System Number 7, which is a protocol internal to ISDN designed to support user access functions.

Finally, although the ink is barely dry on standards for ISDN and although implementations of ISDN are just beginning, plans for a more powerful ISDN, known as broadband ISDN, are underway. Chapter 9 examines this topic and looks at the likely direction of broadband ISDN.

CHAPTER 5
ISDN
OVERVIEW

5-1   A CONCEPTUAL VIEW OF ISDN

ISDN is a massive undertaking in many ways, and it is difficult to provide a concise description of it. To begin to understand ISDN, we look in this section at the concept of ISDN from several different viewpoints:

- Principles of ISDN
- Evolution of the ISDN
- The user interface
- Objectives
- Benefits
- Services
- Architecture

Principles of ISDN

Standards for ISDN are being defined by CCITT, a topic that we explore later in this chapter. Box 5-1, taken from one of the ISDN-related standards, states the principles of ISDN from the point of view of CCITT. Let us look at each of these points in turn.

1. *Support of voice and nonvoice applications using a limited set of standardized facilities*. This principle defines both the purpose of ISDN and the means of achieving it. The ISDN will support a variety of services related to voice communications (telephone calls) and

157

BOX 5-1

CCITT RECOMMENDATION I.120 (1984)

INTEGRATED SERVICE DIGITAL NETWORKS (ISDNs)

1   Principles of ISDN

1.1   The main feature of the ISDN concept is the support of a wide range of voice and non-voice applications in the same network. A key element of service integration for an ISDN is the provision of a range of services (see part II of the I-series of Recommendations) using a limited set of connection types and multipurpose user-network interface arrangements (see parts III and IV of the I-series of Recommendations).

1.2   ISDNs support a variety of applications including both switched and non-switched connections. Switched connections in an ISDN include both circuit-switched and packet-switched connections and their concatenations.

1.3   As far as practicable, new services introduced into an ISDN should be arranged to be compatible with 64 kbit/s switched digital connections.

1.4   An ISDN will contain intelligence for the purpose of providing service features, maintenance and network management functions. This intelligence may not be sufficient for some new services and may have to be supplemented by either additional intelligence within the network, or possibly compatible intelligence in the user terminals.

1.5   A layered protocol structure should be used for the specification of the access to an ISDN. Access from a user to ISDN resources may vary depending upon the service required and upon the status of implementation of national ISDNs.

1.6   It is recognized that ISDNs may be implemented in a variety of configurations according to specific national situations.

2   Evolution of ISDNs

2.1   ISDNs will be based on the concepts developed for telephone ISDNs and may evolve by progressively incorporating additional functions and network features including those of any other dedicated networks such as circuit switching and packet switching for data so as to provide for existing and new services.

2.2   The transition from an existing network to a comprehensive ISDN may require a period of time extending over one or more decades. During this period arrangements must be developed for the interworking of services on ISDNs and services on other networks (see Part I, Section 4 of the I-series).

2.3   In the evolution towards an ISDN, digital end-to-end connectivity will be obtained via plant and equipment used in existing networks, such as digital transmission, time-division multiplex switching and/or space-division multiplex switching. Existing relevant Recommendations for these constituent elements of an ISDN are contained in the appropriate series of Recommendations of CCITT and of CCIR.

2.4   In the early stages of the evolution of ISDNs, some interim user-network arrangements may need to be adopted in certain countries to facilitate early penetration of digital service capabilities.

> i)   Some of those interim arrangements are recommended by CCITT, such as hybrid access arrangements.
>
> ii) Other arrangements corresponding to national variants may comply partly or wholly with I-Series Recommendations. However, the intention is that they are not specifically included in the I-series.

2.5   An evolving ISDN may also include at later stages switched connections at bit rates higher and lower than 64 kbit/s.

nonvoice communications (digital data exchange). These services are to be provided in conformance with standards (CCITT Recommendations) that specify a small number of interfaces and data transmission facilities. The benefit of standards will be explored later in this chapter. For now, we simply state that without such a limitation, a global, interconnected ISDN is virtually impossible.

2. *Support for switched and nonswitched applications*. ISDN will support both circuit switching and packet switching. As we discussed in Part I, there is a place for both technologies. In addition, ISDN will support nonswitched services in the form of dedicated lines.

3. *Reliance on 64-kbps connections*. ISDN is intended to provide circuit-switched and packet-switched connections at 64 kbps. This is the fundamental building block of ISDN. This rate was chosen because, at the time, it was the standard rate for digitized voice, and hence was being introduced into the evolving IDNs. Although this data rate is useful, it is unfortunately restrictive to rely solely on it. Future developments in ISDN will permit greater flexibility.

4. *Intelligence in the network*. An ISDN is expected to be able to provide sophisticated services beyond the simple setup of a circuit-switched call. In addition, network management and maintenance capabilities need to be more sophisticated than in the past. All of this is to be achieved by the use of Signaling System Number 7 and by the use of intelligent switching nodes in the network.

5. *Layered protocol architecture*. The protocols being developed for user access to ISDN exhibit a layered architecture and can be mapped into the OSI model. This has a number of advantages:

- Standards already developed for OSI-related applications may be used on ISDN. An example is X.25 level 3 for access to packet-switching services in ISDN.
- New ISDN-related standards can be based on existing standards, reducing the cost of new implementations. An example is LAP-D, which is based on LAP-B.
- Standards can be developed and implemented independently for various layers and for various functions within a layer. This allows for the gradual implementation of ISDN services at a pace appropriate for a given provider or a given customer base.

6. *Variety of configurations*. More than one physical configuration is possible for implementing ISDN. This allows for differences in national policy (single-source versus competition), in the state of technology, and in the needs and existing equipment of the customer base.

Evolution of ISDN

As we discussed in Chapter 4, ISDN evolves from and with the integrated digital network (IDN). The evolution of the IDN has been driven by the need to provide economic voice communications. The resulting network, however, is also well suited to meet the growing variety of digital data service needs. Whereas the "I" in IDN refers to the integration of digital transmission and switching facilities, the "I" in ISDN refers to the integration of a variety of voice and data transmission services.

The second part of Box 5-1 gives the CCITT view of the way in which ISDN will evolve. Let us look at each of these points in turn.

1. *Evolution from telephone ISDNs*. The intent is that the ISDN evolve from the existing telephone networks.* Two conclusions can be drawn form this point. First, the IDN technology developed for and evolving within existing telephone networks forms the foundation for the services to be provided by ISDN. Second, although other facilities, such as third-party (not the telephone provider) packet-switched networks and satellite links, will play a role in ISDN, the telephone networks will have the dominant role. Although packet switching and satellite providers may be less than happy with this interpretation, the overwhelming prevalence of telephone networks dictates that these networks form the basis for ISDN.

---

* The term "telephone ISDNs" is used in the document. However, there is evidence from other earlier and contemporary CCITT documents (e,g, see Box 5-2) that this is an unfortunate misprint and that the intended term is "telephone IDNs."

2. *Transition of one or more decades.* The evolution to ISDN will be a slow process. This is true of any migration of a complex application or set of applications from one technical base to a newer one. The introduction of ISDN services will be done in the context of existing digital facilities and existing services. There will be a period of coexistence in which connections and perhaps protocol conversion will be needed between alternative facilities and/or services.

3. *Use of existing networks.* This point is simply an elaboration of point 2. For example, ISDN will provide a packet-switched service. For the time being, the interface to that service will be X.25. With the introduction of fast packet switching and more sophisticated virtual call control, there may need to be a new interface in the future.

4. *Interim user-network arrangements.* Primarily, the concern here is that the lack of digital subscriber loops might delay introduction of digital services, particularly in developing countries. With the use of modems and other equipment, existing analog facilities can support at least some ISDN services.

5. *Connections at other than 64 kbps.* The 64-kbps data rate was chosen as the basic channel for circuit switching. With improvements in voice digitizing technology, this rate is unnecessarily high. On the other hand, this rate is too low for many digital data applications. Thus, other data rates will be needed.

The details of the evolution of ISDN facilities and services will vary from one nation to another, and indeed from one provider to another in the same country. These points simply provide a general description, from CCITT's point of view, of the process.

The User Interface

Figure 5-1 is a conceptual view of the ISDN from a user or customer point of view. The user has access to the ISDN by means of a local interface to a digital "pipe" of a certain bit rate. Pipes of various sizes will be available to satisfy differing needs. For example, a residential customer may require only sufficient capacity to handle a telephone and a videotex terminal. An office will typically wish to connect to the ISDN via an on-premise digital PBX, and will require a much higher-capacity pipe.

That more than one size of pipe will be needed is emphasized in Figure 5-2, taken from Recommendation I.410. At the low end of demand would be a single terminal (e.g., a residential telephone) or multiple terminals in some sort of multi-drop arrangement (e.g., a residential telephone, personal computer, and alarm system). Offices are more likely to contain a network of devices attached to a LAN or PBX, with an attachment from that network acting as a gateway to the ISDN.

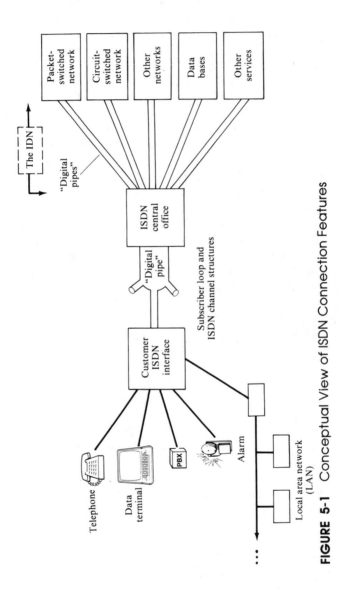

FIGURE 5-1 Conceptual View of ISDN Connection Features

162

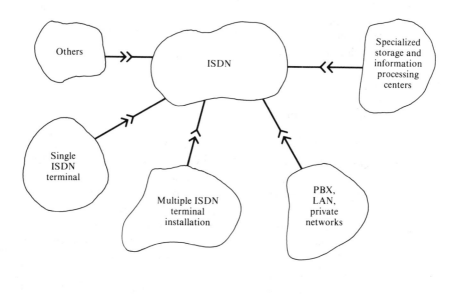

———<←——— ISDN user-network interface

FIGURE 5-2   ISDN User-Network Interface Examples

At any given point in time, the pipe to the user's premises has a fixed capacity, but the traffic on the pipe may be a variable mix up to the capacity limit. Thus a user may access circuit-switched and packet-switched services, as well as other services, in a dynamic mix of signal types and bit rates. The ISDN will require rather complex control signals to instruct it how to sort out the time-multiplexed data and provide the required services. These control signals will also be multiplexed onto the same digital pipe.

An important aspect of the interface is that the user may, at any time, employ less than the maximum capacity of the pipe, and will be charged according to the capacity used rather than "connect time." This characteristic significantly diminishes the value of current user design efforts that are geared to optimize circuit utilization by use of concentrators, multiplexers, packet switches, and other line sharing arrangements.

Objectives

Activities currently under way are leading to the development of a worldwide ISDN. This effort involves national governments, data processing and communication companies, standards organizations, and others. Certain common objectives are, by and large, shared by this disparate group. We list here key objectives.

- Standardization
- Transparency
- Separation of competitive functions
- Leased and switched services
- Cost-related tariffs
- Smooth migration
- Multiplexed support

Standardization is essential to the success of ISDN. Standards will provide for universal access to the network. ISDN-standard equipment can be moved from one location to another, indeed from one country to another, and be plugged into the network. The cost of such equipment will be minimized because of the competition among many vendors to provide the same type of functionality. In addition, the use of a layered protocol architecture and standardized interfaces allows users to select equipment from multiple suppliers and allows changes to be made to a configuration in a gradual, piece-by-piece fashion.

It is also important that the digital transmission service have the property of **transparency;** that is, the service is independent of, and does not affect, the content of the user data to be transmitted. This permits users to develop applications and protocols with the confidence that they will not be affected by the underlying ISDN. Once a circuit or virtual circuit is set up, the user should be able to send information without the provider being aware of the type of information being carried. In addition, user-provided encryption techniques can be employed to provide security of user information.

The ISDN must be defined in a way that does not preclude the **separation of competitive functions** from the basic digital transmission services. It must be possible to separate out functions that could be provided competitively as opposed to those that are fundamentally part of the ISDN. In many countries, a single, government-owned entity will provide all services. Some countries desire (in the case of the United States, require) that certain enhanced services be offered competitively (e.g., videotex, electronic mail). These alternative views are depicted in Figures 5-3 and 5-4 [RUTK82]. Competition promotes innovation and the ability to respond to and satisfy a wide range of user requirements.

The ISDN should provide both **leased and switched services.** This will give the user the greatest range of options in configuring network services, and allow the user to optimize on the basis of cost and performance.

The price for ISDN service should be related to cost, and independent of the type of data being carried. Such a **cost-related tariff** will assure that one type of service is not in the position of subsidizing others. Price distinctions should be related to the cost of providing specific performance and functional characteristics of a service. In this way, distortions are avoided and providers can be driven by customer need rather than some artificial tariff structure.

Because of the large installed base of telecommunications equipment in the networks, and because of customer equipment with interfaces designed for those

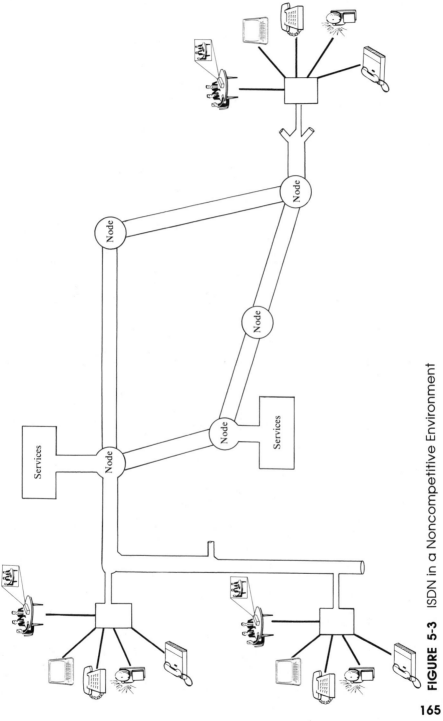

FIGURE 5-3 ISDN in a Noncompetitive Environment

165

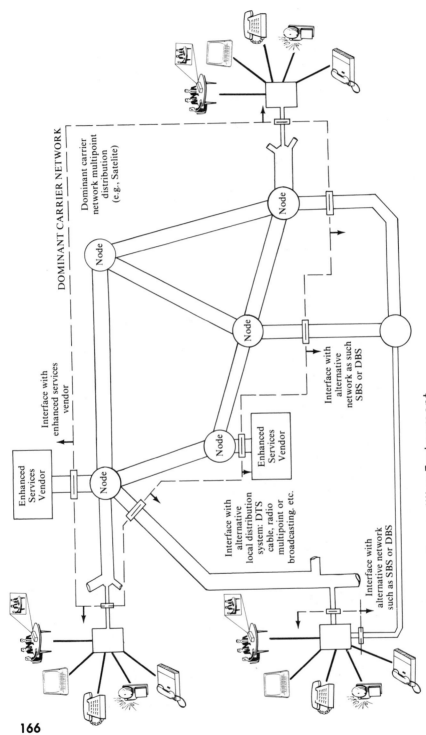

FIGURE 5-4 ISDN in a Competitive Environment

166

networks, the conversion to ISDN will be gradual. Thus, for an extended period of time, the evolving ISDN must coexist with existing equipment and services. To provide for a **smooth migration** to ISDN, ISDN interfaces should evolve from existing interfaces, and interworking arrangements must be designed. Specific capabilities that will be needed include adapter equipment that allow pre-ISDN terminal equipment to interface to ISDN, internetwork protocols that allow data to be routed through a mixed ISDN/non-ISDN network complex, and protocol converters to allow interoperation of ISDN services and similar non-ISDN services.

In addition to providing low-capacity support to individual users, **multiplexed support** must be provided to accommodate user-owned PBX and local area network (LAN) equipment.

There are, of course, other objectives that could be named. Those listed above are certainly among the most important and widely accepted, and help to define the character of the ISDN.

Benefits

The principal benefits of ISDN to the **customer** can be expressed in terms of cost savings and flexibility. The integration of voice and a variety of data on a single transport system means that the user does not have to buy multiple services to meet multiple needs. The efficiencies and economies of scale of an integrated network allow these services to be offered at lower cost than if they were provided separately. Further, the user needs to bear the expense of just a single access line to these multiple services. The requirements of various users can differ greatly in a number of ways: for example, in information volume, traffic pattern, response time, and interface types. The ISDN will allow the user to tailor the service purchased to actual needs to a degree not possible at present. In addition, customers enjoy the advantages of competition among equipment vendors. These advantages include product diversity, low price, and wide availability of services. Interface standards permit selection of terminal equipment and transport and other services from a range of competitors without changes in equipment or use of special adapters. Finally, because the offerings to the customer are based on the ISDN recommendations, which of necessity are slow to change, the risk of obsolescence is reduced.

Network providers, on a larger scale but in a similar way, profit from the advantages of competition, including the areas of digital switches and digital transmission equipment. Also, standards support universality and a larger potential market for services. Interface standards permit flexibility in selection of suppliers, consistent control signaling procedures, and technical innovation and evolution within the network without customer involvement.

Manufacturers can focus research and development on technical applications and be assured that a broad potential demand exists. In particular, the cost of developing VLSI implementations is justified by the potential market. Specialized niches in the market create opportunities for competitive, smaller manufacturers. Significant economies of scale can be realized by manufacturers of all sizes. Interface standards assure that the manufacturer's equipment will be compatible with the equipment across the interface.

Finally, **enhanced service providers,** of, for instance, information retrieval or transaction-based services, will benefit from simplified user access. End users will not be required to buy special arrangements or terminal devices in order to gain access to particular services.

Of course, any technical innovation comes with penalties as well as benefits. The main penalty here is the cost of migration. This cost, however, must be seen in the context of evolving customer needs. There will be changes in the telecommunications offerings available to customers, with or without ISDN. It is hoped that the ISDN framework will at least control the cost and reduce the confusion of migration. Another potential penalty of ISDN is that it will retard technical innovation. The process of adopting a standard is a long and complex one. The result is that by the time a standard is adopted and products are available, more advanced technical solutions have appeared. This is always a problem with standards. By and large, the benefits of standards outweigh the fact that they are always at least a little way behind the state of the art.

Services

The ISDN will provide a variety of services, supporting existing voice and data applications as well as providing for applications now being developed. Some of the most important applications are:

- *Facsimile:* service for the transmission and reproduction of graphics, handwritten and printed material. This type of service has been available for many years, but has suffered from a lack of standardization and the limitations of the analog telephone network. Digital facsimile standards are now available and can be used to transmit a page of data at 64 kbps in 5 seconds.
- *Teletex:* service that enables subscriber terminals to exchange correspondence. Communicating terminals are used to prepare, edit, transmit, and print messages. Transmission is at a rate of one page in 2 seconds at 9.6 kbps.
- *Videotex:* An interactive information retrieval service. A page of data can be transmitted in one second at 9.6 kbps.

Table 5-1 shows the types of services that could be supported by ISDN. These services fall into the broad categories of voice, digital data, text, and image. Most of these services can be provided with a transmission capacity of 64 kbps or less. This rate, as we have mentioned, is the standard rate offered to the user. Some services require considerably higher data rates and may be provided by high-speed facilities outside the ISDN (e.g., cable TV distribution plants) or in future enhancements to ISDN (see Chapter 9 on broadband ISDN).

TABLE 5-1 CANDIDATE SERVICES FOR INTEGRATION

Bandwidth	Service			
	Telephony	*Data*	*Text*	*Image*
Digital voice (64 kbps)	Telephone	Packet-switched data	Telex	
		Circuit-switched data	Teletex	
	Leased circuits	Leased circuits	Leased circuits	
	Information retrieval (by voice analysis and synthesis)	Telemetry	Videotex	
		Funds transfer		Facsimile
		Information retrieval	Information retrieval	Information retrieval
		Mailbox	Mailbox	Surveillance
		Electronic mail	Electronic mail	
		Alarms		
Wide band (>64 kbps)	Music	High-speed computer communication		TV conferencing
				Teletext
				Videophone
				Cable TV distribution

169

TABLE 5-2 BASIC AND ADDITIONAL FACILITIES FOR ISDN SERVICES

Telephony	Data	Teletex	Videotex	Facsimile
		Basic		
National toll access	Automatic dialed call	Incoming call not disturbing local mode	Information retrieval by dialog with a data base	Automatic dialed call
International toll access	Manual dialed call	Message printed on operator demand		Manual dialed call
Malicious call blocking	Automatic answer	Message presentation as in the original		Automatic answer
		Day and hour automatic indication		
		Additional		
Transfer call	Direct call	Delayed messages	Transactions (e.g. reservation, shopping)	Delayed delivery
	Closed user group	Abbreviated address		Multiple destination
Abbreviated dialing	Closed user group with outgoing access	Multiple address		
Rerouting to verbal announcements				
Intermediate call	Calling line identification	Charging indication	Message box service between users	Code, speed, and format conversion for different terminals
Conference call	Called line identification	Telex access	Loading of software from a data base to a terminal	
Camp-on busy	Abbreviated address calling	Graphic mode		
Barring outgoing toll traffic	Barred incoming call		Loading of special character set	
	Multiaddress calling			
Hot line	Detailed billing			
Detailed billing	Transfer call			
Automatic wake-up	Call charging indication			

One of the key aspects of the ISDN will be that it is an "intelligent network." By use of a flexible signaling protocol, the ISDN will provide a variety of network facilities for each service. Table 5-2 gives some examples of planned facilities.

Architecture

Figure 5-5, based on a figure in CCITT Recommendation I.310, is an architectural depiction of ISDN. The ISDN will support a completely new physical connecter for users, a digital subscriber loop, and a variety of transmission services.

The common physical interface provides a standardized means of attaching to the network. The same interface should be usable for telephone, computer terminal, and videotex terminal. Protocols are required to define the exchange of control information between user device and the network. Provision must be made for high-speed interfaces to, for example, a digital PBX or a LAN. The interface supports a *basic* service consisting of three time-multiplexed channels, two at 64 kbps and one at 16 kbps. In addition, there is a *primary* service that provides multiple 64-kbps channels.

The subscriber loop provides the physical signal path from subscriber to ISDN central office. This loop must support full-duplex digital transmission for both basic and primary data rates. Initially, much of the subscriber loop plant will be twisted pair. As the network evolves and grows, optical fiber will be increasingly used.

The ISDN central office connects the numerous subscriber loops to the digital network. This provides access to a variety of lower-layer (OSI layers 1 – 3) transmis-

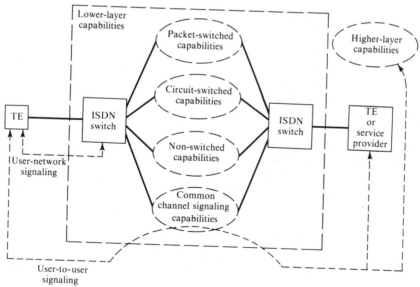

FIGURE 5-5   ISDN Architecture

sion functions, including circuit-switched, packet-switched, and dedicated facilities. In addition, common channel signaling, used to control the network and provide call management, will be accessible to the user. This signaling will allow user-network control dialogue. The use of these control signaling protocols for user-to-user dialogue is a subject for further study within CCITT. By and large, these lower layer functions will be implemented within the ISDN. In some countries with a competitive climate, some of these lower layer functions (e.g., packet switching) may be provided by separate networks that may be reached by a subscriber through ISDN.

There will also be higher-layer (OSI layers 4–7) functions, to support applications such as teletex, facsimile, and transaction processing. These functions may be implemented within ISDN or provided by separate networks, or a mixture of the two.

5-2 ISDN STANDARDS

Although a number of standards organizations are involved in various aspects of ISDN, the controlling body is the International Telegraph and Telephone Consultative Committee (CCITT). In this section, we first look at the rationale for standards, and then examine the ISDN-related standards from CCITT. An appendix to this chapter looks at CCITT itself.

The Importance of Standards

It has long been accepted in the telecommunications industry that standards are required to govern the physical, electrical, and procedural characteristics of communication equipment. With the increasingly digital character of telecommunication networks, and with the increasing prevalence of digital transmission and processing services, the scope of what should be standardized has broadened. As we shall see, the functions, interfaces, and services embodied in ISDN that are subject to standardization cover an extremely broad range.

Although there is no widely accepted and quoted definition of the term standard, the following definition from the 1979 National Policy on Standards for the United States encompasses the essential concept [NSPA79]:

> A prescribed set of rules, conditions, or requirements concerning definition of terms; classification of components; specification of materials, performance, or operation; delineation of procedures; or measurement of quantity and quality in describing materials, product, systems, services, or practices.

[CERN84] lists the following advantages of standards:

- increased productivity and efficiency in industry because of larger scale, low-cost production

- increased competition by allowing smaller firms to market products, readily acceptable by the consumer, without the need for a massive advertising budget
- dissemination of information and the transfer of technology
- expansion of international trade because of the feasibility of exchange of products among countries
- conservation of resources
- increased opportunity for worldwide exchange of information, both voice and data

In the case of ISDN, because of the complexity of ISDN, and because its success depends on the capability of providing true interconnectivity and interoperability, standards are not only advantageous but essential in the introduction of such a network.

The I-Series Recommendations

The development of ISDN is governed by a set of recommendations issued by ISDN, called the I-series of recommendations. These recommendations, or standards, were first issued in 1984. A more complete set was issued in 1988.

It is enlightening to look at the history of CCITT's interest in ISDN. In 1968, CCITT established Special Study Group D (forerunner of today's Study Group XVIII, which has ISDN responsibility within CCITT) to look at a variety of issues related to the use of digital technology in the telephone network. At each Plenary Assembly, the study group was given assignments for the next four-year study period. The first and principal question assigned over this period is shown in Table 5-3. The titles of the first question reflect the evolution of CCITT interest. The focus shifts from digital technology, to integrated digital networks (IDN), to ISDN.

In 1968, Study Group D was set up to study all questions related to the standardization of transmission of pulse-code-modulated (PCM) voice and to coordinate work going on in other groups relating to digital networking. Even at this early stage, there was a vision of an ISDN. Recommendation G.702, issued in 1972, contained the following definition of an integrated services digital network:

TABLE 5-3 QUESTION 1 AS ASSIGNED TO SPECIAL STUDY GROUP D (1968–1976) AND TO STUDY GROUP XVIII (1976–1988)

Study Period	Title of Question 1
1968–1972	Planning of digital systems
1972–1976	Planning of digital systems and integration of services
1976–1980	Overall aspects of integrated digital networks and integration of services
1980–1984	General network aspects of an integrated services digital network (ISDN)
1984–1988	General question on ISDN

An integrated digital network in which the same digital switches and digital paths are used to establish connections for different services, for example, telephony, data.

At this point, there was no information on the type of network that could integrate digital switches and paths, nor how the network could integrate various services. Nevertheless, it was a recognition of the path that could be followed with digital technology

During the next study period (1972 – 1976), there were continuing advances in digital transmission technology. In addition, digital switching equipment began to emerge from the laboratory. Thus the construction of integrated digital networks became a real possibility. Accordingly, the 1976 set of recommendations included specifications dealing with digital switching as well as the specification of a new signaling system (Number 7) designed for use in the forthcoming digital networks. The first question for this period also specifically deals with the integration of services.

In planning for the 1976 – 1980 study period, CCITT recognized that the evolution toward a digital network was underway and was more important than the standardization of individual digital systems and equipment. Thus the focus was on the integration aspects of the digital network and on the integration of services on an IDN. Two key developments that emerged during this study period were:

- The integration of services is based on providing a standardized user-network interface that allows the user to request various services through a uniform set of protocols.
- ISDN will evolve from the digital telephone network.

At the end of this period, the first ISDN standard emerged, entitled Integrated Services Digital Network (ISDN), G.705 (Box 5-2). No other standards on ISDN were issued in 1980; at this point, only the general concept of an ISDN had been developed.

As the next period began (1980 – 1984) ISDN was declared the major concern of CCITT for the upcoming study period. Table 5-4 indicates the set of recommendations that were completed and published in 1984. This initial set of specifications was incomplete and, in some cases, internally inconsistent. Nevertheless, the specification of ISDN by 1984 was sufficient for manufacturers and service providers to begin to develop ISDN-related equipment and to demonstrate ISDN-related services and networking configurations. The 1984 series included this definition of ISDN, retained in the 1988 documents:

An ISDN is a network, in general evolving from a telephony IDN, that provides end-to-end digital connectivity to support a wide range of services, including voice and non-voice services, to which users have access by a limited set of standard multi-purpose user-network interfaces.

Work on the I-series and related recommendations continued in the 1985 – 1988 period. At the beginning of this period, CCITT was significantly restructured

---

BOX 5-2

CCITT RECOMMENDATION G.705 (1980)

INTEGRATED SERVICES DIGITAL NETWORK (ISDN)

The CCITT,

considering

(a)   the measure of agreement that has so far been reached in the studies of Integrated Digital Networks (IDNs) dedicated to specific services such as telephony, data and also of an Integrated Services Digital Network (ISDN),

(b)   the need for a common basis for the future studies necessary for the evolution towards an ISDN,

recommends

that the ISDN should be based on the following conceptual principles:

(1)   The ISDN will be based on and evolve from the telephony IDN by progressively incorporating additional functions and network features including those of any other dedicated networks so as to provide for existing and new services.

(2)   New services introduced into the ISDN should be arranged to be compatible with 64-kbit/s switched digital connections.

(3)   The transition from the existing networks to a comprehensive ISDN may require a period of time extending over one or two decades.

(4)   During the transition period arrangements must be developed for the interworking of services on ISDNs and services on other networks.

(5)   The ISDN will contain intelligence for the purposes of providing service features, maintenance and network management functions. This intelligence may not be sufficient for some new services and may have to be supplemented by either additional intelligence within the network, or possibly compatible intelligence in the customer terminals.

(6)   A layered functional set of protocols appear desirable for the various access arrangements to the ISDN. Access from the customer to ISDN resources may vary depending upon the service required and on the status of evolution of national ISDNs.

Note — Existing relevant Recommendations for some of the constituent elements of the ISDN are contained in Series G, O, Q, and X Recommendations and also in relevant volumes of the CCIR.

TABLE 5-4   THE 1988 CCITT ISDN RECOMMENDATIONS

Recommendation	New/Revision
I.110 General Structure of the I-Series Recommendations	R
I.111 Relationship with Other Recommendations Relevant to ISDNs	R
I.112 Vocabulary of Terms for ISDNs	R
I.113 Vocabulary of Terms for Broadband Aspects of ISDN	N
I.120 Integrated Services Digital Networks	R
I.121 Broadband Aspects of ISDN	N
I.122 Framework for Providing Additional Packet Mode Services	N
I.130 The Method for the Characterization of Telecommunication Services Supported by an ISDN and Network Capabilities of an ISDN	R
I.140 Attributes for the Characterization of Telecommunication Services Supported by an ISDN and Network Capabilities of an ISDN	N
I.141 ISDN Charging Capability Attributes	N

Part II — Service Capabilities

I.200 Guidance to the I.200 Series	N
I.210 Principles of Telecommunication Services Supported by an ISDN and Network Capabilities of an ISDN	R
I.211 Bearer Services Supported by an ISDN	R
I.212 Teleservices Supported by an ISDN	R
I.220 Common Dynamic Description of Basic Telecommunication Services	N
I.221 Common Specific Characteristics of Services	N
I.230 Definition of Bearer Services	N
I.231 Circuit Mode Bearer Services Categories	N
I.232 Packet Mode Bearer Services Categories	N
I.240 Definition of Teleservices	N
I.241 Teleservices Supported by an ISDN	N
I.250 Definition of Supplementary Services	N
I.251 Number Identification Services	N
I.252 Call Offering Services	N
I.253 Call Completion Services	N
I.254 Multiparty Services	N
I.255 Community of Interest Services	N
I.256 Charging Services	N
I.257 Additional Information Transfer Services	N

Part III — Overall Network Aspects and Functions

I.310 ISDN-Network Functional Principles	R
I.320 ISDN Protocol Reference Model	R
I.324 ISDN Network Architecture	N
I.325 Reference Configurations for ISDN Connection Types	N
I.326 Reference Configurations for Relative Network Resource Requirements	N
I.330 ISDN Numbering and Addressing Principles	R
I.331 Numbering Plan for the ISDN Era	R
I.332 Numbering Principles for Interwork Between ISDNs and Dedicated Networks with Different Numbering Plans	N

TABLE 5-4   THE 1988 CCITT ISDN RECOMMENDATIONS (continued)

Recommendation		New/Revision
I.333	Terminal Selection in ISDN	N
I.334	Principles Relating ISDN Numbers/Subaddress to the OSI Reference Model Network Layer Addresses	N
I.335	ISDN Routing Principles	N
I.340	ISDN Connection Types	R
I.350	General Aspects of Quality of Service and Network Performance in Digital Networks, Including ISDN	N
I.351	Recommendations in Other Series, Including Network Performance Objectives that Apply at T Reference Points of an ISDN	N
I.352	Network Performance Objectives for Call Processing Delays	N
Part IV — User-Network Interfaces		
I.410	General Aspects and Principles Relating to Recommendations on ISDN User-Network Interfaces	R
I.411	ISDN User-Network Interfaces — Reference Configurations	R
I.412	ISDN User-Network Interfaces — Interface Structures and Access Capabilities	R
I.420	Basic User-Network Interface	R
I.421	Primary Rate User-Network Interface	R
I.430	Basic User-Network Interface — Layer 1 Specification	R
I.431	Primary Rate User-Network Interface — Layer 1 Specification	R
I.440	ISDN User-Network Interface Data Link Layer — General Aspects	R
I.441	ISDN User-Network Interface Data Link Layer Specification	R
I.450	ISDN User-Network Interface Layer 3 — General Aspects	R
I.451	ISDN User-Network Interface Layer 3 Specification for Basic Call	R
I.452	ISDN User-Network Interface Layer 3 Specification — Generic Procedures for the Control of ISDN Supplementary Services	N
I.460	Multiplexing, Rate Adaptation, and Support of Existing Interfaces	R
I.461	Support of X.21 and X.21 bis and X.20 bis Based DTEs by an ISDN	R
I.462	Support of Packet Mode Terminal Equipment by an ISDN	R
I.463	Support of DTEs with V-Series Type Interfaces by an ISDN	R
I.464	Multiplexing, Rate Adaptation, and Support of Existing Interfaces for Restricted 64 kbit/s Transfer Capability	R
I.465	Support by an ISDN of data terminal equipment with V-Series Type Interfaces with Provision for Statistical Multiplexing	N
I.470	Relationship of Terminal Functions to ISDN	N
Part V — Internetwork Interfaces		
I.500	General Structure of ISDN Interworking Recommendations	N
I.510	Definition and General Principles of ISDN Interworking	N
I.511	ISDN-to-ISDN Layer 1 Internetwork Interface	N
I.515	Parameter Exchange for ISDN Interworking	N
I.520	General Arrangements for Network Interworking between ISDNs	N
I.530	Network Interworking between an ISDN and a Public Switched Telephone Network (PSTN)	N
I.540	General Arrangements for Interworking between Circuit-Switched Public Data Networks (CSPDNs) and ISDNs for the Provision of Data	N

TABLE 5-4 THE 1988 CCITT ISDN RECOMMENDATIONS *(continued)*

Transmission Services

I.550	General Arrangements for Interworking between Packet Switched Public Data Networks (PSPDNs) and ISDNs for the Provision of Data Services	N
I.560	Requirements to be Met in Providing the Telex Service within an ISDN	N

Part VI — Maintenance Principles

I.601	General Maintenance Principles of ISDN Subscriber Access and Subscriber Installation	N
I.602	Application of Maintenance Principles to ISDN Subscriber Installation	N
I.603	Application of Maintenance Principles to ISDN Basic Accesses	N
I.604	Application of Maintenance Principles to ISDN Primary Rate Accesses	N
I.605	Application of Maintenance Principles to Static Multiplexed ISDN Basic Accesses	N

to give a number of its study groups a part of future ISDN work. The dominant function of CCITT became the study of ISDN matters. This is reflected in Table 5-5, which lists ISDN-related questions for the 1985 – 1988 period. Study Group XVIII continues to hold the lead role. The 1988 version of the I-series recommendations are sufficiently detailed to make preliminary ISDN implementations possible in the early 1990s.

TABLE 5-5 QUESTIONS RELATING TO ISDN IN THE 1985 – 1988 ACTIVITY PERIOD

Study Group COM I (Definition, operation and quality of service aspects of telegraph, data transmission and telematic services)

15/1	Definition and operational aspects of ISDN

Study Group COM II (Operation of telephone network and ISDN)

11/II	Human factors issues related to the Integrated Services Digital Network (ISDN)
17/II	Development of the World Numbering Plan for telephone and ISDN application
19/II	Evolution of the telephone routing plan in the ISDN era
31/II	Reference models for ISDN traffic engineering
40/II	Dependability of telecommunication networks

Study Group COM III (General tariff principles including accounting)

22/III	Tariff and accounting principles for the ISDN

Study Group COM IV (Transmission maintenance of international lines, circuits and chains of circuits; maintenance of automatic and semi-automatic networks)

11/IV	Transmission measuring equipment and associated maintenance test access lines
J/IV	Maintenance of digital links and maintenance of ISDNs

TABLE 5-5   QUESTIONS RELATING TO ISDN IN THE 1985-1988 ACTIVITY PERIOD *(continued)*

Study Group COM V (Protection against dangers and disturbances of electromagnetic origin)
(None)

Study Group COM VI (Outside plant)
(None)

Study Group COM VII (Data communication networks)

9/VII	Support of X-series interface DTEs in an ISDN and new interface aspects for data services in ISDNs
10/VII	General principles of interworking
13/VII	Interworking between circuit-switching public data network (CSPDN) and Integrated Services Digital Network (ISDN)
14/VII	Interworking between packet-switched public data network (PSPDN) and Integrated Services Digital Network (ISDN)
25/VII	Principles of maintenance testing in public data networks
26/VII	Maintenance and operation of international links between two public data networks
28/VII	Integration of satellite systems in data communication networks
29/VII	Quality of service in public data networks
31/VII	Numbering plan for public data networks
43/VII	Layers (1-4 of the Reference Model of Open Systems Inter-Connection for CCITT applications
46/VII	Requirements and arrangements for the provision of data services in ISDN

Study Group COM VIII (Terminal equipment for telematic services)

20/VIII	Terminal characteristics and protocols for Telematic services on ISDN
26/VIII	Teleconferencing protocols

Study Group COM IX (Telegraph networks and terminal equipment)
(None)

Study Group COM X (Languages and methods for telecommunications applications)
(None)

Study Group COM XI (ISDN and telephone network switching and signalling)

7/XI	Layer 3 of the digital access signaling system
8/XI	Data link layer of the digital access signaling system
9/XI	Switching functions and signaling information flows for implementation of basic and supplementary services
14/XI	Interworking with land, maritime and aeronautical mobile communications systems
16/XI	Signaling requirements for new transmission equipments
18/XI	Definitions for switching and signaling

Study Group COM XII (Transmission performance of telephone networks and terminals)

5/XII	Speech synthesis/recognition systems
18/XII	Transmission performance of digital systems

Cont.

TABLE 5-5   QUESTIONS RELATING TO ISDN IN THE 1985–1988 ACTIVITY PERIOD *(continued)*

Study Group COM XV (Transmission systems)

3/XV	Equipment for digital transmission of television signals
11/XV	Acoustic echo control
14/XV	Equipment used in the transition period from the analog to the digital networks
24/XV	Characteristics of digital line systems for use in local network
25/XV	Digital equipments for local broadband networks
27/XV	Characteristics of PCM multiplex, ADPCM multiplex and other terminal transmission equipments for voice frequencies
28/XV	Characteristics of digital multiplex equipment and multiplexing arrangements for telephony and other signals
29/XV	Characteristics of 32 kbit/s ADPCM/PCM transcoding equipment
30/XV	Performance characteristics of PCM and ADPCM channels at voice frequencies
31/XV	Digital circuit multiplication equipment

Study Group COM XVII (Data transmission over the telephone network)

1/XVII	Supplement to the vocabulary for data transmission
11/XVII	Support of DTEs with V-series type interfaces on an ISDN
13/XVII	Interchange circuits
yy/XVII	Interconnection of ISDNs and/or PDNs with modern equipped terminals on the PSTN

Study Group COM XVIII (Digital networks including ISDN)

1/XVIII	General question on ISDN
2/XVIII	Definition of service principles
3/XVIII	ISDN architecture functional model
4/XVIII	ISDN protocol reference model
5/XVIII	ISDN connection types
6/XVIII	ISDN-ISDN internetwork interfaces
7/XVIII	Internetworking of ISDNs and other networks
8/XVIII	Numbering and addressing principles
9/XVIII	Charging capabilities in an ISDN
10/XVIII	ISDN routing principles
11/XVIII	General aspects of user-network interfaces
12/XVIII	Layer 1 characteristics of ISDN user-network interfaces
13/XVIII	General aspects of quality of service and network performance in digital networks including ISDN
14/XVIII	Performance objectives for errors and short interruptions
15/XVIII	Performance objectives for timing and controlled slips (synchronization), jitter and wander and propagation delay
16/XVIII	Call and packet processing performance
17/XVIII	Availability performance of digital networks including ISDNs
18/XVIII	Maintenance of digital networks including ISDNs and ISDN digital subscriber lines and subscriber equipments
19/XVIII	Vocabulary for ISDN and general digital network aspects

20/XVIII	Definition of parameters at the network side of NT equipment
21/XVIII	Characteristics of digital sections
22/XVIII	Interworking between different systems based on different standards
23/XVIII	General aspects of interfaces in digital networks
24/XVIII	Network aspects of existing and new levels in the digital hierarchy
25/XVIII	32 kbit/s speech coding
26/XVIII	Wideband speech coding for 64 kbit/s digital paths
27/XVIII	16 kbit/s speech coding
28/XVIII	PCM coding laws according to Recommendation G.711
29/XVIII	Encoding for stored digitized voice
29/XVIII	Network considerations of PCM/ADPCM transcoding equipment
30/XVIII	Digital circuit multiplication (DCM)
31/XVIII	Speech analysis/synthesis techniques
32/XVIII	Speech packetization

Figure 5-6 shows the relationship of the various I-series standards to each other. The 1984 standards contained recommendations in series I.100 through I.400. Some updates and expansions occurred in this series in the 1984–1988 period. The I.500 and I.600 series were left for further study in 1984, and some preliminary work was ready for 1988. In the remainder of this book, we focus on the I.100 through I.400 series; the discussion reflects the 1988 versions of these recommendations.

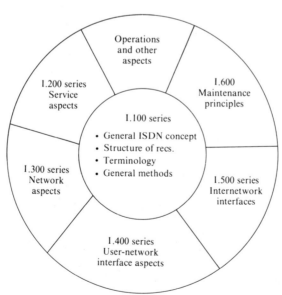

FIGURE 5-6 Structure of I-Series Recommendations

I.100 Series—General Concepts. The I.100 series serves as a general introduction to ISDN. The general structure of the ISDN recommendations is presented as well as a glossary of terms. I.120, reproduced as Box 5-1, provides an overall description of ISDN and the expected evolution of ISDNs. I.130 introduces terminology and concepts that are used in the I.200 series to specify services.

This chapter has covered much of what is in the I.100 series.

I.200 Series—Service Capabilities. The I.200 series is in a sense the most important part of the CCITT ISDN recommendations. Here, the services to be provided to users are specified. We may look on this as a set of requirements that the ISDN must satisfy. In the ISDN glossary (I.112), the term *service* is defined as:

> That which is offered by an Administration or RPOA to its customers in order to satisfy a specific telecommunication requirement.

Although this is a very general definition, the term service has come to have a very specific meaning in CCITT, a meaning that is somewhat different from the use of that term in an OSI context. For CCITT, a standardized service is characterized by [CERN84]:

- complete, guaranteed end-to-end compatibility
- CCITT-standardized terminals, including procedures
- listing of the service subscribers in an international directory
- CCITT-standardized testing and maintenance procedures
- charging and accounting rules

There are three fully standardized CCITT services: telegraphy, telephony, and data. There are four newer CCITT *telematic services* in process of standardization: teletex, facsimile, videotex, and message handling. The goal with all of these services is to ensure high-quality international telecommunications for the end user, regardless of the make of the terminal equipment and the type of network used nationally to support the service.

The I.200 series classifies services into lower-level bearer services and higher-level teleservices. For each service, various attributes are defined, constituting a "laundry list" that is configured by agreement between the subscriber and the provider. Chapter 6 is devoted to the topic of ISDN services.

I.300 Series—Network Aspects. Whereas the I.200 series focuses on the user, in terms of the services provided to the user, the I.300 series focuses on the network, in terms of how the network goes about providing those services. A protocol reference model is presented that, while based on the 7-layer OSI model, attempts to account for the complexity of a connection that may involve two or more users (e.g., a conference call) plus a related common-channel signaling dialogue. Issues such as numbering and addressing are addressed. There is also a discussion of ISDN connection types.

Chapter 7 includes a discussion of ISDN network aspects.

I.400 Series—User-Network Interfaces. The I.400 series deals with the interface between the user and the network. Three major topics are addressed:

- Physical configurations: the issue of how ISDN functions are configured into equipment. The standards specify functional groupings and define reference points between those groupings.
- Transmission rates: the data rates and combinations of data rates to be offered to the user.
- Protocol specifications: the protocols at OSI layers 1 through 3 that specify the user-network interaction.

The first two of these topics are covered in Chapter 7. Chapter 8 deals with ISDN protocols.

5-3 RECOMMENDED READING

The literature of ISDN is growing as rapidly as the field itself. [STAL88b] contains reprints of a number of the key papers. [SCAC86] is an excellent overview. [PAND87] is a good survey article. [RONA87] examines some of the technical, management, and economic issues related to ISDN. [DECI86a and b] contain a number of papers related to ISDN standards and implementation. [ATT87] is an interesting overview from the point of view of one of the major players.

[RUTK85] provides a good summary of the 1984 Recommendations, and addresses the regulatory issues within the United States. Other treatments of the regulatory issues are [HARI86], [FRAN84], and [RUTK82].

5-4 PROBLEMS

5-1 Is an IDN necessary for an ISDN? Sufficient? Explain.

5-2 Elaborate on the statement in Section 5-1 that ISDN is virtually impossible without a limitation on the number of different user-ISDN interfaces and data transmission facilities.

5-3 In Chapter 4, we discussed the concept of a software-defined network and pointed out some of its advantages compared to the traditional private network built on dedicated (leased) lines. With ISDN, the network will have a high degree of intelligence, will be controlled internally with common channel signaling, and may be controlled externally with a common channel signaling interface. Why, then, as stated in Principle 2 (Box 5-1) is there a need for non-switched support?

5-4 It was mentioned in Section 5-1 that user-implemented multidrop lines and multiplexers may disappear. Explain why.

5-5 Compare Recommendation G.705 (Box 5-2) of 1980 with I.120 (Box 5-1) of 1984. What do the differences reveal about the evolution of CCITT thinking with respect to ISDN?

APPENDIX 5A: CCITT

The International Telegraph and Telephone Consultative Committee (CCITT) is a committee of the International Telecommunications Union (ITU), which is itself a United Nations specialized agency [HUMM85]. Hence the members of CCITT are governments. The U.S. representation is housed in the Department of State. The charter of CCITT is "to study and issue recommendations on technical, operating, and tariff questions relating to telegraphy and telephony." Its primary objective is to standardize, to the extent necessary, techniques and operations in telecommunications to achieve end-to-end compatibility of international telecommunication connections, regardless of the countries of origin and destination.

CCITT is organized into 15 study groups that prepare standards, called Recommendations by CCITT. There are three areas of activity concerned with ISDN matters: data communications, telematic services, and integrated services digital networks (ISDN). Telematic services are user-oriented services that involve information transfer, query, and update.

Work within CCITT is conducted in four-year cycles [BELL84]. Every four years, a Plenary Assembly is held. The work program for the next four years is established at the assembly in the form of Questions submitted by the various study groups, based on requests made to the study groups by their members. The assembly assesses the questions, reviews the scope of the study groups, creates new or abolishes existing study groups, and allocates questions to them.

Based on these questions, each study group prepares draft recommendations to be submitted to the next assembly, four years hence. After approval by the assembly, these are published as CCITT Recommendations. If a certain draft recommendation is very urgent, a study group may employ a balloting procedure to gain approval before the end of the four years. In general, however, the process of standardization within CCITT is a slow one.

CHAPTER 6
ISDN
SERVICES

The ISDN will provide a variety of services, supporting existing voice and data applications as well as providing for applications now being developed. In this chapter, we begin by looking at the service capabilities defined in the CCITT ISDN recommendations. We will find that these are somewhat general in nature, and focus on network capabilities needed to support anticipated user requirements. The remainder of the chapter is devoted to a look at three of the most important telecommunications services that ISDN will need to support: digital facsimile, teletex, and electronic mail. We will also examine some of the protocol implications of these services.

6-1   SERVICE CAPABILITIES

The I.200 series of CCITT recommendations, referred to as *service capabilities*, provides a classification and method of description of the telecommunication services supported by ISDN. These services encompass existing services and define additional ones. The purpose of the recommendations is to provide a unifying framework for viewing these services and to set forth the user requirements for ISDN. The series, however, does not impose implementation or configuration guidelines. That is, the way in which the service is to be provided is left open. For example, the description of a teletex service does not presuppose which organization (user, private network, public network, information service provider, etc.) provides the various elements that make up a complete teletex service.

Three types of services are defined by CCITT: bearer services, teleservices, and supplementary services. **Bearer services** provide the means to convey information (speech, data, video, etc.) between users in real time and without alteration of the content of the message. These services correspond to the lower three layers of the OSI model. **Teleservices** combine the transportation function with the information processing function. They employ bearer services to transport data and, in addition, provide a set of higher-layer functions. These higher-layer functions correspond to OSI layers 4 through 7. Whereas bearer services define requirements for, and are provided by, network functions, teleservices include terminal as well as network capabilities. Examples of teleservices are telephony, teletex, videotex, and message handling. Both bearer services and teleservices may be enhanced by **supplementary services.** A supplementary service is one that may be used in conjunction with one or more of the bearer or teleservices. It cannot be used alone. An example is reverse charging. This can be used to reverse charges on a circuit-switched call or a packet-switched virtual call. Reverse charging can also be used with a teleservice, such as the message handling service, to create a "collect message."

In each of these three categories (bearer, teleservice, supplementary), there are a number of specific services defined by CCITT. To characterize and differentiate these various services, a collection of **attributes** have been defined. Each service is characterized by specific values assigned to each descriptive attribute. This method makes it easy to precisely define a service and to compare different services.

Table 6-1 lists the attributes that have so far been defined by CCITT (in I.130), together with the values that they can take on. Most of these terms are self-explanatory; some of the others will be discussed later in this section, in the context of a specific service. One additional comment may be useful. A distinction is made between a communication and a connection. These terms are defined as follows in I.112:

- Communication: The transfer of information according to agreed conventions.
- Connection: A concatenation of transmission channels or telecommunication circuits, switching and other functional units set up to provide for the transfer of signals between two or more points in a telecommunication network, to support a single communication.

TABLE 6-1   ATTRIBUTES AND THEIR VALUES

Attribute	Definition	Values
Information Transfer Mode	Mode for transferring user information	Circuit, Packet
Information Transfer Rate	Bit rate (circuit mode) or throughput (packet mode) between two access points	Appropriate bit rate or throughput

Information Transfer Capability	Used to characterize the transfer of different types of information through ISDN	Unrestricted digital information: sequence of bits with specified bit rate without alteration
		Speech: Digitized speech coded according to a specified encoding rule
		3.1 kHz Audio: Digitized audio with a bandwidth of 3.1 kHz with a specified encoding rule
		7 kHz Audio: as above, for 7 kHz
		15 kHz Audio: as above, for 15 kHz
		Video: Digitized video with a specified encoding rule
Establishment of Communication	Means of establishing and releasing a given communication (transfer of information)	Demand: in response to user request
		Reserved: connection and release times reserved via user request
		Permanent: preestablished connection
Establishment of Connection	Mode of establishment and release of a connection that supports a communication	Switched: set up on demand
		Semipermanent: provided for an indefinite period and pass through a switching network
		Permanent: bypass ISDN exchanges
Symmery	Relationship of information flow between two or more access points	Unidirectional: only one direction
		Bidirectional symmetric: flow characteristics are the same in both directions
		Bidirectional asymmetric: flow characteristics are different in the two directions
Communication Configuration	Spatial arrangement for transferring information between two or more access points	Point-to-point: only two access points
		Multipoint: more than two access points
		Broadcast: *to be defined*
Connection Configuration	Spatial arrangement for transferring information on a connection. Has three sub-attributes	

Cont.

TABLE 6-1 ATTRIBUTES AND THEIR VALUES (continued)

Attribute	Definition	Values
Topology	Arrangement of connection elements	Simple: one connection element Tandem: two or more elements in series to form a connection Parallel: two or more elements in parallel to form a connection Multipoint: *to be defined*
Uniformity	Degree of commonality of the individual connection elements	Uniform: all elements have same attribute values Nonuniform: not uniform
Dynamics	Timing of connection element establishment and release	Concurrent: simultaneous establishment and release of elements Sequential: elements established and released sequentially Add/remove: elements may be added or removed independently
Structure	Capability of delivering information retaining data integrity	8 kHz integrity: all bits submitted are delivered in an equal time interval of 125 μsec Service data unit integrity: all bits submitted as a block are delivered in a corresponding block Unstructured: no guarantee of integrity
Access Channel and Rate	Channels and rates used to transfer user information and/or signaling information	Name of channel and corresponding bit rate
Access Protocol Signaling Access Protocol Information Access Coding/Protocol	Protocol on the signaling and/or user information transfer channel	Appropriate protocol
Supplementary Services Provided	Supplementary service associated with a given telecommunication service	*For further study*
Quality of Service	A group of specific attributes	*For further study*
Connection Performance	Performance attributes related to an ISDN connection	*For further study*

Thus, a communication is a user-oriented concept, and a connection is a network-oriented concept. Those attributes that refer to communication are used to characterize ISDN service, while those attributes that refer to connections are used to characterize ISDN connections. This latter topic will be discussed in the next chapter.

Bearer Services

So far, a total of 12 different bearer services have been defined by ISDN; these are listed in Table 6-2, and Table 6-3 is a list of the possible values for service attributes for these bearer services.

The first five defined services provide for the capability of 64 kbps data transfer. As was mentioned, this data rate is the fundamental building block of ISDN services. The first of these, known as *64 kbps, 8 kHz structured, unrestricted,* is the most general purpose service at that data rate. The term "unrestricted" means that the information is transferred without alteration; this is also known as a transparent bearer service. Users may employ this service for any application that requires a data rate of 64 kbps. Figure 6-1 [SCAC86] illustrates two possible applications. In the first, the user is connecting digital PBX systems and using it to transport voice digitized at 32 kbps. Although 64 kbps is the ISDN standard data rate for digitized voice, sophisticated encoding algorithms make high-quality voice transmission possible at 32 kbps. Thus, the user is saving on data transmission capacity by employing a private encoding algorithm. However, the basic unit of switching within ISDN is 64 kbps; consequently, the two 32-kbps voice channels must be connected to the same

TABLE 6-2   ISDN BEARER SERVICES (I.211)

Circuit-Mode Bearer Services	*Packet-Mode Bearer Services*
• 64 kbps, 8 kHz structured, unrestricted	• Virtual call and permanent virtual circuit
• 64 kbps, 8 kHz structured, speech	• Connectionless on a D channel
• 64 kbps, 8 kHz structured, 3.1 kHz audio	• User signaling
• 64 kbps, 8 kHz structured, alternate speech/unrestricted	
• 64 kbps, 8 kHz structured, alternate speech/3.1 kHz audio	
• 384 kbps, 8 kHz structured, unrestricted	
• 1536 kbps, 8 kHz structured, unrestricted	
• 1920 kbps, 8 kHz structured, unrestricted	
• 2 X 64 kbps, 8 kHz structured, unrestricted	

TABLE 6.3 VALUES FOR ATTRIBUTES CHARACTERIZING BEARER SERVICES

Possible values of attributes								Attributes
circuit					packet			**Information transfer attributes** 1. Information transfer mode
Bit rate kbit/s					Throughput			2. Information transfer rate
64	384	1536	1920	other values for further study	Options for further study			
unrestricted digital information	speech	3.1 kHz audio	7 kHz audio	15 kHz audio	video	Others for further study		3. Information transfer capability
8 kHz integrity		Service data unit integrity			unstructured			4. Structure
demand		reserved			permanent			5. Establishment of communication
point-to-point		multipoint			broadcast			6. Communication configuration
unidirectional		bidirectional symmetric			bidirectional assymetric			7. Symmetry
D(16)	D(64)	✕	B	HO⁻	H11	H12	others for further study	**Access Attributes** 8. Access Channel and rate
I.430/I.431		I.461	I.462	I.463	Others FS			9.1 Signaling access protocol layer 1
I.430/I.431	I.460	I.461	I.462	I.463	G.711	Others FS		9.4 Information access protocol layer 1
I.440/I.441	(CCITT No. 7)	I.462	X.25	Others FS				9.2 Signaling access protocol layer 2
HDLC LAP B	X.25	I.462?		Others FS				9.5 Information access protocol layer 2
I.450/I.451	(CCITT No. 7)	I.461	I.462	X.25	I.463	Others FS		9.3 Signaling access protocol layer 3
T.70-3	X.25	I.462?		Others FS				9.6 Information access protocol layer 3
under study								**General attributes** 10. Supplementary services provided 11. Quality of service 12. Interworking possibilities 13. Operational and commercial

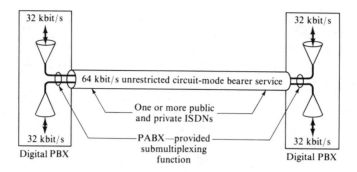

(a) Multiplexed 32-kbps voice channels

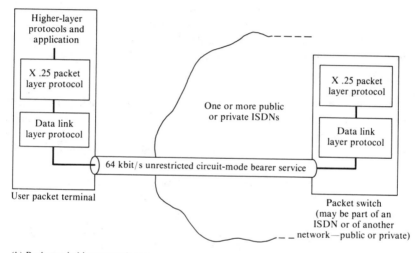

(b) Packet-switching network access

FIGURE 6-1 Example Uses of the 64 kbps, 8kHz structured, unrestricted Service (BART86)

pair of subscribers. That is, it is not possible to use this service to set up two 32-kbps circuits going to two different destinations. Figure 6-1b shows another use of this service. In this case, the 64-kbps circuit is used to connect a host system to a non-ISDN packet-switched network.

The term "8 kHz structured" means that, in addition to bit transmission, a structure is transferred between customers. When one user transmits information to another user, the transmission is accompanied by 8-kHz timing information, which delimits the data in 8-bit units. This 8-kHz structural integrity implies that octets are preserved within the corresponding time interval; that is, an octet is never split across a time interval boundary. This applies in particular to speech which requires the 8 kHz structure in addition to the 64 kbps information flow so as to be able to recognize the octets, which are formed by speech encoding, at the receiving side. In text transmission, character boundaries are preserved. Thus, there is no need for the user to provide an in-band, user-to-user synchronization scheme.

The *64 kbps, 8 kHz structured, speech* service defines a specific structure for the digital signal, namely pulse code modulation (PCM) as defined in CCITT Recommendation G.711. Because the network may assume that the encoded data are speech, it may use processing techniques appropriate for speech, such as analog transmission, echo cancellation, and low bit rate voice encoding. Because these transformations may not be precisely reversible, bit integrity is not guaranteed. However, the received signal should produce a high-quality reproduction of the transmitted voice signal. In other respects, this service is the same as the unrestricted service. The restriction to speech allows the use of processing techniques in the network that may optimize the transmission. Furthermore, the network may perform conversions between digital encoding laws. For example, the G.711 standard specifies two versions of the PCM algorithm, A-law and μ-law. The former is used in North America and Japan; the latter is used in the rest of the world. Thus the voice signal on a connection that crosses these geographic boundaries is automatically converted.

The *64 kbps, 8 kHz structured, 3.1 kHz* service assumes that digitized audio information is being transmitted. This permits routing over analog circuits using codecs, as in the previous service. However, other forms of processing peculiar to speech signals are prohibited. For example, a form of multiplexing known as time-assigned speech interpolation (TASI) exploits the bursty character of speech to multiplex speech channels. This allows thirty speech calls to be squeezed into a T1 24-channel system with no noticeable degradation. However, this technique is not appropriate for nonspeech signals that happen to occupy the voice frequency band, such as digital data that have been passed through a voice-grade modem.

The next two services both involve the alternate transfer of either voice or another capability. There is a requirement for a short (as yet undefined) changeover time when the user requests a change from one service to the alternate service. The next three services provide for high-speed digital transfer, at rates of 384, 1536, and 1920 kbps. These services could be used for a variety of applications, including video, private networking between PBXs, and links between other networks.

The final circuit-mode bearer service is *2 × 64 kbps, 8 kHz structured, unrestricted*. This service provides for the use of two 64-kbps channels that bear some relationship to each other. The details of this service remain to be worked out.

The remaining services are packet-switching types of services. The *virtual call and permanent virtual circuit* service is the traditional packet-network interface allowing both types of virtual circuits; the user attaches to ISDN in the same manner as attaching to a packet-switched network, using X.25. The *connectionless on a D-channel* service provides for a datagram style of packet service. This service might be provided to support applications such as telemetry, alarm, and transaction services, which do not need the connection-oriented service. The access protocol would differ from X.25, and is a subject for further study. The term D channel refers to one of the channel types available with ISDN, as will be discussed in the next chapter. The final packet-mode bearer service, *user signaling*, provides for user-to-user control signaling in a packetized manner. The protocol for this signaling is defined in I.451, and will be described in Chapter 8.

More bearer services, especially at higher data rates, will be defined in the future. However, this mix of services so far defined provides the capability of meeting a wide variety of user requirements and is sufficient for initial implementations of ISDN.

Teleservices

The area of teleservices is significantly less well-developed than that of bearer services. Teleservices are intended to cover a wide variety of user applications over ISDN. The list of services so far defined in I.212 is shown in Box 6-1. In general, they cover applications which are in the nature of terminal-service applications, most of which have been defined by CCITT. This can be contrasted with what might be considered computer-to-computer applications. These latter applications have mostly been defined by ISO, and include file transfer and document architecture.

Table 6-4 is a list of the possible values for service attributes for the teleservices. The lower layer (OSI layers 1 – 3) attributes are essentially the same as for the bearer services. This is because a teleservice relies on a bearer service for information transport across the ISDN. The upper layer attributes form a protocol architecture that maps into OSI layers 4 through 7; this topic is addressed in the next section.

One service conspicuously absent from Box 6-1 is the message-handling service (MHS), defined by the X.400 series of recommendations. This is one of the most important and widely available of the CCITT-defined teleservices, and will be included in future revisions to I.212. We examine this service later in this chapter. Two other important services are also examined: facsimile and teletex.

Supplementary Services

As was mentioned, supplementary services are always associated with a bearer service or teleservice. Each service is defined, and could be implemented, in a manner independent from the bearer services and teleservices with which it might be used. This allows each supplementary service to be used in a uniform fashion, regardless of the bearer service or teleservice that it is supports. For example, the methods of requesting and authorizing reverse charging should be the same for a circuit-switched call or an MHS message.

Box 6- 2 lists the supplementary services that have been defined so far. All of these originated in the telephone world. However, most of them can also be applied to packet-mode bearer services and to some teleservices.

ISDN TELESERVICES

TELEPHONY

Provides 3.1 kHz speech communication. The digital signal follows the agreed encoding laws for speech and the network may use digital signal processing techniques, such as echo cancellation. User information is provided over a B-channel, signaling is provided over the D-channel.

TELETEX

Provides end-to-end text communication using standardized character sets, presentation formats, and communication protocols. The high layer attributes are based on those of the CCITT standardized teletex service (F.200). User information is provided over a B-channel, signaling is provided over the D-channel.

TELEFAX

Provides end-to-end facsimile communication using standardized picture coding, resolution, and communication protocols. The high layer attributes are based on the facsimile Group 4 Recommendations of CCITT. User information is provided over a B-channel, signaling is provided over the D-channel.

MIXED MODE

Provides combined text and facsimile communication (mixed mode) for end-to-end transfer of documents containing mixed information of text and fixed images. The high layer attributes are based on the CCITT Recommendation for the teletex service and facsimile Group 4, mixed mode (F.200, Annex C). User information is provided over a B-channel, signaling is provided over the D-channel.

VIDEOTEX

The videotex service in the ISDN is an enhancement of the existing Videotex service with retrieval and mailbox functions for text (alpha) and graphic (mosaic, geometric, photographic) information.

TELEX

This service provides interactive text communication. The digital signal follows the internationally agreed Recommendations for telex above the ISDN physical layer. User information is transferred over circuit or packet mode bearer channels, signaling is provided over the D-channel.

TABLE 6.4 VALUES FOR ATTRIBUTES CHARACTERIZING TELESERVICES

Possible values of attributes									Service attributes
Refer to Recommendation I.211									Information transfer and access attributes
I.430/I.431	I.461		I.462		I.463		Others FS		9.1 Signaling access protocol layer 1
I.440/I.441	(CCITT No. 7)		I.462		X.25		Others FS		9.2 Signaling access protocol layer 2
I.450/I.451	(CCITT SS No. 7)	I.461	I.462	X.25	I.463		Others FS		9.3 Signaling access protocol layer 3
I.430/I.431	I.460	I.461	I.462	I.463	G.711		Others FS		9.4 Information access protocol layer 1
HDLC LAPB		I.440/I.441	X.25		I.462?		Others FS		9.5 Information access protocol layer 2
T.10		X.25		I.462?		Others FS			9.6 Information access protocol layer 3
Speech	Sound	Text	Fac-simile	Text-Fac-simile	Video tex	Video	Text inter-active	other	10. Type of user information
X.224			T.70			Others			11. Layer 4 protocol
X.225			T.62			Others			12. Layer 5 protocol
T.73	G.711		T.61	T.6	T.100		Others		13. Layer 6 protocol
200	240		300	400		Others			Resolution (Note)
Alpha-mosaic		Geometric		Photographic		Others			Graphic mode (Note)
T.60		T.5		T.72		Others			14. Layer 7 protocol
Under study									General attributes 15—18

Note – If applicable.

6-2 FACSIMILE

A significant class of applications that make use of communications networks are those that involve the transmission of documents and messages. The most common techniques transmit character information, and are suitable for transmitting documents consisting solely of text. Teletex and electronic mail, both discussed later in this chapter, fall into this category. Another technique is to electronically transmit a visual image of the original. A bit-map representation is created of the image, which can include text, graphics, or pictures. This is the approach taken with facsimile.

Facsimile has a number of advantages over other forms of document or message transmission. In addition to printed text, facsimile can transmit pictures,

BOX 6-2

SUPPLEMENTARY SERVICES

USER-TO-USER SIGNALING

Allows two users to exchange information over the signaling channel in association with a circuit-switched call.

CALL FORWARDING UNCONDITIONAL

Permits a served user to have the network send all incoming calls, or just those associated with a specified basic service, addressed to the served user's ISDN number to another number. The served user's originating service is unaffected.

CLOSED USER GROUP

The possibility for a group of users to intercommunicate only amongst themselves or, as required, one or more users may be provided with incoming/outgoing access to users outside the group.

CITYWIDE CENTREX

Allows a subscriber to control the communications capabilities of its user access interfaces. The subscriber's user access interfaces can be served by exchanges or PBXs. With this arrangement a number of capabilities may be made available to subscribers. These include 1) specialized numbering and dialing plans, and 2) call screening. Other possible capabilities, such as simulated private networking, are also envisaged.

DIRECT DIALING IN

Enables a user to call directly to another user on a PBX/Centrex, without attendant intervention, or to call a terminal on a passive bus selectively.

CALL WAITING

Enables a terminal equipment, which is already active in a communication, to notify its user of an incoming call. The user then has the choice of accepting, rejecting, or ignoring the waiting call.

COMPLETION OF CALLS TO BUSY SUBSCRIBER

Allows a calling user A encountering a busy destination B to be notified when the busy destination B becomes not busy and to have the service provider reinitiate the call to the specified destination B if User A desires.

CALLING LINE IDENTIFICATION PRESENTATION

Provides the calling party ISDN number, possibly with additional address information, to the called party.

CALLING LINE IDENTIFICATION RESTRICTION

Restricts presentation of the calling party's ISDN number, possibly with additional address information, to the called party.

LINE HUNTING

Enables incoming calls to a specific ISDN number (or numbers) to be distributed over a group of interfaces or terminals.

THREE PARTY SERVICE

The possibility for a busy subscriber to hold the existing call and make a call to a third party. The following arrangements may then be possible: the ability to switch between the two calls, the introduction of a common speech path between the three parties, and the connection of the other two parties.

CALL TRANSFER

Enables a user to transfer an established incoming or outgoing calling or called party call to a third party. This service is different from the call forward service since, in this case, the call to be transferred must have an established end-to-end connection prior to the transfer.

CREDIT CARD CALLING

Allows automatic charging of communication. The use of a telecommunication card number combined with a confidential code permits a user to charge calls to an account which is independent of the calling line.

---

graphs, drawings, handwritten notes, and anything else that can be put on paper. Also, facsimile saves preparation time because information does not have to be entered into a message system through a keyboard. The paper itself is scanned for patterns of light and dark, which are transmitted to the receiving end.

Although facsimile was developed in 1843 (yes, 1843), it is only since the mid-1970s that the system has come into common use. That use is now growing rapidly, thanks to a number of factors:

- Until recently, there were legal restrictions in some countries inhibiting the use of the public telephone network for facsimile transmission.

- The development and widespread acceptance of CCITT standards is making compatible interworking of facsimile possible on an international scale.
- Facsimile technology has advanced, bringing higher speed, better quality, reduced machine size, reduced machine and transmission costs, and simpler machine operation.
- The advent of the digital facsimile allows a page of information to be easily manipulated by computer systems, stored on disk or tape, and encrypted for security.

With digital facsimile, the role of the facsimile has broadened. In digital form, pages can be transmitted between facsimile machines without ever going through the on-paper stage. A document can be prepared using a graphics package, drawing program, or word processor and handled in digital facsimile form. More sophisticated processing is possible by combining text and graphics capabilities. Thus, the user can easily create and edit text, combine it with charts, pictures, and other graphics, and subsequently treat the whole thing as an electronic or paper image.

Facsimile systems can be classified as either *photographic facsimile*, in which the original copy is reproduced with black, white, and intermediate gray scales, or *document facsimile*, in which only black and white are used. The primary interest in office and telecommunication applications has been in document facsimile, which is the subject of this section.

Traditionally, facsimile equipment operates by a local scan of a page, the transmission of an electronic version of the scanned information to a remote counterpart, and the printing of the same image at the remote location (Figure 6-2). In earlier designs, the scanning and printing processes are synchronized; there is little or no signal storage between the scanner and the printer. In more recent digital designs, buffered facsimile equipment has appeared on the market. And of course, as was mentioned, either the source or destination may be electronic instead of paper.

A variety of technologies have been used for both the scanning and printing processes. Since the focus of this work is communications, we will not examine these alternatives. A good survey on the topic is [KOBA85].

Facsimile Standards

CCITT has classified facsimile equipment for use over public networks into four categories, or groups:

- *Group 1:* The original low-speed analog facsimile technique. Transmission is in analog frequency modulation (FM), with several levels of gray supported as analog midpoints in the white-to-black spectrum. It is suitable for transmission of documents of ISO A4 size (210 × 297 mm; about 8.25 × 11.7 in) at about 4 lines per mm (about 100 lines per inch) in about 6 minutes.

FIGURE 6-2   Facsimile: Generic Block Diagram

- *Group 2:* An improved analog facsimile that employs bandwidth compression techniques to achieve a speed-up of a factor of 2 or more for the same resolution of Group 1. Transmission is duobinary phase modulation (PM), again supporting gray-scale values as well as black and white. Group 2 standards are still widely observed.

- *Group 3:* This is the first digital facsimile standard. This system provides only black and white values, with sampling densities of 200 spots per inch horizontally across the paper and 100 or 200 lines per inch vertically down the page. Group 3 uses a digital encoding scheme and incorporates a means of reducing the redundant information in the document signal prior to modulation. It is assumed that Group 3 transmission is via a modem over an analog telephone network. Transmission time is speeded up by a factor of 3 or more compared to Group 2.

- *Group 4:* Group 4 is also a black/white digital facsimile standard. It is intended for use over digital networks at speeds of up to 64 kbps and with provision for error-free reception. Resolutions of from 200 to 400 pels* per inch are specified. As with Group 3, compression techniques are used to reduce the number of bits transmitted. With Group 4, transmission times drop to a few seconds rather than the minutes of earlier standards.

Groups 1 and 2 were first standardized in 1976; Group 3 in 1980, and Group 4 in 1984. Table 6-5 compares key characteristics of the various CCITT standards. Note that Group 4 facsimile systems are further divided into three classes. Class 1 is a pure facsimile machine. Class 2 is capable of receiving and printing on a document a message transmitted via teletex. Class 3 is capable of transmitting and receiving in teletex and facsimile modes.

Figure 6-3 is a possible organization for a Group 4 facsimile system. The key elements are:

- *Preprocessor:* This takes the input from an analog scanning device and applies a threshold to convert each scan position to black or white.

---

* A *picture element*, or *pel*, is the smallest discrete scanning-line sample of a facsimile system, which contains only black-white information (no gray scales). A *pixel* is a picture element that contains gray-scale information.

TABLE 6-5   CHARACTERISTICS OF CCITT FACSIMILE STANDARDS

Characteristic	Group 1	Group 2	Group 3	Group 4		
				Class 1	Class 2	Class 3
Recommendation	T.2	T.3	T.4	T.5	T.5	T.5
Signal	Analog	Analog	Digital	Digital	Digital	Digital
Horizontal Resolution	3.85 li/mm	3.85 li/mm	7.7 li/mm	200 pels/in	300 pels/in	300 pels/in
Vertical Resolution			7.7 li/mm	200 pels/in	300 pels/in	300 pels/in
Speed	6 min	3 min	<1 min	<10 s	<10 s	<10 s
Network	PSTN	PSTN	PSTN	ISDN	ISDN	ISDN
Data Encoding	N/A	2/3 level spectrum compression	MH, MR	MR	MR	MR
Equipment	Fax	Fax	Fax	Fax	Fax, receive from teletex	fax, teletex

PSTN = Public Switched Telephone Network
MH = Modified Huffman Code
MR = Modified Relative Element Address Designate

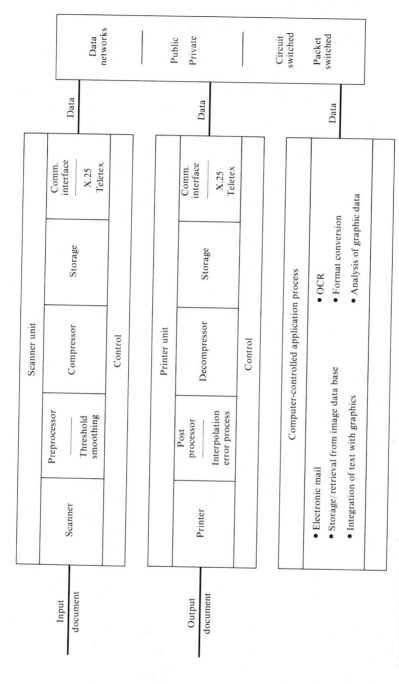

FIGURE 6-3 Group 4 Facsimile: Functional Block Diagram

201

- *Compressor:* The bit matrix representing the picture is compressed to reduce redundant information.
- *Storage:* The source and destination systems must both buffer sufficient compressed data to accommodate uncertainties of the error control system in the data network and terminal/network interface link.
- *Communication Interface:* The Group 4 system can interface to a circuit-switched or packet-switched network, including ISDN.
- *Decompressor:* At the destination, the data stream is decompressed so that the original image can be reproduced.
- *Post-processor:* The decompressed bit matrix may be processed further to improve the image. For example, when the resolution of the printer is greater than that of the scanner, it is possible to interpolate in a manner to provide improved image quality.

The figure also indicates that a number of additional applications, beyond document scan and print, are possible. These include:

- *Electronic mail:* As an alternative to traditional electronic mail systems.
- *Storage/Retrieval from an image data base:* Documents can be stored for later remote printing. Documents can be created using a graphics processor.
- *Format conversion:* from one facsimile standard to another.
- *OCR/Analysis of graphic data:* Images could be transmitted in bit-map form for later processing using pattern recognition and other image processing techniques.

Compression Techniques

Compression techniques are essential to the widespread use of digital facsimile machines. To see this, consider that an A4 page with 200 pel per inch resolution (which is adequate but not unnecessarily high resolution) generates 3,740,000 bits. At 64 kbps, the basic ISDN data rate, this page would take about one minute to transmit. Ultimately, users will expect their systems to operate at a rate similar to that of a copier, or one page every few seconds. To meet this requirement without an inordinately high data rate requires the use of data compression techniques.

There are two broad classes of black-white graphic coding techniques. *Information-preserving techniques* reproduce an exact replica of the original scanned and thresholded binary image. *Approximation techniques* approximate the original image. Both of the compression techniques standardized by CCITT are information-preserving techniques. The two techniques that have been standardized are the Modified Huffman (MH) and Modified READ (MR) algorithms. The MH technique is the default for Group 3, with MR as an option. Group 4 specifies MR. Both techniques are examined in the section. However, to clarify the discussion, we begin with a simpler technique, the Huffman code.

Huffman Encoding. The problem that is addressed by Huffman encoding is this. We wish to construct and transmit a message using N symbols. The simplest technique is to use binary numbers of equal length L to represent each symbol. L will be the smallest number such that:

$$L \geq \log_2 N \text{ bits/symbol}$$

For example, if we wish to use the 26 letters of the alphabet, then $\log_2 (26) = 4.7$, and $L = 5$ bits.

Now, if all of the symbols to be transmitted were equally probable, then this encoding scheme cannot be improved upon. However, if this is not the case, then such a *fixed-length code* is not the most efficient. We would like to use an encoding scheme in which common symbols are assigned short codes and rare symbols are assigned long codes. In this way, the average code length, calculated over the actual transmission, should be reduced.

We can determine how good our *variable-length encoding* scheme is by using a result from information theory. If a source produces N different symbols, then the average information, or entropy, per symbol of the output is:

$$H = -\sum_{k=1}^{N} P_k \log_2 P_k$$

where P_k is the probability of occurrence of the kth symbol. As an example, consider an alphabet of 5 symbols, with respective probabilities of occurrence of 0.4, 0.3, 0.2, 0.04, 0.04, and 0.02. The value of H for this source, using the formula above, is 1.999 bits per symbol. This value is the theoretical minimum value of the number of bits used to encode a source. Because each source symbol must be represented by an integral number of bits, this minimum usually can not be met. However, the Huffman code produces an efficiency very close to the theoretical minimum.

A Huffman code can be constructed as follows. List the symbols in decreasing order of probability. Consider each symbol to be a leaf node in a binary tree to be constructed. Merge the two nodes of lowest probability into a node whose probability is the sum of the two constituent probabilities. At each step, repeat this procedure. The process stops when one unmerged node remains. The result is a binary tree. Label each pair of branches with a zero and a one. The codeword for any symbol is the string of labels from the root node back to the original symbol. Figure 6-4 is an example, using the symbol set defined earlier. Note that straightforward fixed-length encoding would require 3 bits per symbol, whereas Huffman coding is an average of just over 2 bits per symbol.

A Huffman code has the property that no code word is the prefix of any other codeword. Thus, codewords of successive symbols can be concatenated with no punctuation. A proof that the Huffman code is optimum can be found in [GALL68].

Modified Huffman Code. In a typical document, the black and white areas of the image tend to cluster. If we view the document as a sequence of lines, and consider the pattern of black and white on a given line, we observe that there are long

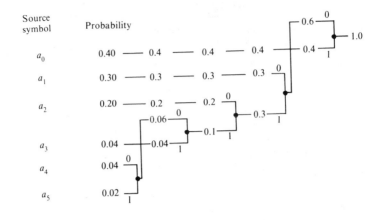

Source symbol	Codework	Length (bits)	Length X probability
a_0	1	1	0.4
a_1	00	2	0.6
a_2	010	3	0.6
a_3	0111	4	0.16
a_4	01100	5	0.2
a_5	01101	5	0.1

2.06

Average codeword length = 2.06 bits/symbol
Entropy of source = 1.999 bits/symbol

FIGURE 6-4   Huffman Coding Example

runs of black (B) and white (W) pels. This property is exploited in a family of techniques referred to as *run-length encoding*. The two-valued input is converted to a many-valued run-length process, and this process is subsequently coded for transmission. In addition, because longer runs of black or white are in general less probable than shorter runs, variable-length coding can be employed to advantage.

The Huffman code, as just described, could be used for the purpose of facsimile encoding. It could be applied to an image one horizontal line at a time to encode the sequence of black and white pels. For example, in Figure 6-5, one scan of the image produces a sequence of W7, B7, W4, B8, W4, B7, W10. If we consider each of these elements as a symbol in a source alphabet, then Huffman encoding can be used to encode the source. However, since CCITT standards require at least

1728 pels per line, the number of different codes and hence the average length of code are very large.

An alternative is the Modified Huffman (MH) encoding technique. MH regards a run-length N as the sum of two terms:

$$N = 64\,m + n; \qquad m = 0, 1, 2, \ldots, 27; \qquad n = 0, 1, 2, \ldots, 63$$

Each run length can now be represented by two values, one for m and one for n, and these values can then be encoded using Huffman encoding. For this purpose, CCITT has defined eight representative documents and calculated the probabilities of the different run-length occurrences. As these probabilities are different for black and white, two sets of probabilities were calculated. From this information two code tables were developed, as shown in Table 6-6. The terminating code is used for run lengths of less than 64. For run lengths greater than 64, a combination of a terminating code (n) and a make-up code (m) is needed. Figure 6-5 shows an example of the application of this code.

There are several additional details concerning this code. Each line ends with a unique code word for end of line (EOL). This is a code word that can never be found in a valid line of data; it therefore facilitates resynchronization after an error burst. Within a line, code words for black and white runs must alternate. However, note that different codes are used for the black and white runs; this provides an additional

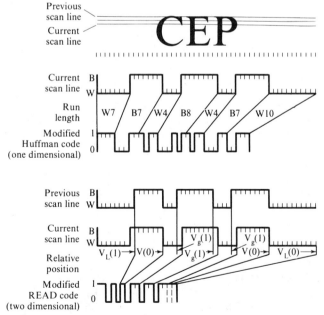

FIGURE 6-5 MH and MR Coding Examples

TABLE 6-6   MODIFIED HUFFMAN CODE TABLE

			Terminating Codewords		
Run Length	White	Black	Run Length	White	Black
0	00110101	0000110111	32	00011011	000001101010
1	000111	010	33	00010010	000001101011
2	0111	11	34	00010011	000011010010
3	1000	10	35	00010100	000011010011
4	1011	011	36	00010101	000011010100
5	1100	0011	37	00010110	000011010101
6	1110	0010	38	00010111	000011010110
7	1111	00011	39	00101000	000011010111
8	10011	000101	40	00101001	000001101100
9	10100	000100	41	00101010	000001101101
10	00111	0000100	42	00101011	000011011010
11	01000	0000101	43	00101100	000011011011
12	001000	0000111	44	00101101	000001010100
13	000011	00000100	45	00000100	000001010101
14	110100	00000111	46	00000101	000001010110
15	110101	000011000	47	00001010	000001010111
16	101010	0000010111	48	00001011	000001100100
17	101011	0000011000	49	01010010	000001100101
18	0100111	0000001000	50	01010011	000001010010
19	0001100	00001100111	51	01010100	000001010011
20	0001000	00001101000	52	01010101	000000100100
21	0010111	00001101100	53	00100100	000000110111
22	0000011	00000110111	54	00100101	000000111000
23	0000100	00000101000	55	01011000	000000100111
24	0101000	00000010111	56	01011001	000000101000
25	0101011	00000011000	57	01011010	000001011000
26	0010011	000011001010	58	01011011	000001011001
27	0100100	000011001011	59	01001010	000000101011
28	0011000	000011001100	60	01001011	000000101100
29	00000010	000011001101	61	00110010	000001011010
30	00000011	000001101000	62	00110011	000001100110
31	00011010	000001101001	63	00110100	000001100111

			Make-Up Codewords		
Run Length	White	Black	Run Length	White	Black
64	11011	0000001111	960	011010100	0000001110011
128	10010	000011001000	1024	011010101	0000001110100
192	010111	000011001001	1088	011010110	0000001110101
256	0110111	000001011011	1152	011010111	0000001110110
320	00110110	000000110011	1216	011011000	0000001110111
384	00110111	000000110100	1280	011011001	0000001010010
448	01100100	000000110101	1344	011011010	0000001010011

512	01100101	0000001101100	1408	011011011	0000001010100
576	01101000	0000001101101	1472	010011000	0000001010101
640	01100111	0000001001010	1536	010011001	0000001011010
704	011001100	0000001001011	1600	010011010	0000001011011
768	011001101	0000001001100	1664	011000	0000001100100
832	011010010	0000001001101	1728	010011011	0000001100101
896	011010011	0000001110010	EOL	000000000001	000000000001

form of error-checking. Finally, by convention, each line begins with a white run length. If the first pel is black, then a white run length of zero is used.

Modified READ Code. The use of modified Huffman encoding significantly reduces the total number of bits that must be transmitted compared to a straightforward transmission of the bit-map image. Further gains in efficiency can be achieved by recognizing that there is a strong correlation between the black-white patterns of two adjacent lines. In fact, for typical facsimile documents, approximately 50 percent of all the B-W and W-B transitions are directly underneath a transition on the previous line, and an additional 25 percent differ by only one pel [SILV87]. Therefore, approximately 75 percent of all transitions can be defined by a relationship that is plus or minus at most one pel from the line above it. This is the underlying basis of the Modified Relative Element Address Designate (MR) Code.

In MR encoding, run lengths are encoded by encoding the position of changing elements, that is elements that are of a different color than the immediately preceding element on the same line. A changing element a_1 is coded in terms of its distance to one of two reference pels: either a preceding changing element a_0 on the same line or a changing element b_1 on the previous line. The selection of a_0 or b_1 depends on the exact configuration, as explained below.

Figure 6-6 illustrates the five changing elements that are defined for this scheme. The encoding procedure is summarized in Table 6-7 and can be defined as follows:

Step 1

a. If the position of b_2 lies to the left of a_1, this is coded using the word 0001. After this encoding, the position of a_1 is shifted to lie under b_2. This is referred to as pass mode. The algorithm resumes at Step 1.

b. If the condition in (a) is not satisfied, go to Step 2.

Step 2

a. If the position of a_1 is within three of the position of b_1 ($|a_1b_1| \le 3$), then a_1 is coded in the vertical mode, after which the old position a_1 becomes the new position a_0, a_2 becomes a_1, and so on.

b. If the position of a_1 is not within three of the position of b_1, then a_1 is coded in the horizontal mode. Following the horizontal mode code 001, a_0a_1 and a_1a_2 are encoded by one-dimensional MH coding. After this, the old position a_2 becomes the new position a_0.

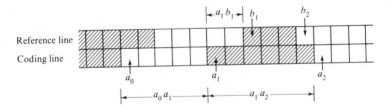

Definition of changing picture elements:

a_0 The reference or starting changing element on the coding line. At the start of the coding line, a_0 is set on an imaginary white changing element just to the left of the first element on the line. During the coding of a line, a_0 is redefined after every encoding.

a_1 The next changing element to the right of a_0 on the coding line.

a_2 The next changing element to the right of a_1 on the coding line.

b_1 The first changing element on the reference line to the right of a_0 and of opposite color to a_0.

b_2 The next changing element to the right of b_1 on the reference line.

FIGURE 6-6   Changing Picture Elements for the MR Technique

Step 1 is used to move the position of b_1 and b_2 along after the exercise of Step 2. Also, Step 1 has the effect of avoiding long run lengths. In Step 2, if the current changing element to be encoded is within three positions of the same transition in the previous line, then the position is encoded with one of seven possible values using MH. This situation will hold most of the time. In the few cases in which a transition in the current line is not within three positions of the same transition in the previous line, the next two runs are encoded using MH (Table 6-6).

TABLE 6.7   MR CODE TABLES

Mode	Elements to be coded		Notation	Code Word
Pass	b_1, b_2		P	0001
Horizontal	a_0a_1, a_1a_2		H	$001 + M(a_0a_1) + M(a_1a_2)$ (see Note)
Vertical	a_1 just under b_1	$a_1b_1 = 0$	V(0)	1
	a_1 to the right of b_1	$a_1b_1 = 1$	$V_R(1)$	011
		$a_1b_1 = 2$	$V_R(2)$	000011
		$a_1b_1 = 3$	$V_R(3)$	0000011
	a_1 to the left of b_1	$a_1b_1 = 1$	$V_1(1)$	010
		$a_1b_1 = 2$	$V_1(2)$	000010
		$a_1b_1 = 3$	$V_1(3)$	0000010

Note — Code M( ) of the horizontal mode represents the code words in Table 6-6

TABLE 6-8   COMPRESSION RATIOS FOR MH AND MR

CCITT Document Number	Normal Resolution (3.85 lines/mm)		Higher Resolution (7.7 lines/mm)	
	MH	MR	MH	MR
1	15.42	22.03	15.42	28.95
2	16.56	38.47	16.59	50.97
3	8.41	14.83	8.42	17.9
4	4.7	5.6	4.71	7.41
5	8.1	12.66	8.11	15.94
6	10.73	26.13	10.75	30.98
7	4.8	5.75	4.8	7.62
8	8.62	22.9	8.61	29.85
Average	8.02	12.27	8.02	15.84

The MR scheme is more sensitive to an error than the MH scheme; the effects of an error could propagate for unpredictable distances. To avoid this, MH encoding is used for every Kth scanning line. CCITT recommends a value of $K = 2$ for a resolution of 3.85 li/mm and $K = 4$ for 7.7 li/mm.

Table 6-8 shows the performance of the MH and MR schemes against a representative set of pages [YASU80]. In both cases, considerable compression is achieved. The compression achieved by MR is clearly superior. Similar results are also reported in [PRAT80].

6-3   TELETEX

Teletex is a relatively new international telecommunication service that provides direct electronic document exchange between such office text machines as electronic typewriters, word processors, and personal computers that are equipped with transmitting and receiving storages. The document exchange occurs directly from the transmit storage of the sending text machine to the receive storage of the receiving machine, independently of concurrent operator text entry or editing. The system provides for a rich set of graphic (printable) and control characters to allow the preparation of text documents to satisfy almost all users of Latin-based alphabets. Teletex can be used with a wide variety of communication networks, including telephone, packet-switched, and ISDN networks.

Teletex is intended to replace the older telex capability. Whereas telex operates at a leisurely 50 bps, a rate of 2400 bps is the default for teletex. Furthermore, teletex offers a much greater selection of graphic and control characters, to allow the exchange of text-based documents, such as letters and memos, rather than simply the text stream allowed with telex.

Characteristics and Functions

The CCITT standards for teletex ensure that teletex terminals and software packages from different manufacturers will be compatible. Recommendation T.60 specifies not only the data rate, but the character set and document characteristics supported by teletex. The key characteristics and functions listed in the recommendation are:

- *Equipment compatibility*: All equipment must implement a common basic set of functions. This assures that all terminals attached to a national or international teletex network can communicate with each other with regard to text and control characters, transmission error control procedures, determination of paper size, and automatic answerback.
- *Unattended operation*: When the receiving terminal is unattended or busy with local operations, it must store and safeguard incoming messages so that no information is lost before it is printed out.
- *Simultaneous terminal usage and document reception*: While the terminal is being used for local typing (e.g., teletex message preparation), it must be capable of receiving and acknowledging incoming messages without interrupting the local operation. Once the local typing is complete, the stored messages are printed out.
- *Compatibility with telex*: A teletex terminal must be capable of receiving and printing telex messages and of operating in telex mode so that it can send messages to a telex terminal. This capability is essential to a smooth migration from telex to teletex.
- *Sheet paper usable area*: In contrast to the typical telex terminal, which uses a continuous roll of paper, teletex terminals use individual sheets of paper. Because both the ISO A4 (210 × 297 mm) and North American (216 × 280 mm; 8.5 × 11 in) paper sizes are in widespread use, the teletex format restricts the usable print area to the area common to both page sizes.

Teletex procedures call for the exchange of reference information before sending a message. This includes call identification and its subset, terminal identification (Figure 6-7). The call identification line identifies the called and calling terminal, the date and time of call origination, and the document and page reference. Each teletex terminal has a unique terminal identification, consisting of four fields. The first field identifies the country and, if necessary, the network within the country. Field 2 identifies the network address of the terminal and is assigned by the network administration. Field 3, which was originally provided to allow terminal subaddressing, is optional; its use is a subject for further CCITT study. Field 4 is an abbreviated name used to identify the owner of the terminal.

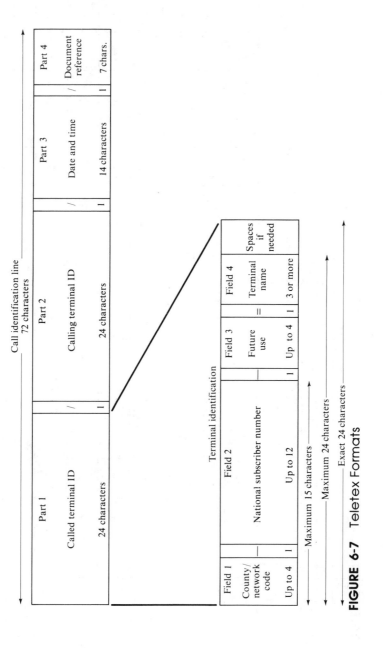

FIGURE 6-7 Teletex Formats

TABLE 6-9 TELETEX PRINTABLE AND CONTROL CHARACTER CODES

b_8	0	0	0	0	0	0	0	0	1	1	1	1	1	1	1	1
b_7	0	0	0	0	1	1	1	1	0	0	0	0	1	1	1	1
b_6	0	0	1	1	0	0	1	1	0	0	1	1	0	0	1	1
b_5	0	1	0	1	0	1	0	1	0	1	0	1	0	1	0	1
b_4 b_3 b_2 b_1	0	1	2	3	4	5	6	7	8	9	10	11	12	13	14	15
0 0 0 0 0			SP	0	@	P		p				°			Ω	K
0 0 0 1 1			!	1	A	Q	a	q			¡	±	´		Æ	æ
0 0 1 0 2			"	2	B	R	b	r			¢	²	`		Đ	đ
0 0 1 1 3			⊕	3	C	S	c	s			£	³	ˇ		ª	ð
0 1 0 0 4			⊕	4	D	T	d	t			$	×	~		Ħ	ħ
0 1 0 1 5			%	5	E	U	e	u			¥	µ	¯			ı
0 1 1 0 6			&	6	F	V	f	v			#	¶	˘		IJ	ĳ
0 1 1 1 7			'	7	G	W	g	w			§	·	˙		Ŀ	ŀ
1 0 0 0 8	BS		(	8	H	X	h	x			¤	÷	¨		Ł	ł

bits	#	0	1	2	3	4	5	6	7	8	9	10	11	12	13	14	15
1 0 0 1	9			)	9	I	Y	i	y					@		Ø	ø
1 0 1 0	10	LF	SUB	*	:	J	Z	j	z					°		Œ	œ
1 0 1 1	11			+	;	K	[	k		PLD	CSI	«	»	˛		º̲	ß
1 1 0 0	12	FF		,	<	L		l		PLU			¼	③̲		Þ	þ
1 1 0 1	13	CR		–	=	M	]	m					½	″		Ŧ	ŧ
1 1 1 0	14			.	>	N		n					¾	˘		Ŋ	ŋ
1 1 1 1	15			/	?	O	⊖̲	o					¿	˙		ʼn	

Note 1 — When interworking with videotex, this code shall have the meaning *delimiter*.

Note 2 — In the 1980 version of this Recommendation code 12/9 was allocated to represent the umlaut mark. The use of this facility is discouraged. Its removal is foreseen in the future.

Note 3 — Non-spacing underline is not a diacritical mark and may be combined with any graphic character of the teletex repertoire.

Note 4 — Teletex terminals should send only the codes 10/6 and 10/8 for graphic characters # and ☐ respectively. When receiving codes 2/3 and 2/4 terminals should interpret them as # and ☐.

Teletex Character Set

Table 6-9 shows the 8-bit encoding of the basic repertoire of teletex characters. Most of the character codes represent graphic, or printable characters. In addition to the Latin alphabet, the graphic character set includes accented letters and umlauts, and nonalphabetic characters, such as decimal digits, punctuation marks, and arithmetic signs.

In addition to printable characters, the teletex standard defines a set of control functions that enable a receiving terminal to produce a document that is identical in contents, layout, and format to that produced by the sending terminal. Each control function is encoded as one or more control characters. The basic repertoire of control characters is listed and defined in Table 6-10. Control characters fall into four categories:

TABLE 6-10　TELETEX BASIC REPETOIRE OF CONTROL FUNCTIONS

Identifier	Name	Definition
		Format Effectors
SP	Space	Advance one character position.
BS	Backspace	Move character position back by one.
LF	Line Feed	Advance to corresponding character position on next line.
FF	Form Feed	Advance to corresponding character position on next page.
CR	Carriage Return	Move to home position on same line.
PLD	Partial Line Down	Make partial vertical offset down. Used to begin subscript or to end superscript.
PLU	Partial Line Up	Make partial vertical offset up. Used to begin superscript or to end subscript.
		Presentation Control
PFS	Page Format Selection	Select vertical or horizontal orientation.
SGR	Select Graphic Rendition	Select default or underlined.
SHS	Select Horizontal Spacing	Select character spacing.
SVS	Select Vertical Spacing	Select line spacing.
		Code Extension
CS1	Control Sequence Introducer	Used to provide additional control functions
		Miscellaneous
SUB	Substitute Character	Used in the place of a character that has been found to be invalid or in error.
IGS	Identify Graphic Subrepertoire	Indicates that a particular subrepertoire of graphic characters is to be used.

- *Format Effectors:* Control the positioning of the printing element.
- *Presentation Control:* Influences the following presentation attributes: page orientation, horizontal and vertical spacing, and use or nonuse of underlining. Each of these functions includes a control character followed by a parameter value.
- *Code Extension:* Used to provide coded representations for additional control functions.
- *Miscellaneous:* Other control functions.

Table 6-9 shows the codes for those control functions represented by a single 8-bit character. The remainder of the control functions require multiple characters; each begins with the code extension character.

In addition to the basic repertoire, additional application-oriented graphic and printable characters may be employed. Several different escape sequences are used to indicate that the teletex message is entering/leaving a nonbasic character set. The standard does not require that a teletex terminal be able to handle these additional characters. A teletex terminal must be able to accept all characters in the basic repertoire, and be able to transmit all or a subset of the basic repertoire.

6-4 Teleservice Protocol Architecture

So far, we have discussed teleservices in general, and looked at two of the most important such services, facsimile and teletex. In terms of the OSI model, the issues we have addressed have primarily been at the presentation and application layers. However, the successful provision of a telecommunication service will require the lower layers as well. To some extent, general-purpose OSI-related standards can be employed to support ISDN teleservices. However, CCITT has found justification for issuing standards for some protocols that are specific to the teleservice requirement.

An overall picture of the protocol architecture for the support of CCITT teleservices is shown in Figure 6-8; those protocol standards that are specific to the teleservices are listed in Table 6-11.

Lower Layer Protocols

Teleservices defined by CCITT are intended for use over a variety of networks; T.70 specifies packet-switched data networks (PSDN), circuit-switched data networks (CSDN), and public-switched telephone networks (PSTN). With a **packet-switched data network,** the three-level X.25 standard discussed in Section 3-7 is employed. With this type of network, teletex messages and facsimile images are transmitted as a sequence of packets.

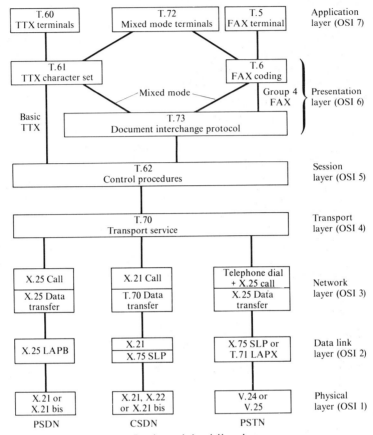

FIGURE 6-8 Teleservice Protocol Architecture

In the **circuit-switched data network** the user obtains a high-speed digital data circuit between the two user endpoints. Two phases of operation need to be distinguished:

- *Call establishment phase:* The 3-level X.21 standard is employed.*
  This is an interface protocol between the subscriber device and the network, used to set up a connection and request network facilities (e.g., reverse charging).
- *Data transfer phase:* Once a circuit is set up between two subscribers, data are passed through the network in a transparent fashion. In effect, the circuit is an OSI layer 1 connection, and layers 2 and above are end-to-end protocols between users. The link layer is the level 2 of the

---

* For a description of X.21, see [STAL88a].

TABLE 6-11 CCITT TELESERVICE PROTOCOLS

OSI Level	CCITT Recommendation	Title	Description
2	T.71	LAPB extended for half-duplex physical level facility	Defines data link layer procedures. Referred to as LAPX.
4	T.70	Network-independent basic transport service for the telematic services	Transport protocol equivalent to OSI Class 0 transport protocol.
5	T.62	Control procedures for teletex and Group 4 facsimile services	Defines the end-to-end session procedures. Corresponds to OSI Session Layer Basic Activity Subset (BAS).
6	T.73	Document interchange protocol for the telematic services	Defines protocol to be used above T.62 when a document is required for mixed-mode and Group 4 facsimile.
6	T.6	Facsimile coding schemes and coding control functions for Group 4 facsimile apparatus	
6	T.61	Character repertoire and coded character sets for the international teletex service	Detailed definitions of the repertoires of graphic characters and control functions. Also describes the means by which supplementary character repertoires are defined.
6	T.5	General aspects of Group 4 facsimile apparatus	Aspects of apparatus that include reducing redundant information in the document signal.
6	T.60	Terminal equipment for use in the teletex service	Addresses issues of data rate, paper format, and character codes.
6	T.72	Terminal capabilities for mixed mode of operation	Defines technical requirements unique to mixed-mode operation.
	F.200	Teletext service	Rules for international service.
	F.161	International facsimile service between subscribers with Group 4 Terminals	Rules for international service.

X.75 standard, which is LAP-B (almost identical to the X.25 LAP-B). The network layer is not really needed since we have, in effect, a direct connection. Accordingly, a very minimal network layer is defined in T.70, which employs a two-octet packet header. The header contains a length indicator and a packet type identifier (only one type has been defined). No protocol functions are performed at this level in the current standard.

The third option specified in T.70 is a **public switched telephone network,** using an analog link. Thus, the physical layer is specified as a modem interface; either a half-duplex or full-duplex modem may be used. If the link is full-duplex, then the data link layer is LAP-B as defined in X.75. If the link is half-duplex, then LAP-X is used. LAP-X is an extension of LAP-B that enforces a half-duplex discipline. At the network layer, a two-stage selection process applies. First, the calling user establishes a physical-level circuit with the called user employing normal telephone procedures. Second, the X.25 call control procedure is used to set up a logical connection between the two users. Strictly speaking, such a logical connection is not needed; however, it is specified to facilitate interworking with packet-switched networks. Once a virtual call is established, the X.25 data transfer capability is used.

In addition to these three types of networks, of course, teleservices will be supported over ISDN. Table 6-4 indicates the protocols that are involved in that context.

Transport and Session Layers

For the transport and session layers, CCITT has specified standards that are compatible with, and subsets of, more general-purpose OSI-related standards.* The transport-layer protocol is specified in T.70, and the session-layer standard, referred to as "Control Procedures for Teletex and Group 4 Facsimile Services," is specified in T.62.

The transport layer is specified in terms of a transport service, provided to the session layer, and a transport protocol that implements the transport service. The transport service definition is very similar to the OSI-based standard. The same OSI-based standard has been issued by CCITT as X.214 and by ISO as ISO 8072. There are only two differences between the T.70 specification and the X.214/ISO 8072 specification:

- The OSI standard includes a service for expedited data, to be delivered as quickly as possible. For the teleservices, this service was not felt to be needed.

---

* For a discussion of the transport and session standards referred to in this section, see [STAL87b] or [STAL88a].

- The T.70 standard explicitly defines an optional error reporting facility. This facility would normally also be present in an OSI service, but it is not specifically defined there.

The transport protocol that implements the transport service is also specified in T.70. This protocol is a subset of the OSI-based protocol defined in X.224 and ISO 8073. Specifically, the T.70 protocol is the same as the OSI transport protocol Class 0. This is the simplest type of transport protocol defined in X.224/ISO 8073. It assumes a reliable network service, and transport connections are mapped one-to-one onto network connections. Flow control and error control are based on network-level flow control and error control, and transport connection release is based on the release of the network connection.

The session layer specification in T.62 is also structured in terms of a session service and a session protocol. As with the transport layer, it is intended that the T.62 specification be compatible with the OSI-based standards, specifically X.215/ISO 8326 for the session service, and X.225/ISO 8327 for the session protocol. The T.62 specifies the use of the basic activity subset (BAS) of the OSI standards. The key elements of T.62 are that it enforces a two-way alternate (half-duplex) form of interaction and that it provides a checkpointing mechanism by which the sender will retain a copy of any transmitted message or document until assured that it is successfully stored at the receiver.

T.62 defines the session connection and termination procedure and the control over the direction of document transfer. Session connection involves a transfer of reference parameters from document sender to document receiver that become the source information for the Call Identification Line. These parameters define the document sender's terminal identification, the date and time of call origination, and an optional session identification to uniquely define each session. Session identification is used for session linkage if a document is prematurely terminated and then continued in a later session. Session connection may also include a negotiation between sender and receiver for optional terminal capabilities (e.g., line spacing), for session capabilities (e.g., number of pages, or checkpoints, that may be transmitted without waiting for a checkpoint response), and for optional private facilities. Document transfer direction control permits document transmission from the called terminal to the calling terminal. Session termination includes both normal and abnormal indications.

Document Interchange Protocol

The presentation layer in the teleservice protocol architecture consists of two sublayers. The upper sublayer specifies the encoding rules for teletex and facsimile document; we have already examined these recommendations. The lower sublayer is an additional presentation-layer capability known as the document interchange protocol.

The document interchange protocol is designed to support the transmission of structured documents, such as produced by mixed-mode terminals. Teletex terminals support the creation, transmission, reproduction, and revision of only character-coded documents. Facsimile terminals allow for the the interchange and reproduction of bit-mapped dot images of documents. However, a document may consist of a mixture of text and images such as logos, signatures, drawings, and photographs. A mixed-mode terminal is one which supports both types of encoding.

The question arises as to why not simply treat a mixed-mode document in facsimile mode. After all, even a document that is nothing but text can be encoded in facsimile mode for transmission and reproduction. There are two motivations for providing a mixed mode capability:

- *Transmission efficiency:* The number of bits required to encode text in teletex form is significantly less than the number of bits required to encode the same amount of text in facsimile form, even if facsimile compression algorithms are used.
- *Document processing:* If the text portion of the document is encoded in teletex mode, then it is possible to use word processing and editing techniques to revise the document.

Figure 6-8 shows the position of the document interchange protocol in the teleservice protocol architecture. The protocol is bypassed for the basic teletex service, avoiding unnecessary processing. Basic Group 4 facsimile uses a very simple form of the protocol without any structuring within a facsimile page, again to avoid unnecessary processing. For mixed-mode documents, the document interchange protocol provides a means for defining the structure of the document and for transmitting the structure and content of the document.

Document Structure. The contents of a document need to be separated into various portions in order to:

- delimit presentation objects, such as pages, to guide the printing or display function;
- delimit logical objects, such as paragraphs and footnotes, to improve reproccessing possibilities;
- use different types of encoding (e.g., 8-bit character code versus MR facsimile code);
- allow processing after communication (e.g., word processing versus bit-map image processing).

To meet these requirements, the document interchange protocol defines a document structure. Actually, there are two structures, each of which is in the form of a tree, and which provide two different but corresponding views upon the content of the document. The layout structure defines the document in terms of layout

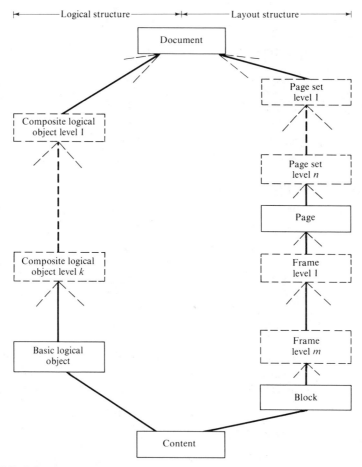

FIGURE 6-9 Document Architecture Model

objects, for their positioning and rendition on the presentation medium. The logical structure defines the document in terms of logical objects serving specific purposes, such as sections, headings, paragraphs, footnotes, and figures. The two structures each define the way in which the contents of the document are organized (Figure 6-9). Some of the key terms used in the document structure definition are listed in Box 6-3.

The **logical structure** mirrors the logical organization of a document. By defining specific elements, such as headers, footnotes, paragraphs, sections, etc., the transmitted document can be manipulated by word processing and image processing software in a sophisticated fashion. This logical order is primarily hierarchical and sequential. A hierarchical order, for example, could consist of sections and subsections, with each subsection consisting of paragraphs, illustrations, footnotes, and so on. In the current version of the document interchange protocol, a structure of zero

BOX 6-3

DOCUMENT INTERCHANGE PROTOCOL TERMS

DOCUMENT

An amount of text that can be interchanged as a unit defined by the originator between applications.

DOCUMENT PROFILE

A set of attributes associated with a document, for the purpose of handling the document as a whole.

CONTENT

The actual information conveyed by the document, independent of layout structure and logical structure.

GRAPHIC ELEMENT

A character, other than a control function, that has a visual representation normally handwritten, printed, or displayed. Graphic characters include simple alphanumeric characters, composite characters (e.g., accented letters), and pictorial characters (e.g., mosaics).

LAYOUT STRUCTURE

The result of dividing and subdividing the content of a document into increasingly smaller parts, on the basis of the presentation, e.g., into pages and blocks.

LOGICAL STRUCTURE

The result of dividing and subdividing the content of a document into increasingly smaller parts, on the basis of the meaning of the content, e.g., chapter, section, paragraph.

DESCRIPTOR

A data element representing a layout object or a logical object.

PAGE

A layout object that is a rectangular area with dimensions equal to the associated interchanged image area.

PAGE SET

A composite layout object corresponding to a sequence of other page sets and/or pages.

BLOCK

A basic layout object corresponding to a rectangular area within a page or within a frame with its sides parallel to the sides of the enclosing page or frame, in which only one category of graphic element is to be imaged.

FRAME

A composite layout object within a page or within another frame with its sides parallel to the sides of the enclosing page or frame, intermediate at one or more levels between the page and the block in a layout structure.

MIXED MODE

A mixed mode capability provides the means of transferring the information content of a document between sender and recipient, where the information content has been encoded using different techniques (e.g., in all forms of facsimile or character coding) and the document structure fully identified enabling the recipient to apply sophisticated editing methods.

or more levels of *composite logical* objects is defined. If there are one or more levels, then a document consists of one or more composite logical objects at the highest level (level 1). At each level, a composite logical object at that level consists of one or more composite logical objects at the next lowest level. This continues until we reach a level of *basic logical objects*, which are objects that are not subdivided and which contain only one category of content (teletex or facsimile). At present, no further details about logical structure are included in the standard; it is an area for further study.

Before a document can be printed or displayed, its **layout structure** must be defined. The graphic elements of the content associated with the logical objects must be arranged within certain layout areas that represent the layout objects. During printing or display, these areas are then mapped onto a physical presentation medium. The layout structure is also a tree structure. In the layout structure, a document is considered to consist of one or more *pages*. If there is more than one page, then the pages are grouped into one or more *page sets*. Individual pages may have different layouts (e.g., title page versus body pages), and a page set may share some common attributes. For example, each page set may represent a chapter, and the headings of each chapter are different (as in this book). Each page consists of one or more *blocks*, each of which contains one category of graphic element. The dimensions and position of each block are specified. In addition, the blocks may be organized into one or more levels of *frames*, which are also characterized by dimensions and position. The difference between a frame and a block is that the latter may not contain subordinate elements but must consist of text or a facsimile image.

Within a page, frames and blocks may be positioned in such a way that they intersect partially or fully. When blocks overlap, the overlap may be either transparent or opaque. In the latter case, the order of overlap must be specified to determine which block is "on top."

In addition to organizing a document into a tree structure, each element in the structure has associated attributes. The attributes plus the structure define the document. In general, we can categorize the attributes of layout objects as follows:

- *Identification attributes*: specifying the type of object (page, block, etc.) and identifying the individual object.
- *Structure attributes*: specifying the hierarchical relationship between objects and the correspondence between layout objects and content portions.
- *Positioning attributes*: specifying the dimensions and positions of objects and overlay characteristics.
- *Presentation attributes*: specifying how the content of the object is to be imaged, e.g., character spacing, line spacing, resolution.

Table 6-12 lists the attributes of layout objects and the additional attributes of blocks. In some cases, an attribute has one or more default values, and these are indicated. The term BMU that appears in the table stands for Basic Measurement Unit. This is based on the resolution of the output medium; typically, one BMU corresponds to one pel.

Document Interchange Format. The document interchange protocol provides a structure for characterizing a document. This may be viewed as an abstract representation of the document. To transmit a document, the contents, structure, and associated attributes must be encoded into a format that is recognized by both parties. In T.73, this is referred to as the document interchange format. The document interchange format consists of a sequence of protocol elements. Protocol elements of three types are distinguished: document profile descriptor, layout descriptor, and text unit.

The **document profile descriptor** includes information relating to the document as a whole. The descriptor consists of a number of protocol elements, including an identification of the entire document, presentation capabilities (such as required terminal type: teletex, Group 4 facsimile, mixed mode), and related information such as author and date of creation. Following the document profile descriptor is a series of **layout descriptors,** each of which consists of one or more protocol elements. A layout descriptor represents a layout object and contains the values of its associated attributes, including attributes that indicate the place of this object in the

TABLE 6-12   ATTRIBUTES OF LAYOUT OBJECTS

(a) Blocks

Content Type	D *(character box)*
Attributes of character box content type	
Character path	D (0°)
Line progression	D (270°)
Character box orientation	D (0°)
Character box size	D (24.40 BMU as in S.61)
Character baseline offset	D (14 BMU, S.61)
Character spacing	D (24 BMU, S.61)
Line spacing	D (40 BMU)
Alignment	D (left aligned)
Line layout	not yet defined
Initial offset	D (0.26 BMU)
Graphic rendition	D (as in S.61)
Attributes of photographic content type	
Pel path	D (0°)
Line progression	D (270°)
Resolution	D (1 pel/BMU)
Initial offset	D (0.0 BMU)

(b) Layout Objects and Content Portions

Layout Objects	
Object type	M
Object identifier	O
Reference is corresponding generic object	M
References to subordinate objects	O
References to content portions	O
User-readable comments	O
Default value lists	O
Position	D (0.0 BMU)
Dimensions	D (page dimens.)
Overlay characteristics	D (transparent)
Presentation attributes	
Content portions	
Content portion identifier	O
Type of coding	D (S.61, T.b)
Number of pels per line	D
Compression	D (as in T.b)
Alternative graphic renditions	O

D defaultable	M mandatory
( ) standard default value	O optional

layout structure. Finally, there is a **text unit** for each content portion (content of a block). Each text unit contains protocol elements containing the values of the associated attributes, as well as one or more protocol elements that contain the actual contents to be transmitted for storage, printing and/or display.

To transmit this sequence of protocol elements, each element must be encoded according to the formating rules in T.73. Each elementary protocol unit is encoded as three components: the identifier, the length, and the contents. The identifier is the name of the element, which designates the data type and governs the interpretation of the contents. The length specifies the length of the contents in octets. The contents, of course, is the actual value of the protocol element.

Thus, to transmit a document using the document interchange protocol, it is first necessary to describe both the structure and content of the document, together with associated attributes. The document's content, structure, and attributes, are then represented by a series of protocol elements. Finally, each protocol element is encoded following the rules of the document interchange format. The transmitted document can now be properly interpreted by the recipient.

6-5   MESSAGE HANDLING SYSTEMS

The final teleservice that we will examine in this chapter is referred to by CCITT as a message handling system. It is essentially an electronic mail capability. Although teletex illustrates some of the aspects of an electronic mail system, it does not provide the full range of functions and services usually associated with electronic mail. In many cases, the teletex service will prove adequate. However, in other cases, a more complete electronic mail system is required. We begin this section with a discussion of electronic mail in general. We then look at the CCITT standards in this area.

Electronic Mail

One of the deadliest wasters of time in the office is a phenomenon known as "telephone tag." Mr. X calls Ms. Y, who is away from her desk. Some time later Y returns the call but X is out or on another line. X is now "it" and must return Y's return to X's call. And so on. . . . Independent studies have shown that over 70 percent of all business telephone calls do not reach the intended recipient on the first try [MAR179]. The problem is that the caller and callee must both be at their phones and available to answer at the same time. If the caller could simply write a note and leave it on the callee's desk, the problem could be avoided. Electronic mail provides a way to do this.

Electronic mail addresses another problem as well: the office paper explosion. Offices generate a tremendous amount of paperwork, most of it in the form of internal memos and reports: over 80 percent of all business documents are textual and/or numeric (no graphics) and originate and remain within the same organization [POTT77].

Electronic mail, also known as a computer-based message system (CBMS), is a facility that allows users at terminals to compose and exchange messages. The messages need never exist on paper unless the user (sender or recipient) desires a paper copy of the message. Some electronic mail systems serve only users on a single computer; others provide service across a network of computers. In this section, we briefly look at the functionality of single-system electronic mail, then turn our attention to the more interesting (for this book) case of network electronic mail. Finally, the CCITT X.400 family of standards is described.

Single-System Electronic Mail. The simplest, and by far the most common, form of electronic mail is the single-system facility. This facility allows all the users of a shared computer system to exchange messages. Each user is registered on the system and has a unique identifier, usually the person's last name. Associated with each user is a mailbox. The electronic mail facility is an application program available to any user logged on to the system. A user may invoke the electronic mail facility, prepare a message, and "send" it to any other user on the system. The act of sending simply involves putting the message in the recipient's mailbox. The mailbox is actually an entity maintained by the file management system, and is in the nature of a file directory. One mailbox is associated with each user. Any "incoming" mail is simply stored as a file under that user's mailbox directory. The user may later go and fetch that file to read the message. The user reads messages by invoking the mail facility and "reading" rather than "sending." In most systems, when the user logs on, he or she is informed if there is any new mail in that user's mailbox.

A basic electronic mail system performs four functions:

- *Creation:* A user creates and edits a message, generally using a rudimentary editing capability. Most systems also allow the user to create a message using the system editor or a word processor, and then incorporate the resulting file as the body of the message.
- *Sending:* The user designates the recipient (or recipients) of the message, and the facility stores the message in the appropriate mailbox(es).
- *Reception:* The intended recipient may invoke the electronic mail facility to access and read the delivered mail.
- *Storage:* Both sender and recipient may choose to save the message in a file for more permanent storage.

Because we are interested in the networking aspects of electronic mail, the topic of basic user services will not be further pursued here. More detail can be found in [HIRS85] and [BARC81].

Network Electronic Mail. With a single-system electronic mail facility, messages can only be exchanged among users of that particular system. Clearly, this is too limited. In a distributed environment, we would like to be able to exchange messages with users attached to other systems. Thus, we would like to treat electronic mail as an application-layer protocol that makes use of lower-layer protocols to transmit messages.

Figure 6-10 suggests the internal system architecture required. Let us refer to a single-system mail facility as a *native mail* facility. For native mail, three major modules are needed. Users will interact with native mail via terminals; hence, terminal-handling software is needed. Mail is stored as files in the file system, so file-handling software is needed. Finally, there must be a native mail package that contains all the logic for providing mail-related serives to users.

To extend this system to *network mail*, two more modules are needed. Since we are going to communicate across some sort of network or transmission system, communication I/O logic is needed; in the most general case, this would encompass layers 1 through 6 of the OSI model. Mail transfer logic is also needed, that knows how to invoke the communications function, to specify the network address of the recipient, and to request whatever communication services are needed (e.g., priority). Note in the figure that the user does not directly interact with the mail transfer module. Ideally, the user interface for local and remote mail should be the same. If the user designates a local recipient, the message is stored in a local mailbox. If a remote recipient is designated, the native mail module passes the message to the mail transfer module for transmission across the network. Incoming mail from the network is routed to the appropriate mailbox and henceforth treated the same as other messages in the mailbox.

Many vendors now offer a network version of their basic electronic mail facility. However, this will only allow the user to send mail to users on systems of the same vendor. As in other areas, standards are needed. It is to these standards that we now turn our attention.

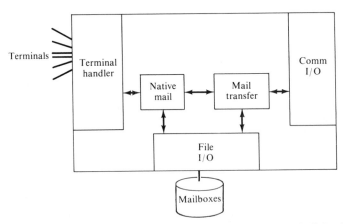

FIGURE 6-10 Conceptual Structure of an Electronic Mail System

The CCITT X.400 Family of Standards

In 1984, CCITT issued a family of standards for Message Handling Systems (MHS) that encompass the requirements of what we have referred to as network electronic mail. The standards do not deal with the user interface or the services available directly to the user (what we have referred to as native mail). They do, however, specify what services are available for use in sending messages across the network and thus provide the base for building the user interface.

Table 6-13 lists the eight recommendations that comprise the X.400 family. Most of the standards deal with, in OSI terms, the application layer. The only exception is X.409, which is a presentation-layer service [POPE84]. All of the recommendations fit into the framework of an MHS model, which is described in X.400. We describe that model first, and then look at some of the key aspects of the specifications of services and protocols.

TABLE 6-13   THE CCITT X.400 FAMILY OF STANDARDS FOR MESSAGE HANDLING SYSTEMS

Number	Title	Description
X.400	System model-service elements	Defines the message handling system model consisting of user agents and message transfer agents, discusses naming and addressing, defines interpersonal messaging and message transfer services, and discusses protocol layering
X.401	Basic service elements and optional user facilities	Divides services into required; essential optional; and additional optional
X.408	Encoded information type conversion rules	Specifies the rules for converting from one type of encoded information to another; examples: IA5 (ASCII), telex, teletex, videotex, Group 3 Facsimile
X.409	Presentation transfer syntax and notation	Defines a binary encoding scheme and an associated notation for data structures used in transferring messages
X.410	Remote operations and reliable transfer server	Defines how remote terminals interact with a MHS network and defines how MHS protocols use the session layer
X.411	Message transfer layer	Specifies protocols at the Message Transfer Sublayer
X.420	Interpersonal messaging user agent layer	Specifies the protocol for the Interpersonal Messaging Sublayer and specifies the format for memo headers and multipart body types
X.430	Access protocol for teletex terminals	Specifies the access protocol required to support teletex terminals.

Message Handling System Model. The message handling system model is defined in X.400. This model provides a framework for all of the other recommendations, and is illustrated in Figure 6-11. The model defines two types of entities: *user agent* (UA) and *message transfer agent* (MTA). The user agent operates on behalf of a user. It interacts directly with the user, performs functions for preparing messages and submitting messages for routing to the destination(s). In the process, the source UA interacts with destination UAs, which perform the delivery function. The UAs also assist the user in dealing with other message functions, such as filing, replying, retrieving, and forwarding. The UA submits messages to an MTA for transmission across the network. The X.400 series specifies the interaction of the UA with MTA and other UA entities, but does not specify the interaction between the UA and its user.

The message transfer agent (MTA) accepts messages from UAs for delivery to other UAs. Sometimes, the MTA that accepts submission of a message also performs delivery. In other cases, it is necessary for the MTA to route the message, and the message is relayed through a series of MTAs to the destination. For example, if only some MTAs have access to the proper long-distance communications paths, a message addressed to a distant UA might be relayed in several stages. Using relays also eliminates the need to have all UAs and MTAs available on a 24-hour basis. This store-and-forward action makes it feasible to treat electronic mail components like any other office equipment that gets turned off at night.

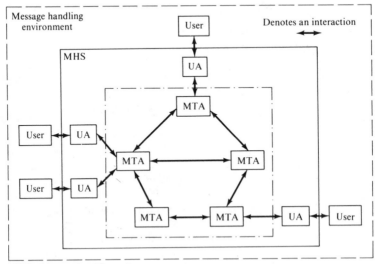

MHS = Message handling system
MTS = Message transfer system
MTA = Message transfer agent
UA = User agent

FIGURE 6-11 Functional View of X.400 Model

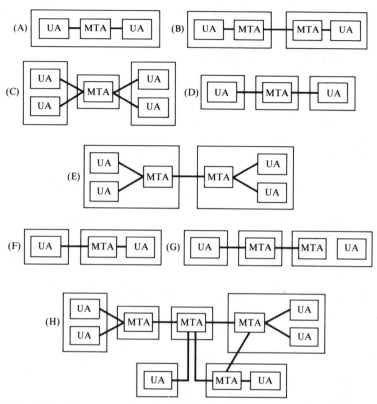

FIGURE 6-12 Example Physical Realizations of an Electronic Mail System

A message handling system consisting of UAs and MTAs can be physically organized in a number of ways. Figure 6-12 and the following discussion, which are based on [DEUT86], suggest several possibilities.

The UA and MTA functions may be implemented on a single system (example A). This is just the single-system electronic mail facility described above. Example B illustrates an electronic mail facility for a collection of single-user personal computers or workstations, which might be connected with a local area network. Each workstation has sufficient processing power to implement both UA and MTA functions, and sufficient storage to temporarily buffer incoming and outgoing messages.

In both examples C and D, the end-user systems include only the UA function, and these systems are all connected through a central system that acts as a switch for routing messages between end-user systems. In the case of C, shared minicomputers could be used as end-user systems, while in the case of D, the end-user systems would be personal computers. In both cases, a server system exists; the connection to the server could either be across a local network or by means of point-to-point links in a star topology. These architectures are very modular and flexible. The architecture can be expanded by adding more end-user systems and more servers as needed. This approach could be used to provide a distributed, private electronic mail facility for a corporation.

Example E illustrates the growth of a facility based on systems of the type shown in example A. This architecture could be used in the case of a network of fairly large systems, such as super-minicomputers and mainframes. An organization may have one of each at several dispersed locations, and use this architecture for tying together the electronic mail facilities provided by each system. An alternative to E is, of course, to stick with architecture A: have one very large central system and tie terminal users into it from remote locations. However, placing a system near each concentration of users would likely reduce communications costs.

Examples F through H show some heterogeneous architectures. The advantage of a heterogeneous approach is that an electronic mail facility can be designed to meet the requirements of different user populations operating on a diverse hardware base. As long as the common UA and MTA services are specified and the interactions between modules are standardized, such architectures are feasible.

Finally, we should note that the connections among separate systems can be any form of communications facility, including point-to-point links and the various kinds of communications networks.

The X.400 Protocol Architecture. As was mentioned, the message-handling facility defined in the X.400 series is primarily an application-layer service. As such, it must rely on lower-layer entities to provide a complete communications capability. The architecture which incorporates the X.400 services is illustrated in Figure 6-13.

The application-layer functionality is divided into two sublayers: a user application sublayer, that provides interpersonal messaging services, and a message transfer sublayer. The user application sublayer contains user application entities (UAEs). A UAE is simply the embodiment of the protocol-related functions of a single UA. UAEs cooperate to provide the services of the user application sublayer, known as interpersonal messaging services. An example of a service at this sublayer is receipt notification, in which a message's originator is notified after a particular recipient has read the message.

The protocol that is used for interaction between UAEs is known as the P2 protocol (Table 6-14). Two types of protocol data units (PDUs) are defined: those that convey a user message, and those that convey status reports. In the former case, the protocol data unit consists of the user message plus a header, known as the *heading*. The heading contains the following fields:

- Message ID
- Originator
- Authorizing Users

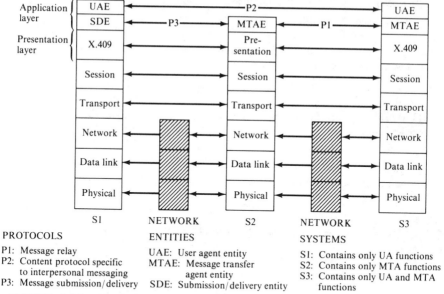

FIGURE 6-13 X.400 Protocol Architecture

- Primary Recipients
- Copy Recipients
- Blind Copy Recipients
- In-Reply-To Reference
- Obsoletes Reference
- Cross References
- Subject
- Expiration Date
- Reply By
- Reply to Users
- Importance
- Sensitivity
- Autoforwarded

Some of these fields are self-explanatory; others will be explained in the context of services, below.

The status report PDUs contain no user information, just a header with the following fields:

- Receipt or Nonreceipt Information
- User PDU Message ID
- Actual Recipient

TABLE 6-14   PROTOCOLS DEFINED WITHIN X.400

Message Transfer Protocol (P1) — X.411

P1 provides for relaying of messages and other interactions between the various message transfer agent entities (MTAEs). It thus serves as the backbone switching protocol. Protocol elements are termed message protocol data units (MPDUs).

Submission and Delivery Protocol (P3) — X.411

P3 enables a user agent (UA) that is remote from its message transfer agent (MTA) to obtain access to the message transfer layer services. In effect, P3 is a remote procedure call protocol. Protocol elements are termed operations protocol data units (OPDUs).

Interpersonal Messaging Protocol (P2) — X.420

P2 provides the interactions between the user agent entities for exchanging messages. Protocol elements are termed user agent protocol data units.

Teletex Access Protocol (P5) — X.430

P5 defines the communications for teletex terminal access to the message handling system.

- Intended Recipient
- Code Conversion Indication

The message transfer sublayer of the X.400 application layer contains two kinds of entities: message transfer agent entities (MTAEs) and submission/delivery entities (SDEs). An MTAE embodies the protocol-related functions of a single MTA. MTAEs cooperate to provide the services of the message transfer sublayer. An example of a service at this sublayer is delivery notification, in which a message's originator is notified after a message has been successfully delivered to a particular recipient's UA.

The protocol that is used for interaction between MTAEs is known as the P1 protocol. This protocol is used to transfer a message from the originator's MTAE to the recipient's MTAE through zero or more intermediate MTAEs. The protocol is also used, if the service has been requested, for transferring a notification of delivery or nondelivery back to the originator's MTAE. Of course, if the originator and recipient share the same MTAE (Figure 6-12a,c,d,f), then this protocol is not needed.

Three types of protocol data units are defined: user, delivery report, and probe. The user PDU consists of the user agent sublayer PDU plus a header, known as the *envelope* (Figure 6-14). The envelope contains the information needed for handling the message, including a network name for the recipient that will allow routing, a unique identifier, and information on how to process the PDU, such as the priority and whether a delivery report is required. The delivery report includes a header that consists of a unique identifier, the name of the originator that submitted the message to which this report refers, and trace information, which indicates the route that the delivery report followed. The body of the delivery report PDU includes the identifier

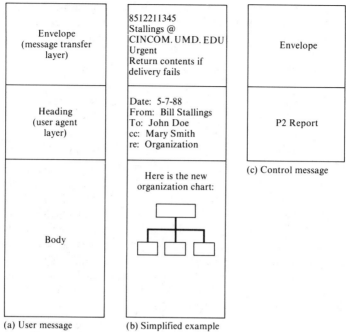

FIGURE 6-14 X.400 Message Structure

of the original user PDU plus information about the delivery. This may include such items as the trace of the original user PDU, billing information, and, of course, whether delivery was successful.

The probe PDU is similar to the envelope portion of a user PDU. Its purpose is to determine if a particular delivery is possible without actually sending a user message. Delivery reports will be returned on probe PDUs.

An MTAE is present in a system that only includes the MTA function. As such, it acts solely as a relay. An MTAE may also be present in a system that includes a UA, in which case the interaction between the UA and the MTA is beyond the scope of the standard; it is to be implemented to satisfy the objectives (e.g., cost, performance) associated with that system. However, as we have seen (Figure 6-12), there are systems that include the UA function but not the MTA function. In this case, we need a protocol that allows the UAE to remotely invoke the services of its MTAE. This protocol, P3, is in effect a remote procedure call protocol, and the entities that engage in this protocol are the MTAE and the submission/delivery entity (SDE). The latter makes the services of the message transfer sublayer available to its UAE. When a UAE requests a message transfer sublayer service, the SDE passes the request primitive and its parameters to the MTAE in the form of a PDU that contains a code for the primitive and a list of the parameters. Similarly, the MTAE uses a P3 PDU to pass an indication primitive and its parameters to the UAE via the SDE.

X.400 Services.   As with most communications standards, the X.400 series specifies not only protocols but the services to be provided to users. In this case the users are either terminal users who invoke electronic mail facilities, or application programs that exchange messages. Corresponding to the two protocol sublayers discussed above, the services are grouped into message transfer services and interpersonal messaging services.

For both sets of services, the services are divided into three categories: basic, essential optional, and additional optional. *Basic* services are inherent in the message-handling system and must be implemented. The remaining services are known as optional user facilities which may be invoked at the option of the user, in some cases on a per-message basis and in others for an agreed contractual period. *Essential optional user facilities* must be offered by the service provider; that is, the provider must offer the option, but it is up to the user to select or not select the option. Finally, *additional optional user facilities* may or may not be offered by the provider.

Table 6-15 lists the services provided by the message transfer sublayer. The layer attempts to deliver messages to one or more intended recipients, and can be asked to notify the originator's UAE of the success or failure of each attempt. This layer may also invoke presentation-layer transformations on behalf of the user agent sublayer. The originator may request that delivery take place no earlier than a specified time. The recipient may request that a message be temporarily held in the system prior to delivery. In addition, the originator may designate a message as urgent.

Interpersonal messaging services are provided at the user-agent sublayer, and listed in Table 6-16. In this case, optional services receive two designations, one for origination and one for reception. Note that many of the services that are additional (need not be offered) for origination are essential for reception. For example, UAs are not required to allow a user to mark a message as private, but must be able to appropriately handle a received message marked private. There are many services at this sublayer. Among the most fundamental are specification of primary and secondary recipients and the subject of the message. Other services have to do with how to handle the message and instructions for notification.

6-6   SUMMARY

The requirements that guide the design and implementation of ISDN can be expressed in terms of telecommunications services. These services are the reason for the existence of ISDN or any network. Thus it is important to be clear about what services are to be provided and, in detail, what characteristics and attributes that the user expects to have associated with these services. Once this is known, the network capabilities needed to support the services can be determined.

CCITT has specified these services as part of the I-series of recommendations. Two types of services are defined: bearer services and teleservices. Bearer services are the lower-level functions responsible for transferring data between subscribers

TABLE 6-15 MESSAGE TRANSFER LAYER SERVICES (X.401)

Basic Services

Access management	Enables UA to submit and have messages delivered to it
Content type indication	Specified by originating UA
Converted indication	Specifies any conversions performed on message being delivered
Submission/delivery time stamp	Submission and delivery time are supplied with each message
Message identification	Unique identifier for each message
Nondelivery notification	Message cannot be delivered
Registered encoded information types	Allows UA to specify types that can be delivered to it
Original encoded information types	Specified by submitting UA and supplied to receiving UA

Essential Optional Services

Alternate recipient allowed	Deliver to alternate if designated recipient cannot be found
Deferred delivery	Deliver no sooner than specified date and time
Deferred delivery cancellation	Abort delivery of deferred message
Delivery notification	Notify originator of successful delivery
Disclosure of other recipients	Disclose list of recipients to recipient
Grade of delivery selection	Request urgent, normal, or nonurgent
Multidestination delivery	Specify more than one recipient
Conversion prohibition	Prevents MTS from conversion
Probe	Determines if a message could be deliverable

Additional Optional Services

Prevention of nondelivery notification	Suppress potential nondelivery notice
Return of contents	Return message contents if nondelivery
Explicit conversion	Specifies particular conversion
Implicit conversion	Perform necessary conversion on all messages without explicit instruction
Alternate recipient assignment	Requests designation of requesting UA as alternate recipient
Hold for delivery	Requests that messages intended for this UA be held in MTS until later time

across ISDN. These services correspond to layers 1 through 3 of the OSI model. CCITT has defined these services quite explicitly. Teleservices are the actual user-visible services that are supported across ISDN. These services correspond to

TABLE 6-16   INTERPERSONAL MESSAGING SERVICES (X.401)

Basic Services

IP-message identification	Assign reference identifier to each message content sent or received
Typed body	Allows nature and attributes of message body to be conveyed along with body.

Essential Optional Services
(for both origination and reception)

Originator indication	Identifies the user that sent message
Primary and copy recipients indication	Allows UA to specify primary and secondary recipients
Replying IP-message indication	Specifies an earlier message to which this is a reply
Subject indication	Description of message

Additional (for origination) and
Essential (for reception) Optional
Services

Blind copy recipient indication	List of recipients whose identities are not to be disclosed to primary or copy recipients
Autoforwarded indication	Marks a message as containing an automatically-forwarded message
Authorizing users indication	Indicates one or more persons who authorized the message
Expiry date indication	Conveys a date and time after which the originator considers the message invalid
Cross-referencing indication	Specifies one or more other messages related to this one
Importance indication	Specifies low, normal, or high
Obsoleting indication	Specifies previous messages that are obsolete and superseded by this one
Sensitivity indication	Specifies personal, private, or company-confidential
Reply request indication	Asks for response; may also specify date and time and other recipients
Forwarded IP-message indication	Marks a message as containing a forwarded message
Body part encryption indication	Body part of message is encrypted
Multipart body	Enables sending message with multiple parts, each with its own attributes

Additional Optional Services
(for both orignation and reception)

Nonreceipt notification	Requests that originator be informed if message is not received by its intended recipient
Receipt notification	Requests that originator be notified of receipt of message by intended recipient

layers 4 through 7 of the OSI model and make use of the bearer services. Strictly speaking, the protocols that are part of the teleservices are not part of and are not visible to a communications network, including ISDN. However, there are several reasons for addressing teleservices in the context of ISDN. First, both teleservices and bearer services make use of a common set of supplementary services (e.g., reverse charging), and a uniform means of specifying and invoking those services is useful. Second, the nature of a teleservice will determine the nature of the bearer service used, and standards on the interrelationships are useful.

In addition to a general description of teleservices, this chapter reviews three of the most important teleservices. *Teletex* is a message preparation and delivery service that is an upgrade to *telex*. *Group 4 facsimile* is a digital facsimile service that provides high-speed image transfer using sophisticated image compression techniques. CCITT has also standardized mixed-mode terminals that can prepare and display/print images consisting of both text and images. To assist in the efficient transmission and in the processing of such documents, the document interchange protocol has been developed. This protocol allows the definition of the structure and attributes of a mixed-mode document. Finally, the X.400 standards on *message handling systems* define a sophisticated electronic mail facility.

6-7 RECOMMENDED READING

[KAHL86] is a review of CCITT standards on ISDN service capabilities (I.200 series). The subject is also addressed in [RUTK85].

[KOBA85] is a good survey of facsimile technology and CCITT standardization of it. [RYAN87] is also a good discussion, with an emphasis on CCITT-compliant products. Good discussions of MH and MR compression techniques are provided in [JAYA84] and [NETR88]. [BODS86] looks at the throughput of Group 4 facsimile over ISDN and packet-switched networks. The teletex standard is presented in [HELM82] and [MOOR83]; a discussion can also be found in [BLAC87]. The document interchange protocol is discussed in [NEME85], [HORA85], and [HORA84].

An excellent survey of the X.400 standards is [DEUT86]. Other worthwhile articles are [CUNN84] and [CUNN85]. [SCHU87] discusses implementation issues relating to X.400. A discussion of X.409 can be found in [STAL87b].

6-8 PROBLEMS

6-1   In the United States, there has been considerable thought given to the types of telecommunication services that should be subject to government regulation of price and quality, and those that should be offered competitively with little or no regulation. Two important efforts in this regard are the Computer Inquiry II by the Federal Communications Commission (FCC) and the

Modification of Final Judgement (MFJ) which resulted in the break-up of AT&T. In Computer Inquiry II, the FCC defined the following terms:

Basic Service   limited to the common carrier offering of transmisison capacity for the movement of information.

Enhanced Service   any offering over the telecommunications network which is more than a basic transmission service. Such services employ computer processing applications that act on the format, content, code, protocol or similar aspects of the subscriber's transmitted information; provide the subscriber additional, different , or restructured information; or involve subscriber interaction with stored information.

The MFJ produced the following definitions:

Telecommunication Service   the transmissions, between or among points specified by the user, of information of the user's choosing, without change in the form or content of the information as seen and received, by means of electromagnetic transmission, with or without benefit of any closed transmission medium, including all instrumentalities, facilities, apparatus, and services (including the collection, storage, forwarding, switching, and delivery of such information) essential to such transmission.

Information Service   a capability for generating, acquiring, storing, transforming, processing, retrieving, utilizing, or making available information which may be conveyed via telecommunications, except that such service does not include any use of such capability for the management, control, or operation of a telecommunciations system or the management of a telecommunications service.

Compare these two pairs of definitions with these definitions from I.112:

Bearer Service   a type of telecommunication service that provides the capability for the transmission of signals between user-network interfaces.

Teleservice   a type of telecommunication service that provides the complete capability, including terminal equipment functions, for communication between users according to protocols established by agreement between Administrations and/or RPOAs.

6-2   Consider Figure 6-3. With the Group 4 recommendation, the compressor/ decompressor and communication interface modules are standardized. Do you think that the preprocessor/postprocessor modules are also standardized? Justify your answer.

6-3   Consider a binary source that produces symbols x1 and x2 with probabilities 0.8 and 0.2 respectively.

a. What is the entropy H?

b. A simple binary code will produce an output of 1 bit per symbol, which is considerably above the entropy. A rate closer to H can be achieved by a combination of encoding delay and variable-length encoding. We look at all possible source sequences of length 2, and assign codewords to each of the four sequences. Show the Huffman code for this scheme and compute the average codeword length.

6-4   Consider a source with four symbols whose probabilites of occurrence are 0.5, 0.25, 0.125, and 0.125.

a. What is the entropy H?

b. Develop the Huffman code. What is the average codeword length?

6-5   Consider a high-resolution facsimile document of 2376×1728 two-level pels.

a. Without data compression, how long will it take to transmit this page over a 4800-bps line?

b. To transmit the message over a 4800-bps line in one minute, what compression ratio is required?

6-6   Suppose the document of Problem 6-5 is encoded using MR, achieving a compression ratio of 10 pels/bit. Assume that transmission errors do not propagate beyond one horizontal line. If there is to be no more than 1 degraded line per document on the average, what (approximately) is the acceptable value for the probability of a random bit error?

6-7   Suppose that a document has 150×200 mm of text with 0.5 char/mm and 0.24 lines of text per mm (not to be confused with scanning lines). Assume digitization of 400×400 pels per mm. If the document is transmitted as text, 8-bit teletex characters are used. Ignoring protocol overhead, compare the message transmission time of teletex, uncompressed facsimile, and facsimile compressed at a ratio of 10 pels/bit over a 64-kbps ISDN line.

6-8   Consider a document with the following logical structure: The document consists of one section; the section consists of three paragraphs of text. The same document has the following layout structure: The document consists of two pages. Each page contains two blocks of text. The second paragraph is split across a page boundary. Draw the combined logical and layout structure for this document. Hint: Show the logical structure with the root at the top, and the layout structure with the root at the bottom, and join the two trees with a common content portion.

6-9   It is clear from Figure 6-13 that there is not an end-to-end transport connection between the originator and recipient of a message. Why not?

6-10   Protocol P1 provides that a message envelope and its contents be transmitted from one MTAE to another. The standard specifies that the message envelope and the message content be transmitted as a single P1 PDU. Several other mechanisms are possible. The sending MTAE could transmit the message envelope first, wait for approval from the second MTAE, and then transmit the message content. A third method is to transmit the message envelope first, one parameter at at time, waiting for a positive acknowledgment after each parameter. For example, the recipient list might be transmitted first, then handling instructions, and so on. Discuss the relative advantages and disadvantages of each method.

6-11   Electronic mail systems differ in the manner in which multiple recipients are handled. In some systems, the originating UA or MTA makes all the necessary copies and these are sent out independently. An alternative approach is to determine the route for each destination first. Then a single message is sent out on a common portion of the route and copies are only made when the routes diverge; this process is referred to as *mail-bagging*. Discuss the relative advantages and disadvantages of the two methods.

CHAPTER 7
ISDN ARCHITECTURE

This chapter looks at a variety of issues related to ISDN architecture as seen by the user. On the whole, the user need not be concerned with the internal functioning or mechanisms of an ISDN. However, the user is concerned with the nature of the interface and the way in which services are requested and provided. This is an area that is continuing to evolve as new services are developed and as agreements are reached concerning the nature of the interface. We can expect that by the time the 1992 version of the ISDN recommendations are issued, considerably greater detail will be available.

Four technical areas are examined in this chapter:

- *Transmission structure:* the way in which logical channels providing bearer services are organized for transmission over the local loop.
- *User-network interfaces:* the way in which user-ISDN interactions are organized functionally, and how this guides the actual equipment configuration and the definition of the user-ISDN interface.
- *Addressing:* the way in which a calling user specifies the called user so that the network can perform routing and delivery functions.
- *Interworking:* the capability for an ISDN subscriber to establish a connection to a subscriber on a non-ISDN network.

7-1 TRANSMISSION STRUCTURE

ISDN Channels

The digital pipe between the central office and the ISDN subscriber will be used to carry a number of communication channels. The capacity of the pipe, and therefore the number of channels carried may vary from user to user. The transmission structure of any access link will be constructed from the following types of channels:

- *B channel*: 64 kbps
- *D channel*: 16 or 64 kbps
- *H channel*: 384, 1536, or 1920 kbps

The **B channel** is a user channel that can be used to carry digital data, PCM-encoded digital voice, or a mixture of lower-rate traffic, including digital data and digitized voice encoded at a fraction of 64 kbps. In the case of mixed traffic, all traffic of the B channel must be destined for the same endpoint; that is, the elemental unit of circuit switching is the B channel. If a B channel consists of two or more subchannels, all subchannels must be carried over the same circuit between the same subscribers. Three kinds of connections can be set up over a B channel:

- *Circuit-switched*: this is equivalent to switched digital service, available today. The user places a call and a circuit-switched connection is established with another network user. An interesting feature is that the call establishment does not take place over the B channel, but is done using common-channel signaling.
- *Packet-switched*: the user is connected to a packet-switching node, and data are exchanged with other users via X.25.
- *Semipermanent*: this is a connection to another user set up by prior arrangement, and not requiring a call establishment protocol. This is equivalent to a leased line.

The designation of 64 kbps as the standard user channel rate highlights the fundamental disadvantage of standardization. The rate was chosen as the most effective for digitized voice, yet the technology has progressed to the point at which 32 kbps or even less will produce equally satisfactory voice reproduction. To be effective, a standard must freeze the technology at some defined point. Yet by the time the standard is approved, it may already be obsolete.

The **D channel** serves two main purposes. First, it carries common-channel signaling information to control circuit-switched calls on associated B channels at the user interface. In addition, the D channel may be used for packet-switching or low-speed (e.g., 100 bps) telemetry at times when no signaling information is waiting. Table 7-1 summarizes the types of data traffic to be supported on B and D channels.

H channels are provided for user information at higher bit rates. The user may use such a channel as a high-speed trunk or subdivide the channel according to the user's own TDM scheme. Examples of applications include fast facsimile, video, high-speed data, high-quality audio, and multiplexed information streams at lower data rates.

TABLE 7-1 ISDN CHANNEL FUNCTIONS

B Channel (64 kbps)	D Channel (16 kbps)
Digital voice	Signaling
64 kbps PCM	Basic
Low bit rate (32 kbps)	Enhanced
High-speed data	Low-speed data
Circuit-switched	Videotex
Packet-switched	Terminal
Other	Telemetry
Facsimile	Emergency services
Slow-scan video	Energy management

These channel types are grouped into transmission structures that are offered as a package to the user. The best-defined structures at this time (Figure 7-1) are the basic channel structure (basic access) and the primary channel structure (primary access).

Basic access consists of two full-duplex 64-kbps B channels and a full-duplex 16-kbps D channel. The total bit rate, by simple arithmetic, is 144 kbps. However, framing, synchronization, and other overhead bits bring the total bit rate on a basic access link to 192 kbps; the details of these overhead bits are presented in Chapter 8. The basic service is intended to meet the needs of most individual users, including residential subscribers and very small offices. It allows the simultaneous use of voice and several data applications, such as packet-switched access, a link to a central alarm service, facsimile, teletex, and so on. These services could be accessed through a single multifunction terminal or several separate terminals. In either case, a single physical interface is provided. Most existing two-wire local loops can support this interface [GIFF86].

In some cases, one or both of the B channels remain unused. This results in a $B + D$ or D interface, rather than the $2B + D$ interface. However, to simplify the network implementation, the data rate at the interface remains at 192 kbps. Never-

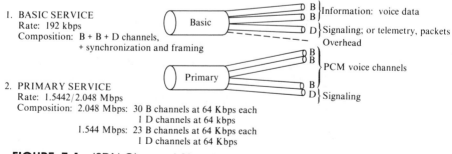

1. BASIC SERVICE
   Rate: 192 kbps
   Composition: B + B + D channels,
   + synchronization and framing

2. PRIMARY SERVICE
   Rate: 1.5442/2.048 Mbps
   Composition: 2.048 Mbps: 30 B channels at 64 Kbps each
   1 D channels at 64 kbps
   1.544 Mbps: 23 B channels at 64 Kbps each
   1 D channels at 64 Kbps

FIGURE 7-1 ISDN Channel Structures

theless, for those subscribers with more modest transmission requirements, there may be a cost savings in using a reduced basic interface.

Primary access is intended for users with greater capacity requirements, such as offices with a digital PBX or a LAN. Because of differences in the digital transmission hierarchies used in different countries, it was not possible to get agreement on a single data rate. The United States, Canada, and Japan make use of a transmission structure based on 1.544 Mbps; this corresponds to the T1 transmission facility of AT&T. In Europe, 2.048 Mbps is the standard rate. Both of these data rates are provided as a primary interface service. Typically, the channel structure for the 1.544-Mbps rate will be 23 B channels plus one 64-kbps D channel and, for the 2.048-Mbps rate, 30 B channels plus one 64-kbps D channel. Again, it is possible for a customer with lesser requirements to employ fewer B channels, in which case the channel structure is $nB + D$, where n ranges from 1 to 23 or from 1 to 30 for the two primary services. Also, a customer with high data rate demands may be provided with more than one primary physical interface. In this case, a single D channel on one of the interfaces may suffice for all signaling needs, and the other interfaces may consist solely of B channels ($24B$ or $31B$).

The primary interface may also be used to support H channels. Some of these structures include a 64-kbps D channel for control signaling. When no D channel is present, it is assumed that a D channel on another primary interface at the same subscriber location will provide any required signaling. The following structures are recognized:

- *Primary rate interface H0 channel structures*: This interface supports multiple 384-kbps H0 channels. The structures are $3H0 + D$ and $4H0$ for the 1.544-Mbps interface and $5H0 + D$ for the 2.048-Mbps interface.
- *Primary rate interface H1 channel structures*: The H11 channel structure consists of one 1536-kbps H11 channel. The H12 channel structure consists of one 1920-kbps H12 channel and one D channel.
- *Primary rate interface structures for mixtures of B and H0 channels*: Consists of zero or one D channels plus any possible combination of B and H0 channels up to the capacity of the physical interface (e.g., $3H0 + 5B + D$ and $3H0 + 6B$).

Rate Adaption and Multiplexing

The principal means of transmitting user data is the B channel, which operates at a data rate of 64 kbps. However, it is desirable to be able to support subscriber devices on the B channel that operate at data rates of less than 64 kbps. There are two reasons for this. First, much existing equipment, such as terminals and personal computers, operates at data rates of less than 64 kbps. In the long run, equipment will be built with ISDN interfaces, but this existing equipment must be accommodated during the transition period.

The second reason has to do with the advantages of multiplexing. As we have pointed out, in the current version of the ISDN standards, the entire B channel is the fundamental unit of circuit switching. That is, even if a B channel is logically divided into a number of subchannels, all of the subchannels must be carried on a single circuit between the same pair of subscribers. Even so, a subscriber may have several devices attached to an ISDN interface and wish to connect two or more of them to the same destination. For example, a residential user might want to connect to his or her office and make use of a personal computer and a facsimile at the same time. It will be cheaper if all of this traffic can be carried on one B channel. Furthermore, if all of the data traffic to the office is multiplexed on one B channel, the other B channel of the resident's basic interface is free for sending and receiving telephone calls.

Thus two separate concepts are involved in our discussion: rate adaption and multiplexing. We look at each of these in turn.

Rate Adaption. Rate adaption is the function of adapting a terminal with a data rate of less than 64 kbps to a data rate of 64 kbps. For **circuit-switched connections** over the B channel, there are three cases:

- *Single bit stream of 8, 16, or 32 kbps:* the first 1, 2, or 4 bits, respectively, of each octet transmitted on the B channel are used, with the remaining 7, 6, or 4 bits set to 1.
- *Single bit stream at another rate of less than 32 kbps:* the signal is first converted to a bit stream of 8, 16, or 32 kbps by bit padding; superfluous bits are added in a structured fashion. The resulting bit stream is then adapted to 64 kbps, as above.
- *Single bit stream of between 32 kbps and 64 kbps:* the signal is converted to 64 kbps by bit padding.

The first case is illustrated in Figure 7-2. Data is transmitted on the B channel as a stream of octets at a rate of 64 kbps or, equivalently, 8000 octets per second. For an 8-kbps subscriber device, a terminal adaptor (TA) works as follows. Data from the subscriber arrive at the TA at a rate of 8 kbps. Each incoming bit is transmitted in an octet in which the first bit of the octet is a user data bit and the remaining 7 bits are each set to binary one. For data arriving from the ISDN side, the first bit of each incoming octet is passed on to the terminal and the remaining 7 bits are discarded. A similar adaption procedure is followed for terminals operating at 16 kbps and 32 kbps.

For the second case listed above, a two-stage adaption process is followed (Figure 7-3). The user data rate is first converted to an intermediate ISDN rate (8, 16, or 32 kbps), and then converted from this intermediate rate to 64 kbps. The advantage of using a two-stage technique is that the second stage could be reversed (e.g., from 64 kbps to 8 kbps) somewhere in the network for the purpose of conserving loop or trunk capacity. As a service offering, this could carry a lower tariff rate [COLL83].

| b | 1 | 1 | 1 | 1 | 1 | 1 | 1 |

(a) 8-kbps stream

| b | b | 1 | 1 | 1 | 1 | 1 | 1 |

(b) 16-kbps stream

| b | b | b | b | 1 | 1 | 1 | 1 |

(c) 32-kbps stream

FIGURE 7-2 Allocation of Bits in B Channel Octet for Rate Adaption

The second half of the rate adaption, labeled RA2 in Figure 7-3, is the same as that described above for adapting 8, 16, or 32 kbps to 64 kbps. The first half, labeled RA1, involves the creation of a frame, with only some of the bits in the frame carrying user data. As a specific example, consider the adaption of a user rate of 2400 bps to an intermediate ISDN rate of 8 kbps, which is illustrated in Table 7-2. The conversion is implemented by means of an 80-bit frame structure. Although the data transmitted out of the RA1 module is a constant bit stream, it is considered to consist of a stream of 80-bit frames. The bits of the frame are as follows:

1. The first octet is all zeros. The first bit of the remaining nine octets is one. This provides a means of synchronization.
2. The sixth octet contains a one followed by a set of "E-bits," E1, E2, . . . , E7. These bits are used to indicate the user data rate. At

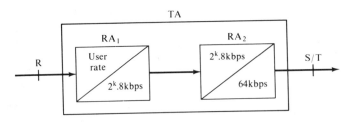

R,S,T = Reference points
RA$_i$ = Rate adaptation functions
TA = Terminal adapter

FIGURE 7-3 Rate Adaption

TABLE 7-2   ADAPTION OF 2400 bps USER RATE TO 8 kbps INTERMEDIATE RATE

Octet	Bits							
1	0	0	0	0	0	0	0	0
2	1	D1	D1	D2	D2	D3	D3	S
3	1	D4	D4	D5	D5	D6	D6	X
4	1	D7	D7	D8	D8	D9	D9	S
5	1	D10	D10	D11	D11	D12	D12	S
6	1	1	1	0	E4	E5	E6	E7
7	1	D13	D13	D14	D14	D15	D15	S
8	1	D16	D16	D17	D17	D18	D18	X
9	1	D19	D19	D20	D20	D21	D21	S
10	1	D22	D22	D23	D23	D24	D24	S

D = data bits
S = status bits
E = user data rate indication
X = reserved for future use

present only the first three bits are used for this purpose; the remaining bits are reserved for future use. The code 110 for E1 E2 E3 indicates that the user data rate is 2400 bps.

3. The S bits are status bits that convey channel-associated status information. The exact nature of these bits depends on the physical interface between the subscriber terminal and the terminal adaptor.
4. The X bits are unused and reserved for future use.
5. Each data bit is repeated. This repetition is not strictly necessary; it acts to fill in unneeded bit positions. These positions could also have been filled in with arbitrary bits.

Each frame contains 24 user data bits. Since we have an 8-kbps output data rate and 80-bit frames, the rate of transmission of frames is 100 frames per second; therefore, the rate of transmission of user data is 2400 bps, as required. In general, we can summarize the function of the RA1 module in Figure 7-3 as follows. Define:

* F = the number of bits in the frame
* F_u = the number of data bits in the frame
* R_u = the user data rate
* R_f = the desired rate of transmission, in frames per second
* R = the desired rate of transmission, in bits per second

Two formulas must be satisfied:

$$F \times R_f = R$$

and

$$Ru/R_f = F_u \text{ with no remainder}$$

The final case listed above is the adaption of a data rate between 32 kbps and 64 kbps to 64 kbps. In this case, only the first stage of Figure 7-2 is needed.

So far, we have discussed the case of circuit-switched connections. With this type of connection, there is a transparent transmission of data between the two subscribers. With rate adaption, it is still necessary that the two subscribers operate at the same data rate. For example, a terminal operating at 2400 bps can be rate adapted to 64 kbps. One could attempt to connect this terminal through ISDN to a 4800-bps computer port which is also rate-adapted to 64 kbps. However, the computer will transmit data at 4800 bps and the terminal's adaptor expects and requires that the incoming 64 kbps stream contains only user data at a rate of 2400 bps. Thus, the traditional circuit-switching requirement, that the data rate of both users connected to the same circuit must be the same, applies in ISDN.

One final point about the circuit-switching rate adaption. The user data rate is identified during the call setup, which takes place via common-channel signaling on the D channel. The following user data rates are supported: 0.6, 1.2, 2.4, 3.6, 4.8, 7.2, 8, 9.6, 14.4, 16, 19.2, 32, 48, and 56 kbps. During the call setup phase, the network will assure that the data rate of the two subscribers is the same; otherwise the connection request is rejected.

Let us now look at the case of **packet-switched connections** over the B channel. In this case, the subscriber does not have a direct circuit to another subscriber. Rather, the subscriber has a circuit connection to a packet-switched node and communicates with other packet-switching subscribers via X.25. Here again, we may be faced with the case of a preexisting subscriber device that operates at a data rate of less than 64 kbps. CCITT Recommendation I.462 suggests two ways of performing rate adaption: interframe flag stuffing and the two-stage method of Figure 7-3.

Recall from Figure 3-11 that X.25 packets are transmitted in LAP-B frames. If the data rate of the subscriber device is less than 64 kbps, then a terminal adaptor can function as follows. LAP-B frames are accepted from the subscriber at the subscriber's data rate and buffered in the TA. Each frame is then transmitted onto the B channel at 64 kbps. Since frames are being transmitted faster than they are generated, there will be gaps. These gaps are filled with additional flag octets (01111110). When frames are received from the network at 64 kbps, they are buffered and delivered to the subscriber at the subscriber's data rate. Excess flag octets between frames are discarded. This process is known as *interframe flag stuffing*. With this procedure, the network cannot distinguish between packet-mode devices operating at 64 kbps and those operating at less than 64 kbps. Therefore, the D-channel signaling used to connect a device to a packet-switching node indicates a data rate of 64 kbps.

The alternative approach is the *two-stage rate adaption* of Figure 7-3. In this case, the bits transmitted by the subscriber are embedded into the 80-octet structure described earlier, and the D-channel signaling indicates the user data rate. With this technique, the packet-switching node to which the subscriber is linked must match the data rate of the subscriber. This is clearly less flexible than the interframe flag stuffing approach, and the latter is recommended by CCITT.

Multiplexing. Multiplexing, in the context of this section, is the function of combining traffic from multiple terminals, each with a data rate of less than 64 kbps, onto a single B channel at 64 kbps. For **circuit switched connections,** there are two cases:

- *Multiple bit streams of 8, 16, and/or 32 kbps:* bits from different streams, up to a total of 64 kbps, are interleaved within each octet.
- *Multiple bit streams of rates other than 8, 16, or 32 kbps:* the signals are first converted into bit streams of 8, 16, or 32 kbps, and then multiplexed as above.

For the first case, there are two approaches defined in I.460. With *fixed format multiplexing,* the following rules are observed:

- an 8-bps bit stream may occupy any bit position; a 16-kbps bit stream may occupy bit positions (1, 2), (3, 4), (5, 6), or (7, 8); a 32-kbps bit stream may occupy bit positions (1, 2, 3, 4) or (5, 6, 7, 8).
- a subrate stream occupies the same bit position(s) in each successive B channel octet.
- all unused bit positions are set to binary one.

If this procedure is used, and the data substreams are added one at a time, it is possible that the 64-kbps capacity will not be effectively utilized. For example, if bit positions 1 and 8 are used to support two 8-kbps substreams, then a 32-kbps substream can not be added even though the capacity is available. An approach which avoids this is *flexible format multiplexing.* The following rules are observed:

- an attempt is made to accommodate a new subrate stream using the fixed format procedure.
- if this attempt fails, the new subrate stream is added by inserting each successive bit of the new stream into the earliest available bit position in the B channel octet.
- a subrate stream occupies the same bit position(s) in each successive B channel octet.
- all unused bit positions are set to binary one.

This procedure always allows subrate streams to be multiplexed up to the 64-kbps limit of the B channel. The fixed format procedure is simpler to implement and should be used if the mixture of subrate streams is known in advance. When the mixture is dynamic, CCITT recommends the use of the more complex flexible format procedure.

The second case listed above is that of multiple bit streams of rates other than 8, 16, or 32 kbps. In this case, a two-stage approach is used. First, each stream is rate-adapted to 8, 16, or 32 kbps. Second, the resulting streams are multiplexed as described previously.

7-2   USER-NETWORK INTERFACES

Reference Points and Functional Groupings

To define the requirements for ISDN user access, an understanding of the anticipated configuration of user premises equipment and of the necessary standard interfaces is critical. The first step is to group functions that may exist on the user's premises in ways that suggest actual physical configurations. Figure 7-4 shows the CCITT approach to this task, using:

- *Functional groupings*: certain finite arrangements of physical equipment or combinations of equipment.
- *Reference points*: conceptual points used to separate groups of functions.

An analogy with the OSI model might be useful at this point. The principal motivation for the 7-layer OSI architecture is that it provides a framework for standardization. Once the functions to be performed in each layer are defined, protocol standards can be developed at each layer. This effectively organizes the standards work and provides guidance to software and equipment providers. Furthermore, by defining the services that each layer provides to the next higher layer, work in each layer can proceed independently. So long as the interface between two layers remains stable, new and different technical approaches can be provided within one layer without an impact on neighboring layers. In the case of ISDN, the architecture on the subscriber's premises is broken up functionally into groupings

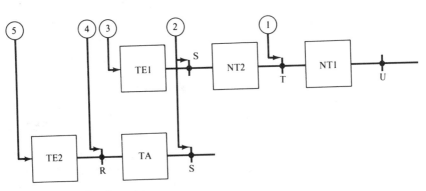

R,S,T = Reference interface points
TE1 = Terminal equipment type 1
TE2 = Terminal equipment type 2
TA = Terminal adaptor
NT1 = Network termination 1
NT2 = Network termination 2

FIGURE 7-4   ISDN Reference Points and Functional Groupings

separated by reference points. This permits interface standards to be developed at each reference point. Again, this effectively organizes the standards work and provides guidance to the equipment providers. Once stable interface standards exist, technical improvements on either side of an interface can be made without impact on adjacent functional groupings. Finally, with stable interfaces, the subscriber is free to procure equipment from different suppliers for the various functional groupings, so long as the equipment conforms to the relevant interface standards.

Let us consider first the functional groupings. **Network termination 1** (NT1) includes functions that may be regarded as belonging to OSI layer 1, that is functions associated with the physical and electrical termination of the ISDN on the user's premises (Table 7-3). The NT1 may be controlled by the ISDN provider and forms a boundary to the network. This boundary isolates the user from the transmission technology of the subscriber loop and presents a new physical connector interface for user device attachment. In addition, the NT1 will perform line maintenance functions such as loopback testing and performance monitoring. The NT1 supports multiple channels (e.g., 2B + D); at the physical level, the bit streams of these channels are multiplexed together, using synchronous time-division multiplexing. Finally, the NT1 interface might support multiple devices in a multidrop arrangement. For example, a residential interface might include a telephone, personal computer, and alarm system, all attached to a single NT1 interface via a multidrop line. For such a configuration, the NT1 includes a contention resolution algorithm to control access to the D channel; this algorithm is described in Chapter 8.

Network termination 2 (NT2) is an intelligent device that may include, depending on the requirement, up through OSI layer 3 functionality. NT2 can perform switching and concentration functions. Examples of NT2 are a digital PBX,

TABLE 7-3   FUNCTIONS OF ISDN FUNCTIONAL GROUPINGS

NT1	NT2	TE
line transmission termination	layers 2 and 3 protocol handling	protocol handling
line maintenance and performance monitoring	layers 2 and 3 multiplexing	maintenance functions
timing	switching	interface functions
power transfer	concentration	connection functions to other equipment
layer 1 multiplexing	maintenance functions	
interface termination including multidrop termination employing layer 1 contention resolution	interface termination, and other layer 1 functions	

a terminal controller, and a LAN. For example, a digital PBX can provide NT2 functions at layers 1, 2, and 3. A simple terminal controller can provide NT2 functions at only layers 1 and 2. A simple time-division multiplexer can provide NT2 functions at only layer 1. An example of a switching function is the construction of a private network using semipermanent circuits among a number of sites. Each site could include a PBX that acts as a circuit switch or a host computer that acts as a packet switch. The concentration function simply means that multiple devices, attached to a digital PBX, LAN, or terminal controller may transmit data across ISDN.

Terminal equipment refers to subscriber equipment that make use of ISDN. Two types are defined. **Terminal equipment type 1** (TE1) refers to devices that support the standard ISDN interface. Examples are digital telephone, integrated voice/data terminals, and digital facsimile equipment. **Terminal equipment type 2** (TE2) encompasses existing non-ISDN equipment. Examples are terminals with a physical interface such as RS-232 and host computers with an X.25 interface. Such equipment requires a **terminal adaptor** (TA) to plug into an ISDN interface. We have already seen one example of a terminal adaptor (Figure 7-3).

The definitions of the functional groupings also define, by implication, the reference points. **Reference point T** (terminal) corresponds to a minimal ISDN network termination at the customer's premises. It separates the network provider's equipment from the user's equipment. **Reference point S** (system) corresponds to the interface of individual ISDN terminals. It separates user terminal equipment from network-related communications functions. **Reference point R** (rate) provides a non-ISDN interface between user equipment that is not ISDN-compatible and adaptor equipment. Typically, this interface will comply with an X series or V series CCITT recommendation. The final reference point illustrated in Figure 7-4 is **reference point U** (user). This interface describes the full-duplex data signal on the subscriber line. At the present time, this reference point is not defined in I.411, which states:

> there is no reference point assigned to the transmission line, since an ISDN user-network interface is not envisaged at this location.

Earlier drafts of I.411, up through 1981, defined such a reference point. In 1981, this definition was dropped without explanation, to be replaced by the flat assertion above, which survived into the 1984 final version of I.411, and has not subsequently been removed. Despite this statement, it is clear that at least in the United States, the U interface will be present. The issue involved is one which clearly illustrates that a difference in philosophy concerning the degree of competitiveness in ISDN provision can have detailed technical impact. It is therefore worthy of a brief elaboration.

To begin, let us consider why the T reference point was defined by CCITT as occurring between an NT1 and an NT2, rather than combining these two functional groups and defining the loop transmission system as the standard user-network interface. It was felt that there must be a decoupling of customer premises equipment from network technology, configuration, and evolution. This would allow customers to preserve their investment in user equipment and software while the capabilities and performance characteristics of the network evolve. Because the subscriber loop transmission system is the most expensive single part of ISDN, continuing technical evolution in that area is essential to provide high-performance, low-cost network service. Furthermore, the technology in this area is changing rapidly, and there are a number of possible solutions to the technical challenges presented by the subscriber loop (e.g., echo cancellation versus time-compression multiplexing). Accordingly, it is not desirable to define an interface directly at the subscriber loop, which in turn defines the loop transmission technology.

Within the United States, however, the consequences of Computer Inquiry II (see Section 1-3) dictate an opposite conclusion. In addition to drawing a distinction between basic and enhanced services, Computer II defined a distinction between network equipment and customer premises equipment, and mandated that the latter must be available to users independently of the network provider. Indeed, network services providers are forbidden from supplying customer premises equipment as a part of the basic network. The FCC determined that what it referred to as Network Channel Terminating Equipment (NCTE) is customer premises equipment. Accordingly, service providers must provide a standardized interface that allows the customer to procure NCTE devices from other vendors.

The problem for ISDN planning arises in that the NCTE and NT1 units are analogous if not identical. Therefore, the concept of the NT1 being part of the network is contrary to Computer II. The FCC commented on this issue in its first report on ISDN, issued in 1984:

Our NCTE decision as applied to ISDN implicitly requires that an interface to the input of the NT1 be established. Stated alternatively, our NCTE decision requires that there be established an interface to the loop, to which customer-premises equipment may be connected.

It appears clear that an interface to the loop facilities will be required to facilitate the provision of equipment or capabilities comparable to the NT1 by subscribers in the United States. Since ISDN has been directed towards arriving at relatively uniform international recommendations governing ISDN, it may prove appropriate for the CCITT to arrive at a suitable definition of a U interface to facilitate this. To avoid potential confusion and inconsistency of domestic implementations of ISDN with the international recommendations, it would be desirable for the international ISDN planning efforts to include sufficient flexibility as they evolve to accommodate the U interface concept. Therefore, we urge that this matter be pursued in the continuing ISDN planning efforts.

Currently, there is considerable work within the U.S. standards groups affiliated with CCITT to develop U interface standards, with the current focus on echo cancellation techniques. This work will eventually result in U.S. standards. At this time, it is not clear whether these standards will be adopted by CCITT.

Service Support

The structure defined in Figure 7-4 can be related to the ISDN services. This helps to further clarify the distinction between bearer services and teleservice, while also clarifying the implications of the functional groupings and reference points.

Bearer services supported by ISDN are accessed at points 1 and/or 2 (reference points T and S). In both cases, the basic service concept is identical. Thus, for example, a bearer service of *circuit-mode 64-kbps 8 kHz-structure unrestricted* can be supplied at either reference point. The choice between access points 1 and 2 depends on the configuration of the communications equipment at the customer premises.

At access point 4 (reference point R), other standardized services (e.g., X series and V series interfaces) may be accessed. This allows terminals not conforming to the ISDN interface standards to be used in conjunction with the bearer services. For such terminals, a terminal adapter is required to adapt the existing standard to the ISDN standard. Such adaption can include data rate, analog-to-digital, or other interface characteristics.

Access points 3 and 5 provide access to teleservices. ISDN teleservices incorporating terminals which conform to ISDN standards are accessed at access point 3. Teleservices which make use of terminals based on existing non-ISDN standards are accessed at point 5. For these services, as with the bearer services, a terminal adaptor may be required.

Access Configurations

Based on the definitions of functional groupings and reference points, various possible configurations for ISDN user-network interfaces have been proposed by CCITT. These are shown in Figure 7-5. Note that on the customer's premises there may be interfaces at S and T, at S but not T, at T but not S, or at a combined S-T interface. The first case (S and T) is the most straightforward; one or more pieces of equipment correspond to each functional grouping. Examples were given above when the functional groupings were defined.

In the second case (S but not T), the functions of NT1 and NT2 are combined. In this case, the line termination function is combined with other ISDN interface functions. Two possible situations are reflected by this arrangement. In many countries without competitive provision of telecommunications services, the ISDN provider will provide the NT1 function. If that same provider also offers computer, local area network, and/or digital PBX equipment, the NT1 functions can be integrated into this other equipment. In the United States, the NT1 function is not an integral part of the ISDN offering and can be supplied by a number of vendors. In this case, a LAN or digital PBX vendor might integrate the NT1 function into its equipment.

In the third case (T but not S) the NT2 and terminal (TE) functions are combined. One possibility here is a host computer system that supports users but also

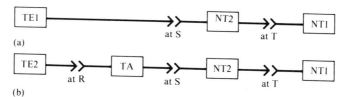

(a)

(b)

Configurations where ISDN physical interfaces occur at reference points S and T

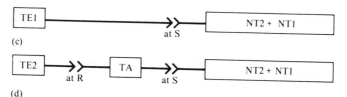

(c)

(d)

Configurations where ISDN physical interfaces occur at reference point S only

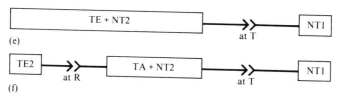

(e)

(f)

Configurations where ISDN physical interfaces occur at reference point T only

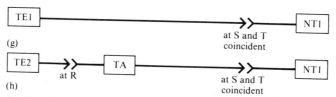

(g)

(h)

Configurations where a single ISDN physical interface occurs at a location where both reference points S and T coincide

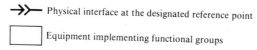

FIGURE 7-5   Examples of Physical Configurations

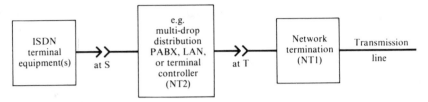

(a) An implementation (see Figure 7.5a) where ISDN physical interfaces occur at reference points S and T.

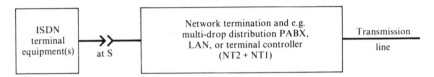

(b) An implementation (see Figure 7.5c) where an ISDN physical interfaces occur at reference point S but not T

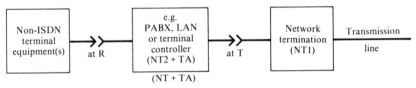

(c) An implementation (see Figure 7.5f) where an ISDN physical interface occurs at reference point T but not S.

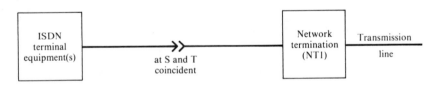

(d) An implementation (see Figure 7.5g) where a single ISDN physical interface occurs at a location where both reference points S and T coincide

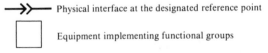

— Physical interface at the designated reference point

Equipment implementing functional groups

FIGURE 7-6 Examples of Implementation of NT1 and NT2 Functions

acts as a packet switch in a private packet-switching network that uses ISDN for trunking. Another possibility is that terminal equipment is supported by non-ISDN-standard interfaces. This latter possibility is illustrated in Figure 7-5c and discussed below.

The final configuration (combined S-T interface) illustrates a key feature of ISDN interface compatibility: an ISDN subscriber device, such as a telephone, can connect directly to the subscriber loop terminator or into a PBX or LAN, using the same interface specifications and thus ensuring portability.

Figure 7-6 provides examples of the ways in which a customer may implement the NT1 and NT2 functions. These examples illustrate that a given ISDN function can be implemented using various technologies, and that different ISDN functions can be combined in a single device. For example: Figure 7-6c illustrates that a LAN can interface to ISDN using a primary or basic access interface, while the user devices make use of a very different interface (e.g., a token-ring LAN interface).

One additional set of configurations is suggested by CCITT. These cover cases in which the subscriber has more than one device at a particular interface point, but not so many devices that a separate PBX or LAN is warranted. In these cases, it is possible to have multiple physical interfaces at a single reference point. Examples are shown in Figure 7-7. Figure 7-7a and b show multiple terminals connected to the network, either through a multidrop line or through a multiport NT1. These cases are not intended to require that individual terminals can talk to each other, as in a LAN, but rather that each terminal can communicate with the network.

Figure 7-7c and d provide multiple connections between TE1s and NT2. The two figures more or less correspond to PBX and LAN, respectively. Figure 7-7e shows the case of multiple NT1 equipment, whereas Figure 7-7f shows a case in which NT1 provides a layer 1 multiplexing of multiple connections.

The final two configurations indicate that either S or T, but not both, need not correspond to a physical interface in a particular configuration. We have already referred to the combination of NT1 and NT2. In addition, an NT2 can be equipped with the capability to attach TE2 equipment directly.

7-3 ADDRESSING

In the worldwide public telephone network, calls are placed based on the telephone number of the called party. For worldwide telephone connectivity, each subscriber must have a unique telephone number, and the network must be able to determine the location of the subscriber based on that number. A telephone number supports two important functions:

- it routes the call;
- it activates the necessary procedures for proper call charging.

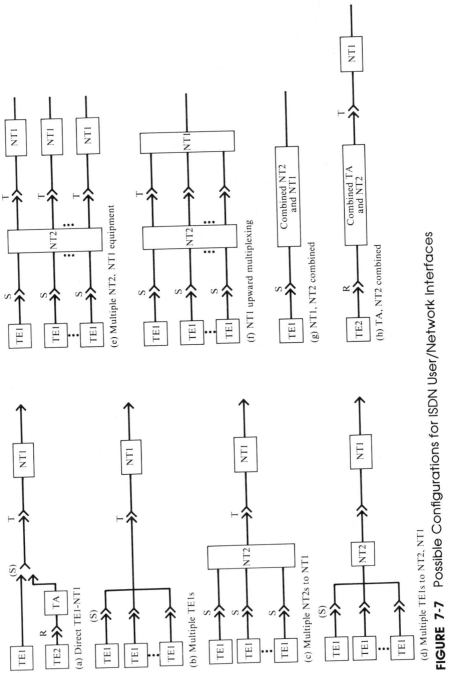

FIGURE 7-7 Possible Configurations for ISDN User/Network Interfaces

Similarly, a numbering plan is needed for ISDN. The numbering scheme for ISDN should be based on the following requirements:

- It should be easily understood and used by the subscriber.
- It should be compatible with existing and planned switching equipment.
- It should allow for expansion of the size of the subscriber population.
- It should facilitate interworking with existing public network numbering schemes.

As work on ISDN proceeded through the early 1980s, there was considerable sentiment that ISDN numbering should be based on the current numbering plan for telephony, embodied in CCITT E.163. However, E.163 allows for only 12 decimal digits and was felt to be inadequate for the large number of subscribers anticipated for ISDN. ISDN must accommodate not only telephones but a large population of data devices. The result was the adoption of a numbering scheme that is an enhancement of E.163.

The ISDN numbering plan is presented in I.330 and I.331, and embodies the following principles:

- As mentioned, it is an enhancement of E.163. In particular, the telephone country code specified in E.163 is used to identify countries in the ISDN numbering plan.
- It is independent of the nature of the service (e.g., voice or data) or the performance characteristics of the connection.
- It is a sequence of decimal digits (not alphanumeric).
- Interworking between ISDNs requires only the use of the ISDN number.

ISDN Address Structure

CCITT makes a distinction between a number and an address. An **ISDN number** is one which relates to the ISDN network and ISDN numbering plan. It contains sufficient information for the network to route a call. Typically, but not always, an ISDN number corresponds to the subscriber attachment point to the ISDN, i.e., to the T reference point. An **ISDN address** comprises the ISDN number and any mandatory and/or optional additional addressing information. This additional information is not needed by the ISDN to route the call, but is needed at the subscriber site to distribute the call to the appropriate party. Typically, but not always, an ISDN address corresponds to an individual terminal, i.e., to the S reference point. This situation is illustrated in Figure 7-8a, which shows a number of terminals connected to an NT2 (e.g., a PBX or LAN). The NT2 as a whole has a unique ISDN number, while each individual terminal has an ISDN address. Another way to express the distinction between ISDN numbers and addresses is that an ISDN number is associated with a D channel, which provides common-channel signaling for a number of subscribers, each of which has an ISDN address.

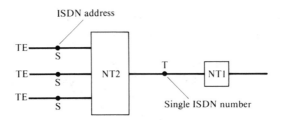

(a) Single ISDN number at T interface

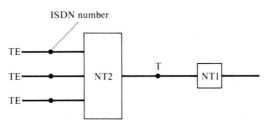

(b) Direct dialing-in

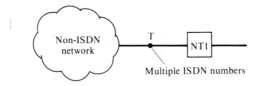

(c) Non-ISDN network

FIGURE 7-8   ISDN Addressing

Other correspondences between reference points and ISDN numbers and addresses are possible; these are discussed below.

Figure 7-9 shows the format of the ISDN address. An address in this format would appear in call setup messages communicated in common-channel signaling protocols such as Signaling System Number 7. The elements of the address are:

- *Country code:* specifies the destination country (or geographic area) of the call. It is composed of a variable number of decimal digits (1 to 3) and is defined in Recommendation E.163 (existing telephony numbering plan).
- *National destination code:* is of variable length and a portion of the National ISDN number. If subscribers within a country are served by more than one ISDN and/or public switched telephone network (PSTN), it can be used to select a destination network within the

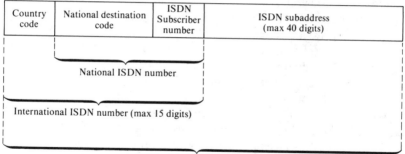

FIGURE 7-9 Structure of the ISDN Address

specified country. It can also be used in a trunk code (area code) format to route the call over the destination network to a particular region of the network. The NDC code can, where required, provide a combination of both of these functions.

- *ISDN subscriber number:* is also of variable length and constitutes the remainder of the National ISDN Number. Typically, the subscriber number is the number to be dialed to reach a subscriber in the same local network or numbering area.
- *ISDN subaddress:* provides additional addressing information and is a maximum of 40 digits in length. The subaddress is not considered part of the numbering plan but constitutes an intrinsic part of the ISDN addressing capability.

The national destination code plus the ISDN subscriber number form a unique national ISDN number within a country. This plus the country code form the international ISDN number, which is at present limited to a maximum of 15 digits. CCITT is considering expanding this to 16 or 17 digits. The ISDN subaddress is added to the international ISDN number to form an ISDN address with a maximum of 55 digits.

Address Information

Figure 7-8a shows the most straightforward way of employing ISDN numbers and addresses: Each T reference point is assigned an ISDN number, and each S reference point is assigned an ISDN address. The last field of the ISDN address, known as the subaddress, allows multiple subscribers to be discriminated at the subscriber site in a fashion that is transparent to the network. As an example, consider a site consisting of a digital PBX supporting some number of telephones. The national ISDN number for the PBX could be 617-543-7000. To address a local telephone with extension number 678, a remote caller would need to dial 617-543-

7000-678. The ISDN would route the call based on the first 10 digits; the remaining 3 digits would be used by the PBX to connect the call to the appropriate extension.

An alternative use of numbers and addresses is suggested by Figure 7-8b. In this case, a number of terminals each have their own ISDN number. This feature is referred to as **direct dialing-in** (DDI). With DDI, the numbering scheme for local terminals is built into the national scheme. For example, again suppose a digital PBX with a main number of 543-7000, with an extension to that PBX of 678. To dial the extension directly from the outside, a user would dial 543-7678, and the 543-7XXX block would be lost for use except for 999 extension possibilities for that PBX. DDI is simpler for the subscriber than subaddressing, since fewer digits are needed to place a call. With DDI, the ISDN still routes on the basis of the ISDN number. In addition, the last few digits forming the end of the ISDN number are transferred to the called subscriber's installation. The number of digits used varies and depends upon the requirement of the called subscriber's equipment and the capacity of the numbering plan used. DDI must be used sparingly to assure that sufficient ISDN numbers are available to support all subscribers.

It is possible to combine DDI and subaddressing. This would allow direct dialing-in to certain intermediate equipment on site, such as terminal concentrators, with the subaddress used to discriminate devices attached to the intermediate equipment.

Another alternative is to assign multiple ISDN numbers to a single reference point. For example, at an ISDN interface, a user might have an attachment to a non-ISDN network, such as a private packet-switching network (Figure 7-8c). Although physically, there is only a single attachment point to the ISDN, it might be desirable to provide visibility to ISDN of a number of the devices on the private network, by assigning a unique ISDN number to each.

Numbering Interworking

For some extended transition period, there will be a number of public networks in addition to ISDN, including public switched telephone networks (PSTN), and public data networks, such as X.25 packet-switching networks and telex networks. A variety of standards have been issued that deal with the address structure and address assignment for these various networks. Unfortunately, although these standards have been developed with knowledge of the others, they are not compatible with each other nor with the ISDN numbering plan. This creates the problem of how addressing can be performed between an ISDN subscriber and a subscriber on another network which has a connection to ISDN.

Other Address Structures.   Figure 7-10 illustrates the address structure for the major international public network standards. The international PSTN standard, E.163, makes use of a 12-digit number. The country code is the same as the country code used in ISDN. The national significant number of the PSTN corresponds to

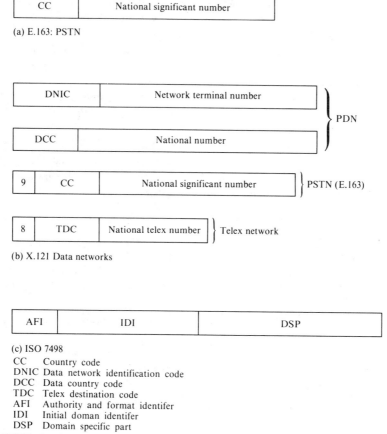

CC	National significant number

(a) E.163: PSTN

DNIC	Network terminal number

DCC	National number

} PDN

9	CC	National significant number

} PSTN (E.163)

8	TDC	National telex number

} Telex network

(b) X.121 Data networks

AFI	IDI	DSP

(c) ISO 7498

CC   Country code
DNIC Data network identification code
DCC   Data country code
TDC   Telex destination code
AFI   Authority and format identifer
IDI   Initial doman identifer
DSP   Domain specific part

FIGURE 7-10 International Network Numbering

the national ISDN number, although the latter may contain three more digits. Thus, E.163 and the ISDN standard (I.330 and I.331) are reasonably compatible.

X.121 provides a standard for public data networks. As can be seen, there are a number of variations, depending on the network. If a data terminal is accessed through a public data network, then the E.163 number, prefixed by a 9, is used. For public data networks, a data country code is used, which unfortunately is not the same as a telephone country code. Nor is the national data number related in any way to the national telephone number. The telex numbering scheme also bears no relation to E.163 or I.33x.

Finally, ISO has developed an international numbering scheme in the context of the OSI model. The authority and format identifier (AFI) portion of the ISO address defines one of six subdomains of the global network addressing domain:

- A set of four domains, each of which corresponds to a type of public telecommunications network (i.e., packet-switched, telex, PSTN, and ISDN), all of which are administered by CCITT.
- An ISO geographic domain that is allocated and corresponds to individual countries. ISO member bodies within each country are responsible for assigning these addresses.
- An ISO international organization domain that is allocated and corresponds to different international organizations (e.g., NATO).

In addition, the AFI specifies the format of the IDI part and the structure of the DSP part. The initial domain identifier is the initial (and perhaps only) part of the actual address, and is interpreted according to the value of the AFI. Finally, the DSP part, if any, provides additional addressing information.

For ISDN networks, the AFI has a value of 44 for ISDN numbers expressed as decimal digits, and 45 for ISDN numbers expressed as binary numbers. The latter is not standard ISDN procedure, but may be employed by a user in an OSI context; in that case, the number would have to be converted to decimal for use by ISDN. In general, the international ISDN number is identical to the initial domain identifier, and the ISDN subaddress is identical to the domain specific part of the ISO address.

Interworking Strategies.   From the point of view of ISDN addressing, interworking is defined as a procedure whereby an ISDN subscriber can set up a call to subscribers or services terminated on other public networks. Two general approaches are possible: single-stage and two-stage selection.

With the **single-stage approach,** the calling party designates the address of the called party in the call setup procedure. This address contains sufficient information for:

- ISDN to route the call to a point at which the called network attaches to ISDN.
- the called network to route the call to the called party.

CCITT suggests two ways in which single-stage addresses could be constructed. In the first method, the address begins with a prefix that identifies the particular network to be accessed; the remainder of the address is in the format used by that network (Figure 7-11a). In this approach, the calling address would have to identify the called numbering plan as part of the calling procedure. An example of such a prefix is the authority and format indicator of the ISO address structure. In the ISDN signaling protocol (I.451), to be discussed in Chapter 8, there is in fact a place in the call setup address field for such a code, known as the numbering plan identification field.

An alternative address structure for the single-stage approach is one which conforms to the ISDN address structure. In this case, some national destination

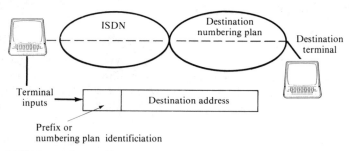

(a) Single-stage interworking

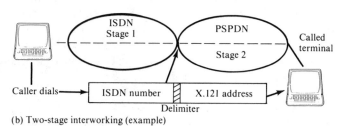

(b) Two-stage interworking (example)

FIGURE 7-11 Strategies for Numbering Interworking

codes (NDC; see Figure 7-9) could be specially assigned for interworking purposes. This is a less general solution than the prefix approach, as the number of available NDCs is limited.

With the **two-stage approach,** the first stage of selection provides the calling party access via ISDN to an interworking unit (IWU) associated with the point of attachment of the called network to the ISDN. The calling party uses an ISDN number to set up a connection to the IWU. When a connection is established, the IWU responds. The necessary address information for the called party on that particular network is then forwarded, as a second stage of selection, through the ISDN and the IWU to complete the call in the non-ISDN network (Figure 7-11b).

The main disadvantages of the two-stage approach are:

- Additional digits must be dialed by the caller.
- The caller must employ two numbering plans.
- A delimiter or pause is necessary between the two stages (e.g., a second dial tone).

For these reasons, CCITT prefers the one-stage approach but allows the two-stage approach.

7-4   INTERWORKING

It is clear that there is never likely to be a single, monolithic, worldwide ISDN. In the near term, there will be a variety of non-ISDN public networks operating, with the need for the subscribers on these networks to connect to subscribers on ISDN networks. Even in the case of different national ISDNs, differences in services or the attributes of services may persist indefinitely. Accordingly, CCITT has begun to address the issue of the interworking of other networks with ISDN.

One issue related to interworking, that of interworking between numbering plans, was discussed in the preceding section. The interworking of numbering plans allows an ISDN subscriber to identify a non-ISDN subscriber for the purpose of establishing a connection and using some service. However, for successful communication to take place there must be agreement on, and the capability to provide, a common set of services and mechanisms. To provide compatibility between ISDN and existing network components and terminals, a set of interworking functions must be implemented. Typical functions include:

- Provide interworking of numbering plans.
- Match physical-layer characteristics at the point of interconnection between the two networks.
- Determine if network resources on the destination network side are adequate to meet the ISDN service demand.
- Map control signal messages such as services identification, channel identification, call status, and alerting between the ISDN's common-channel signaling protocol and the called network's signaling protocol, whether the latter is inchannel or common channel.
- Ensure service and connection compatibility.
- Provide transmission structure conversion, including information modulation technique and frame structure.
- Maintain synchronization (error control, flow control) across connections on different networks.
- Collect data required for proper billing.
- Coordinate operation and maintenance procedures to be able to isolate faults.

Thus interworking may require the implementation of a set of interworking functions, either in ISDN or the network attached to ISDN. The approach identified by CCITT for standardizing the interworking capability is to define additional reference points associated with interworking and to standardize the interface at that reference point. This is a sound strategy that should minimize the impact both on ISDN and on other networks. The inclusion of these additional reference points is illustrated in Figure 7-12. As before, ISDN-compatible customer equipment attaches to ISDN via the S or T reference point. The following additional reference points are defined:

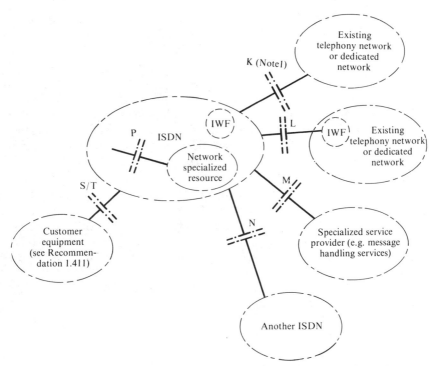

Note 1 — Different interface specifications will exist at the K reference point depending on the type of network.

Note 2 — The specification of interfaces at the K, L, M, N and P reference points need further study.

FIGURE 7-12 Reference Points Associated with the Interconnection of Customer Equipment and Other Networks to an ISDN

- K: Interface with an existing telephone network or other non-ISDN network requiring interworking functions. The functions are performed by ISDN.
- L: As with K, but it is the responsibility of the other network to perform the interworking functions.
- M: A specialized network, such as teletex or MHS. In this case, an adaption function may be needed, to be performed in the specialized network.
- N: Interface between two ISDNs. Some sort of protocol is needed to determine the degree of service compatibility.
- P: There may be some specialized resource that is provided by the ISDN provider but that is clearly identifiable as a separate component or set of components.

As yet, the work in this area is not far advanced. Although these reference points have been defined the details of the interworking functions and of the interface standards at the reference points have not been worked out. This section provides a brief overview of some of the issues involved.

ISDN-ISDN Interworking

The simplest case of interworking involves two ISDNs. If the two ISDNs provide identical bearer services and teleservices, then no interworking capabilities are required. However, it may be the case that the two networks differ in the attribute values that they support for one or more services. In that case, interworking is needed. The interworking would occur in two phases. In the *control phase*, a service negotiation takes place in order to reach a service agreement. A service agreement can be reached if the maximum common service that can be provided across the two networks equals or exceeds the minimum service that the caller will accept. If agreement is reached, then the connection is established, which involves splicing together connections from the two ISDNs to form a single connection from the user's point of view. User-to-user communication can then take place in the *user phase*.

Figure 7-13 illustrates the call negotiation procedure used to reach service agreement. The following steps are involved:

1. A call from TEx to ISDN2 is routed to IWF1.
2. IWF1 communicates with IWF2 and determines whether the requested service (indicated by bearer capability) of the calling user is supported by ISDN2, using a service list in IWF2. If the compatibility is satisfied, network interworking between ISDN1 and ISDN2 begins.
3. If the service compatibility does not exist, IWF2 (or IWF1) negotiates with the calling user to change or abandon the service request.
4. With a changed service request, step 2 or 3 is repeated until service compatibility is satisfied or the effort abandoned.
5. When the connection between TEx and TEy is established, low-level compatibility (bearer) and high-level compatibility (teleservice) is examined on an end-to-end basis. The network does not participate in this procedure but agreement between ISDNs concerning user-to-user information transfer method might be required.

Thus, it is first necessary to determine if the two ISDNs can support the required attributes of the caller's requested bearer service. Then, the end-to-end compatibility between the two users is determined.

ISDN-PSTN Interworking

In many countries, digitization of the existing public switched telephone network (PSTN) has been ongoing for a number of years, including implementation of digital transmission and switching facilities and the introduction of common-

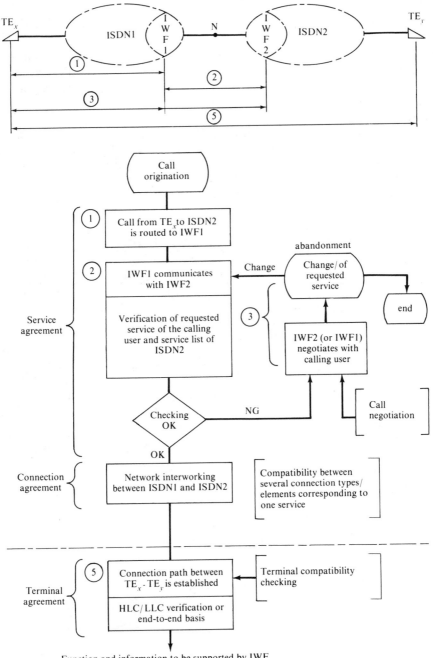

FIGURE 7-13 Call Negotiation Procedure in ISDN-ISDN Interworking

channel signaling. The availability of digital subscriber loops has lagged the introduction of these other digital aspects. In any case, such networks exhibit some
overlap with the capabilities of a full ISDN but lack some of the services that an
ISDN will support. Thus, it will be necessary for some time to provide interworking
between ISDN and PSTN facilities.

Table 7-4 (from I.530) identifies the key characteristics of an ISDN and a
PSTN, indicating possible interworking functions to accommodate dissimilar characteristics. Some sort of negotiation procedure, similar to that depicted in Figure
7-13 will be needed to establish connections.

TABLE 7-4   KEY ISDN AND PSTN CHARACTERISTICS

	ISDN	*PSTN*	*Interworking Functions*
Subscriber interface	Digital	Analog	a
User-network signaling	Out-of-band (I.441/I.451)	Mainly in-band (e.g., DTMF)	b, e
User terminal equipment supported	Digital TE (ISDN NT, TE1 or TE2 + TA)	Analog TE (e.g., dial pulse telephones, PABXs modem-equipped DTEs)	c
Interexchange signaling	SS No. 7 ISDN user part (ISUP)	In-band (e.g., R1, R2, No. 4, No. 5) or out-of-band (e.g., No. 6, No. 7 TUP)	d, e
Transmission facilities	Digital	Analog/digital	a
Exchange types	Digital	Analog/digital	f
Information transfer mode	Circuit/packet	Circuit	f
Information transfer capability	Speech, digital unrestricted, 3.1 kHz audio, video, etc.	3.1 kHz audio (voice/voiceband data)	f

where:
a)   analog-to-digital and digital-to-analog conversion on transmission facilities;
b)   mapping between PSTN signals in the subscriber access and I.451 messages for
     intra-exchange calls;
c)   support of communication between modem-equipped PSTN DTEs and ISDN
     terminals;
d)   conversion between the PSTN signaling system and Signaling System No. 7 ISDN
     user part;
e)   mapping between signals in the ISDN subscriber (I.441, I.451) access and PSTN
     in-band interexchange signaling (e.g., R1);
f)   further study required.

7-5   RECOMMENDED READING

Not much literature is yet available on the topics in this chapter. [LUET86] provides a general overview. [RUMS86] discusses the terminal adaption functions. [RUTK85] provides a good discussion of the need for a U reference point. [ROBI84], [COLL83], and [DECI82] examine aspects of the ISDN transmission structure and ISDN user-network interfaces.

7-6   PROBLEMS

7-1 List all of the approved interface structures for the primary rate interface. Don't forget combinations that include H channels.

7-2 An ISDN customer has offices at a number of sites. A typical office is served by two 1.544-Mbps digital pipes. One provides circuit-switched access to ISDN; the other is a semipermanent connection to another user site. The on-premises equipment consists of a digital PBX plus a host computer system with an X.25 capability. The user has three requirements:

- telephone service
- a private packet-switched network for data
- video teleconferencing at 1.544 Mbps

How might the user allocate capacity optimally to meet these requirements?

7-3 What is the percentage overhead on the basic channel structure?

7-4 Construct tables similar to Table 7-2 for the following data rate adaptions:
   a. 600 bps to 8 kbps
   b. 1200 bps to 8 kbps
   c. 4800 bps to 8 kbps
   c. 9600 bps to 16 kbps
   d. 19.2 kbps to 64 kbps
   e. 48 kbps to 64 kbps
   f. 56 kbps to 64 kbps

7-5 In the discussion of rate adaption, it was suggested that the two-stage procedure could save network capacity, since a conversion of, say 8 kbps to 64 kbps could be reversed in the network. Since all of the subchannels of a single B channel must be carried on the same ISDN circuit between the same pair of subscribers, what opportunity for such savings is possible?

7-6 Subscriber X sets up a 64-kbps circuit-switched connection to subscriber Y over a B channel. Over time, various subchannels of traffic are carried between X and Y on the B channel. The pattern of traffic is: add 8 kbps; add 32 kbps; add 16 kbps; subtract 32 kbps; add 16 kbps; subtract 8 kbps; add 32 kbps.

Using flexible format multiplexing, show the assignment of B-channel octet bits over time.

7-7 In Figure 7-4, there is no access point defined for reference point U. One reason for this is that CCITT has not yet recognized this interface. However, if and when this interface is incorporated in the CCITT recommendations, is it appropriate to talk about accessing services (bearer or teleservices) at this reference point, or is this a primitive level of interfacing below the level at which services become visible to the subscriber?

7-8 For each of the configurations of Figure 7-7, indicate the possible correspondences between ISDN numbers and ISDN addresses on the one hand, and reference point on the other.

7-9 What is the difference between direct dialing-in (Figure 7-8b) in which there are multiple ISDN numbers, one for each of multiple S reference points, and the use of multiple ISDN numbers at a single T reference point?

CHAPTER 8

ISDN
PROTOCOLS

This chapter looks at the communication protocols peculiar to ISDN that are required for user access to ISDN and for the functioning of ISDN. We begin with an overall look at the protocol architecture for user access to ISDN. This architecture makes clear what functions and services are provided by ISDN and how, through the OSI architecture, the ISDN-related protocols fit into the overall communications requirements of subscriber systems. Next, we look at the types of connections supported by ISDN and the protocols used in the setup and maintenance of these connections. The next three sections look at the specific user access protocols defined for ISDN. The physical layer specifies both the basic access and primary access interfaces. LAP-D is the data link control protocol developed for the D channel. The I.451 call control protocol allows the user to exercise call control on B channels by means of a D-channel protocol. The chapter closes with a look at an internal ISDN protocol, the SS7 ISDN User Part, which is a key element in providing ISDN support to subscribers.

8-1 ISDN PROTOCOL ARCHITECTURE

The development of standards for ISDN includes, of course, the development of protocols for interaction between ISDN users and the network and for interaction between two ISDN users. It would be desirable to fit these new ISDN protocols into the OSI framework, and to a great extent this has been done. However, there are certain requirements for ISDN that are not met within the current structure of OSI.

Examples of these are:

- **Multiple related protocols:** The primary example of this is the use of a protocol on the D channel to set up, maintain, and terminate a connection on a B channel.
- **Multimedia calls:** ISDN will allow a call to be set up that allows information flow consisting of multiple types, such as voice, data, facsimile, and control signals.
- **Multipoint connections:** ISDN will allow conference calls.

These and other functions are not directly addressed in the current OSI specification. However, the basic 7-layer framework appears valid even in the ISDN context and the issue is more one of specific functionality at the various layers. The issue of the exact relationship between ISDN and OSI remains one for further study.

Figure 8-1 suggests the relationship between OSI and ISDN. As a network, ISDN is essentially unconcerned with user layers 4–7. These are end-to-end layers employed by the user for the exchange of information. Network access is concerned only with layers 1–3. Layer 1, defined in I.430 and I.431, specifies the physical interface for both basic and primary access. Since the B and D channels are multiplexed over the same physical interface, these standards apply to both types of channels. Above this layer, the protocol structure differs for the two channels.

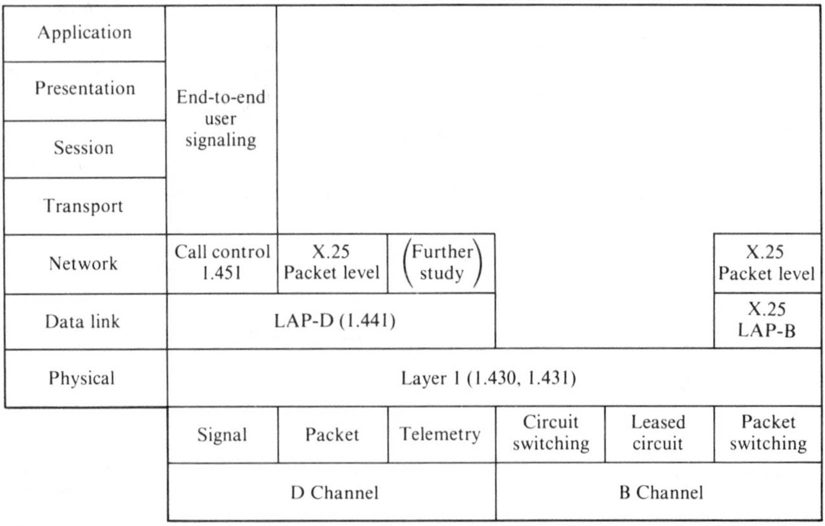

Application							
Presentation	End-to-end user signaling						
Session							
Transport							
Network	Call control I.451	X.25 Packet level	(Further study)				X.25 Packet level
Data link	LAP-D (1.441)						X.25 LAP-B
Physical	Layer 1 (I.430, I.431)						
	Signal	Packet	Telemetry	Circuit switching	Leased circuit	Packet switching
	D Channel			B Channel		

FIGURE 8-1 Layered Protocol Structure at the ISDN User-Network Interface

For the D-channel, a new data link layer standard, LAP-D has been defined. All transmission on this channel is in the form of LAP-D frames that are exchanged between the subscriber equipment and an ISDN switching element. Three applications are supported: control signaling, packet-switching, and telemetry. For control signaling, a call control protocol has been defined (I.451). This protocol is used to establish, maintain, and terminate connections on B channels. Thus it is a protocol between the user and the network. Above layer 3, there is the possibility for higher-layer functions associated with user-to-user control signaling. These are a subject for further study. The D channel can also be used to provide packet switching services to the subscriber. In this case, the X.25 level 3 protocol is used, and X.25 packets are transmitted in LAP-D frames. The X.25 level 3 protocol is used to establish virtual circuits on the D channel to other users, and to exchange packetized data. The final application area, telemetry, is a subject for further study.

The B channel can be used for circuit switching, semipermanent circuits, and packet-switching. Let us consider circuit switching first. The D channel is used to set up a circuit between two ISDN users. Once the circuit is set up, it may be used for data transfer between the users. Recall from Chapter 2 that a circuit-switched network provides a transparent data path between communication stations. To the attached stations, it appears that they have a direct full-duplex link with each other. They are free to use their own formats, protocols, and frame synchronization. Hence, from the point of view of ISDN, layers 2 – 7 are not visible nor specified. The same line of reasoning applies to semipermanent circuits. In the case of packet-switching, a circuit-switched connection is set up on the B channel between the user and a packet-switched node using the D channel control protocol. Once the circuit is set up on the B channel, the user employs X.25 levels 2 and 3 to establish a virtual circuit to another user over that channel and to exchange packetized data.

8-2   ISDN Connections

ISDN provides three types of service for end-to-end communication:

- Circuit-switched calls over the B channel
- Packet-switched calls over the B channel
- Circuit-switched calls over the D channel

Circuit Switching

The network configuration and protocols for circuit switching involve both the B and D channels. The B channel is used for the transparent exchange of user data. The communicating users may use any protocols they wish for end-to-end communication. The D channel is used to exchange control information between the user and the network for call establishment and termination, and access to network facilities.

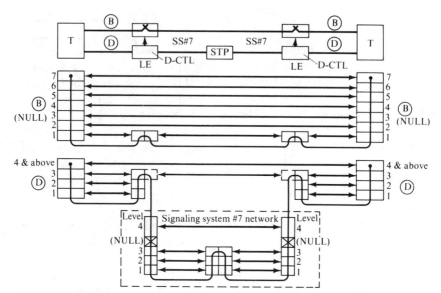

FIGURE 8-2   Network Configuration and Protocols for Circuit Switching

Figure 8-2 depicts the protocol architecture that implements circuit switching (see Table 8-1 for a key to Figures 8-2 through 8-4). The B channel is serviced by an NT1 or NT2 using only layer 1 functions. The end users may employ any protocol, although generally layer 3 will be null. On the D channel, a three-layer network access protocol is used, and is explained below. Finally, the process of establishing a

TABLE 8-1   KEY TO FIGURES 8-2 THROUGH 8-4

B = An ISDN B channel
D = An ISDN D channel
T = Terminal
D-CTL = D-channel controller
SS 7 = CCITT signaling system 7
STP = Signaling transfer point
(Null) = Channel not present
7, 6, 5, 4, 3, 2, 1 = Layers in ISO basic reference model
LEVEL = Levels in SS 7
LE = Local exchange
TE = Transit exchange
PSF = Packet-switching facility
Horizontal line = Peer-to-peer protocol
Vertical line = Layer-to-layer data flow

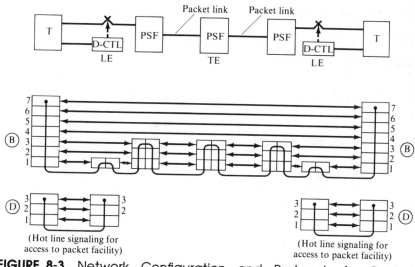

FIGURE 8-3 Network Configuration and Protocols for Packet Switching Using B Channel with Circuit-Switched Access

circuit through ISDN involves the cooperation of switches internal to ISDN to set up the connection. These switches interact using Signaling System Number 7.

Packet Switching

The ISDN must also permit user access to packet-switched services for data traffic (e.g., interactive) that is best serviced by packet switching. Figures 8-3 and 8-4 show two possibilities.

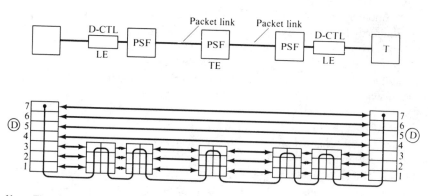

Note: There is another possibility: that LE is transparent to layer 3.

FIGURE 8-4 Network Configuration and Protocols for Packet Switching for D Channel

The first possibility is high-speed (64 kbps) packet-switched access via the **B channel.** Figure 8-3 depicts a scenario in which the ISDN provides a circuit-switched link to a value-added packet-switching node. The local user interface need only perform physical layer functions to maintain a transparent connection between the user and the packet-switching node. The latter two entities communicate use X.25 layers 2 and 3.

There are two sets of variations to consider, one set concerned with the nature of the connection from the user to the packet-switching node, and the other concerned with the nature of the packet-switching service. The connection between the user (via a B channel) and the packet-switching node with which it communicates may be either semipermanent or circuit-switched. In the former case, the connection is always there and the user may freely invoke X.25 to set up a virtual circuit to another user. In the latter case, the D channel is involved, and the following sequence of steps occurs:

- The user requests, via the D-channel call control protocol (I.451), a circuit-switched connection on the B channel to a packet-switching node.
- The connection is set up using SS7 and the user is notified via the D channel.
- The user sets up a virtual circuit to another user via the X.25 call establishment procedure on the B channel (described in Chapter 3).
- The user terminates the virtual circuit using X.25 on the B channel.
- After one or more virtual calls on the B channel, the user is done, and signals via the D channel to terminate the circuit-switched connection to the packet switching node.
- The connection is terminated via SS7.

Another source of variability is whether the packet-switching service is provided directly by the ISDN provider or is provided by a separate packet-switching network. In either case, a semipermanent or circuit-switched connection is possible. One observable difference is that ISDN-provided packet switching via the B channel allows the establishment of virtual circuits to users employing the D channel for packet switching.

Packet-switching service can also be obtained on the **D channel.** For D-channel access, the ISDN provides a packet-switching capability as part of the network. The D channel provides a semipermanent connection to a packet-switching node within the ISDN. The user employs the X.25 level 3 protocol as is done in the case of a B-channel virtual call. Since the D channel is also used for control signaling, some means is needed to distinguish between X.25 packet traffic and ISDN control traffic. This is accomplished by means of the link layer addressing scheme explained below.

8-3   PHYSICAL LAYER

The ISDN physical layer is presented to the user at either reference point S or T (Figure 7-4). In either case, the following functions are included as physical layer (OSI layer 1) functions:

- Encoding of digital data for transmission across the interface.
- Full-duplex transmission of B-channel data.
- Full-duplex transmission of D-channel data.
- Multiplexing of channels to form basic or primary access transmission structure.
- Activation and deactivation of physical circuit.
- Power feeding from network termination to the terminal.
- Terminal identification.
- Faulty terminal isolation.
- D-channel contention access.

The last function is needed when there is a multipoint configuration for basic access; this is described below.

The nature of the physical interface and functionality differs for basic and primary user-network interfaces. We examine each in turn.

Basic User-Network Interface

The layer 1 specification for the basic user-network interface is defined in Recommendation I.430. Recall that the basic interface supports a 2B + D channel structure at 192 kbps. In this section, we examine three key aspects of the basic interface:

- encoding for transmission
- framing for multiplexing
- contention resolution for multidrop configurations.

Data Encoding.   At the interface between the subscriber and the network terminating equipment (T or S reference point), digital data are exchanged using full-duplex transmission. A separate physical line is used for the transmission in each direction. Hence we need not concern ourselves with echo cancellation or time-compression multiplexing techniques to achieve full-duplex operation. Because the distances are relatively short, and because all of the equipment is on the subscriber's premises, it is far easier to use two separate physical circuits than to use any other technique for full-duplex operation.

The physical layer must specify the nature of the signals on the two circuits that will represent binary zero and binary one. The most common and easiest way to transmit digital signals is to use two different voltage levels for the two binary digits. For example, the absence of voltage (which is also the absence of current) could be used to represent 0, whereas a constant positive voltage could be used to represent 1. More typically, a negative voltage (low) is used to represent 0, and a positive voltage (high) is used to represent 1. The latter technique, shown in Figure 8-5a is known as Non-Return to Zero (NRZ).

There are several disadvantages to NRZ transmission. If a long string of 0s or 1s occur, it is possible for a loss of synchronization to occur, since it will be difficult for the receiver to determine where one bit ends and the next bit begins. If the receiver's clock is slightly off from the transmitter's clock, then there will be an accumulating drift so that errors in sampling a long string of 1s or 0s occur. Also, there is a direct-current (dc) component during each bit time that will accumulate if 1s or 0s predominate. This produces undesirable spectral qualities that degrade signal integrity. Furthermore, the dc component can cause plating or other deterioration at attachment contacts.

To overcome these problems, some form of signal encoding is needed. The form chosen for the basic rate interface is known as **pseudoternary coding.** In this scheme, a binary 1 is represent by no line signal and a binary 0 is represented by a positive or negative pulse (Figure 8-5b). The binary 0 pulses must alternate in polarity. The term pseudoternary arises due to the use of three encoded signal levels to represent two-level (binary) data. We can see several advantages to this approach. First, there will be no loss of synchronization if a long string of 0s occurs. Each 0 introduces a transition, and the receiver can resynchronize on that transition. A long string of 1s would still be a problem but, as we shall see, the basic interface framing structure includes extra 0s to avoid this problem. Second, since the 0 signals alternate in voltage from positive to negative, there is no net dc component. Also, the bandwidth of the resulting signal is considerably less than the bandwidth for NRZ.

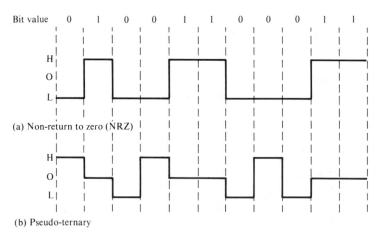

FIGURE 8-5 Digital Signal Encoding

Finally, the pulse alternation property provides a simple means of error detection. Any isolated error, whether it deletes a pulse or adds a pulse, causes a violation of this property.

Thus, there is significant advantage to the use of pseudoternary coding over NRZ. Of course, as with any engineering design decision, there is a tradeoff. With pseudoternary coding, the line signal may take on one of three levels, but each signal element, which could represent $\log_2 3 = 1.58$ bits of information, bears only one bit of information. Thus pseudoternary is not as efficient as NRZ coding. We have introduced redundancy into the signal to overcome some of the technical problems with NRZ.

Framing and Multiplexing. The basic access structure consists of two 64-kbps B channels and one 16-kbps D channel. These channels, which produce a load of 144 kbps, are multiplexed over a 192-kbps interface at the S or T reference point. The remaining capacity is used for various framing and synchronization purposes.

As with any synchronous time-division multiplexed (TDM) scheme, basic access transmission is structured into repetitive, fixed-length frames. In this case, each frame is 48 bits long; at 192 kbps, frames must repeat at a rate of one frame every $250\,\mu$sec. Figure 8-6 shows the frame structure; the lower frame is transmitted by the subscriber's terminal equipment (TE) to the network (NT1 or NT2); the upper frame is transmitted from the NT1 or NT2 to the TE. The pseudoternary coding is illustrated. Frame synchronization is such that each frame transmitted from a TE toward the NT is later than the frame in the opposite direction by two bit-times.

Each frame of 48 bits includes 16 bits from each of the two B channels and 4 bits from the D channel. The remaining bits have the following interpretation. Let us first consider the frame structure in the TE-to-NT direction. Each frame begins with a framing bit (F) that is always transmitted as a positive pulse. This is followed by a dc balancing bit (L) that is set to a negative pulse to balance the voltage. The F-L pattern thus acts to synchronize the receiver on the beginning of the frame. The specification dictates that, following these first two bit positions, the first occurrence of a zero bit will be encoded as a negative pulse. After that, the pseudoternary rules is observed. The next eight bits (B1) are from the first B channel. This is followed by another dc balancing bit (L). Next comes a bit from the D channel, followed by its balancing bit. This is followed by the auxiliary framing bit (F_A) which is set to zero unless it is to be used in a multiframe structure, as explained below. There follows another balancing bit(L), eight bits (B2) from the second B channel, and another balancing bit (L). This is followed by bits from the D channel, first B channel, D channel again, second B channel and the D channel yet again, with each group of channel bits followed by a balancing bit.

The frame structure in the NT-to-TE direction is similar to the frame structure for transmission in the TE-to-NT direction. The following new bits replace some of the dc balancing bits. The D-channel echo bit (E) is a retransmission by the NT of the most recently received D bit from the TE; the purpose of this echo is

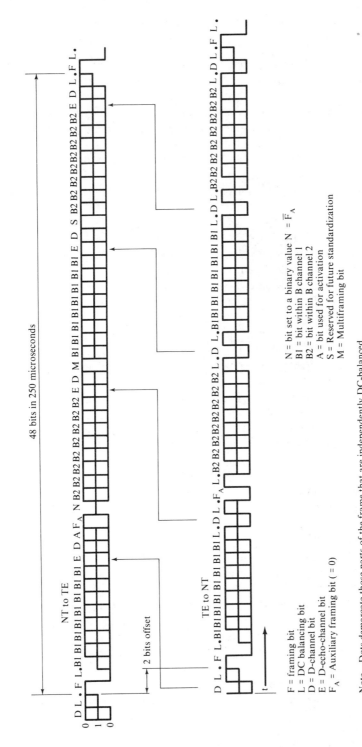

FIGURE 8-6 Frame Structure at Reference Points S and T for Basic Rate

F = framing bit
L = DC balancing bit
D = D-channel bit
E = D-echo-channel bit
F_A = Auxiliary framing bit (= 0)

N = bit set to a binary value N = $\overline{F}_A$
B1 = bit within B channel 1
B2 = bit within B channel 2
A = bit used for activation
S = Reserved for future standardization
M = Multiframing bit

Note—Dots demarcate those parts of the frame that are independently DC-balanced.
Note—The F_A bit in the direction TE to NT is used as a Q bit in every fifth frame if the Q channel capability is applied.

explained below. The activation bit (A) is used to activate or deactivate a TE, allowing the device to come on line or, when there is no activity, to be placed in low-power-consumption mode. The N bit, always set to one, is reserved for future use in multiframing. The M bit may be used for multiframing as explained below. The S bit is reserved for other future standardization requirements.

A recently-added feature of the basic interface specification is the provision for an additional channel for traffic in the TE-to-NT direction, called the Q channel. At present, the use of the Q channel is for further study. However, the current version of I.430 provides the structure for the Q channel. To implement the Q-channel, a multiframe structure is established by setting the M bit (NT to TE direction) to binary 1 on every twentieth frame. In the TE-to-NT direction, every F_A bit in every fifth frame is a Q bit. Thus in each 20-frame multiframe there are 4 Q bits.

Multidrop Configurations.   With the basic access interface, it is possible to have more than one TE device in a passive-bus configuration. Figure 8-7 shows the allowable configurations. The simplest is a point-to-point configuration, with only one TE. In this configuration, the maximum distance between the NT equipment and the TE is on the order of 1 km. The second configuration is an ordinary passive bus, which has traditionally been referred to as a multidrop line. This kind of configuration imposes limitations on the distances involved. This has to do with the way in which signal strength is determined.

When two devices exchange data over a link, the signal strength of the transmitter must be adjusted to be within certain limits. The signal must be strong enough so that, after attenuation and signal impairment across the medium, it meets the receiver's minimum signal strength requirements and maintains an adequate signal-to-noise ratio. On the other hand, the signal must not be so strong as to overload the circuitry of the transmitter, which creates harmonics and nonlinear effects. With a point-to-point link, the principal factor to take into account is the length of the medium. With a multidrop link, each tap into the bus creates losses and distortions. Accordingly, for a given data rate and transmission medium, a multidrop line will need to be shorter than a point-to-point line. In the case of the basic access interface, CCITT specifies a maximum distance somewhere between 100 and 200 meters, with a maximum of 8 TEs connected at random points along the interface cable.

The length of the short passive bus is also limited by the differential round trip delay in signal propagation. Because the devices are connected at various points, the NT receiver must cater for pulses arriving with different delays from various terminals. To maintain receiver synchronization, the limit of 100 to 200 meters is needed. A greater length can be achieved if all of the devices are clustered together at the far end of the line (Figure 8-7c). With this extended bus configuration, a maximum length of 500 meters, with a maximum differential distance between terminals of 25–50 meters is possible.

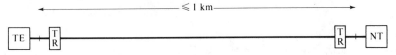

(a) Point-to-point

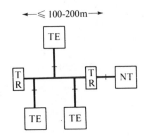

(b) Short passive bus

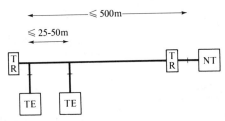

(c) Extended passive bus

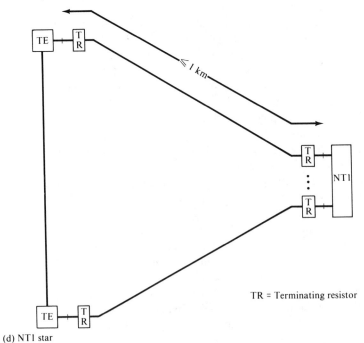

(d) NT1 star

TR = Terminating resistor

FIGURE 8-7 Basic Interface Wiring Configurations

With the configurations of Figure 8- 7b and c, there is a contention problem. In the case of the two B channels, no additional functionality is needed, since each channel is dedicated to a particular TE at any given time. However, the D channel is shared by all TEs for control signaling and D-channel packet transmission. For incoming data, we will see that the LAP-D addressing scheme is sufficient to sort out the proper destination TE for each frame. For outgoing data, some sort of contention resolution protocol is needed to assure that only one device at a time attempts to transmit.

The D-channel contention-resolution algorithm has the following elements:

1. When a subscriber device has no LAP-D frames to transmit, it transmits a series of binary ones on the D channel. Using the pseudo-ternary encoding scheme, this corresponds to the absence of line signal.

2. The NT, on receipt of a D channel bit, reflects back the binary value as a D-channel echo bit (Figure 8-6).

3. When a terminal is ready to transmit a LAP-D frame, it listens to the stream of incoming D-channel echo bits. If it detects a string of 1-bits of length equal to a threshold value X_i, then it may transmit. Otherwise, the terminal must assume that some other terminal is transmitting, and wait.

4. It may happen that several terminals are monitoring the echo stream and begin to transmit at the same time, causing a collision. To overcome this condition, a transmitting TE monitors the echo bits and compares them to its transmitted bits. If a discrepancy is detected, the terminal ceases to transmit and returns to a listen state.

The electrical characteristics of the interface (i.e., 1-bit = absence of signal) are such that any user equipment transmitting a 0-bit will override user equipment transmitting a 1-bit at the same instant. This arrangement ensures that one device will be guaranteed successful completion of its transmission.

The algorithm also includes a primitive priority mechanism based on the threshold value X_i. Signaling information is given priority over packet information. Within each of these two priority classes, a station begins at normal priority and then is reduced to lower priority after a transmission. It remains at the lower priority until all other terminals have had an opportunity to transmit. The values of X_i are 8 and 9 1-bits for signal information and 10 and 11 for packet information.

The final configuration illustrated in Figure 8-7 is the star configuration. This configuration permits multiple TEs but requires only point-to-point wiring. In this configuration, the NT1 must include digital logic to provide for the operation of the D-channel echo. The NT1 must transmit the same echo bit over all NT1-to-TE lines. The value of the echo bit is 0 if any of the incoming D bits is 0; otherwise it is 1. On the network side, the NT1 must merge the transmissions from all of the TEs to form a single 192 kbps stream.

Primary User-Network Interface

The primary interface, like the basic interface, multiplexes multiple channels across a single transmission medium. In the case of the primary interface, only a point-to-point configuration is allowed. Typically, the interface exists at the T reference point with a digital PBX or other concentration device controlling multiple TEs and providing a synchronous TDM facility for access to ISDN. Two data rates are defined for the primary interface: 1.544 Mbps and 2.048 Mbps.

Interface at 1.544 Mbps.   The ISDN interface at 1.544 Mbps is based on the North American DS-1 transmission structure, which is used on the T1 transmission service. Figure 8-8a illustrates the frame format for this data rate. The bit stream is structured into repetitive 193-bit frames. Each frame consists of 24 8-bit time slots and a framing bit. The same time slot repeated over multiple frames constitutes a channel. At a data rate of 1.544 Mbps, frames repeat at a rate of one every 125 μsec, or 8000 frames per second. Thus each channel supports 64 kbps. Typically, the transmission structure is used to support 23 B channels and 1 D channel. As discussed in Chapter 7, other assignments can be made, include 24 B channels or various combinations of H channels.

The framing bit is used for synchronization and other management purposes. A multiframe structure of 24 193-bit frames is imposed, and Table 8-2 shows the assignment of values to the 24 framing bits across the 24-frame multiframe. Six of the bits form a frame alignment signal, with the code 001011, which repeats every multiframe. The purpose is to provide a form of synchronization. If for some reason, the receiver becomes one or more bits out of alignment with the transmitter, it will fail to detect the alignment signal and hence will detect the misalignment. The

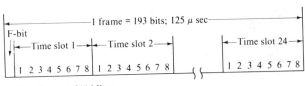

(a) Interface at 1.544 Mbps

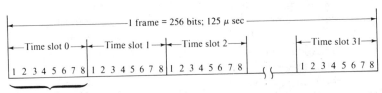

(b) Interface at 2.048 Mbps

FIGURE 8-8   Primary Access Frame Formats

TABLE 8-2 ASSIGNMENT OF VALUES TO FRAMING BITS IN 1.544-Mbps INTERFACE

Multiframe Frame Number	Multiframe Bit Number	F-Bits		
			Assignments	
		FAS	Note 1	Note 2
1	0	—	m	—
2	193	—	—	e_1
3	386	—	m	—
4	579	0	—	—
5	772	—	m	—
6	965	—	—	e_2
7	1158	—	m	—
8	1351	0	—	—
9	1544	—	m	—
10	1737	—	—	e_3
11	1930	—	m	—
12	2123	1	—	—
13	2316	—	m	—
14	2509	—	—	e_4
15	2702	—	m	—
16	2895	0	—	—
17	3011	—	m	—
18	3281	—	—	e_5
19	3474	—	m	—
20	3667	1	—	—
21	3860	—	m	—
22	4053	—	—	e_6
23	4246	—	m	—
24	4439	1	—	—

FAS: Frame alignment signal (. . . 001011 . . .).

Note 1 — The use of the m-bits is for further study (for example, for maintenance and operational information).

Note 2 — The use of the bits e_1 to e_6 is for further study.

remaining bits are currently not assigned in the standard, but they may possibly be used in the future. For example, the bits designated as e_i bits could be used as a 6-bit cyclic redundancy check (CRC) of the framing bits.

The coding scheme that is used with the 1.544-Mbps interface is known as *bipolar with 8-zeros substitution* (B8ZS). As with the basic interface, the coding scheme is based on a pseudo-ternary code. In this case, the code, referred to as bipolar, is as follows: binary 0 is represent by no line signal and a binary 1 is represented by a positive or negative pulse. The binary 1 pulses must alternate in polarity. Note that the assignment of codes to binary 0 and 1 is the reverse of that for the basic interface. The drawback of the bipolar code is that a long string of zeros may result in loss of synchronization. To overcome this problem the bipolar encoding is amended with the following rules (Figure 8-9):

- If an octet of all zeros occurs and the last voltage pulse preceding this octet was positive, then the eight zeros of the octet are encoded as 000+-0-+.
- If an octet of all zeros occurs and the last voltage pulse preceding this octet was negative, then the eight zeros of the octet are encoded as 000-+0+-.

This technique forces two code violations of the bipolar code, an event unlikely to be caused by noise or other transmission impairment. The receiver recognizes the pattern and interprets the octet as consisting of all zeros.

Interface at 2.048 Mbps.   The ISDN interface at 2.048 Mbps is based on the European transmission structure of the same data rate. Figure 8-8b illustrates the frame format for this data rate. The bit stream is structured into repetitive 256-bit frames. Each frame consists of 32 8-bit time slots. The first time slot is used for framing and synchronization purposes; the remaining 31 time slots support user channels. At a data rate of 2.048 Mbps, frames repeat at a rate of one every 125 μsec, or 8000 frames per second. Thus each channel supports 64 kbps. Typically, the transmission structure is used to support 30 B channels and 1 D channel. As discussed in Chapter 7, other assignments can be made, including 31 B channels or various combinations of H channels.

Table 8-3 shows the use of the bits in time slot 0. The frame alignment signal occupies positions 2 to 8 in channel time slot 0 of every frame. This signal, which is

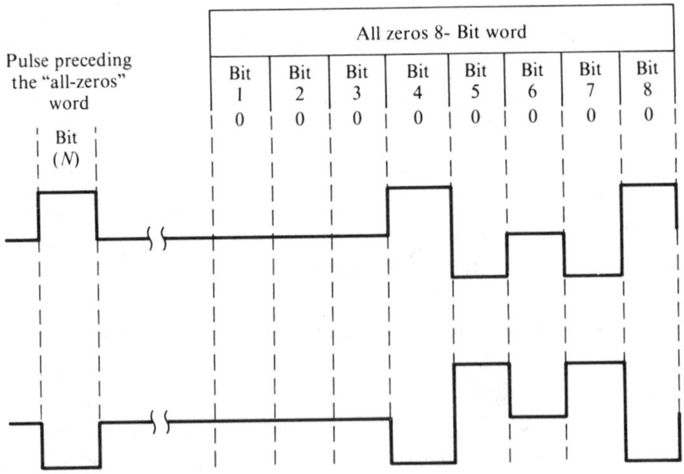

FIGURE 8-9   Bipolar with 8-Zero Substitution (B8ZS)

TABLE 8-3 ASSIGNMENT OF VALUES TO FRAMING BITS IN 2.048-Mbps INTERFACE

Alternate frames \ Bit Number	1	2	3	4	5	6	7	8
Frame containing the frame alignment signal	S_i (Note 1)	0	0	1	1	0	1	1
				Frame alignment signal				
Frame not containing the frame alignment signal	S_i (Note 1)	1 (Note 2)	A (Note 3)	S_n	S_n	S_n	S_n	S_n
						(Note 3)		

Note 1 — S_i; — The use will be defined at a later stage.
Note 2 — This bit is fixed at 1 to assist in avoiding simulations of the frame alignment signal.
Note 3 — The use of these bits will be defined at a later stage.

0011011, is used for alignment in the same fashion as the frame alignment signal on the 1.544-Mbps interface. The S_i bits are not defined at this time; one possible use is for a 4-bit CRC procedure. The A bit is currently not defined; one possible use is for a remote alarm indication. In an alarm condition, it would be set to 1. The S_n bits are spare bits with no currently contemplated use.

The coding scheme that is used with the 2.048-Mbps interface is known as the *high-density bipolar — 3 zeros* (HDB3) code (Table 8-4). As before, it is based on the use of bipolar encoding. In this case, the scheme replaces strings of four zeros with sequences containing one or two pulses. In each case, the fourth zero is replaced with a code violation. In addition, a rule is needed to ensure that successive violations are of alternate polarity so that no dc component is introduced. Thus, if the last violation was positive, this violation must be negative and vice versa. This table shows that this condition is tested for by determining whether the number of pulses since the last violation is even or odd and determining the polarity of the last pulse before the occurrence of the four zeros.

8-4 LAP-D

All traffic over the D channel employs a link-layer protocol known as LAP-D (Link Access ProtocolD) channel. We look first at the services that LAP-D provides to the network layer, and then at various elements of the LAP-D protocol.*

Services

The purpose of LAP-D is to convey user information between layer 3 entities across ISDN using the D-channel. The LAP-D service will support:

- Multiple terminals at the user-network installation (e.g., see Figure 8-7)
- Multiple layer 3 entities (e.g., X.25 level 3, I.451)

The LAP-D standard provides two forms of service to LAP-D users: the unacknowledged information transfer service and the acknowledged information

TABLE 8-4   HDB3 SUBSTITUTION RULES

Polarity of Preceding Pulse	Number of Bipolar Pulses (ones) Since Last Substitution	
	Odd	Even
−	000 −	+ 00 +
+	000 +	− 00 −

---

* The basic link control functions of flow control, error detection, and error control, which are part of the LAP-D protocol, are discussed in Appendix A.

transfer service. The **unacknowledged information transfer service** simply provides for the transfer of frames containing user data with no acknowledgment. The service does not guarantee that data presented by one user will be delivered to another user, nor does it inform the sender if the delivery attempt fails. The service does not provide any flow control or error control mechanism. This service supports both point-to-point (deliver to one user) or broadcast (deliver to a number of users). This service allows for fast data transfer and is useful for management procedures such as alarm messages and messages that need to be broadcast to multiple users.

The **acknowledged information transfer service** is the more common one, and is similar to the service offered by LAP-B and HDLC. With this service, a logical connection is established between two LAP-D users. Three phases occur: connection establishment, data transfer, and connection termination. During the *connection establishment phase*, the two uses agree to exchange acknowledged data. One user issues a connection request to the other. If the other is prepared to engage in a logical connection, then the request is acknowledged affirmatively, and a logical connection is established. In essence, the existence of a logical connection means that the LAP-D service provider at each end of the connection will keep track of the frames being transmitted and those being received, for the purposes of error control and flow control. During the *data transfer phase*, LAP-D guarantees that all frames will be delivered in the order that they were transmitted. During the *connection termination phase*, one of the two users requests termination of the logical connection.

LAP-D Protocol: Basic Characteristics

The LAP-D protocol is modeled after the LAP-B protocol used in X.25 and on HDLC. Both user information and protocol control information and parameters are transmitted in frames. Corresponding to the two types of service offered by LAP-D, there are two types of operation:

- *Unacknowledged operation:* Layer 3 information is transferred in unnumbered frames. Error detection is used to discard damaged frames, but there is no error control or flow control.
- *Acknowledged operation:* Layer 3 information is transferred in frames that include sequence numbers and that are acknowledged. Error control and flow control procedures are included in the protocol. This type is also referred to in the standard as multiple-frame operation.**

** In the 1984 version of I.440, another form of acknowledged operation, known as *single-frame operation*, was also defined. With this form, the stop-and-wait flow control technique was used, allowing only one frame to be outstanding at a time. In contrast, the multiple-frame form uses the sliding-window flow control technique, which allows multiple frames to be outstanding at a time (see Appendix A for a discussion of these flow control techniques). Because of lack of support, single-frame operation was subsequently dropped from the recommendation.

These two types of operation may coexist on a single D channel. With the acknowledged operation it is possible to simultaneously support multiple logical LAP-D connections. This is analogous to the ability in X.25 level 3 to support multiple virtual circuits.

Frame Structure

All user information and protocol messages are transmitted in the form of frames. Figure 8-10 depicts the structure of the LAP-D frame. Let us examine each of these fields in turn.

Flag Fields.   Flag fields delimit the frame at both ends with the unique pattern 01111110. A single flag may be used as the closing flag for one frame and the opening flag for the next. On both sides of the user-network interface, receivers are continuously hunting for the flag sequence to synchronize on the start of a frame. While receiving a frame, a station continues to hunt for that sequence to determine the end of the frame. As with the signaling link level of Signaling System Number 7,

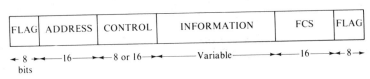

(a) Frame format

C/R = Command/response
SAPI = Service access point identifier
TEI = Terminal endpoint identifier

(b) Address field format

N(S) = Transmitter send sequence number
N(R) = Transmitter receive sequence number
S = Supervisory function bit
M = Modifier function bit
P/F = Poll/final bit

(c) Control field formats

FIGURE 8-10   LAP-D Formats

LAP-D uses bit-stuffing to provide transparency. The transmitter inserts a 0 bit after all sequences of five contiguous 1 bits to ensure that a flag is not simulated within the frame. The receiving LAP-D entity examines the frame contents between the opening and closing flag sequences and discards any 0 bit that directly follows five contiguous 1 bits (see Figure 4-10).

Address Field.   LAP-D has to deal with two levels of multiplexing. First, at a subscriber site, there may be multiple user devices sharing the same physical interface. Second, within each user device, there may be multiple types of traffic: specifically, packet-switched data and control signaling. To accommodate these levels of multiplexing, LAP-D employs a two-part address, consisting of a terminal endpoint identifier (TEI) and a service access point identifier (SAPI).

Typically, each user device is given a unique **terminal endpoint identifier** (TEI). It is also possible for a single device to be assigned more than one TEI. This might be the case for a terminal concentrator. TEI assignment occurs either automatically when the equipment first connects to the interface, or manually by the user. In the latter case, care must be taken that multiple equipment attached to the same interface do not have the same TEI. The advantage of the automatic procedure is that it allows the user to change, add, or delete equipment at will without prior notification to the network administration. Without this feature, the network would be obliged to manage a data base for each subscriber that would need to be updated manually. Table 8-5 shows the assignment of TEI numbers.

The **service access point identifier** (SAPI) identifies a layer 3 user of LAP-D, and thus corresponds to a layer 3 protocol entity within a user device. Four

TABLE 8-5   SAPI AND TEI ASSIGNMENTS

a. SAPI Assignments

SAPI Value	Related Layer 3 or Management Entity
0	Call control procedures
1	Reserved for packet mode communication using I.451 call control procedures
16	Packet communication conforming to X.25 level 3
63	Layer 2 management procedures
All others	Reserved for future standardization

b. TEI Assignments

TEI Value	User Type
0-63	Nonautomatic TEI assignment user equipment
64-126	Automatic TEI assignment user equipment
127	Used during automatic TEI assignment

values have been assigned, as shown in Table 8-4a. A SAPI of 0 is used for call control procedures for managing B channel circuits; the value 16 is reserved for packet-mode communication on the D channel using X.25 level 3; and a value of 63 is used for the exchange of layer 2 management information. The most recent assignment, made in 1988, is the value of 1 for packet-mode communication using I.451. This could be used for user-user signaling.

The SAPI values are unique within a TEI. That is, for a given TEI, there is a unique layer 3 entity for a given SAPI. Thus the TEI and the SAPI together uniquely identify a layer 3 user at a subscriber site. The TEI and SAPI together are also used to uniquely identify a logical connection; in this context, the combination of TEI and SAPI is referred to as **data link connection identifier** (DLCI). At any one time, LAP-D may maintain multiple logical connections, each with a unique DLCI. Thus, at any one time, a layer three entity may have only one LAP-D logical connection. Figure 8-11 provides an example. It shows five independent logical connections over a single D-channel interface, terminating in two TEs on the user side of the interface.

The address field format is illustrated in Figure 8-10b. The SAPI and TEI fields refer to the address of the subscriber layer 3 entity. On transmission, the layer 3 entity includes this address in the frame. Frames arriving from the network have this address, and the LAP-D entity uses the address to deliver the user data to the appropriate layer 3 entity. In addition, the address field includes a **command/ response** (C/R) bit. As explained below, all LAP-D messages are categorized as either commands or responses, and this bit is used to indicate which type of message is contained in the frame.

Control Field. LAP-D defines three types of frames, each with a different control field format. **Information transfer frames** (I-frames) carry the data to be transmitted for the user. Additionally, flow and error control data, using the go-back-N ARQ mechanism, are piggybacked on an information frame. **Supervisory frames** (S-frames) provide the ARQ mechanism when piggybacking is not used. **Unnumbered frames** (U-frames) provide supplemental link control functions and are also used to support unacknowledged operation. The first one or two bits of the control field serves to identify the frame type. The remaining bit positions are organized into subfields as indicated in Figure 8-10c. Their use is explained in the discussion of LAP-D operation, below.

All of the control field formats contain the poll/final bit (P/F). In command frames, it is referred to as the P bit, and is set to 1 to solicit (poll) a response frame from the peer LAP-D entity. In response frames, it is referred to as the F bit, and is set to 1 to indicate the response frame transmitted as a result of a soliciting command.

Information Field. The information field is present only in I-frames and some unnumbered frames. The field can contain any sequence of bits but must consist of an integral number of octets. The length of the information field is variable up to some system-defined maximum. In the case of both control signaling and packet information, I.441 specifies a maximum length of 260 octets.

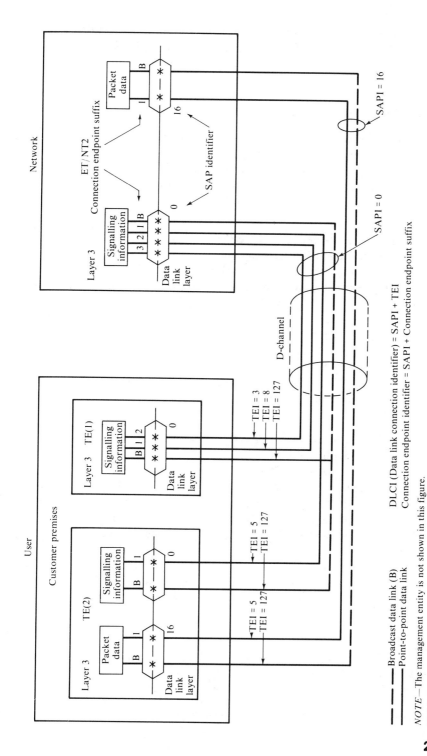

NOTE—The management entity is not shown in this figure.

FIGURE 8-11 Overview Description of the Relation Between SAPI, TEI, and Data Link Connection Endpoint Identifier (I.440)

297

Frame Check Sequence Field.   The frame check sequence (FCS) is an error-detecting code calculated from the remaining bits of the frame, exclusive of flags. The code used is the CRC-CCITT code defined in Appendix A.

Acknowledged Operation

The acknowledged operation of LAP-D consists of the exchange of I-frames, S-frames, and U-frames between a subscriber TE and the network over the D channel. The various commands and responses defined for these frame types are listed in Table 8-6. In describing LAP-D operation, we will discuss these three types of frames.

Connection Establishment.   A logical connection may be requested by either the network or the subscriber by transmitting a SABME* frame. Generally, this will be in response to a request from a layer 3 entity. The SABME frame contains the TEI and the SAPI of the layer 3 entity to which connection is requested. The peer LAP-D entity receives the SABME frame and passes up a connection request indication to the appropriate layer 3 entity. If the layer 3 entity responds with an acceptance of the connection, then the LAP-D entity transmits a UA frame back to the other side. When the UA is received, signifying acceptance, the LAP-D entity passes a confirmation up to the requesting user. If the destination user rejects the connection request, its LAP-D entity returns a DM frame, and the receiving LAP-D entity informs its user of the rejection.

Data Transfer.   When the connection request has been accepted and confirmed the connection is established. Both sides may begin to send user data in I-frames, starting with sequence number 0. The N(S) and N(R) fields of the I-frame are sequence numbers that support flow control and error control. A LAP-D entity sending a sequence of I-frames will number them sequentially, modulo 128, and place the sequence number in N(S). N(R) is the piggybacked acknowledgment for I-frames received; it enables the LAP-D entity to indicate which number I-frame it expects to receive next.

The S-frames are also used for flow control and error control. Sliding-window flow control and go-back-N ARQ error control are used. The receive ready (RR) frame is used to acknowledge the last I-frame received by indicating the next I-frame

---

* This stands for Set Asynchronous Balanced Mode (ABM) Extended. It is used in HDLC to choose the ABM mode, which involves two peer entities, as opposed to a primary and a secondary, and to select extended sequence number length of 7 bits, as opposed to the default value of 3 bits. Both ABM and 7-bit sequence numbers are mandatory in LAP-D acknowledged operation. Thus, this is simply a connection request command, but the same terminology is retained for consistency.

TABLE 8-6   LAP-D COMMANDS AND RESPONSES

Name	Control Field Encoding	C/R	Description
	Information Transfer Format		
I (Information)	0-N(S)--P-N(R)--	C	Exchange user data
	Supervisory Format		
RR (Receive Ready)	10000000*-N(R)--	C/R	Positive ack; ready to receive I frame
RNR (Receive Not Ready)	10100000*-N(R)--	C/R	Positive ack; not ready to receive
REJ (Reject)	10010000*-N(R)--	C/R	Negative ack; go back N
	Unnumbered Format		
SABME (Set Asynchronous Balanced Mode)	1111P110	C	Request logical connection
DM (Disconnected Mode)	1111F000	R	Unable to establish or maintain logical connection
UI (Unnumbered Information)	1100P000	C	Used for unacknowledged information transfer service
DISC (Disconnect)	1100P010	C	Terminate logical connection
UA (Unnumbered Acknowledgment)	1100F110	R	Acknowledge SABME or DISC
FRMR (Frame Reject)	1110F001	R	Reports receipt of unacceptable frame
XID (Exchange Identification)	1111*101	C/R	Exchange identification information

* = P/F bit

expected. The RR is used when there is no reverse user traffic to carry a piggybacked acknowledgment. Receive not ready (RNR) acknowledges an I-frame, as with RR, but also asks the peer entity to suspend transmission of I-frames. When the entity that issued RNR is again ready, it sends an RR. REJ initiates the go-back-N ARQ. It indicates that the last I-frame received has been rejected and that retransmission of all I-frames beginning with number N(R) is required.

Disconnect.   Either LAP-D entity can initiate a disconnect, either on its own initiative if there is some sort of fault, or at the request of its layer 3 user. The LAP-D entity issues a disconnect on a particular logical connection by sending a DISC frame to the peer entity on the connection. The remote entity must accept the disconnect by replying with a UA and informing its layer 3 user that the connection has been terminated. Any outstanding unacknowledged I-frames may be lost, and their recovery is the responsibility of higher layers.

Miscellaneous Functions.   The frame reject (FRMR) frame is used to indicate that an improper frame has arrived — one that somehow violates the protocol. One or more of the following conditions have occurred:

- The receipt of a control field that is undefined (not one of the control field encodings listed in Table 8-6) or not implemented.
- The receipt of an S-frame or U-frame with incorrect length.
- The receipt of an invalid N(R); the only valid N(R) is in the range from the sequence number of the last acknowledged frame to the sequence number of the last transmitted frame.
- The receipt of an I-frame with an information field that exceeds the maximum established length.

The effect of the FRMR is to abort the connection. Upon receipt of an FRMR, the receiving entity may try to reestablish the connection using the connection establishment procedure described earlier.

The exchange identification (XID) frame is used for two stations to exchange information relating to connection management. When a peer entity receives an XID command, it responds with an XID response. The actual information exchanged is beyond the scope of the standard.

Examples of Acknowledged Operation.   In order to better understand the acknowledged operation, several examples are presented in Figure 8-12. The examples all make use of the vertical time sequence diagram [CARL80]. It has the advantages of showing time dependencies and illustrating the correct send-receive relationship. Each arrow represents a single frame transiting a data link between TE and NT. Each arrow includes a legend that specifies the frame name, the setting of the P/F bit, and, where appropriate, the values of N(R) and N(S). The setting of the P or F bit is 1 if the designation is present and 0 if absent.

Figure 8-12a shows the frames involved in link setup and disconnect. In the example, the TE is requesting the connection; a similar sequence occurs if the NT requests the connection. The data link entity for the TE issues an SABME command to the other side and starts a timer, T200 (see Table 8-7, below). The other LAP-D entity, upon receiving the SABME returns a UA response and sets local variables and counters to their initial values. The initiating entity receives the UA response, sets its variables and counters, and stops the timer. The logical connection is now active, and both sides may begin transmitting frames. Should the T200 expire without a response, the originator will repeat the SABME, as illustrated. This would be repeated until a UA or DM is received or until, after a given number of tries (N200), the entity attempting initiation gives up and reports failure to a management entity. In this case, higher-layer intervention is necessary. The same figure (Figure 8-12a) shows the disconnect procedure. One side issues a DISC command, and the other responds with a UA response.

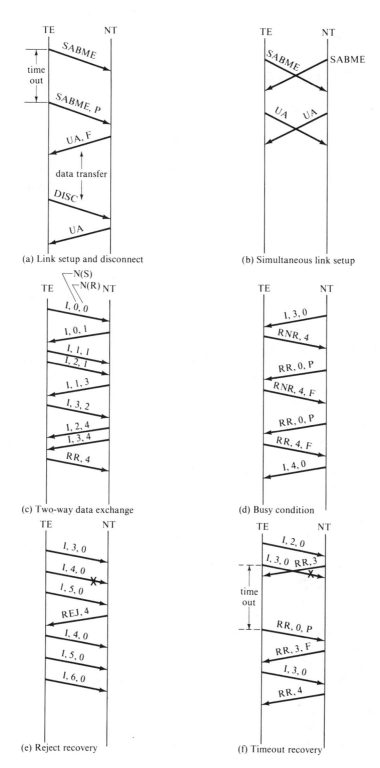

FIGURE 8-12 LAP-D Operation

LAP-D is a balanced mode of operation, meaning that the NT and TE entities have equal status. Thus it is possible that both sides may attempt to set up a logical connection to the same TEI and SAPI user at about the same time. Figure 8-12b illustrates that this situation is resolved by having both sides respond to the incoming SABME, and then setting up the logical connection.

Figure 8-12c illustrates the full-duplex exchange of I-frames. When an entity sends a number of I-frames in a row with no incoming data, then the receive sequence number is simply repeated (e.g., I,1,1; I,2.1 in the TE-to-NT direction). When an entity receives a number of I-frames in a row with no outgoing frames, then the receive sequence number in the next outgoing frame must reflect the cumulative activity (e.g., I,1,3 in the NT-to-TE direction). Note that, in addition to I-frames, data exchange may involve supervisory frames.

Figure 8-12d shows an operation involving a busy condition. Such a condition may arise because a LAP-D entity is not able to process I-frames as fast as they are arriving, or the intended user is not able to accept data as fast as they arrive in I-frames. In either case, the entity's receive buffer fills up and it must halt the incoming flow of I-frames using an RNR command. In this example, the TE issues an RNR, which requires the NT to halt transmission of I-frames. The station receiving the RNR will usually poll the busy station at some periodic interval by sending an RR with the P bit set. This requires the other side to respond with either an RR or an RNR. When the busy condition has cleared, the TE returns an RR, and I-frame transmission from NT can resume.

An example of error recovery using the REJ command is shown in Figure 8-12e. In this example, the TE transmits I-frames numbered 3, 4, and 5. Number 4 suffers an error. The NT detects the error and discards the frame. When the NT receives I-frame number 5, it discards this frame because it is out of order, and sends an REJ with an N(R) of 4. This causes the TE entity to initiate retransmission of all I-frames sent, beginning with frame 4. It may continue to send additional frames after the retransmitted frames.

An example of error recovery using a timeout is shown in Figure 8-12f. In this example, the NT transmits I-frame number 3 as the last in a sequence of I-frames. The frame suffers an error. The NT detects the error and discards it. However, the NT cannot send an REJ. This is because there is no way to know on which logical connection the damaged frame was sent or, indeed, whether or not it was even an I-frame. If an error is detected in a frame, all of the bits of that frame are suspect, and the receiver has no way to act upon it. The transmitter, however, started a timer (T200) as the frame was transmitted. This timer has a duration long enough to span the expected response time. When the timer expires, the station initiates recovery action. This is usually done by polling the other side with an RR command with the P bit set, to determine the status of the other side. Since the poll demands a response, the entity will receive a frame containing an N(R) field and be able to proceed. In this case, the response indicates that frame 3 was lost, which the TE retransmits.

These examples are not exhaustive. However, they should give the reader a good feel for the behavior of LAP-D.

Unacknowledged Operation

Unacknowledged operation provides for the exchange of user data with no form of error control or flow control. The user information (UI) frame is used to transmit user data. When a LAP-D user wishes to send data, it passes the data to its LAP-D entity, which passes the data in the information field of a UI frame. When this frame is received, the information field is passed up to the destination user. There is no acknowledgment returned to the other side. However, error detection is performed and frames in error are discarded.

Management Functions

There are two functions related to link management that apply to the LAP-D entity as a whole, rather than to a particular connection or user of LAP-D. These are for TEI management and for parameter negotiation.

TEI Management.   The TEI management capability provides for automatic TEI assignment procedures. These procedures may be invoked for newly-connected TE equipment at a specific user-network interface, so that no manual setting of a TEI value is necessary. The initiation of TEI assignment is triggered by one of two events. First, if equipment is connected to the user-network interface, and the user attempts either unacknowledged data transfer or the establishment of a logical connection, the LAP-D entity suspends action on the request until a TEI assignment takes place. Or, second, the user side layer management entity may initiate the TEI assignment procedures for its own reasons. In either case, the user LAP-D entity transmits a UI frame with an SAPI of 63, a TEI of 127, and an information field that contains two subfields: message type and reference number. The message type is identity request. The reference number is a random number used to differentiate among a number of simultaneous identity requests by different user equipment. If the network side is able to assign an unused TEI value in the range 64 to 126, then it responds with a UI frame with an SAPI of 63, a TEI of 127, and an information field that contains three subfields: message type, reference number, and action indicator. The reference number is equal to the value received from the user, the message type is identity assigned, and the action indicator is the assigned TEI value. If the network is unable to assign a TEI, it returns a UI with a message type of identity denied.

In addition to automatic TEI assignment, there are procedures for checking the value of an existing TEI assignment and removing a TEI assignment. These procedures also make use of UI frames.

Parameter Negotiation.   Associated with LAP-D operation are certain key parameters. Each parameter is assigned a default value in the standard, but provisions are made for the negotiation of other values. The parameters and their default values are listed in Table 8-7. If a LAP-D entity wishes to use a different set of values for a

TABLE 8-7 LAP-D SYSTEM PARAMETERS

Parameter	Default Value	Definition
T200	1 second	Time to wait for an acknowledgment to a frame before initiating recovery
T201	=T200	Minimum time between TEI identity check messages
T202	2 seconds	Minimum time between TEI identity request messages
T203	10 seconds	Maximum time with no frames exchanged
N200	3	Maximum number of retransmission of a frame
N201	260 octets	Maximum length of information field
N202	3	Maximum number of retransmissions of TEI identity request message
k	1 for 16-kbps packet; 3 for 16-kbps signaling 7 for 64 kbps	Maximum number of outstanding I-frames

particular logical connection, it may issue an XID frame, with the desired values contained in subfields of the information field. The other side responds with an XID containing the list of parameter values that the peer can support. Each value must be in the range between the default value and the requested value.

8-5 LAYER 3 USER-NETWORK INTERFACE

For call control signaling, the D-channel layer 3 interface is defined in Recommendations I.450 and I.451. It specifies procedures for establishing connections on the B channels that share the same interface to ISDN as the D channel. It also provides user-to-user control signaling over the D channel.

Terminal Types

Two basic types of user terminals are supported by ISDN: functional and stimulus. **Functional terminals** are considered to be intelligent devices and can employ the full range of I.451 messages and parameters for call control. All signaling information is sent in a single control message (en bloc sending). **Stimulus terminals** are devices with a rudimentary signaling capability. A simple digital telephone is an example of a stimulus terminal. Messages sent to the network by a stimulus terminal are usually generated as a direct result of actions by the terminal user (e.g., handset lifted, key depression) and in general do little more than describe the event which has taken place at the man–machine interface. Thus, stimulus terminals transmit signaling information one event or one digit at a time (overlap sending). Signaling messages sent by the network to a stimulus terminal contain explicit instruction regarding the operations to be performed by the terminal (e.g., connect B channel, start alerting). For stimulus terminals, control functions are centralized in the exchange and functional expansion, if any, will be realized by changes in the exchange.

Messages

The process of establishing, controlling, and terminating a call occurs as a result of control signaling messages exchanged between the user and the network over a D channel. A common format is used for all messages defined in I.451, illustrated in Figure 8-13a. Three fields are common to all messages:

- *Protocol discriminator:* used to distinguish messages for user-network call control from other message types. The only other message type so far defined is X.25 level 3 packets. Additional message types may be defined later.
- *Call reference:* identifies the B-channel call to which this message refers. As with X.25 virtual circuit numbers, it has only local significance. The call reference field comprises 3 subfields. The length subfield specifies the length of the remainder of the field in octets. Provisionally, this length is one octet for a basic rate interface, and two octets for a primary rate interface. The flag indicates which end of the LAP-D logical connection initiated the call.
- *Message type:* identifies which I.451 message is being sent. The contents of the remainder of the message depend on the message type.

Following these three common fields, the remainder of the message consists of a sequence of zero or more information elements, or parameters. These contain

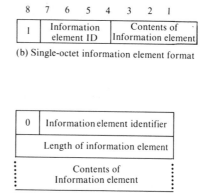

(a) General message format

(b) Single-octet information element format

(c) Variable-length information element format

FIGURE 8-13   I.451 Formats

TABLE 8-8 ISDN USER-NETWORK INTERFACE I.451 MESSAGES

Message	Parameters	Function
	Call Establishment Messages	
ALERTing	Cause, Channel identification, Terminal capabilities, Display, Redirecting address, User-user information	Sent by called TE and by network to calling TE to indicate that the called TE has begun to notify human user of the incoming call. Sent by called stimulus TE to indicate reception of SETUP message.
CALL PROCeeding	Cause, Channel identification, Display	Sent by network to calling TE to indicate that call establishment has been initiated.
CONNect	Cause, Connected address, Channel identification, CCITT-standardized facilities, Network-specific facilities, Terminal capabilities, Display, Switchhook, Redirecting address, User-user information	Sent by called TE and by network to calling TE to indicate call acceptance by the called TE.
CONNect ACKnowledge	Channel identification, Display, Signal	Sent by network to called TE to acknowledge reception of CONNect message.
SETUP	Bearer capability, Channel identification, CCITT-standardized facilities, Network-specific facilities, Terminal capabilities, Display, Keypad, Signal, Switchhook, Origination address, Destination address, Redirecting address, Transit Network selection, Low layer compatibility, High layer compatibility, User-user information	Sent by calling TE and by network to called TE to request call establishment.
SETUP ACKnowledge	Cause, Channel identification, CCITT-standardized facilities, Network-specific facilities, Display, Signal	Sent by network to calling TE and (primary interface) called TE to network to acknowledge SETUP but to request more information before proceeding.
	Call Information Phase Messages	
RESume	Call identity, Channel identification, Terminal capabilities	Sent by TE to request resumption of previously suspended call.
RESume ACKnowledge	Channel identification	Sent by network to indicate that requested call has been reestablished.
RESume REJect	Cause	Sent by network to indicate failure to resume suspended call.

Message	Information Elements	Description
SUSPend	Call identity	Sent by TE to request suspension of a call.
SUSPend ACKnowledge	Display	Sent by network to indicate that call has been suspended.
SUSPend REJect	Cause, Display	Sent by network to indicate failure of requested call suspension.
USER INFOrmation	More data indication, Display, User-user information	Sent by TE to network and then by network to another TE to transfer information between the two TEs.

Call Disestablishment Messages

Message	Information Elements	Description
DETach	CCITT-standardized facilities, network-specific facilities, Display, User-user information	Sent by TE or network to indicate that the B channel should be released but that call reference information should be retained. Can be used to obtain accounting information after completion of a call.
DETach ACKnowledge	—	Acknowledges DETach and confirms release of channel.
DISConnect	Cause, Display, User-user information	Sent by either TE or network to indicate call is completed and the receiver is invited to release the channel and call reference.
RELease	Cause, Display, Signal, User-user information	Sent by either TE or network to indicate that the channel and call reference are released. Usually the response to a DISConnect message.
RELease COMplete	Cause, Display, Signal	Sent by either TE or network to indicate acceptance of RELease message and that the channel and call reference are released.

Miscellaneous Messages

Message	Information Elements	Description
CANCel	CCITT-standardized facilities, network-specific facilities	Sent by TE to request discontinuation of a facility.
CANCel ACKnowledge	—	Sent by network to indicate that the facility named in a CANcel message has been discontinued.
CANCel REJect	Cause	Sent by network to indicate failure to discontinue a facility.

Cont.

TABLE 8-8 ISDN USER-NETWORK INTERFACE I.451 MESSAGES Continued

Message	Parameters	Function
CONgestion CONtrol	Congestion level, Cause, Display	Sent by network or TE to set or release flow control of user-to-user signaling messages.
FACility	CCITT-standardized facilities, network-specific facilities, Display, Origination address	Sent by TE to request a network facility and by network when activation of a facility requires user agreement.
FACility ACKnowledge	Display	Sent by network to indicate that requested facility has been activated and by TE to indicate agreement to the use of a facility.
FACility REJect	Cause, Display	Sent by network or TE to indicate rejection of a facility request.
INFOrmation	Channel identification, CCITT-standardized facilities, Network-specific facilities, Display, Keypad, Keypad echo, Signal, Destination address, Transit network selection	Sent by network or TE to provide additional information.
REGister	CCITT-standardized facilities, network-specific facilities	Sent by TE to request a long-term network facility and network when activation of a long-term facility requires user agreement.
REGister ACKnowledge	Display	Sent by network to confirm user facility registration and by TE to indicate agreement to requested facility registration.
REGister REJect	Cause, Display	Sent by network or TE to indicate rejection of a facility registration request.
STATUS	Cause, Call state	Sent by TE or network at any time during a call when an unexpected message is received or to report any other call conditions.

additional information to be conveyed with the message. Thus, the message type specifies a command or response, and the details are provided by the information elements. Some information elements must always be included with a given message (mandatory), and others are optional (additional). Two formats for information elements are used, as indicated in Figures 8-13b and c.

Table 8-8 lists all of the I.451 messages, together with their parameters. A brief definition of each parameter is provided in Box 8-1. The messages can be divided into four categories. **Call establishment messages** are used to initially set up a call. This group includes messages between the calling terminal and the network (SETUP, SETUP ACK, CALL PROC, CONN) and between the network and the called terminal (SETUP, ALERT, CONN, CONN ACK). These messages support the following services:

- Set up a B-channel call in response to user request.
- Provide particular network facilities for this call.
- Inform calling user of the progress of the call establishment process.

Once a call has been set up, but prior to the disestablishment (termination) phase, **call information phase messages** are sent between user and network. One of the messages in this group allows the network to relay, without modification, information between the two users of the call. The nature of this information is beyond the scope of the standard, but it is assumed that it is control signaling information that can't or should not be sent directly over the B-channel circuit. The remainder of the messages allow users to request the suspension and later resumption of a call. When a call is suspended, the network remembers the identity of the called parties and the network facilities supporting the call, but deactivates the call so that no additional charges are incurred and so that the corresponding B channel is freed up. Presumably, the resumption of a call is quicker and cheaper than the origination of a new call.

Call disestablishment messages are sent between user and network in order to terminate a call. Finally, there is a variety of **miscellaneous messages** that may be sent between user and network at various stages of the call. Some may be sent during call setup; others may be sent even though no calls exist. The primary function of these messages is to negotiate network features (supplementary services).

Circuit-Switched Call Example

Figure 8-14, taken from I.451, is an example of the use of the protocol to set up a B-channel circuit-switched telephone call. We will follow this example through to give the reader an idea of the use of the I.451 protocol.

The process begins when a calling subscriber lifts the handset. The ISDN-compatible telephone insures that the D channel is active before itself generating a dial tone (not shown). When the subscriber keys in the called number (not shown), the telephone set accumulates the digits, and when all are keyed in, sends a SETUP

BOX 8-1

PARAMETERS FOR I.451 MESSAGES

BEARER CAPABILITY

Indicates provision, by the network, of one of the bearer capabilities defined in I.201. Includes specification of rate adaption if used.

CALL IDENTITY

Used to identify a suspended call. It is assigned at the start of call suspension.

CALL STATE

Describes the current status of a call, such as active, detached, and disconnect request.

CAUSE

Used to describe the reason for generating certain messages, to provide diagnostic information in the event of procedural errors and to indicate the location of the cause originator. The location is specified in terms of which network originated the cause.

CCITT-STANDARDIZED FACILITIES

Indicates which binary facilities standardized by CCITT are being invoked. Binary facilities are those which do not require a parameter; they are either present or absent. Examples of facilities are: delivery of origination address barred, reverse charging, and various X.25 facilities, such as fast select.

CHANNEL IDENTIFICATION

Identifies channel/subchannel within the interface (e.g., which B channel).

CONGESTION LEVEL

Describes the congestion status of the call. Currently, only receiver ready and receiver not ready values are defined.

CONNECTED ADDRESS

Indicates which address is connected to a call. This may be different from origination or destination address because of changes (e.g., call redirection) during the call. The address field includes an indication of numbering plan plus the actual address. Allowable numbering plans include ISDN, X.121, telephony (E.163), and telex (F.69).

DESTINATION ADDRESS

Identifies called party. Address structure as indicated for connected address.

DISPLAY

Supplies additional information coded in IA5 (International Alphabet 5, also known as ASCII) characters. Intended for display on user terminal.

HIGH LAYER COMPATIBILITY

To be used to check the compatibility at layers 4 through 7 of the caller and called users. The use and coding of this parameter is for further study.

KEYPAD

Conveys IA5 characters entered by means of a terminal keypad.

KEYPAD ECHO

Conveys to the user characters received by the network via Keypad.

LOW LAYER COMPATIBILITY

Used for compatibility checking. Includes information transfer capability, information transfer rate, and protocol identification at layers 1 through 3.

MORE DATA INDICATION

Transferred between users by the network. The use of this flag is not supervised by the network. Its intended use is to permit one user to alert another that more data is coming in an additional USER INFO message.

NETWORK-SPECIFIC FACILITIES

Allows the specification of facilities peculiar to a particular network.

ORIGINATION ADDRESS

Identifies called party. Address structure as indicated for connected address.

REDIRECTING ADDRESS

Identifies destination address from which call redirection/diversion/transfer was invoked. Address structure as indicated for connected address.

Cont.

BOX 8-1 *continued*

SIGNAL

Conveys indications causing a stimulus mode terminal to generate tones and alerting signals. Example values are dial tone on, ring back tone on, busy tone on, and tones off.

SWITCHHOOK

Indicates the state of the stimulus mode terminal switchhook to the network. Values are on-hook and off-hook.

TERMINAL CAPABILITIES

Used by stimulus mode terminals to indicate their capabilities to the network. Values include type 1 (only one B channel may be connected at a time per data link layer address) and type 2 (multiple B channels may be connected at a time per data link layer address).

TRANSIT NETWORK SELECTION

Identity of a network that connection should use to get to final destination. This parameter may be repeated within a message to select a sequence of networks through which a call must pass.

USER-USER INFORMATION

Used to transfer information between ISDN users that should not be interpreted by the network(s).

message over the D channel to the exchange. This message triggers two activities at the local exchange. First, using signaling system number 7 (SS7), the local exchange sends a message through the network that results in designating a route for the requested call and allocating resources for that call. Second, the exchange sends back a CALL PROC message indicating that call setup is underway. The exchange may also request more information from the caller (via SETUP ACK and INFO). When the SS7 message reaches the remote exchange, it sends a SETUP message to the called telephone. The called telephone accepts the call by sending an ALERT message to the network and generating a ringing tone. The ALERT message is transmitted all the way back to the calling telephone set. When the called party lifts

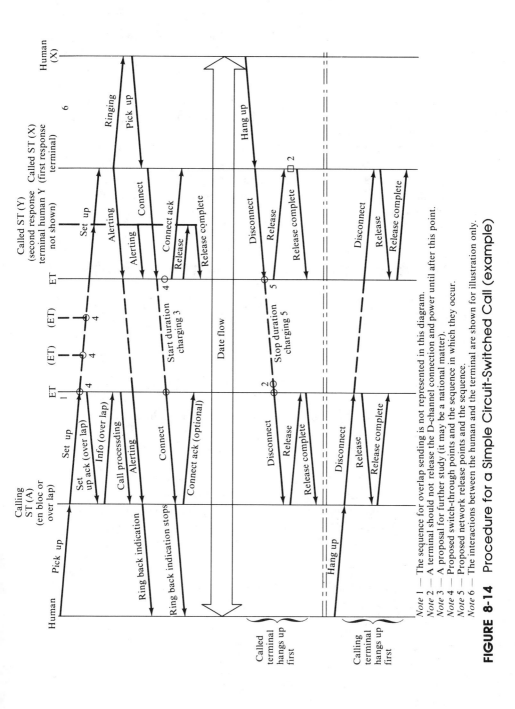

Note 1 — The sequence for overlap sending is not represented in this diagram.
Note 2 — A terminal should not release the D-channel connection and power until after this point.
Note 3 — A proposal for further study (it may be a national matter).
Note 4 — Proposed switch-through points and the sequence in which they occur.
Note 5 — Proposed network release points and the sequence.
Note 6 — The interactions between the human and the terminal are shown for illustration only.

FIGURE 8-14 Procedure for a Simple Circuit-Switched Call (example)

313

the handset, the telephone sends a CONN message to the network. The local exchange sends a CONN ACK message to its subscriber and forwards the CONN message to the calling exchange, and it in turn forwards it to the calling telephone. The B-channel circuit is now available for the called and calling telephone.

Once the circuit is set up, the digitized voice data are exchanged over the B channel. Additional signaling messages, such as call information phase messages, may be transmitted during this period.

Call termination begins when one of the telephone users hangs up. This causes a DISC message to be sent from the telephone to the exchange. The exchange responds with a REL message and when the telephone sends REL COM the B channel is released. The complementary action takes place at the other telephone-network interface.

8-6   ISDN USER PART OF SIGNALING SYSTEM NUMBER 7

The ISDN user part (ISUP) of Signaling System No. 7 (see Figure 4-8) defines the functions, procedures, and interexchange signaling information flows required to provide circuit-switched services and associated user facilities for voice and nonvoice calls over ISDN. We can state three requirements for the ISUP:

- It must rely on the message transfer part or network service part of SS7 for the transmission of messages.
- Its design must be flexible to accommodate future enhancements of ISDN capabilities.
- It must interwork with the user-network I.451 call control protocol.

This last point highlights the distinction between the ISUP, which is defined in CCITT Recommendations Q.761–Q.766, and I.451. The call control protocol defined in I.451 refers to common channel control signaling facilities open to use by the ISDN subscriber. I.451 is used by the subscriber to set up calls to other subscribers with associated user facilities. ISUP refers to signaling facilities employed by the network provider on behalf of the ISDN user. Thus, ISDN communicates with the ISDN user (subscriber) via 1.451 for the purpose of call control, and uses ISUP internal to the network to implement subscriber call control requests. The term "user part" is unfortunate since this does not refer to the ISDN user; rather, it refers to the fact that the ISUP is a user of the lower layers of SS7.

Messages

The network procedures for establishing, controlling, and terminating a call occur as a result of ISUP messages exchanged between exchanges and signal transfer points within the network. A common format is used for all messages defined in

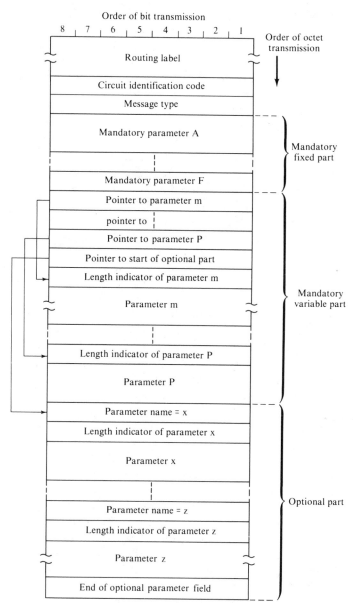

FIGURE 8-15 Message Format for ISDN User Part

ISUP, illustrated in Figure 8-15. The message consists of fields organized into the following parts:

- *Routing label:* referred to as the standard label in Figure 4-9. This label indicates the source and destination points of the message. The label also includes a signaling link selection field, used in load sharing across multiple physical links.
- *Circuit identification code:* specifies the circuit to which this message relates.
- *Message type:* identifies which ISUP message is being sent. The content of the remainder of the message depends on the message type.
- *Mandatory fixed part:* contains those parameters that are mandatory for a particular message type and of fixed length. The position, length, and order of the parameters is uniquely defined by the message type.
- *Mandatory variable part:* contains those parameters that are mandatory for a particular message type and of variable length. Each parameter requires a pointer and a length indicator as well as a parameter value.
- *Optional part:* contains those parameters that may or may not occur for a particular message type. Each parameter requires a name and length indicator as well as a parameter value.

Box 8-2 lists all of the ISUP messages, together with a brief definition. The messages can be divided into nine categories. **Forward address messages** are used to set up a circuit. In addition to identifying the exchange endpoints, these messages allow for the specification of the desired characteristics of the call. These messages propagate in a forward direction, from the exchange originating the call to the exchange that is the destination point. **General setup messages** are used during the call establishment phase. They provide a means of transferring any additional information required during call setup, plus a means for checking that a circuit which straddles more than one ISDN maintains the desired characteristics across all networks. **Backward setup messages** support the call setup process and initiate accounting and charging procedures. **Call supervision messages** are additional messages that might be needed in the process of call establishment. This group includes indications of whether the call was answered or not and the capability to support manual intervention between ISDNs that cross national boundaries. **Circuit supervision messages** relate to an already-established circuit. Three key functions are supported. A circuit may be released, which terminates the call. A circuit may be suspended and later resumed. Finally, a circuit may be established which is not currently being used for a call. In this case it is possible to block the circuit so that outgoing calls on the circuit are prevented, saving the circuit for incoming calls. In the case of a group of circuits that are treated as a single unit for control, **circuit group supervision messages** perform similar functions. **In-call modification messages** are used to alter characteristics or associated network facilities of an active call. The category of **node-to-node messages** includes two quite different facilities.

BOX 8-2
ISDN USER PART MESSAGES

FORWARD ADDRESS

Initial Address

Sent in forward direction to initiate seizure of an outgoing circuit and to transmit address and related information.

Subsequent Address

May be sent following Initial Address message to convey additional calling party address information.

GENERAL SETUP

Information Request

Requests additional call-related information.

Information

Conveys additional call-related information.

Continuity

Sent in forward direction to indicate continuity of the preceding speech circuit to the following international exchange.

BACKWARD SETUP

Address Complete

Sent in backward direction to indicate that all the address information required for routing the call to the called party has been received.

Charging

Conveys accounting and/or call charging information.

CALL SUPERVISION

Answer

Sent in backward direction to indicate that the call has been answered.

Forward Transfer

Sent in the forward direction on semiautomatic calls when the outgoing international exchange operator wants the help of an operator at the incoming international exchange.

Cont.

BOX 8-2 *continued*

Unsuccessful Backward Setup Information

Sent in the backward direction to indicate that call setup was unsuccessful for the reason given in the message. May include information for call forwarding or rerouting.

CIRCUIT SUPERVISION

Release

Indicates that the circuit identified in the message is being released.

Delayed Release

Indicates that the subscriber has disconnected but that the network is holding the connection.

Released

Sent following the transmission of a Release message, to indicate that the circuit has been released and is ready to be put in the idle state on receipt of the Release Complete message.

Release Complete

Sent in response to a Released message when the circuit concerned has been brought into the idle condition.

Continuity Check Request

Sent by an exchange for a circuit on which a continuity check is to be performed, to the exchange at the other end of the circuit, requesting continuity checking equipment to be attached.

Reset Circuit

Sent to release a circuit when, because of a fault, it is unknown whether a Released or Release Complete message is appropriate. If, at the receiving end, the circuit is blocked, reception of this message should cause the condition to be removed.

Blocking

Sent for maintenance purposes to the exchange at the other end of a circuit, to cause subsequent outgoing calls on that circuit to be blocked.

Unblocking

Sent to the exchange at the other end of a circuit to cancel, in that exchange, the blocked condition caused by a previous Blocking message.

Blocking Acknowledgment

Response to a Blocking message, indicating that the circuit has been blocked.

Unblocking Acknowledgment

Response to an Unblocking message, indicating that the circuit has been unblocked.

Pause

Indicates that the subscriber's terminal has been temporarily disconnected.

Resume

Indicates that the subscriber, after having sent a Pause message, is reconnected.

CIRCUIT GROUP SUPERVISION

Circuit Group Blocking

Sent for maintenance purposes to the exchange at the other end of a group of circuits, to cause subsequent outgoing calls on that group of circuits to be blocked.

Circuit Group Unblocking

Sent to the exchange at the other end of a group of circuits to cancel, in that exchange, the blocked condition caused by a previous Circuit Group Blocking message.

Circuit Group Blocking Acknowledgment

Response to a Circuit Group Blocking message, indicating that the group of circuits has been blocked.

Circuit Group Unblocking Acknowledgment

Response to a Circuit Group Unblocking message, indicating that the group of circuits has been unblocked.

Reset Circuit Group

Sent to release a group of circuits when, because of a fault, it is unknown which of the clearing signals is appropriate for each of the circuits in the group. Circuits that are blocked at the receiving end should be unblocked on receiving this message.

Cont.

BOX 8-2 *continued*

Reset Circuit Group Acknowledge

Response to a Reset Circuit Group message, indicating either that the group of circuits has been reset or that resetting has been started and that the resulting status will be reported.

IN-CALL MODIFICATION

Call Modification Request

Indicates a calling or called party request to modify the characteristics of an established call (e.g., from data to voice).

Call Modification Completed

Response to a Call Modification Request message indicating that the requested call modification has been completed.

Reject Connect Modify

Response to a Call Modification Request message indicating that the requested call modification has been rejected.

Facility Request

Sent from an exchange to another exchange or to a data base to request activation of a facility.

Facility Accepted

Sent to an exchange from an exchange or data base indicating that the requested facility has been invoked.

Facility Deactivated

Sent to deactivate a previously invoked facility.

Facility Reject

Sent to an exchange from an exchange or data base indicating that the facility request has been rejected.

Facility Information

Sent to request or respond to a request for additional information related to a given facility.

NODE-TO-NODE

Closed User Group Selection and Validation Request

Sent to a data base by an originating local exchange prior to setting up a closed user group call to request information regarding the validity of the call.

Closed User Group Selection and Validation Response

Sent by a data base in response to a Closed User Group Selection and Validation Request indicating whether the call is valid.

Pass Along

Used to transfer information between two signaling points along the same signaling path as that used to establish a physical connection between those two points.

USER-TO-USER

User-to-user Information

This message is for further study.

One facility relates to the management of closed user groups. Such groups can be set up so that incoming or outgoing or both types of calls are forbidden except between members of the group. The other facility is a passalong capability, explained below. Finally, there is a **user-to-user message** which has not been fully defined by CCITT.

Example

Figure 8-16, taken from Q.764, is an example of the use of the protocol to set up a B-channel circuit-switched telephone call. We will follow this example through to give the reader an idea of the use of the ISUP protocol.

Call Establishment.   The process within the ISDN is triggered by an I.451 SETUP message on the D channel between an ISDN user and an exchange, which becomes the originating exchange for this call. The SETUP message contains the information about the characteristics of the requested call and the associated network facilities required. If the exchange determines that the called party is on another exchange, then the first hop on the route to that exchange is determined, and an Initial Address message is sent to this intermediate exchange. This message contains the ISDN number of the called party, the type of connection required (e.g., 64-kbps transparent), the identity of the selected physical circuit to the succeeding exchange and its characteristics. The Initial Address message is then sent to the exchange on

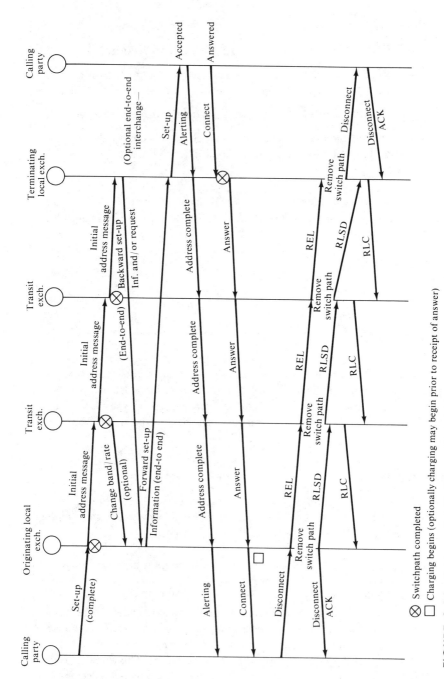

FIGURE 8-16 Successful Ordinary Call (en bloc operation)

which the selected outgoing link terminates. At each transit, or intermediate exchange, the Initial Address message is received and analyzed. Based on the destination address and other routing information, the transit exchange makes a routing decision, selects the appropriate outgoing link, and transmits the Initial Address message to the next exchange. A connection is set up between the incoming and outgoing paths. This process continues until the Initial Address message reaches the terminating, or destination, exchange. If the terminating exchange requires additional information, it sends a Backward Setup message. For example, the calling party address may be required at the destination exchange but not be included in the Initial Address Message. The terminating exchange will determine the identity of the party to be connected. If the connection is allowed, the exchange notifies the called party of the incoming call with an I.451 SETUP message on a D channel, containing any information received in the Initial Address message that is relevant to the called party.

When the terminal device begins alerting the user, it returns an I.451 ALERT message. When this is received by the local exchange, it sends an Address Complete message back through the ISDN to the originating exchange. This message serves several purposes:

- It is an acknowledgment to the originating exchange that a connection has been established.
- It indicates that the called party was found to be idle and is being alerted.
- It may carry charging information.
- It may contain a request to the originating exchange to forward additional call-related information.

When the Address Complete message is received by the originating exchange, it sends an I.451 ALERT message to the calling party.

When the called party answers, an I.451 CONN message is sent to the terminating exchange, which sends an Answer message back through the ISDN to the originating exchange, which issues an I.451 CONN to the calling party. At both ends, the user-network B channel is connected to the internal ISDN circuit. Charging, if applicable, begins.

Call Release.   The release procedures are based on a three-message (Release, Released, Release Complete) approach in which the Release message is transmitted through the network as quickly as possible. In this example we show a release initiated by the calling party. The same procedures are used whether the release is initiated by the called or calling party.

The process is triggered by an I.451 DISC message on the D channel between the calling party and the local exchange. On receipt of this message, the exchange immediately starts the release of the switched path that supports the B-channel circuit and, at the same time, sends a Release message to the succeeding exchange. This message is passed through the network to all intermediate exchanges and the terminating exchange. The Release message is intended to inform the exchanges involved in the call as quickly as possible that the call-related circuit connections are to be released.

Meanwhile, at the originating exchange, when the path has been fully disconnected, three actions are taken:

- Send an I.451 REL message to the calling subscriber to indicate that the B-channel circuit has been released.
- Send a Released message to the succeeding exchange to indicate that the circuit has been released.
- Start a timer T_1 to ensure that a Release Complete message is received within a specified time.

At each intermediate exchange, the receipt of a Release message causes the following actions:

- Start a timer T_{12} to ensure that a Released message is received from the preceding exchange.
- Send a Release message to the succeeding exchange.
- Disconnect the switched path.
- When the path has been fully disconnected, send a Released message to the succeeding exchange.
- Start a timer T_1 to ensure receipt of a Release Complete message.
- When a Released message is received from the preceding exchange, return a Release Complete message to the preceding exchange.

At the terminating exchange, the receipt of a Release message causes the following actions:

- Issue an I.451 DISC message to the called subscriber.
- Start a timer T_{12} to ensure receipt of a Released message.
- Disconnect the switched path.
- When a Released message is received from the preceding exchange, return a Release Complete message to the preceding exchange.

The timers are used in the following way. If a Release Complete message is not received within T_1, the exchange will repeat the Released message. If repeated transmissions of Released are not acknowledged, the exchange sends a Reset Circuit message and alerts maintenance personnel. If a Released message is not received within T_{12}, the exchange sends a Reset Circuit message and alerts maintenance personnel.

The use of the three messages satisfies the requirements for both speed and reliability. The Release message is sent through the network as quickly as possible so that all exchanges can begin to release the resources dedicated to the circuit. The

Released and Release Complete messages ensure that the circuit is in fact released throughout the network.

End-to-End Signaling

End-to-end signaling is defined as the capability to transfer signaling information directly between the end points of a circuit-switched connection or between signaling points that are not interconnected by a circuit-switched connection. End-to-end signaling is used typically between the ISUPs located in call originating and terminating exchanges. It can be used to request or respond to requests for additional call-related information or to transfer user-to-user information transparently through the network.

If the end-to-end signaling relates to an existing connection, it may be achieved by the **passalong method.** With this method, signaling information is sent along the signaling path of a previously established physical connection. The message is passed along the route of transit exchanges that constitute the circuit path. No information processing occurs at a transit exchange, which simply forwards the information to the next exchange. With this method, the ISUP makes direct use of the message transfer part of SS7 (Figure 4-8).

The passalong method makes use of an end-to-end connection which is set up whenever a circuit is established between two subscribers. The end-to-end connection consists of a number of connection sections which run in parallel with and use the same identification code as the circuits sections that comprise the user's circuit. Thus, when a call is placed, two connections are established across ISDN. One is a circuit that supports the user's B-channel traffic, and the other is an SS7 end-to-end connection. These two connections follow the same route through the network but are separate dedicated connections.

An alternative method for end-to-end signaling is the **signaling connection control part (SCCP) method.** This method, which makes use of the SCCP protocol of SS7, can be used whether or not there is a circuit established between the message originating and terminating exchanges. In this case, the route taken by end-to-end signaling messages is determined by SCCP and may not relate to any user circuit.

Services

The basic service provided by the ISDN user part is the setup and release of a simple circuit-switched call. In addition the following supplementary services are supported:

- closed user group
- user access to calling party address identification
- user access to called party address identification
- redirection of calls

- connect when free and waiting allowed
- call completion to busy subscribers
- malicious call identification

The **closed user group** service enables a subscriber to belong to one or more closed user groups. In its basic form, a closed user group permits the subscribers belonging to the group to communicate with each other but precludes communication with all other subscribers. Thus, the members of the group are protected from unauthorized access (into or out of the group). A subscriber may belong to zero, one, or more closed user groups. In addition to the basic service, there are extensions that may be defined:

- *Closed user group with outgoing access:* This enables the subscriber in a closed user group to make outgoing calls to the open part of the network (i.e., subscribers not belonging to any closed user group) and to subscribers belonging to other closed user groups with the incoming access capability.
- *Closed user group with incoming access:* This enables the subscriber in a closed user group to receive incoming calls from the open part of the network and from subscribers belonging to other closed user groups with the outgoing access capability.
- *Incoming calls barred within a closed user group:* This enables the subscriber in a closed user group to originate calls to subscribers in the same group but precludes the reception of incoming calls from subscribers in the same group.
- *Outgoing calls barred within a closed user group:* This enables the subscriber in a closed user group to receive calls from subscribers in the same group but prevents the subscriber from originating calls to subscribers in the same group.

When this facility is in use, the originating and terminating exchanges must verify that a call is allowable before establishing that call, either by accessing information stored locally in the exchange or by access to some sort of centralized data base. In the latter case, the Closed User Group Selection and Validation Request and Response messages are used to communicate with the data base.

User access to calling party address identification is a service that enables a subscriber to be informed on incoming calls of the address of the calling party, unless the calling party restricts access to this information. The information may be contained in the Initial Address message. If not, the terminating exchange requests the information either by setting an appropriate indication in the Address Complete message or by generating an Information Request message. In either case, the originating exchange returns the requested information in an Information message. Similarly, **user access to called party address identification** is a service that enables a caller to be informed on outgoing calls of the identity of the user to which the call has been connected. The originating exchange requests this information either by setting an appropriate indication in the Initial Address message or by generating an Information Request message. The requested information may be returned either in the Address Complete message or in a separate Information message.

The **redirection of calls** service redirects incoming calls addressed to a particular number to an alternate number. The redirection occurs only when the facility is activated by the subscriber at the called number.

A user subscribing to the **connect when free and waiting allowed** service is assigned a number of waiting positions at the local exchange at which incoming calls can wait when the access line(s) to the user is busy. This enables the calling party to wait for completion of the call until the called party becomes free. During waiting, the connection is maintained. A similar service is the **call completion to busy subscribers** service. This enables a calling party encountering the busy condition to complete the call automatically when the called party becomes free. After a call failure, the originating exchange transmits a Facility Request message to the terminating exchange, requesting the call completion to busy subscribers facility. The terminating exchange accepts the request by returning a Facility Accepted message. These messages must be sent using SCCP since no connection exists. Once the called subscriber is free, the terminating exchange sends a Facility Information message to the originating exchange, which proceeds to try the call again by sending out an Initial Address message.

The **malicious call identification** service provides the network with access to the calling party address identification. This information is delivered to the terminating exchange but not to the called user. It is used by the network administration to analyze suspicious calls.

8-7 SUMMARY

A variety of protocols are needed for the use of ISDN. These protocols can be divided into three categories:

- *User-to-user protocols*: These are end-to-end protocols within the OSI architecture between subscribers, making use of ISDN as a data transport mechanism. These protocols are not of direct concern to ISDN except that they require specific services from ISDN.
- *User-to-network protocols*: These allow the user to access ISDN and are the focus of this chapter. They include the physical layer specification for both basic and primary access, LAP-D, and the I.451 call control protocol.
- *Internal network protocols*: These are protocols operating within the network to support the user services, and are transparent to the subscriber. A family of protocols known as Signaling System Number 7

have been developed specifically for the common channel signaling function in ISDN. In this chapter the ISDN user part of SS7 is reviewed.

8-8   RECOMMENDED READING

[DUC85] and [POTT85] discuss the ISDN protocol architecture. The ISDN physical layer is discussed in [JULI86] and [FALE87]. The latter also discusses LAP-D and I.451. A detailed technical discussion of pseudoternary coding can be found in [BELL82a]. [RUFF87] and [LEE86] provide discussions of the 1.544-Mbps interface. There is a good discussion of LAP-D in [SCAC86]; [CHEN87] discusses various implementation approaches. [KANO86] discusses both LAP-D and I.451. [APPE86] covers the ISDN user part of SS7; this is also discussed in [RONA87], which contrasts the roles of I.451 and the ISDN user part.

8-9   PROBLEMS

8-1   Why, in Figure 8-1 is it assumed that layer 3 on the B channel is null? Under what circumstances will it not be null?

8-2   In Section 8-3, rate adaption was not included in the list of physical layer functions? Should it be on the list? Justify your answer.

8-3   Develop a state diagram (finite state machine) representation of pseudoternary coding.

8-4   Consider the following signal encoding technique. Binary data are presented as input, a_m, $m = 1, 2, 3, \ldots$. Two levels of processing occur.
First, a new set of binary numbers are produced:

$$b_m = a_m + b_{m-1} \bmod 2$$

These are then encoded as

$$c_m = b_m - b_{m-1}$$

On reception, the original data are recovered by

$$a_m = c_m \bmod 2$$

a. Verify that the received values of a_m equal the transmitted values of a_m.
b. What sort of encoding is this?

8-5   Figure 8-6 indicates that, with the exception of the first occurrence of the L bit in a D-channel frame, all subsequent L bits have either zero voltage or a positive voltage, but not a negative voltage. Why?

8-6   Demonstrate that the last nonzero pulse of a D-channel frame is always positive. Note that the first pulse of the following frame is also positive. Is there an advantage to that?

8-7   What is the data rate on the Q channel?

8-8   In the discussion of D-channel contention resolution, it was stated that a station remains at lower priority until all other terminals have had a chance to transmit. In the standard (I.430) it states that the value of the lower level of priority is changed back to the value of the higher level of priority when the TE observes a string of 1-bits on the echo stream of length equal to the value of the lower level of priority. Does this in fact guarantee that all other terminals have had a chance to transmit?

8-9   For the B8ZS coding scheme to be effective, the probability of occurrences of more than one code violation (two pulses in a row with the same polarity) due to an error must be quite small. What is the probability of the occurrence of more than one code violation in 8 bits for an error rate per bit of 10^{-6}? For an error rate of 10^{-3}?

8-10   What is the percentage overhead for each of the two primary rate interfaces?

8-11   Assume that a LAP-D entity has sent six I-frames over a new logical connection, and followed this with a poll (RR with the P bit set). What will be the N(R) count back from the peer entity after the last frame? (Assume error-free operation.)

8-12   Create a merged diagram from Figures 8-14 and 8-16.

8-13   For each of the five closed user group facilities, give an example of an application in which the facility would be useful.

8-14   Could the ISDN User Part be used instead of the I.451 call control protocol to provide control signaling for the subscriber? Justify your answer.

CHAPTER 9

BROADBAND ISDN

As we saw in Chapter 5, the planning for ISDN began as far back as 1976 and is only now moving from the planning stage to prototypes and actual implementations. It will be many years before the full spectrum of ISDN services is widely available, and there will continue to be refinements and improvements to ISDN services and network facilities. It may then surprise the reader to know that, with the ink hardly dry on the first definitive set of ISDN standards (the 1988 recommendations), much of the planning and design effort is now directed toward a network concept that will be far more revolutionary than ISDN itself. This new concept has been referred to as **broadband ISDN** (BISDN).

In one of its first working documents on BISDN, draft Recommendation I.1yx, CCITT modestly defines BISDN as "a service requiring transmission channels capable of supporting rates greater than the primary rate." Behind this innocuous statement lies plans for a network and set of services that will have far more impact on business and residential customers than ISDN. With BISDN, services, especially video services, requiring data rates orders of magnitudes beyond those that can be delivered by ISDN, will become available. To contrast this new network and these new services from the original concept of ISDN, that original concept is now being referred to as **narrowband ISDN.**

The primary triggers for evolving toward the BISDN include an increasing demand for high bit rate services, especially image and video services, and the evolution of technology to support those services. The key developments in technology are:

- Optical fiber transmission systems that can offer low-cost high-data-rate transmission channels for network trunks and for subscriber lines.

331

- Microelectronic circuits that can offer high-speed, low-cost building blocks for switching, transmission, and subscriber equipment.
- High-quality video monitors and cameras that can, with sufficient production quantities, be offered at low cost.

These advances in technology will result in the integration of a wide range of communications facilities and the support of, in effect, universal communications with the following key characteristics:

- Worldwide exchange between any two subscribers in any medium or combination of media.
- Retrieval and sharing of massive amounts of information from multiple sources, in multiple media, among people in a shared electronic environment.
- Distribution, including switched distribution, of a wide variety of cultural, entertainment, and educational materials to home or office, virtually on demand.

CCITT is in the early stages of work on BISDN, and it is expected to be the mid to late 1990s before BISDN facilities begin to be introduced. Accordingly, this chapter presents a preliminary view. We begin with a look at the services of a broadband ISDN, and follow this with a look at BISDN architecture.

9-1   BROADBAND SERVICES

When the capacity available to the ISDN user is increased substantially, then the range of services that it can support also increases substantially. CCITT classifies the services that could be provided by a BISDN into interactive services and distribution services (Figure 9-1). **Interactive services** are those in which there is a two-way exchange of information (other than control signaling information) between two subscribers or between a subscriber and a service provider. These include conversational services, messaging services, and retrieval services. **Distribution services** are those in which the information transfer is primarily one way, from service provider to BISDN subscriber. These include broadcast services, for which the user has no control over the presentation of the information, and cyclical services (explained below), which allow the user some measure of presentation control. Table 9-1, from draft CCITT Recommendation I.1yx, lists each of these five categories together with possible applications and characteristics. Let us look at each of these subcategories in turn.

Conversational Services

Conversational services provide the means for bidirectional dialogue communication with bidirectional, real-time (not store-and-forward) end-to-end information transfer between two users or between a user and a service provider host. These

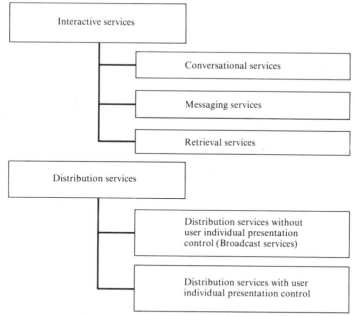

FIGURE 9-1   Broadband Services

services support the general transfer of data specific to a given user application. That is, the information is generated by and exchanged between users; it is not "public" information.

This category encompasses a wide range of applications and data types. Table 9-1 divides these into moving pictures (video), data, and document. In the long run, perhaps the most important category of BISDN service is video conversational services, and perhaps the most important of these services is video telephony. Video telephony simply means that the telephone instrument includes a video transmit and receive/display capability so that dial-up calls include both voice and live picture. The first use of this service is likely to be the office environment. It can be used in any situation where the visual component of a call is advantageous, including sales, consulting, instruction, negotiation, and the discussion of visual information, such as reports, charts, advertising layouts, and so on. As the cost of videophone terminals decline, it is likely that this will be a popular residential service as well.

Another video conversational service is videoconference. The simplest form of this service is a point-to-point capability, which can be used to connect conference rooms. This differs from videophone in the nature of the equipment used. Accordingly, the service must specify the interface and protocols to be used to assure compatible equipment between conference rooms. A point-to-point videoconference would specify additional features such as facsimile and document transfer and the use of special equipment such as electronic blackboards. A different sort of videoconference is a multipoint service. This would allow participants to tie together

TABLE 9-1 POSSIBLE BROADBAND SERVICES IN ISDN[1]

Service-classes	Type of Information	Examples of Broadband Services	Applications	Some Possible Attribute Values[7,8]	Proposed Categorization	
					Teleservice	Bearer Service
Conversational services	Moving pictures (video) and sound	Broadband[2] Video-telephony (incl. point-to-point-video-conference)	Communication for the transfer of voice (sound), moving pictures, and video-scanned still images and documents between two locations (person-to-person, person-to-group, group-to-group)[3]	—Demand/reserved/permanent —Point-to-point —Bidirectional symmetric/bidirectional asymmetric —(Value for information transferrate is under study)	X	
		Broadband[2] Multipoint-Videoconference	Multipoint communication for the transfer of voice (sound), moving pictures, and video-scanned still images and documents between more than two locations (person-to-person, person-to-group, group-to-group)[3]	—Demand/reserved/permanent —Multipoint —Bidirectional symmetric/bidirectional asymmetric	X	
		Videosurveillance	—Building security —Traffic monitoring	—Demand/reserved/permanent —Point-to-point/multipoint —Bidirectional asymmetric/unidirectional	X	

Category	Service	Applications	Attributes		
	Video/audio information transmission service	— TV signal transfer — Video/audio dialogue	— Demand/reserved/permanent — Point-to-point/multipoint — Bidirectional symmetric/bidirectional asymmetric	X	

Data	High speed unrestricted digital information transmission service	— High speed data transfer
		  • LAN interconnection
		  • Computer-computer interconnection
		— Transfer of video and other information types
		— Still image transfer
		— Data file transfer
			— Demand/reserved/permanent
			— Point-to-point/multipoint
			— Bidirectional symmetric/bidirectional asymmetric
				X	

	High volume file transfer service		— Demand — Point-to-point/multipoint — Bidirectional symmetric/bidirectional asymmetric		X
	High speed teleaction	— Real time control — Telemetry — Alarms		X	X
Document	High speed telefax	User-to-user transfer of text, images, drawings, etc.	— Demand — Point-to-point/multipoint — Bidirectional symmetric/bidirectional asymmetric		X

Cont.

TABLE 9-1 POSSIBLE BROADBAND SERVICES IN ISDN[1] *(continued)*

Service-classes	Type of Information	Examples of Broadband Services	Applications	Some Possible Attribute Values[7,8]	Proposed Categorization	
					Teleservice	*Bearer Service*
		Document communication service	User-to-user transfer of mixed documents[4]	—Demand —Point-to-point/multipoint —Bidirectional symmetric/bidirectional asymmetric	X	
Messaging services	Moving pictures (video) and sound	Video mail service	Electronic mailbox service for the transfer of moving pictures and accompanying sound	—Demand —Point-to-point/multipoint —Bidirectional asymmetric/unidirectional (for further study)	X	
	Document	Document mail service	Electronic mail box service for "mixed" documents[4]	—Demand —Point-to-point/multipoint —Bidirectional asymmetric/unidirectional (for further study)	X	
Retrieval services	Text, data, graphics, sound, still images, moving pictures	Broadband videotex	—Videotex incl. moving pictures —Remote education and training —Telesoftware —Teleshopping —Advertising	—Demand —PT-PT —Bidirectional asymmetric	X	

	Service	Application	Attributes	
	Video retrieval service	— News retrieval — Entertainment purposes — Remote education and training	— Demand/reserved — Point-to-point/multipoint — Bidirectional asymmetric[6]	X
	High resolution image retrieval service	— Entertainment purposes — Remote education and training	— Demand/reserved — Point-to-point/multipoint — Bidirectional asymmetric[6]	X
	Document retrieval service	"Mixed documents" retrieval from information centers, archives, etc.[4,5]	— Demand — Point-to-point/multipoint[6] — Bidirectional asymmetric	X
Distribution services without user individual presentation control — Video	Existing quality TV distribution service (PAL, SECAM, NTSC)	TV program distribution	— Demand (selection)/permanent — Broadcast — Bidirectional asymmetric/unidirectional	X
	Extended quality TV distribution service — Enhanced definition TV distribution service — High quality TV . . .	TV program distribution	— Demand (selection)/permanent — Broadcast — Bidirectional asymmetric/unidirectional	X
	High definition TV distribution service	TV program distribution	— Demand (selection)/permanent — Broadcast	X

TABLE 9-1 POSSIBLE BROADBAND SERVICES IN ISDN¹ *(continued)*

Service-classes	Type of Information	Examples of Broadband Services	Applications	Some Possible Attribute Values[7,8]	Proposed Categorization	
					Teleservice	Bearer Service
		Pay-TV (pay-per-view, pay-per-channel)	TV program distribution	—Bidirectional asymmetric/unidirectional —Demand (selection)/permanent —Broadcast/multipoint	X	
	Text, graphics, still images	Document distribution service	—Electronic newspaper —Electronic publishing	—Bidirectional asymmetric/unidirectional —Demand (selection)/permanent —Broadcast/multipoint	X	
	Data	High speed unrestricted digital information distribution service	Distribution of unrestricted data	—Bidirectional asymmetric/unidirectional[6] —Permanent —Broadcast —Unidirectional		X
	Moving pictures and sound	Video information distribution service	Distribution of video/audio signals	—Permanent —Broadcast —Unidirectional		X

Distribution services with user individual presentation control	Text, graphics, sound, still images	Full channel broadcast videotex	— Remote education and training — Advertising — News retrieval — Telesoftware	— Permanent — Broadcast — Unidirectional	X

Note 1: In this table only those broadband teleservices and bearer services are considered which may require higher transfer capacity than that of the H1 capacity. Teleservices for sound retrieval, sound mail applications, and visual services with reduced or highly reduced resolutions are not listed.

Note 2: This terminology indicates that a redefinition regarding existing terms has taken place. The new terms may or may not exist for a transition period.

Note 3: The realization of the different applications may require the definition of different quality classes.

Note 4: "Mixed document" means that a document may contain text, graphic, still, and moving picture information as well as voice annotation.

Note 5: Special high-layer functions are necessary if post-processing after retrieval is required.

Note 6: Further study is required to indicate whether the point to multipoint connection represents in this case a main application.

Note 7: At present packet mode is dedicated to non-realtime applications. Depending on the final definition of the packet transfer mode further applications may appear. The application of this attribute value requires further study.

Note 8: For the moment this column merely highlights some possible attribute values to give a general indication of the characteristics of these services. The full specification of these services will require a listing of all values which will be defined for broadband services in CCITT Rec. I.2xx.

single videophones in a conference connection, without leaving their workplaces, using a video conference server within the network. Such a system would support a small number (e.g., five) of simultaneous users. Either one participant would appear on all screens at a time, as managed by the video conference server, or a split screen technique could be used.

A third variant of video conversational service is video surveillance. This is not a distribution service since the information delivery is limited to a specific, intended subscriber. This form of service can be unidirectional; if the information is simple video images generated by a fixed camera, then the information flow is only from video source to subscriber. A reverse flow would come into play if the user had control over the camera (change orientation, zoom, etc.). The final example listed in the table is video/audio information transmission service. This is essentially the same capability as video telephony. The difference is that a higher quality image may be required. For example, computer animation that represents a detailed engineering design may require much higher resolution than ordinary human-to-human conversation.

The next type of conversational service listed in Table 9-1 is for data. In this context, data mean arbitrary information whose structure is not visible to ISDN. Examples of applications that would use this service [ARMB86]:

- File transfer in a distributed architecture of computer and storage systems (load sharing, back-up systems, decentralized databases, etc.).
- Large-volume or high-speed transmission of measured values or control information.
- Program downloading.
- Computer-aided design and manufacturing (CAD/CAM).
- Connection of local area networks (LANs) at different locations.

Finally, there is the conversational transfer of documents. This could include very high resolution facsimile or the transfer of mixed documents that might include text, facsimile images, voice annotation, and/or a video component. Two types of applications are likely here: a document transfer service for the exchange of documents between users at workstations, and a document storage system, based on the document transfer service, which provides document servers for the filing, update, and access of documents by a community of users.

Messaging Services

Messaging services offer user-to-user communication between individual users via storage units with store-and-forward, mailbox and/or message handling (e.g., information editing, processing and conversion) functions. In contrast to conversational services, messaging services are not in real time. Hence, they place lesser demands on the network and do not require that both users be available at the same time. Analogous narrowband services are X.400 and teletex.

One new form of messaging service that could be supported by ISDN is video mail, analogous to today's electronic mail (text/graphic mail) and voice mail. Just as electronic mail replaces the mailing of a letter, so video mail replaces mailing a video cassette. This may become one of the most powerful and useful forms of message communication. Similarly, a document mail service allows the transmission of mixed documents, containing text, graphics, voice, and/or video components.

Retrieval Services

Retrieval services provide the user with the capability to retrieve information stored in information centers that are, in general, available for public use. This information is sent to the user on demand only. The information can be retrieved on an individual basis; that is, the time at which an information sequence is to start is under the control of the user.

An analogous narrowband service is videotex. This is an interactive system designed to service both home and business needs. It is a general-purpose data base retrieval system that can use the public switched telephone network or an interactive metropolitan cable TV system. Figure 9-2 depicts a typical system. The videotex provider maintains a variety of data bases on a central computer. Some of these are public data bases provided by the videotex system. Others are vendor-supplied services, such as a stock market advisory. Information is provided in the form of pages of text and simple graphics.

Broadband videotex is an enhancement of the existing videotex system [SUGI88]. The user would be able to select sound passages, high-resolution images of TV standard, and short video scenes, in addition to the current text and simplified graphics. Examples of broadband videotex services:

- retrieval of encyclopedia entries
- results of quality tests on consumer goods
- computer-supported audio-visual entries
- electronic mail-order catalogs and travel brochures with the option of placing a direct order or making a direct booking

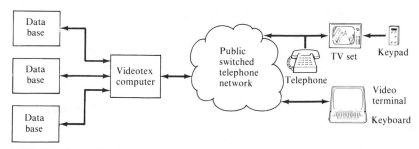

FIGURE 9-2 A Typical Videotex System

Another retrieval service is video retrieval. With this service, a user could order full-length films or videos from a film/video library facility. Since the provider may have to satisfy many requests, bandwidth considerations dictate that only a small number of different video transmissions can be supported at any one time. A realistic service would offer perhaps 500 movies/videos for each two-hour period. Using a 50-Mbps video channel, this would require a manageable 25-Gbs transmission capacity from video suppliers to distribution points [WEIN87]. The user would be informed by the provider at what time the film will be available to be viewed or transmitted to the subscriber's video recorder.

Distribution Services without User Presentation Control

Services in this category are also referred to as broadcast services. They provide a continuous flow of information which is distributed from a central source to an unlimited number of authorized receivers connected to the network. Each user can access this flow of information but has no control over it. In particular the user cannot control the starting time or order of the presentation of the broadcasted information. All users simply tap into the flow of information.

The most common example of this service is broadcast television. Currently, broadcast television is available from network broadcast via radio waves and through cable television distribution systems. With the capacities planned for BISDN, this service can be integrated with the other telecommunications services. In addition, higher resolutions can now be achieved and it is anticipated that these higher-quality services will also be available via BISDN.

An example of a nonvideo service is an electronic newspaper broadcast service. This would permit the transmission of facsimile images of newspaper pages to subscribers who had paid for the service.

Distribution Services with User Presentation Control

Services in this class also distribute information from a central source to a large number of users. However, the information is provided as a sequence of information entities (e.g., frames) with cyclical repetition. So, the user has the ability of individual access to the cyclical distributed information and can control start and order of presentation. Due to the cyclical repetition, the information entities, selected by the user, will always be presented from the beginning.

An analogous narrowband service is teletext (not to be confused with teletex; see Chapter 6), which is depicted in Figure 9-3. Teletext is a simple one-way system that uses unallocated portions of the bandwidth of a broadcast TV signal. At the transmission end, a fixed set of pages of text is sent repeatedly in round-robin fashion. The receiver consists of a special decoder and storage unit, a keypad for user entry,

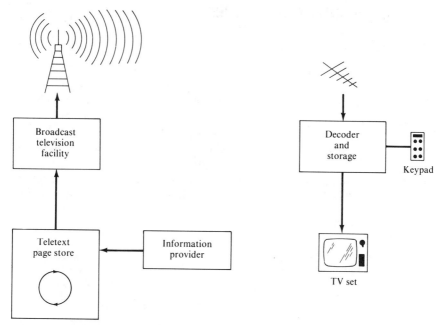

FIGURE 9-3   A Typical Teletext System

and an ordinary TV set. The user keys in the number of the page desired. The decoder reads that page from the incoming signal, stores it, and displays it continuously until instructed to do otherwise. Typically, pages of teletext form a tree pattern with higher-level pages containing menus that guide the selection of lower-level pages. Thus, although the system appears interactive to the user, it is actually a one-way broadcast of information. Since only a small portion of the TV signal bandwidth is used for this purpose, the number of pages is limited by a desire to reduce access time. A typical system will support a few hundred pages with a cycle time of a few tens of seconds.

Teletext is oriented primarily to the home market, with different sets of pages offered on different channels. Examples of information presented by such a system are stock market reports, weather reports, news, leisure information, and recipes.

With BISDN, an enhancement to teletext known as cabletext can be provided. Whereas teletext uses only a small portion of an analog TV channel, cabletext would use a full digital broadband channel for cyclical transmission of pages with text, images, and possible video and audio passages. As an electronic newspaper that uses public networks, or as an in-house information system for trade fairs, hotels, and hospitals, cabletext will provide low-cost access to timely and frequently-requested information. A typical system might allow access to 10,000 pages with a cycle time of 1 second [ARMB87].

9-2   BISDN ARCHITECTURE

Requirements

In order to get some sense of what is required for a broadband ISDN, we need to look at the requirements it must satisfy. As a first step, the BISDN services presented in Section 9-1 provide a qualitative description of requirements. To decide on the transmission structure, we need some ideas of the data rate requirements of the subscriber. Figure 9-4 [WEIN87] provides an estimate. As can be seen, the potential range of data rates is wide. The figure also gives estimated durations of calls, which is also a factor in network design.

Another estimate of data rate requirements is shown in Table 9-2 [CASA87]. Note that the values here differ from those in Figure 9-4. In both cases, the numbers

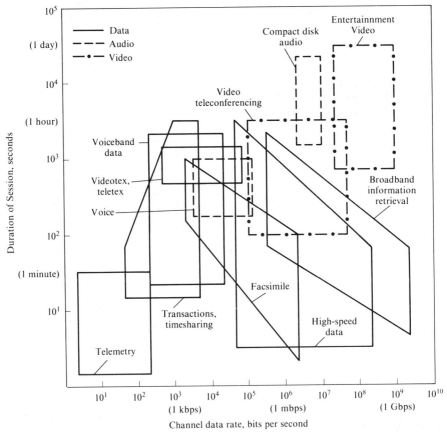

FIGURE 9-4   Data Rate and Duration of Potential Broadband ISDN Services

TABLE 9-2 TRAFFIC CHARACTERISTICS OF B-ISDN

Services	Bit Rate (kbit/s)		Call Duration (secs)		Burstiness	
	Min	Max	Min	Max	Min	Max
Communicative services						
Dialog						
• Telephony	64	64	10^2	10^2	0.3	1
• Videotelephony	64	70.10^3	10^2	10^2	0.5	1
• Telemetry	10^{-2}	10	1	10	0.01	0.1
• Teletex	10	10				
• Facsimile (Group 4)	64	64		10^2	1	1
• Videosurveillance	10	30.10^3	10^3	10^4	0.1	1
• Videoconference	10^3	70.10^3	10^3	10^4	0.5	1
Retrieval						
• Videotex	1	64	10^2	10^3	0.1	1
• Broadband videotex	10^3	70.10^3	10^2	10^3	0.1	
Messaging						
• Voice mail	16	64	10	10^2	0.3	0.5
• Video mail	10^3	70.10^3	10	10^3	0.1	0.5
• Electronic mail	10	10	10^2		0.5	
Distributive services						
• HiFi sound	768	768	10^3	10^4	1	
• TV	30.10^3	70.10^3	10^3	10^4	1	
• High definition TV	140.10^3	565.10^3	10^3	10^4	1	

can only be estimates for the projected services, and the differences point out the uncertainty in planning that will face BISDN designers. The table also includes the useful parameter of burstiness, which is the ratio between the time during which information is sent and the time for which the channel is occupied. This quantity provides guidance on the type of switching technology (circuit switching versus packet switching) appropriate for BISDN.

It is worth elaborating briefly on the data rate requirements for video transmission, since it is video that will drive the overall data rate requirement. The transmission of an analog video signal requires on the order of 6 MHz bandwidth. Using straightforward digitization techniques, the data rate required for digital video transmission can be as much as 1 Gbps. This is clearly too high even for a network based on optical fiber and high-speed switches. Two complementary approaches are used to reduce bit rate requirements:

- Use data compression techniques that remove redundancy or unnecessary information.
- Allow for distortions that are least objectionable to the human eye.

Knowing what information is necessary and the types of acceptable distortion requires an in-depth understanding of the image source to be coded and of human vision. With this knowledge, one can apply various coding techniques and engineering trade-offs to achieve the best image possible.

What is acceptable in terms of image quality and in terms of data rate is a function of application. For example, videophone and videoconferencing require both transmission and reception. To limit the engineering requirements at the subscriber site, we would like to drastically limit the video transmission data rate. Fortunately, in the case of videophone, the resolution required, especially for residential applications, is modest, and in the case of both videoconference and videophone the rate of change of the picture is generally low. This latter property can be exploited with interframe redundancy compression techniques, as opposed to merely the intraframe compression techniques used in systems such as facsimile.

CCITT has defined five levels of quality for video images, as shown in Table 9-3. The table also indicates the current state of the art for digital encoding of such images. The bottom two categories (D and E) are often referred to as low bit rate encoding systems, which are defined as systems that transmit at data rates of about 2 Mbps or less [HASK87]. These quality levels are targeted at the videoconference and videophone applications. For quality level D, there is reduced resolution compared to broadcast television and reduced ability to track movement. In general, this produces acceptable quality. However, if there is rapid movement in the scene being televised, this will appear as jerky, discontinuous movement on the viewer's screen. Furthermore, if there is a desire to transmit a high-resolution graphics image (e.g., during a presentation at a videoconference), then the resolution on the screen may be inadequate. To overcome this latter problem, the transmitter should be capable of switching between a full-motion, lower-resolution transmission and a freeze-frame, higher-resolution transmission at the same data rate.

TABLE 9-3   BIT RATES FOR COMPRESSED VIDEO TRANSMISSION

Service Quality	Description	Data Rate (Mbps)
A	High definition television (HDTV)	$92 - >200$
B	Digital component-coding signal	$30/45 - 145$
C	Digitally-coded NTSC, PAL, SECAM for distribution	$20 - 45$
D	Reduced spatial resolution and movement portrayal	$0.384 - 1.92$
E	Highly-reduced spatial resolution and movement portrayal	0.064

At the present time, a data rate of 64 kbps, produces a noticeably inferior picture, designated quality level E. This data rate may be acceptable for videophone. However, the distinction between levels D and E may disappear as advances in coding technology continue. As an example of the pace of change, 64-kbps video codecs introduced in late 1986 were of equal quality to 1.544-Mbps codecs introduced in 1982 [KIM86]. By the time that BISDN is deployed, the need for the data rates of category D may disappear.

Quality level C corresponds to the quality of analog broadcast television today. Quality level B is, known as digital component coding or extended definition television, provides improved quality but retains the same number of lines and ratio of screen height to width of current analog broadcast television standards. In this technique, the analog television signal is broken up into components (usually the color components — red, green, blue). Each component is then separately digitally encoded and the resulting signals are time-division multiplexed. Traditional encoding techniques perform digitization on the original analog signal (known as the composite signal). It turns out that the component coding technique provides superior performance. The development of this system was undertaken with the direct-broadcast satellite application in mind, but it is certainly appropriate to BISDN.

Finally, the highest-quality standard is known as high-definition television (HDTV). This system is comparable in resolution to 35-mm film projection and will put the quality of TV reception in the home and office at the level of the cinema. With HDTV, not only is the resolution greater, but the system will support wider screens, more along the lines of cinema screens in height-width ratio.

You will note that Table 9-3 provides a rather large range of data rates within most of the categories. This is for two reasons. First, the technology of digital video coding is evolving rapidly, and this table attempts to predict the rates needed in the mid-1990s. Second, a distinction is made between two types of signals:

- *contribution*, where the signal is transferred between studios and is subject to post-production studio processing

- *distribution*, where the signal is distributed for viewing and is not subject to such processing

Generally, a higher degree of compression can be applied for contribution rather than distribution signals.

The estimates in Figure 9-4 and Table 9-2 show that broadband services require the network to handle a wide range of call types, from those with short holding times (e.g., file transfer) to those with long holding times (e.g., distributive services), and at a wide range of data rates. Also, it is to be expected that many of these services will show the same busy-hour characteristics of narrowband ISDN services, with peaks during business hours.

From a consideration of capacity, a more detailed list of requirements can be drawn up. Table 9-4, from [CASA87], suggests the requirements that BISDN must satisfy.

TABLE 9-4 REQUIREMENTS FOR BROADBAND ISDN

Aspects	BISDN requirements
Service	Support for narrowband and broadband signals including full motion video of different service quality from high definition TV to highly reduced resolution video Distributive and communicative service capability Point-to-point and point-to-multipoint connections
Network	Compliance with OSI network architecture reference model including subnetworks and gateways Ability to accommodate different traffic patterns and different routing for the same multimedia communication (e.g., voice and video) Ability to be transparent or to provide value-added services (e.g., encryption, speed and format conversion) Smooth transition from narrowband ISDN Same numbering for all services to each subscriber access point Unique signaling channel for each subscriber access point
Switching	Ability to support multirate switched and nonswitched connections Network structure independent of switching mode
Transmission	Provision of a channel bandwidth up to 140 Mbit/s per service (e.g., compressed HDTV) Subscriber line bit rate range between 140 Mbit/s and 565 Mbit/s (at T reference point)
User	Dynamic allocation of access channels (bandwidth) from the user Attractive tariff structure
Operational	Simple operation and maintenance Simple extension and reconfiguration procedures Maximum use of existing infrastructures.

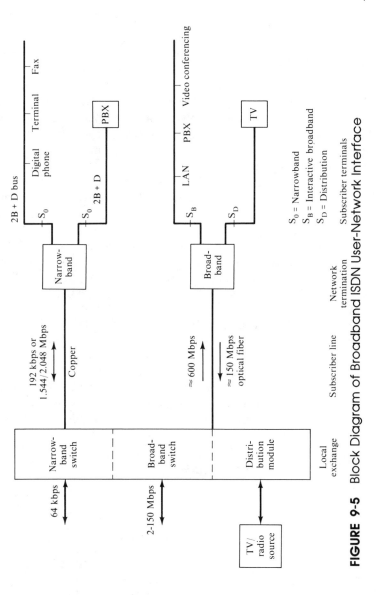

FIGURE 9-5 Block Diagram of Broadband ISDN User-Network Interface

Network Characteristics

The BISDN will differ from a narrowband ISDN in a number of ways. To meet the requirement for high-resolution video, an upper channel rate of approximately 150 Mbps will be needed. To simultaneously support one or more interactive services and distributive services, a total subscriber line rate of about 600 Mbps is needed. In terms of today's installed telephone plant, this is a stupendous data rate to sustain. The only appropriate technology for widespread support of such data rates is optical fiber. Hence, the introduction of BISDN depends on the pace of introduction of fiber subscriber loops.

Internal to the network, there is the issue of the switching technique to be used. The switching facility will have to be capable of handling a wide range of different bit rates and traffic parameters (e.g., burstiness). Despite the increasing power of digital circuit-switching hardware and the increasing use of optical fiber trunking, it may be difficult to handle the large and diverse requirements of BISDN with circuit-switching technology. For this reason, there is increasing interest in the fast packet switching, often referred to as asynchronous transfer mode (ATM), as the basic switching technique for BISDN [BAUW87], [HUI87], [NOJI87], [TAKE87].

Figure 9-5 is a general depiction of the BISDN user access architecture. The local exchange to which subscribers attach must be able to handle both BISDN and ISDN subscribers. ISDN subscribers can be supported with twisted pair at the basic and primary access rates. For BISDN subscribers, optical fiber will be used. The data rate from network to subscriber will need to be approximately 600 Mbps in order to handle multiple video distributions, such as might be required in an office environment. The data rate from subscriber to network would normally need to be much

TABLE 9-5   NARROWBAND CHANNELS AND PROPOSED BROADBAND CHANNELS

Channel	Data Rate	Application
		Narrowband
D	16 or 64 kbps	control signaling; packet-switched data
B	64 kbps	circuit- and packet-switched data, voice, facsimile
H0	384 kbps	data, voice, facsimile, compressed video
H11	1.536 Mbps	PBX access, compressed video, high-speed data
H12	1.920 Mbps	PBX access, compressed video, high-speed data
		Broadband
H2	30–45 Mbps	Full-motion video for conferencing, video telephone, or video messaging
H3	60–70 Mbps	Not identified
H4	120–140 Mbps	Bulk data transfer of text, facsimile, enhanced video information

TABLE 9-6 EXAMPLES OF USER-NETWORK INTERFACE STRUCTURE, BASED ON PROPOSALS FROM SEVERAL ADMINISTRATIONS

	1 to 4	1	4	4	1 to 4	6	3
Number of Broadband Channels	1 to 4	1	4	4	1 to 4	6	3
Speed of Broadband Channels (Mbit/s)	34–140	140	140	140	140	70	30.720 92.160
Number of B-Channels	2	2	30	2	2^2	30	m
Number of D-Channels	1	1	1	1	1	1	1
Speed of D-Channels (kbit/s)	16 or 64	16	64	16 or 64	≥ 64	64	16 or 64
Other channels, No., type	None	4 H_{12}	16 H_{12}	None	2^2	---	$n \cdot H_1$
Bus or Pt. to Pt.	Both	Both	Both	Both	---	Pt-Pt	Both
Packet mode included	Yes	Yes	Yes	Yes	Yes	?	Yes
Symmetrical	Yes[1]	Yes	Yes/No	No	Yes[1]	No	Yes[1]
Total Bit rate at T reference point (Mbit/s)	145	155	600	560	150/600	560/70	100

[1] Access capability can be asymmetrical.

[2] B, H_0, H_1 and broadband channels can be derived on a per call basis.

less, since the typical subscriber does not initiate distribution services. A rate of about 150 Mbps or less is probably adequate.

With this sort of configuration in mind, CCITT has been working on the definition of new channel types, with a final standardization due in 1992. Currently, three new channel types have been proposed by CCITT, as shown in Table 9-5. Of course, these channels must be organized into a transmission structure at the user interface. As yet, no single structure has emerged for standardization. Table 9-6 gives examples of structures under consideration.

9-3   SUMMARY

Although the development and deployment of ISDN is still in its early stages, planners and designers are already looking toward a much more revolutionary change in telecommunications: the broadband ISDN. Advances in terminal technology, optical fiber transmission technology, and switching technology, together with a rising demand for information-rich services are accelerating the telecommunications environment through ISDN to a BISDN before the end of the century. Just as the capacity of BISDN is several orders of magnitude greater than ISDN, its impact will also be greater.

9-4   RECOMMENDED READING

As yet, there is comparatively little literature on the subject of broadband ISDN. Some worthwhile articles are [MINZ87], [WEIN87], [SAZE87], [ANDR87], and [CASA87]. [ARMB87] and [ARMB86] are good discussions of BISDN services. The *IEEE Journal on Selected Areas in Communications* has devoted two issues to the subject. The July 1986 issue [OHNS86] discusses a broad range of issues, including services, components, transmission, switching, architectures, and terminals. The October 1987 issue [WHIT87] is devoted to broadband switching. [STAL90] provides a discussion of the application of BISDN services.

A discussion of current video technologies, including extended definition and high definition, is provided by [GAGG87]. [STEN86] addresses approaches to video transmission on B-ISDN.

9-5   PROBLEMS

9-1   Is there a need to enhance or otherwise modify Signaling System Number 7 to support broadband ISDN?

9-2   Is there a need to enhance or otherwise modify the I.451 call control protocol to support broadband ISDN?

9-3 In many developed countries, a substantial investment has been made in coaxial cable installation to support cable TV distribution to home and office.

a. Can this installed plant, rather than optical fiber, become the subscriber loop for BISDN?

b. If not, why not maintain this separate network for TV distribution rather than attempting to incorporate all communications services under BISDN?

APPENDIX A

FLOW CONTROL, ERROR DETECTION, AND ERROR CONTROL

Fundamental to the operation of a data communications facility are the mechanisms of flow control, error control, and error detection. These mechanisms are found in levels 2 and 3 of X.25, in the signaling link level of Signaling System Number 7, and in LAP-D. They are also found in a number of other protocols, such as HDLC. This appendix examines the basic principles of these mechanisms. Their application in X.25, SS7, and ISDN is presented at the appropriate points in the main part of this book.

A-1 FLOW CONTROL

Flow control is a technique for assuring that a transmitting entity does not overwhelm a receiving entity with data. The receiver will typically allocate a data buffer of some maximum length. When data are received, the receiver must do a certain amount of processing (e.g., examine the header and remove it) before passing the data to a higher-level user. In the absence of flow control, the receiver's buffer may fill up and overflow while it is processing old data.

In this section, we examine mechanisms for flow control in the absence of errors. The model we will use is depicted in Figure A-1a. Data are sent as a sequence of blocks. We will refer to the block as a *protocol data unit* (PDU) to emphasize that the exact nature of the block depends on the protocol involved. In X.25 level 2 and in LAP-D, the term *frame* is used; In the signaling link level of Signaling System Number 7, the term *signal unit* is used; and in X.25 level 3, the term *packet* is used. In any case, we assume that all PDUs that are transmitted are successfully received; no PDUs are lost and none arrive with errors. Furthermore, PDUs arrive in the same

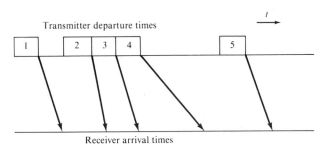

(a) Error-free transmission

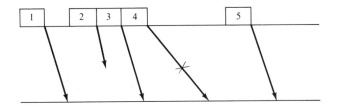

(b) Transmission with losses and errors

FIGURE A-1   Model of Frame Transmission

order in which they are sent. However, each transmitted PDU suffers an arbitrary and variable amount of delay before reception.

The simplest form of flow control, known as **stop-and-wait flow control**, works as follows. A source entity transmits a PDU. After reception, the destination entity indicates its willingness to accept another PDU by sending back an acknowledgment to the PDU just received. The source must wait until it receives the acknowledgment before sending the next PDU. The destination can thus stop the flow of data by simply withholding acknowledgment. This procedure works fine and, indeed, can hardly be improved upon when a message is sent as one contiguous block of data. However, it is often the case that a source will break up a large block of data into smaller blocks and send these one at a time. This is done for one or more of the following reasons:

- The buffer size of the receiver may be limited.
- On a multipoint line (such as may be found using LAP-D), it is usually desirable not to permit one station to occupy the line for very long, thus causing long delays at the other stations.]
- On a shared network (such as an X.25 packet-switching network), the network may impose a maximum packet size.
- The longer the transmission, the more likely that there will be an error, necessitating retransmission of the entire block. With smaller blocks, errors are detected sooner, and a smaller amount of data needs to be retransmitted.

With the use of multiple PDUs for a single message, the stop-and-wait procedure may be inadequate. The essence of the problem is that only one PDU at a time
can be in transit. In situations where the bit length of the link is greater than the PDU
length, serious inefficiencies result. This is illustrated in Figure A-2; in the figure the
transmission time (the time it takes for a station to transmit a PDU) is normalized to
one, and the propagation delay (the time it takes for a bit to propagate from sender to
receiver) is expressed as the variable a. Note that most of the time, most of the line
is idle.

Efficiency can be greatly improved by allowing multiple PDUs to be in transit
at the same time. Let us examine how this might work for two stations, A and B,
connected via a full-duplex link. Station B allocates buffer space for n PDUs instead
of the one discussed above. Thus B can accept n PDUs, and A is allowed to send n
PDUs without waiting for an acknowledgment. To keep track of which PDUs have
been acknowledged, each is labeled with a sequence number. B acknowledges a
PDU by sending an acknowledgment that includes the sequence number of the next
PDU expected. This acknowledgment also implicitly announces that B is prepared
to receive the next n PDUs beginning with the number specified. This scheme can
also be used to acknowledge multiple PDUs. For example, B could receive PDUs 2,
3, and 4, but withhold acknowledgment until PDU 4 has arrived. By then returning
an acknowledgment with sequence number 5, B acknowledges PDUs 2, 3, and 4 at
one time. A maintains a list of sequence numbers that it is allowed to send and B
maintains a list of sequence numbers that it is prepared to receive. Each of these lists
can be thought of as a *window* of PDUs. The operation is referred to as **sliding-
window flow control.**

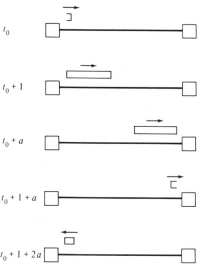

FIGURE A-2 Stop-and-Wait Link Utilization

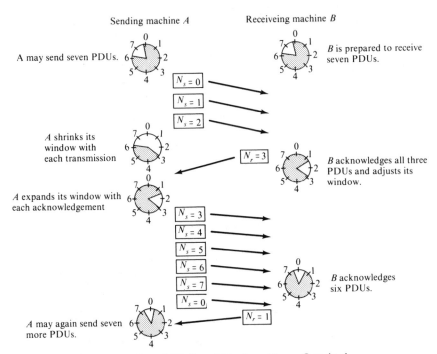

FIGURE A-3   Example of Sliding-Window Flow Control

Several additional comments need to be made. First, since the sequence number to be used occupies a field in the PDU, it is clearly of bounded size. For a k-bit field, the sequence number can range from 0 to $2^k - 1$. Accordingly, PDUs are numbered modulo 2^k; that is after sequence number $2^k - 1$, the next number is zero. Second, the maximum size of the window is some number $n \leq 2^k - 1$. The limitation to $2^k - 1$ rather than 2^k has to do with the error control mechanism, and will be justified in due course.

An example of this mechanism is shown in Figure A-3. The example assumes a 3-bit sequence number field and a maximum window size of seven. Initially, A and B have windows indicating that A may transmit seven PDUs. After transmitting three PDUs without acknowledgment, A has shrunk its window to four PDUs. When PDU 2 is acknowledged, A is back up to permission to transmit seven PDUs.

Figure A-4, which shows the efficiency implications of this mechanism, is to be contrasted with the stop-and-wait mechanism illustrated in Figure A-3. If the maximum window size, n, is a little greater than twice the round-trip propagation delay $(n > 2a + 1)$, then it is possible to utilize the link to the fullest.* Even for

---

* Recall that the time to transmit one PDU is normalized to one time unit, and the propagation time is the variable a. Hence the time to transmit n PDUs in succession is n time units.

smaller window sizes, the utilization of the link is clearly superior to that of stop-and-wait.

The mechanism so far described does indeed provide a form of flow control: the receiver must only be able to accommodate n PDUs beyond the one it has last acknowledged. To supplement this, most protocols also allow a station to completely cut off the flow of PDUs from the other side by sending a Receive Not Ready (RNR) message, which acknowledges former PDUs but forbids transfer of future PDUs. Thus, RNR 5 means: "I have received all PDUs up through number 4 but am

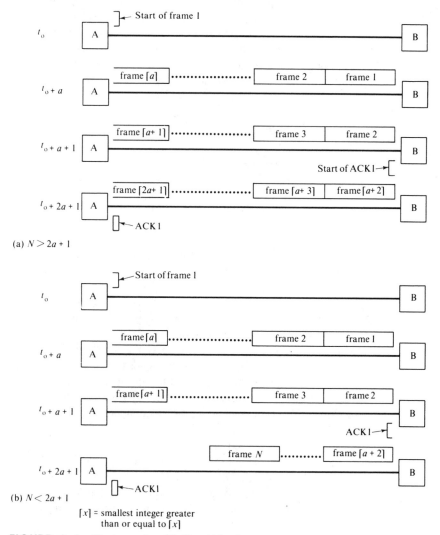

FIGURE A-4   Timing of a Sliding Window Protocol

unable to accept any more." At some subsequent point, the station must send a normal acknowledgment to reopen the window.

So far, we have discussed transmission in one direction only. If two stations exchange data, each needs to maintain two windows: one for transmit and one for receive, and each side needs to send the data and acknowledgments to the other. To provide efficient support for this requirement, a feature known as *piggybacking* is typically provided. Each data *PDU* includes a field that holds the sequence number of that PDU plus a field that holds the sequence number used for acknowledgment. Thus, if a station has data to send and an acknowledgment to send, it sends both together in one PDU, saving communication capacity. Of course, if a station has an acknowledgment but no data to send, it send a separate *acknowledgment PDU*. If a station has data to send but no new acknowledgment to send, it must repeat the last acknowledgment that it sent. This is because the data PDU includes a field for the acknowledgment number and some value must be put into that field. When a station receives a duplicate ACK, it simply ignores it.

A-2   ERROR DETECTION

The Error Detection Process

Any data transmission is subject to errors. In transmitting across a data link, signal impairments, such as the following, may alter the contents of a unit of data [STAL88a]:

- *Attenuation:* The strength of the signal decreases with distance over any transmission medium. With sufficient attenuation, it becomes difficult for the receiver to recover the data from the received signal.
- *Attenuation distortion:* Attenuation is an increasing function of frequency. Thus, frequency components of a signal are differentially affected, which introduces distortion into the signal.
- *Delay distortion:* The velocity of propagation of a signal through a wire medium varies with frequency; the velocity tends to be highest near the center frequency of the signal and fall off toward the two edges of the signal's bandwidth. This causes the signal energy from one bit time to spill into the time slots of neighboring bits, a phenomenon known as intersymbol interference.
- *Noise:* Noise is any unwanted signal that combines with, and hence, distorts the signal intended for reception. Varieties include thermal noise, intermodulation noise, crosstalk, and impulse noise.
- *Collisions:* In a multipoint link, if two stations transmit at the same time, their signals overlap and neither signal can be successfully received.

Because of these impairments, a protocol entity (e.g., LAP-D, X.25 level 2, SS7 signaling link level) may receive a PDU from the other side in which some bits have changed value. Accordingly, some form of error detection is needed to avoid delivering incorrect data to the user.

The error detection process is illustrated in Figure A-5. On transmission, a calculation is performed on the bits of the PDU to be transmitted; the result, called an **error-detecting code,** is inserted as an additional field in the frame. On reception, the same calculation is performed on the received bits and the calculated result is compared to the value stored in the incoming frame. If there is a discrepancy, the receiver assumes that an error has occurred and discards the PDU.

The Cyclic Redundancy Check

One of the most common, and one of the most powerful, of the error-detecting codes is the cyclic redundancy check (CRC). It is used in X.25 level 2, SS7 signaling link level, and LAP-D. We first examine the operation of this code, and then look at its effectiveness.

CRC Operation.   Given a k-bit block of data, the transmitter generates an n-bit sequence, known as a *frame check sequence* (FCS) so that the resulting frame, consisting of $k + n$ bits is exactly divisible by some predetermined number. The receiver then divides the incoming frame by the same number and, if there is no remainder, assumes that there was no error.

To clarify the above, we present the procedure in several ways:

- Modulo 2 arithmetic.
- Polynomials.
- Shift registers and exclusive-or gates.

First, we work with binary numbers and modulo 2 arithmetic. Modulo 2 arithmetic uses binary addition with no carries, which is just the exclusive-or operation.

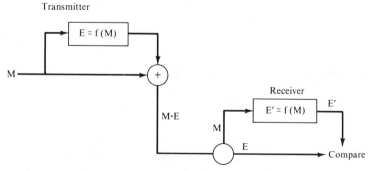

M = Message
E, E' = Error-detecting code
f = Error-detecting code function

FIGURE A-5 Error Detection

Examples

$$
\begin{array}{r}
1111 \\
+\,1010 \\
\hline
0101
\end{array}
\qquad
\begin{array}{r}
11001 \\
\times\quad 11 \\
\hline
11001 \\
11001 \\
\hline
101011
\end{array}
$$ ∎

Now define:

> $T = (k + n)$-bit PDU to be transmitted, with $n < k$
> $M = k$-bit message, the first k bits of T
> $F = n$-bit FCS, the last n bits of T
> $P =$ pattern of $n + 1$ bits; this is the predetermined divisor mentioned above

We would like T/P to have no remainder. It should be clear that

$$T = 2^n M + F$$

That is, by multiplying M by 2^n, we have in effect shifted it to the left by n bits and padded out the result with 0s. Adding F gives us the concatenation of M and F, which is T. Now we want T to be exactly divisible by P. Suppose that we divided $2^n M$ by P:

$$\frac{2^n M}{P} = Q + \frac{R}{P} \qquad\qquad \text{(A-1)}$$

There is a quotient and a remainder. Since division is binary, the remainder is always one bit less than the divisor. We will use this remainder as our FCS. Then

$$T = 2^n M + R$$

Question: Does this R satisfy our condition? To see that it does, consider

$$\frac{T}{P} = \frac{2^n M + R}{P}$$

substituting equation (A-1), we have

$$\frac{T}{P} = Q + \frac{R}{P} + \frac{R}{P}$$

However, any binary number added to itself modulo 2 yields zero. Thus

$$\frac{T}{P} = Q + \frac{R + R}{P} = Q$$

There is no remainder, and therefore T is exactly divisible by P. Thus the FCS is easily generated. Simply divide $2^n M$ by P and use the remainder as the FCS. On reception, the receiver will divide T by P and will get no remainder if there have been no errors.

A simple example of the procedure is now presented:

1.   Given

$$\text{Message } M = 1010001101 \text{ (10 bits)}$$
$$\text{Pattern } P = 110101 \text{ (6 bits)}$$
$$\text{FCS } R = \text{to be calculated (5 bits)}$$

2.   The message is multiplied by 2^5, yielding 101000110100000.
3.   This product is divided by P:

```
                    1101010110 ← Q
P → 110101 101000110100000 ← 2ⁿM
           110101
            111011
            110101
             111010
             110101
              111110
              110101
               101100
               110101
                110010
                110101
                 1110 ← R
```

4.   The remainder is added to $2^n M$ to give $T = 101000110101110$, which is transmitted.
5.   If there are no errors, the receiver receives T intact. The received PDU is divided by P:

```
                  1101010110
    110101 101000110101110
           110101
            111011
            110101
             111010
             110101
              111110
              110101
               101111
               110101
                110101
                110101
                   00
```

Since there is no remainder, it is assumed that there have been no errors.

The pattern P is chosen to be one bit longer than the desired FCS, and the exact bit pattern chosen depends on the type of errors expected. At minimum, both the high- and low-order bits of P must be 1.

The occurrence of an error is easily expressed. An error results in the reversal of a bit. Mathematically, this is equivalent to taking the exclusive-or of the bit and $1: 0 + 1 = 1; 1 + 1 = 0$. Thus the errors in an $(n + k)$-bit PDU can be represented by an $(n + k)$-bit field with 1's in each error position. The resulting frame T_r can be expressed as

$$T_r = T + E$$

where

T = transmitted frame
E = error pattern with 1s in positions where errors occur
T_r = received frame

The receiver will fail to detect an error if and only if T_r is divisible by P, that is, if and only if E is divisible by P. Intuitively, this seems an unlikely occurrence.

A second way of viewing the CRC process is to express all values as polynomials in a dummy variable X with binary coefficients. The coefficients correspond to the bits in the binary number. Thus for $M = 110011$, we have $M(X) = X^5 + X^4 + X + 1$, and for $P = 11001$, we have $P(X) = X^4 + X^3 + 1$. Arithmetic operations are again modulo 2. The CRC process can now be described as:

1. $\dfrac{X^n M(X)}{P(X)} = Q(X) + \dfrac{R(X)}{P(X)}$

2. $T(X) = X^n M(X) + R(X)$

Four versions of $P(X)$ are widely used:

$$CRC\text{-}12 = X^{12} + X^{11} + X^3 + X^2 + X + 1$$
$$CRC\text{-}16 = X^{16} + X^{15} + X^2 + 1$$
$$CRC\text{-}CCITT = X^{16} + X^{12} + X^5 + 1$$
$$CRC\text{-}32 = X^{32} + X^{26} + X^{23} + X^{22} + X^{16} + X^{12} + X^{11}$$
$$+ X^{10} + X^8 + X^7 + X^5 + X^4 + X^2 + X + 1$$

The CRC-12 system is used for transmission of streams of 6-bit characters and generates a 12-bit FCS. Both CRC-16 and CRC-CCITT are popular for 8-bit characters, in the United States and Europe respectively, and both result in a 16-bit FCS. This would seem adequate for most applications, although CRC-32 is specified as an option in some point-to-point synchronous transmission standards.

As a final representation, Figure A-6 shows that the CRC process can easily be implemented as a dividing circuit consisting of exclusive-or gates and a shift register. The circuit is implemented as follows:

1.   The register contains n bits, equal to the length of the FCS.

Key: [ ] 1 bit shift register

(+) : Exclusive OR (modulo 2 addition)

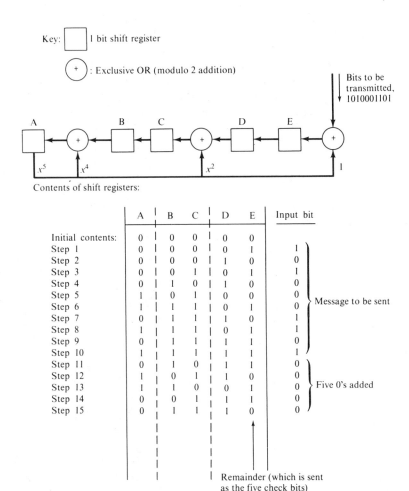

Contents of shift registers:

	A	B	C	D	E	Input bit	
Initial contents:	0	0	0	0	0		
Step 1	0	0	0	0	1	1	
Step 2	0	0	0	1	0	0	
Step 3	0	0	1	0	1	1	
Step 4	0	1	0	1	0	0	
Step 5	1	0	1	0	0	0	
Step 6	1	1	1	0	1	0	Message to be sent
Step 7	0	1	1	1	0	1	
Step 8	1	1	1	0	1	1	
Step 9	0	1	1	1	1	0	
Step 10	1	1	1	1	1	1	
Step 11	0	1	0	1	1	0	
Step 12	1	0	1	1	0	0	
Step 13	1	1	0	0	1	0	Five 0's added
Step 14	0	0	1	1	1	0	
Step 15	0	1	1	1	0	0	

Remainder (which is sent as the five check bits)

FIGURE A-6   Circuit with Shift Registers for Dividing by the Polynomial $(X^5 + X^4 + X^2 + 1)$

2. There are up to n exclusive-or gates.
3. The presence or absence of a gate corresponds to the presence or absence of a term in the divisor polynomial, $P(X)$.

In this example, we use:

$$\text{Message } M = 1010001101; \ M(X) = X^9 + X^7 + X^3 + X^2 + 1$$
$$\text{Divisor } P = 110101; \ P(X) = X^5 + X^4 + X^2 + 1$$

which were used earlier in the discussion.

The process begins with the shift register cleared (all zeroes). The message, or dividend, is then entered, one bit at a time, starting with the most significant (leftmost) bit. Since no feedback occurs until a 1 dividend bit arrives at the most significant end of the register, the first four operations are simple shifts. Whenever a 1 bit arrives at the left end, a 1 is subtracted (exclusive-or) from the second and fifth bits on the next shift. This is identical to the binary long division process illustrated earlier. The process continues through all the bits of the message, plus four zero bits. These latter bits account for shifting M to the left four positions to accommodate the FCS. After the last bit is processed, the shift register contains the remainder (FCS), which can then be transmitted.

At the receiver, the same logic is used. As each bit of M arrives it is inserted into the shift register at A. If there have been no errors, the shift register should contain the bit pattern for R at the conclusion of M. The transmitted bits of R now begin to arrive, and the effect is to zero out the register so that, at the conclusion of reception, the register contains all 0s.

CRC Effectiveness.   The measure of effectiveness of any error-detecting code is what percentage of errors it detects. In the case of CRC, effectiveness is most easily determined by using the polynomial representation. Consider, as before, that we are transmitting a block $T(X)$. When this block is transmitted, one or more bits may be altered by transmission impairments. The pattern of error bits may be represented by another polynomial $E(X)$. Thus the actual received pattern is $T(X) + E(X)$. Now, if this received pattern is divisible by $P(X)$, then the error will not be detected. We have:

$$\frac{T(X) + E(X)}{P(X)} = \frac{T(X)}{P(X)} + \frac{E(X)}{P(X)} = \frac{Q(X)\,E(X)}{P(X)}$$

Thus, the received pattern, when divided by $P(X)$, will produce a remainder only if $E(X)$ produces a remainder. Conversely, an error will remain undetected if $E(X)$ is divisible by $P(X)$. It can be shown that all of the following errors are not divisible by $P(X)$ and hence are detectable [MART73]:

- All single-bit errors.
- All double-bit errors, as long as $P(X)$ has at least three terms.
- Any odd number of errors, as long as $P(X)$ contains a factor $(X + 1)$.
- Any burst error for which the length of the burst is less than the length of the divisor polynomial $P(X)$; that is, less than or equal to the length of the FCS.
- Most larger burst errors.

Let us examine each of these assertions in turn.

1. Single-Bit Errors
A single bit error can be represented by $E(X) = X^i$ for some i less than the total message length $(i < k + n)$. We have said that for $P(X)$, both the first and last terms

must be nonzero. Thus $P(X)$ has at least two terms and cannot divide the one-term $E(X)$.

2. Double-Bit Errors

A double-bit error can be represented by $E(X) = X^i + X^j = X^i(1 + X^{j-i})$ for some i and j with $i < j$. To avoid a remainder $P(X)$ must exactly divide either X^i or $(1 + X^{j-i})$. We have shown that it does not divide X^i. If the polynomial has at least three terms, it cannot divide the two-term $(1 + X^{j-i})$ either. All of the CRC codes in common use have at least three terms.

3. Odd Number of Errors

Assume that $E(X)$ has an odd number of terms and is divisible by $(X + 1)$. Then we can express $E(X)$ as $E(X) = (X + 1)F(X)$. Then $E(1) = (1 + 1)F(x) = 0$, since $1 + 1 = 0$ in modulo two arithmetic. But any polynomial expression $E(X)$ will have the value $E(1) = 0$ if and only if it contains an even number of terms. Thus $E(X)$ with an odd number of terms is not divisible by $(X + 1)$ and any polynomial $P(X)$ with that factor will detect the error. Again, all of the CRC codes in common use have $(X + 1)$ as a factor.

4. Burst Errors

A burst error refers to a string of bits within a message in which at least the first and last bits of the string are in error. Thus, a burst error of length j is a string of bits beginning and ending with 1 and containing intervening 1s and 0s. For example, if $E(X)$ represents the error pattern 00000101001100000, then there is a burst error of length 7.

A burst error can be expressed as $E(X) = X^i(X^{j-1} + \cdots + 1) = X^iG(X)$ where i expresses how far the burst is shifted from the right-hand end. For our example,

$$E(X) = X^{10} + X^8 + X^5 + X^4$$
$$= X^4(X^6 + X^4 + X + 1)$$

Since X^i is not divisible by $P(X)$, the error will go undetected only if the second factor, $G(X)$, is exactly divisible by $P(X)$. In the case of a burst error of length less than the length of the polynomial ($j < n + 1$), $P(X)$ will not divide the $G(X)$ since $P(X)$ is of higher order.

Now consider the case where the length of the burst error exactly equals the length of the polynomial ($j = n + 1$). In this case, the error will go undetected only if $G(X) = P(X)$. We already know that the first and last terms of both $G(X)$ and $P(X)$ are nonzero. Therefore, the remaining $n - 1$ bits of the two expressions must be equal. If we assume all bit errors are equally likely, then the probability that $G(X) = P(X)$ is $(1/2)^{n-1}$. Thus, for CRC-16 or CRC-CCITT, the probability of an undetected error is $(1/2)^{15} = 0.0000305$, given that the block contains a burst of length 17 bits (a very rare event).

Finally, when the number of bits in the burst is greater than the length of the polynomial ($j > n + 1$), then a number of different values of $G(X)$ will be divisible by $P(X)$. If $G(X)$ is exactly divisible by $P(X)$, we can write:

$$\frac{G(X)}{P(X)} = Q(X)$$

where $Q(X)$ is the quotient obtained by dividing $G(X)$ by $P(X)$. Now, $G(X)$ is a polynomial of degree $j - 1$, and $P(X)$ is a polynomial of degree n. Thus the degree of $Q(X)$ is $(j - 1) - n$. The number of bits that correspond to $Q(X)$ is therefore $j - n$. We know that the first and last bit are one. The remaining $j - n - 2$ bits may take either binary value. This means that there are 2^{j-n-2} values of $G(X)$ that are exactly divisible by $P(X)$. Given a burst error of length j, then there are a total of 2^{j-2} possible values of $G(X)$. Thus the fraction of burst errors of length j that will go undetected is:

$$\frac{2^{j-n-2}}{2^{j-2}} = (1/2)^n$$

Again, for CRC-16 and CRC-CCITT, the probability of an undetected error is $(1/2)^{16} = 0.0000153$, given that the block contains a burst of length greater than 17 bits.

These results are summarized in Table A-1.

A-3   ERROR CONTROL

Error control refers to mechanisms to detect and correct errors that occur in the transmission of protocol data units (PDUs). The model that we will use, which covers the typical case, is illustrated in Figure A-1b. As before, data are sent as a sequence of PDUs; PDUs arrive in the same order in which they are sent; and each transmitted PDU suffers an arbitrary and variable amount of delay before reception. In addition, we admit the possibility of two types of errors:

- *Lost PDU*: A PDU fails to arrive at the other side. In the case of a network, the network may simply fail to deliver a packet. In the case of a direct point-to-point data link, a noise burst may damage a frame to the extent that the receiver is not aware that a frame has been transmitted.
- *Damaged PDU*: A recognizable PDU does arrive but some of the bits are in error (have been altered during transmission).

TABLE A-1   EFFECTIVENESS OF THE CYCLIC REDUNDANCY CHECK (CRC)

Type of Error	Probability of Detection
Single bit errors	1.0
Two bits in error (separate or not)	1.0
Odd number of bits in error	1.0
Error burst of length less than $(n + 1)$ bits	1.0
Error burst of $(n + 1)$ bits	$1 - (1/2)^{n-1}$
Error burst of greater than $(n + 1)$ bits	$1 - (1/2)^n$

The most common techniques for error control are based on some or all of the following ingredients:

- *Error Detection:* The destination detects and discards PDUs that are in error, using the techniques described in the preceding section.
- *Positive acknowledgment:* The destination returns a positive acknowledgment to successfully received, error-free PDUs.
- *Retransmission after timeout:* The source retransmits a PDU that has not been acknowledged after a predetermined amount of time.
- *Negative acknowledgment and retransmission:* The destination returns a negative acknowledgment to PDUs in which an error is detected. The source retransmits such PDUs.

Collectively, these mechanisms are all referred to as **automatic repeat request** (ARQ). The two most common forms of ARQ are go-back-N ARQ and selective-repeat ARQ. Both of these forms are based on the use of the sliding-window flow control technique described in Section A-1. We examine each of these in turn.

Go-back-N ARQ. In go-back-N ARQ, a station may send a series of PDUs sequentially numbered modulo some maximum value. The number of unacknowledged PDUs outstanding is determined by window size, using the sliding-window flow control technique. While no errors occur, the destination will acknowledge (ACK) incoming PDUs as usual. If the destination station detects an error in a PDU, it sends a negative acknowledgment (NAK) for that PDU. The destination station will discard that PDU and all future incoming PDUs until the PDU in error is correctly received. Thus the source station, when it receives a NAK, must retransmit the PDU in error plus all succeeding PDUs that had been transmitted in the interim.

Consider that station A is sending PDUs to station B. After each transmission, A sets an acknowledgement timer for the PDU just transmitted. The go-back-N technique takes into account the following contingencies:

1. Damaged PDU. There are three subcases:
    (a) A transmits PDU i. B detects an error and has previously successfully received PDU $(i - 1)$. B sends a NAK i, indicating that frame i is rejected. When A receives this NAK, it must retransmit PDU i and all subsequent PDUs that it has transmitted.
    (b) PDU i is lost in transit. A subsequently sends PDU $(i + 1)$. B receives PDU $(i + 1)$ out of order, and sends a NAK i.
    (c) PDU i is lost in transit and A does not soon send additional PDUs. B receives nothing and returns neither an ACK or a NAK. A will time out and retransmit PDU i.
2. Damaged ACK. There are two subcases:
    (a) B receives PDU i and sends ACK $(i + 1)$, which is lost in transit. Since ACKs are cumulative (e.g., ACK 6 means that all PDUs

through 5 are acknowledged), it may be that A will receive a subsequent ACK to a subsequent PDU that will do the job of the lost ACK before the associated timer expires.
(b) If A's timer expires, A retransmits PDU *i* and all subsequent PDUs.
3.   Damaged NAK. If a NAK is lost, A will eventually time out on the associated PDU and retransmit that PDU and all subsequent PDUs.

Figure A-7 shows the PDU flow for go-back-N ARQ on a full-duplex line, assuming a 3-bit sequence number.

In the section of flow control, we mentioned that for a *k*-bit sequence number field, which provides a sequence number range of 2^k, the maximum window size is limited to 2^{k-1}. This has to do with the interaction between error control and acknowledgment. Consider that if data are being exchanged in both directions, station *B* must send a piggybacked acknowledgment to station *A*'s PDUs in the data PDUs being transmitted by *B*, even if the acknowledgment has already been sent. As we have mentioned, this is because *B* must put some number in the acknowledgment field of its data PDUs. As an example, assume a 3-bit sequence number size. Suppose a station send PDU 0 and gets back an ACK 1, and then sends PDUs 1, 2, 3, 4, 5, 6, 7, 0 and gets another ACK 1. This could mean that all eight PDUs were received correctly and the ACK 1 is a cumulative acknowledgment. It could also mean that all eight PDUs were damaged in transit, and the receiving station is repeating its previous ACK 1. The problem is avoided if the maximum window size is limited to 7 ($2^3 - 1$).

Selective-Repeat ARQ.   With selective-repeat ARQ, the only PDUs retransmitted are those that receive a NAK or which time out. Figure A-8, which exhibits

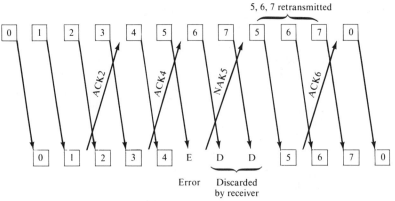

FIGURE A-7 Go-back-N ARQ

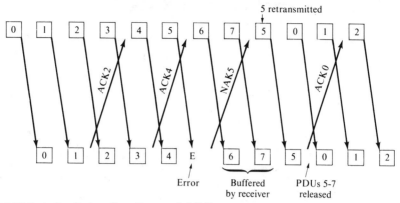

FIGURE A-8   Selective Repeat ARQ

the same error pattern as Figure A-7, illustrates selective repeat. This would appear to be more efficient than the go-back-N approach, since it minimizes the amount of retransmission. On the other hand, the receiver must contain storage to save post-NAK PDUs until the PDU in error is retransmitted, and contain logic for reinserting that PDU in the proper sequence. The transmitter, too, will require more complex logic to be able to send PDUs out of sequence. Because of such complications, the selective-reject ARQ is rarely implemented.

The window size requirement is more restrictive for selective-repeat than for go-back-N. We have seen that for a sequence number space of 2^k, the maximum window size for go-back-N is 2^{k-1}. Now consider the case of a 3-bit sequence number size (sequence space is eight) using selective repeat. Allow a window size of seven, and consider the following scenario [TANE81]:

1. Station A sends PDUs 0 through 6 to station B.
2. Station B receives and acknowledges all seven PDUs.
3. Because of a long noise burst, all seven acknowledgments are lost.
4. Station A times out and retransmits PDU 0.
5. Station B has already advanced its receive window to accept PDUs 7, 0, 1, 2, 3, 4, and 5. Thus it assumes that PDU 7 has been lost and that this is a new PDU 0, which it accepts.

The problem with the foregoing scenario, for selective repeat ARQ, is that there is an overlap between the sending and receiving windows. To overcome the problem, the maximum window size should be no more than half the range of sequence numbers. In the scenario above, if only four unacknowledged PDUs may be outstanding, no confusion can result.

A-4   A COMPARISON OF PROTOCOLS

In this book, we examine four protocols that make use of some or all of the flow and error control mechanisms described in this appendix:

- X.25 level 2 (LAP-~~D~~) ℬ
- X.25 level 3
- SS7 signaling link level
- LAP-D

Table A-2 compares these protocols in terms of various aspects of flow control and error control. For flow control, SS7 and LAP-D provides for the use of 7-bit sequence numbers and a maximum window size of 127 signal units. The other protocols in the table provide the option of 3-bit or 7-bit sequence numbers, and the corresponding maximum window size of 7 or 127. The choice is made at the time of connection setup. All of the protocols employ piggybacking, when possible, for acknowledgment.

Note that no error detection is performed by X.25 level 3. The level 3 protocol relies on the level 2 protocol (LAP-B) to assure that all received packets are free of bit errors. However, error control mechanisms are still needed to account for lost packets. For the other three protocols, all at the link level, the CRC-CCITT divisor is used:

$$P(X) = X^{16} + X^{12} + X^5 + 1$$

TABLE A-2   A COMPARISON OF VARIOUS PROTOCOLS

Feature	SS7 Signaling Link Level	LAP-D	LAP-B	X.25 Level 3
Sequence number field (bits)	7	7	3 or 7	3 or 7
Piggybacking	Yes	Yes	Yes	Yes
Maximum window size	127	127	7 or 127	7 or 127
CRC Code*	CRC-CCITT	CRC-CCITT	CRC-CCITT	None
ARQ type	Go-back-N, Cyclic retransmission	Go-back-N	Go-back-N	Go-back-N
Bit stuffing	Yes	Yes	Yes	No
Address Field	None	16 bits	8 bits	12 bits

* Note: The CRC calculation involves a bit inversion; see text.

Several refinements are added to the process described in Section A-2. Specifically, the 16-bit FCS is defined to be the ones complement of $R(X)$, where

$$R(X) = [X^{16}M(X) + X^kL(X)]/P(X)$$

with

$$L(X) = X^{15} + X^{14} + X^{13} + \cdots + X^2 + X + 1$$

and

$$k = \text{number of bits in } M$$

The addition of $X^kL(X)$ to $X^{16}M(X)$ is equivalent to inverting the first 16 bits of $M(X)$. It can be accomplished in a shift register implementation, such as Figure A-6, by presetting the register to all ones initially, instead of all zeros. This term is present to detect erroneous addition or deletion of zero bits at the leading end of $M(X)$. The procedure described in Section A-2 will produce the same result for two messages that differ only in the number of leading zeros. The complementing of $R(X)$ by the transmitter at the completion of the division insures that the transmitted sequence has a property that permits the receiver to detect addition or deletion of trailing zeros that may appear as a result of errors. Again, the procedure described in Section A-2 will produce the same result at the receiver for two transmissions that differ only in the number of trailing zeros.

At the receiver, the reverse operations must be done to perform error detection. Using a shift register implementation, the initial content of the receiver's register is set to all ones. If there have been no transmission errors, the final remainder after division of the incoming bits, including the FCS, by $P(X)$ will be the unique 16-bit sequence:

0001110100001111

Thus, instead of comparing the result to the received FCS, the receiver computes a value and compares it to this unique bit pattern.

Returning to Table A-2, we can see that all of the protocols use Go-back-N ARQ for error control. In addition, SS7 signaling link level employs a cyclic retransmission scheme.

Several other characteristics of the four protocols are worth comparison. All of the link-level protocols use bit stuffing. This is needed because all of these protocols use flags for marking the beginning and end of PDUs. For X.25 level 3, no flag is employed and bit stuffing is not required. Finally, the protocols differ in the manner in which addresses are handled. There is no address field in the SS7 signaling link level protocol. Addressing usually serves no purpose on point-to-point links; a signal unit transmitted by one side is intended for the other side. LAP-B also makes use of point-to-point links and could do without an address field. However, LAP-B is intended to be compatible with HDLC, which allows multipoint configurations and which therefore requires an address field. LAP-D, provides a 16-bit address field that include a service access point identifier and a terminal endpoint identifier. Finally, X.25 level 3 employs a 12-bit virtual circuit number for addressing purposes.

A-5 RECOMMENDED READING

A number of books cover the topic of error detection. [MCNA88], [MART73], and [BERT87] are especially readable. [PETE61] is also a good presentation. The CRC algorithm is usually implemented in hardware, but is sometimes implemented in software. In the latter case, an algorithm that treats data 8 bits at a time rather than one bit at a time is considerably more efficient. Two approaches are discussed in [PERE83] and [GRIF87].

Clear discussions of flow control and error control can be found in [MART81] and [BERT87]. The latter provides clear proofs that the various algorithms actually work as intended. Good survey articles on the subject are [LIN84] and [BERL87]. [STAL88a] and [STAL86] provide a simple technique for calculating the efficiency of the various flow and error control techniques. More sophisticated analyses can be found in [BERT87] and [STUC85].

A-6 PROBLEMS

A-1   What is the purpose of using modulo 2 arithmetic in computing an FCS rather than binary arithmetic?

A-2   Using the CRC-CCITT polynomial, generate the 16-bit FCS for the message consisting of a one followed by 15 zeros.

A-3   Explain in words why the shift register implementation of CRC will result in all zeros at the receiver if there are no errors. Demonstrate by example.

A-4   For $P = 110011$ and $M = 11100011$, find the FCS.

A-5   In Section A-1, the variable a was defined to be the propagation time given that the transmission time is normalized to one. Another way of saying this is that $a = $ (propagation time)/(transmission time).
(a) Show that, for stop-and-wait flow control, the maximum utilization of the link is equal to $1/(1 + 2a)$.
(b) Show that for sliding window flow control, the maximum utilization of the link is 1 if $n > (2a + 1)$, and is $n/(2a + 1)$ if $n < (2a + 1)$.

A-6   Explain how the procedure outlined in Section A-4 detects erroneous addition or deletion of zero bits at the beginning or end of a message?

A-7   An alternative to ARQ is the use of an error-correcting code. Such a code not only detects errors but enables the receiver to correct them. Does this accomplish the same thing as ARQ?

A-8   Selective repeat ARQ has a major advantage and a major disadvantage compared to go-back-N ARQ. Discuss the tradeoffs involved.

A-9 In go-back-N ARQ, if a PDU is received out of order, it is discarded. However, such a PDU contains a piggybacked acknowledgment. Give an example in which the protocol will deadlock if each side ignores receive sequence numbers in discarded packets.

A-10 The following statement is made in the LAP-B specification:

> If a DCE or DTE, due to a transmission error, does not receive (or receives and discards) a single I frame or the last I frame(s) in a sequence of I frames, it will not detect an $n(S)$ sequence error condition and therefore, will not transmit a REJ frame.

An I frame is simply a data PDU. Explain this statement. Does it present a potential problem?

APPENDIX B
THE OSI REFERENCE MODEL

One of the most important concepts in data communications is the open systems interconnection (OSI) reference model. This model serves as a framework within which communication protocol standards are developed. It also serves as a frame of reference for talking about data communications. Although the ISDN recommendations represent a separate effort from OSI and OSI-related standards, the ISDN protocols do fit within the OSI framework. This appendix provides an overview of the OSI model.

B-1 MOTIVATION

When work is done that involves more than one computer, additional elements must be added to the system: the hardware and software to support the communication between or among the systems. Communications hardware is reasonably standard and generally presents few problems. However, when communication is desired among heterogeneous (different vendors, different models of same vendor) machines, the software development effort can be a nightmare. Different vendors use different data formats and data exchange conventions. Even within one vendor's product line, different model computers may communicate in unique ways.

As the use of computer communications and computer networking proliferates, a one-at-a-time special-purpose approach to communications software development is too costly to be acceptable. The only alternative is for computer vendors to adopt and implement a common set of conventions. For this to happen, a set of

BOX B-1

PURPOSE OF THE OSI MODEL (ISO84)

The purpose of this International Standard Reference Model of Open Systems Interconnection is to provide a common basis for the coordination of standards development for the purpose of systems interconnection, while allowing existing standards to be placed into perspective within the overall Reference Model.

The term Open Systems Interconnection (OSI) qualifies standards for the exchange of information among systems that are "open" to one another for this purpose by virtue of their mutual use of the applicable standards.

The fact that a system is open does not imply any particular systems implementation, technology, or means of interconnection, but refers to the mutual recognition and support of the applicable standards.

It is also the purpose of this International Standard to identify areas for developing or improving standards, and to provide a common reference for maintaining consistency of all related standards. It is not the intent of this International Standard either to serve as an implementation specification, or to be a basis for appraising the conformance of actual implementations, or to provide a sufficient level of detail to define precisely the services and protocols of the interconnection architecture. Rather, this International Standard provides a conceptual and functional framework which allows international teams of experts to work productively and independently on the development of standards for each layer of the Reference Model of OSI.

international or at least national standards must be promulgated by appropriate organizations. Such standards have two effects:

- Vendors feel encouraged to implement the standards because of an expectation that, because of wide usage of the standards, their products would be less marketable without them.
- Customers are in a position to require that the standards be implemented by any vendor wishing to propose equipment to them.

It should become clear from the ensuing discussion that no single standard will suffice. The task of communication in a truly cooperative way between applications on different computers is too complex to be handled as a unit. The problem must be decomposed into manageable parts. Hence, before one can develop standards, there should be a structure or *architecture* that defines the communications tasks.

This line of reasoning led the International Organization for Standardization (ISO) in 1977 to establish a subcommittee to develop such an architecture. The result was the *Open Systems Interconnection* reference model, which is a framework for defining standards for linking heterogeneous computers. The OSI model provides the basis for connecting *open* systems for distributed applications processing. The term open denotes the ability of any two systems conforming to the reference model and the associated standards to connect.

Box B-1 extracted from the basic OSI document [ISO84] summarizes the purpose of the model.

B-2   CONCEPTS

A widely accepted structuring technique, and the one chosen by ISO, is *layering*. The communications functions are partitioned into a vertical set of layers. Each layer performs a related subset of the functions required to communicate with another system. It relies on the next lower layer to perform more primitive functions and to conceal the details of those functions. It provides services to the next higher layer. Ideally, the layers should be defined so that changes in one layer do not require changes in the other layers. Thus, we have decomposed one problem into a number of more manageable subproblems.

The task of the ISO subcommittee was to define a set of layers and the services performed by each layer. The partitioning should group functions logically, should have enough layers to make each layer manageably small, but should not have so many layers that the processing overhead imposed by the collection of layers is burdensome. The principles by which ISO went about its task are summarized in Box B-2. The resulting OSI reference model has seven layers, which are listed with a brief definition in Table B-1. Box B-3 provides ISO's justification for the selection of these layers.

Table A-3 defines, in general terms, the functions that must be performed in a system for it to communicate. Of course, it takes two to communicate, so the same set of layered functions must exist in two systems. Communication is achieved by having the corresponding *(peer)* layers in two systems communicate. The peer layers communicate by means of a set of rules or conventions known as a *protocol*. The key elements of a protocol are:

- *Syntax:* Includes such things as data format and signal levels.
- *Semantics:* Includes control information for coordination and error handling.
- *Timing:* Includes speed matching and sequencing.

Figure B-1 illustrates the OSI model. Each system contains the seven layers. Communication is between applications in the systems, labeled AP X and AP Y in the figure. If Ap X wishes to send a message to AP Y, it invokes the application layer (layer 7). Layer 7 establishes a peer relationship with layer 7 of the target machine, using a layer 7 protocol. This protocol requires services from layer 6, so the two layer

BOX B-2
PRINCIPLES USED IN DEFINING THE OSI LAYERS (ISO84)

1. Do not create so many layers as to make the system engineering task of describing and integrating the layers more difficult than necessary.
2. Create a boundary at a point where the description of services can be small and the number of interactions across the boundary are minimized.
3. Create separate layers to handle functions that are manifestly different in the process performed or the technology involved.
4. Collect similar functions into the same layer.
5. Select boundaries at a point that past experience has demonstrated to be successful.
6. Create a layer of easily localized functions so that the layer could be totally redesigned and its protocols changed in a major way to take advantage of new advances in architectural, hardware, or software technology without changing the services expected from and provided to the adjacent layers.
7. Create a boundary where it may be useful at some point in time to have the corresponding interface standardized.
8. Create a layer where there is a need for a different level of abstraction in the handling of data (e.g., morphology, syntax, semantics).
9. Allow changes of functions or protocols to be made within a layer without affecting other layers.
10. Create for each layer boundaries with its upper and lower layer only.

Similar principles have been applied to sublayering:

11. Create further subgrouping and organization of functions to form sublayers within a layer in cases where distinct communication services need it.
12. Create, where needed, two or more sublayers with a common and therefore minimal functionality to allow interface operation with adjacent layers.
13. Allow bypassing of sublayers.

TABLE B-1 THE OSI LAYERS

Layer	Definition
1. Physical	Concerned with transmission of unstructured bit stream over physical link; involves such parameters as signal voltage swing and bit duration; deals with the mechanical, electrical, and procedural characteristics to establish, maintain, and deactivate the physical link
2. Data link	Provides for the reliable transfer of data across the physical link; sends blocks of data (frames) with the necessary synchronization, error control, and flow control
3. Network	Provides upper layers with independence from the data transmission and switching technologies used to connect systems; responsible for establishing, maintaining, and terminating connections
4. Transport	Provides reliable, transparent transfer of data between end points; provides end-to-end error recovery and flow control
5. Session	Provides the control structure for communication between applications; establishes, manages, and terminates connections (sessions) between cooperating applications
6. Presentation	Performs generally useful transformations on data to provide a standardized application interface and to provide common communications services; examples: encryption, text compression, reformatting
7. Application	Provides services to the users of the OSI environment; examples: transaction server, file transfer protocol, network management

6 entities use a protocol of their own, and so on down to the physical layer, which actually passes the bits through a transmission medium.

Note that there is no direct communication between peer layers except at the physical layer. Even at that layer, the OSI model does not stipulate that two systems be directly connected. For example, a packet-switched or circuit-switched network may be used to provide the communications link. This point should become clearer below, when we discuss the network layer.

The attractiveness of the OSI approach is that it promises to solve the heterogeneous computer communications problem. Two systems, no matter how different, can communicate effectively if they have the following in common.

- They implement the same set of communications functions.
- These functions are organized into the same set of layers. Peer layers must provide the same functions, but note that it is not necessary that they provide them in the same way.
- Peer layers must share a common protocol.

To assure the above, standards are needed. Standards must define the functions and services to be provided by a layer (but not how it is to be done — that may

JUSTIFICATION OF THE OSI LAYERS (ISO84)

a. It is essential that the architecture permit usage of a realistic variety of physical media for interconnection with different control procedures (e.g., V.24, V.25, X.21, etc.). Application of principles, 3, 5, and 8 [Box B-2] leads to identification of a *Physical Layer* as the lowest layer in the architecture.

b. Some physical communication media (e.g., telephone line) require specific techniques to be used to transmit data between systems despite a relatively high error rate (i.e., an error rate not acceptable for the great majority of applications). These specific techniques are used in data-link control procedures, which have been studied and standardized for a number of years. It must also be recognized that new physical communication media (e.g., fiber optics) will require different data-link control procedures. Application of principles 3, 5, and 8 leads to identification of a *Data Link Layer* on top of the Physical Layer in the architecture.

c. In the open systems architecture, some systems will act as the final destination of data. Some systems may act only as intermediate nodes (forwarding data to other systems). Application of principles 3, 5, and 7 leads to identification of a *Network Layer* on top of the Data Link Layer. Network-oriented protocols, such as routing, for example, will be grouped in this layer. Thus, the Network Layer will provide a connection path (network-connection) between a pair of transport-entities, including the case where intermediate nodes are involved.

d. Control of data transportation from source end-system to destination end-system (which is not performed in intermediate nodes) is the last function to be performed to provide the totality of the transport-service. Thus, the upper layer in the transport-service part of the architecture is the *Transport Layer*, on top of the Network Layer. This Transport Layer relieves higher layer entities from any concern with the transportation of data between them.

e. There is a need to organize and synchronize dialogue, and to manage the exchange of data. Application of principles 3 and 4 leads to the identification of a *Session Layer* on top of the Transport Layer.

f. The remaining set of general interest functions are those related to representation and manipulation of structured data for the benefit of application programs. Application of principles 3 and 4 leads to identification of a *Presentation Layer* on top of the Session Layer.

g. Finally, there are applications consisting of application processes that perform information processing. An aspect of these applications processes and the protocols by which they communicate comprise the *Application Layer* as the highest layer of the architecture.

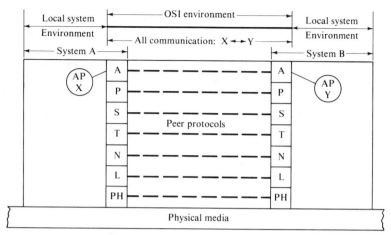

FIGURE B-1   The OSI Environment

differ from system to system). Standards must also define the protocols between peer layers (each protocol must be identical for the two peer layers). The OSI model, by defining a 7-layer architecture, provides a framework for defining these standards.

Some useful OSI terminology is illustrated in Fig. B-2. For simplicity, any layer is referred to as the *(N) layer*, and names of constructs associated with that layer are also preceded by (N). Within a system, there are one or more active entities in each layer. An *(N) entity* implements functions of the (N) layer and also the protocol for communicating with (N) entities in other systems. An example of an entity is a process in a multiprocessing system. Or it could simply be a subroutine. There might be multiple identical (N) entities, if this is convenient or efficient for a given system. There might also be differing (N) entities, corresponding to different protocol standards at that level. Each (N) entity implements a protocol for communicating

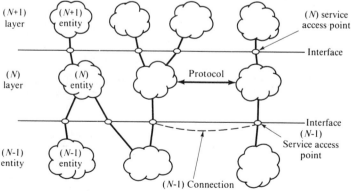

FIGURE B-2   The Layer Concept

with (N) entities in other systems. Each entity communicates with entities in the layers above and below it across an interface. The interface is realized as one or more *service access points* (SAPs).

To clarify these terms as well as some functions common to all layers, refer to Fig. B-3. The functions we wish to discuss are:

- Encapsulation
- Segmentation
- Connection establishment
- Flow control
- Error control
- Multiplexing

First, consider the most common way in which protocols are realized, which is by a process of *encapsulation*. When AP X has a message to send to AP Y, it transfers those data to a (7) entity in the application layer. A *header* is appended to the data that contains the required information for the peer layer 7 protocol; this is referred to as an encapsulation of the data. The original data, plus the header, is now passed as a

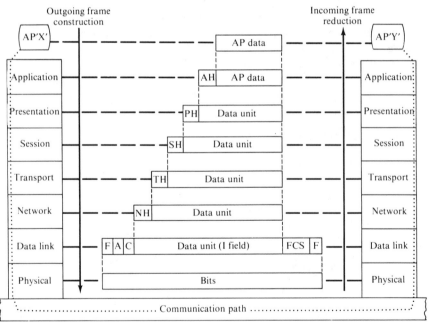

FIGURE B-3   OSI Operation

unit to layer 6. The (6) entity treats the whole unit as data, and appends its own header (a second encapsulation). This process continues down through layer 2, which generally adds both a header and a trailer, the function of which is explained later. This layer 2 unit, called a *frame*, is then transmitted by the physical layer onto the transmission medium. When the frame is received by the target system, the reverse process occurs. As the data ascend, each layer strips off the outermost header, acts on the protocol information contained therein, and passes the remainder up to the next layer.

At each stage of the process, a layer may segment the data unit it receives from the next higher layer into several parts, to accommodate its own requirements. These data units must then be reassembled by the corresponding peer layer before being passed up.

When two peer entities wish to exchange data, this may be done with or without a prior *connection*. A connection can exist at any layer of the hierarchy. In the abstract, a connection is established between two (N) entities by identifying a connection endpoint, $(N-1)$ CEP, within an $(N-1)$ SAP for each (N) entity. A connection facilitates flow control and error control. *Flow control* is a function performed by an (N) entity to limit the amount or rate of data it receives from another (N) entity. This function is needed to ensure that the receiving (N) entity does not experience overflow. *Error control* refers to mechanisms to detect and correct errors that occur in the transmission of data units between peer entities.

Multiplexing can occur in two directions. *Upward* multiplexing means that multiple (N) connections are multiplexed on, or share, a single $(N-1)$ connection. This may be needed to make more efficient use of the $(N-1)$ service or to provide several (N) connections in an environment where only a single $(N-1)$ connection exists. *Downward* multiplexing, or *splitting*, means that a single (N) connection is built on top of multiple $(N-1)$ connections, the traffic on the (N) connection being divided among the various $(N-1)$ connections. This technique may be used to improve reliability, performance, or efficiency.

B-3 LAYERS

Physical Layer

The *physical layer* covers the physical interface between devices and the rules by which bits are passed from one to another. The physical layer has four important characteristics:

- Mechanical
- Electrical
- Functional
- Procedural

Examples of standards at this layer are RS-232-C, RS-449/422/423, and portions of X.21.

Data Link Layer

Although the physical layer provides only a raw bit stream service, the *data link layer* attempts to make the physical link reliable and provides the means to activate, maintain, and deactivate the link. The principal service provided by the link layer to the higher layers is that of error detection and control. Thus, with a fully functional data link layer protocol, the next higher layer may assume virtually error-free transmission over the link. If communication is between two systems that are not directly connected, however, the connection will comprise a number of data links in tandem, each functioning independently. Thus, the higher layers are not relieved of an error control responsibility.

Examples of standards at this layer are HDLC, LAP-B, LAP-D, and LLC.

Network Layer

The basic service of the *network layer* is to provide for the transparent transfer of data between transport entities. It relieves the transport layer of the need to know anything about the underlying data transmission and switching technologies used to connect systems. The network service is responsible for establishing, maintaining, and terminating connections across the intervening communications facility.

It is at this layer that the concept of a protocol becomes a little fuzzy. This is best illustrated with reference to Fig. B-4, which shows two stations that are communicating, not via direct link, but via a packet-switched network. The stations have

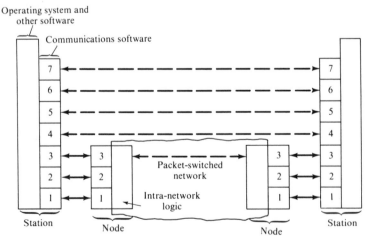

FIGURE B-4   Communication Across a Network

direct links to the network nodes. The layer 1 and 2 protocols are station-node protocols (local). Layers 4 through 7 are clearly protocols between (N) entities in the two stations. Layer 3 is a little bit of both.

The principal dialogue is between the station and its node; the station sends addressed packets to the node for delivery across the network. It requests a virtual circuit connection, uses the connection to transmit data, and terminates the connection. All of this is done by means of a station-node protocol. Because packets are exchanged and virtual circuits are set up between two stations, however, there are aspects of a station-station protocol as well.

There is a spectrum of possibilities for intervening communications facilities to be managed by the network layer. At one extreme, the simplest, there is a direct link between stations. In this case, there may be little or no need for a network layer, because the data link layer can perform the necessary functions of managing the link. Between extremes, the most common use of layer 3 is to handle the details of using a communication network. In this case, the network entity in the station must provide the network with sufficient information to switch and route data to another station. At the other extreme, two stations might wish to communicate but are not even connected to the same network. Rather they are connected to networks that, directly or indirectly, are connected to each other. One approach to providing for data transfer in such a case is to use an internet protocol (IP) that sits on top of a network protocol and is used by a transport protocol. IP is responsible for internetwork routing and delivery, and relies on a layer 3 at each network for intranetwork services. IP is sometimes referred to as "layer 3.5."

The best known example of layer 3 is the X.25 layer 3 standard. The X.25 standard refers to itself as an interface between a station and a node (using our terminology). In the context of the OSI model, it is actually a station-node protocol.

Transport Layer

The purpose of layer 4 is to provide a reliable mechanism for the exchange of data between processes in different systems. The *transport layer* ensures that data units are delivered error-free, in sequence, with no losses or duplications. The transport layer may also be concerned with optimizing the use of network services and providing a requested quality of service to session entities. For example, the session entity might specify acceptable error rates, maximum delay, priority, and security. In effect, the transport layer serves as the user's liaison with the communications facility.

The size and complexity of a transport protocol depends on the type of service it can get from layer 3. For a reliable layer 3 with a virtual circuit capability, a minimal layer 4 is required. If layer 3 is unreliable, the layer 4 protocol should include extensive error detection and recovery. Accordingly, ISO has defined five classes of transport protocol, each oriented toward a different underlying service.

Session Layer

The *session layer* provides the mechanism for controlling the dialogue between presentation entities. At a minimum, the session layer provides a means for two presentation entities to establish and use a connection, called a *session*. In addition it may provide some of the following services:

- *Dialogue type*: This can be two-way simultaneous, two-way alternate, or one-way.
- *Recovery*: The session layer can provide a checkpointing mechanism, so that if a failure of some sort occurs between checkpoints, the session entity can retransmit all data since the last checkpoint.

Presentation Layer

The presentation layer offers application programs and terminal handler programs a set of data transformation services. Services that this layer would typically provide include:

- *Data translation*: Code and character set translation.
- *Formatting*: Modification of data layout.
- *Syntax selection*: Initial selection and subsequent modification of the transformation used.

Examples of presentation protocols are data compression, encryption, and virtual terminal protocol. A virtual terminal protocol converts between specific terminal characteristics and a generic or virtual model used by application programs.

Application Layer

The *application layer* provides a mean for application processes to access the OSI environment. This layer contains management functions and generally useful mechanisms to support distributed applications. Examples of protocols at this level are virtual file protocol and job transfer and manipulation protocol.

B-4   PERSPECTIVES ON THE OPEN SYSTEMS INTERCONNECTION MODEL

Figure B-5 provides two useful perspectives on the OSI architecture. The annotation along the right side suggests viewing the seven layers in three parts. The lower three layers contain the logic for a host to interact with a network. The host is

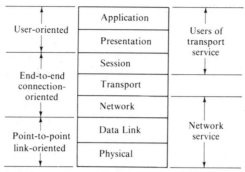

FIGURE B-5 Perspectives on the OSI Architecture

attached physically to the network, uses a data link protocol to reliably communicate with the network, and uses a network protocol to request data exchange with another device on the network and to request network services (e.g., priority). The X.25 standard for packet-switched networks actually encompasses all three layers. Continuing from this perspective, the transport layer provides a reliable end-to-end connection regardless of the intervening network facility. Finally, the upper three layers, taken together, are involved in the exchange of data between end users, making use of a transport connection for reliable data transfer.

Another perspective is suggested by the annotation on the left. Again, consider host systems attached to a common network. The lower two layers deal with the link between the host system and the network. The next three layers are all involved in transfer data from one host to another. The network layer makes use of the communication network facilities to transfer data from one host to another; the transport layer assures that the transfer is reliable; and the session layer manages the flow of data over the logical connection. Finally, the upper two layers are oriented to the user's concerns, including considerations of the application to be performed and any formatting issues.

B-5   RECOMMENDED READING

[STAL87b] provides an in-depth examination of the OSI model, plus a discussion of protocol standards at each layer. [STAL88a] and [TANE81] also cover the OSI model, with more emphasis on the technology of protocols at each layer rather than the standards themselves. A more informal account can be found in [MART81]. Good articles on the subject are [VOEL86}, [ASCH86], and [FOLT81]. [STAL87c] contains reprints of key articles covering OSI and the standards at each layer.

B-6   PROBLEMS

B-1   List the major disadvantages with the layered approach to protocols.

B-2   Based on the principles enunciated in Box B-2, design an architecture with eight layers and make a case for it. Design one with six layers and make a case for that.

B-3   Two blue armies are each poised on opposite hills preparing to attack a single red army in the valley. The red army can defeat either of the blue armies separately but will fail to defeat both blue armies if they attack simultaneously. The blue armies communicate via an unreliable communication system (a foot soldier). The commander, with one of the blue armies, would like to attack at noon. His problem is this: If he sends a message ordering the attack, he cannot be sure it will get through. He could ask for acknowledgment but the acknowledgment might not get through. Is there a protocol that the two blue armies can use to assure victory?

B-4   In Figure B-3, exactly one protocol data unit (PDU) in layer N is encapsulated in a PDU at layer $(N - 1)$. It is also possible to break one N-layer PDU into multiple $(N - 1)$-layer PDUs (segmentation) or to group multiple N-layer PDUs into one $(N - 1)$-layer PDU (blocking).

(a)   In the case of segmentation, is it necessary that each $(N - 1)$-layer PDU contain a copy of the N-layer header?

(b)   In the case of blocking, is it necessary that each N-layer PDU retain its own header, or can the data be consolidated into a single N-layer PDU with a single N-layer header?

B-5   A broadcast network is one in which a transmission from one station is automatically received by all other stations. An example is a local network. Discuss the need or lack of need for a network layer (OSI layer 3) in a broadcast network.

GLOSSARY

Some of the definitions in this glossary are taken from CCITT Recommendation I.112, *Vocabulary of Terms for ISDN*, 1988; these are indicated by a "†" next to the term. Others are taken from U. S. Federal Standard 1037A, *Glossary of Telecommunication Terms*, 1986; these are indicated by a "*" next to the term.

Access Protocol.†   A defined set of procedures that is adopted at an interface at a specified reference point between a user and a network to enable the user to employ the services and/or facilities of that network.

Analog Data.*   Data represented by a physical quantity that is considered to be continuously variable and whose magnitude is made directly proportional to the data or to a suitable function of the data.

Analog Signal.   A continuously varying electromagnetic wave that may be propagated over a variety of media.

Analog Transmission.   The transmission of analog signals without regard to content. The signal may be amplified, but there is no intermediate attempt to recover the data from the signal.

Application Layer.   Layer 7 of the OSI model. This layer determines the interface of the system with the user and provides useful application-oriented services.

Automatic Repeat Request (ARQ).   A feature that automatically initiates a request for retransmission when an error in transmission is detected.

Bandwidth.*   The difference between the limiting frequencies of a continuous frequency band.

Basic Access.†   A term used to describe a simple standardized combination of access channels that constitute the access arrangements for the majority of ISDN users.

Bell Operating Company (BOC).   Before the divestiture of AT&T, the 22 Bell Operating Companies were AT&T subsidiaries that built, operated, and maintained the local and intrastate networks and provided most of the day-to-day service for customers. After divestiture, the BOCs retain their identity within seven regional companies (RBOCs) and are responsible for local service as defined by local access and transport areas (LATAs).

Bit Stuffing. The insertion of extra bits into a data stream to avoid the appearance of unintended control sequences.

Broadband ISDN (BISDN). A second generation of ISDN. The key characteristic of broadband ISDN is that it provides transmission channels capable of supporting rates greater than the primary ISDN rate.

Centrex.† A service offered by operating telephone companies which provides, from the telephone company office, functions and features comparable to those provided by a PBX.

Circuit Switching. A method of communicating in which a dedicated communications path is established between two devices through one or more intermediate switching nodes. Unlike packet switching, digital data are sent as a continuous stream of bits. Data rate is guaranteed, and delay is essentially limited to propagation time.

Codec. Coder-decoder. Transforms analog data into a digital bit stream (coder), and digital signals into analog data (decoder).

Common Carrier. In the United States, companies that furnish long-distance telecommunication services to the public. Common carriers are subject to regulation by federal and state regulatory commissions.

Common Channel Signaling.† A method of signaling in which signaling information relating to a multiplicity of circuits, or function or for network management, is conveyed over a single channel by addressed messages.

Communications Architecture. The hardware and software structure that implements the communications function.

Cyclic Redundancy Check (CRC). An error-detecting code in which the code is the remainder resulting from dividing the bits to be checked by a predetermined binary number.

Data Circuit-Terminating Equipment (DCE). In a data station, the equipment that provides the signal conversion and coding between the data terminal equipment (DTE) and the line. The DCE may be separate equipment or an integral part of the DTE or of intermediate equipment. The DCE may perform other functions that are normally performed at the network end of the line.

Datagram. In packet switching, a self-contained packet, independent of other packets, that does not require acknowledgment and that carries information sufficient for routing from the originating data terminal equipment (DTE), without relying on earlier exchanges between the DTEs and the network.

Data Link Layer. Layer 2 of the OSI model. Converts an unreliable transmission channel into a reliable one.

Data Terminal Equipment (DTE).* Equipment consisting of digital end instruments that convert the user information into data signals for transmission, or reconvert the received data signals into user information.

Digital Data.* Data represented by discrete values or conditions.

Digital PBX. A private branch exchange (PBX) that operates internally on digital signals. Thus, voice signals must be digitized for use in the PBX.

Digital Signal. A discrete or discontinuous signal, such as a sequence of voltage pulses.

Digital Transmission. The transmission of digital data or analog data that have been digitized, using either an analog or digital signal, in which the digital content is recovered and repeated at intermediate points to reduce the effects of impairments, such as noise, distortion, and attenuation.

Digitize.* To convert an analog signal to a digital signal.

Encapsulation.   The addition of control information by a protocol entity to data obtained from a protocol user.

Error Detecting Code.*   A code in which each data signal conforms to specific rules of construction, so that departures from this construction in the received signal can be automatically detected.

Error Rate.*   The ratio of the number of data units in error to the total number of data units.

Exchange Area.   A geographical area within which there is a single uniform set of charges for telephone service. A call between any two points within an exchange area is a local call.

Facsimile.   A system for the transmission of images. The image is scanned at the transmitter, reconstructed at the receiving station and duplicated on some form of paper.

Fast Packet Switching.   An approach to packet switching that attempts to exploit the high capacity of current digital transmission services. Formats and procedures are designed to minimize packet processing time.

Flow Control.   A function performed by a receiving entity to limit the amount or rate of data sent by a transmitting entity.

Frame Check Sequence.   An error-detecting code inserted as a field in a block of data to be transmitted. 'The code serves to check for errors upon reception of the data.

Frequency-Division Multiplexing (FDM).   Division of a transmission facility into two or more channels by splitting the frequency band transmitted by the facility into narrower bands, each of which is used to constitute a distinct channel.

Full-Duplex Transmission.   Transmission of data in both directions at the same time.

Functional Group.†   A set of functions that may be performed by a single equipment.

Half-Duplex Transmission.   Data transmitted in either direction, one direction at a time.

Header.   System-defined control information that precedes user data.

Inchannel Signaling.   A technique in which the same channel is used to carry network control signals as is used to carry the call to which the control signals relate.

Integrated Digital Network (IDN).   The integration of transmission and switching functions using digital technology in a circuit-switched telecommunications network.

Integrated Services Digital Network (ISDN).   Planned worldwide telecommunication service that will use digital transmission and switching technology to support voice and digital data communications.

Layer.   A conceptual region that embodies one or more functions between an upper and a lower logical boundary.

Local Access and Transport Areas (LATA).   A geographic area generally equivalent to a Standard Metropolitan Statistical Area. The territory served by the Bell system was divided into approximately 160 LATAs at divestiture. Intra-LATA services are provided by the Bell Operating Companies.

Local Loop.   A transmission path, generally twisted pair, between the individual subscriber and the nearest switching center of a public telecommunications network. Also referred to as a subscriber loop.

Modem.   Modulator/Demodulator. Transforms a digital bit stream into an analog signal (modulator) and vice versa (demodulator).

Multiplexing.*   In data transmission, a function that permits two or more data sources to share a common transmission medium such that each data source has its own channel.

Network Layer.   Layer 3 of the OSI model. Responsible for routing data through a communication network.

Network Terminating Equipment (NTE). A grouping of ISDN functions at the boundary between the ISDN and the subscriber.

Open Systems Interconnection (OSI) Reference Model. A model of communications between cooperating devices. It defines a 7-layer architecture of communication functions.

Packet Switching. A method of transmitting messages through a communications network, in which long messages are subdivided into short packets. Each packet is passed from source to destination through intermediate nodes. At each node, the entire message is received, stored briefly, and then passed on to the next node.

Physical Layer. Layer 1 of the OSI model. Concerned with the electrical, mechanical, and timing aspects of signal transmission over a medium.

Picture Element (pel). The smallest discrete scanning line sample of a facsimile system, which contains only black/white information (no gray shading information is used).

Piggybacking. The inclusion of an acknowledgment of a previously-received protocol data unit in an outgoing protocol data unit.

Ping-Pong Transmission Technique. See *Time-Compression Multiplexing.*

Pixel. * A picture element that contains gray scale information.

Point-to-point. A configuration in which two stations share a transmission path.

Postal, Telegraph, and Telephone (PTT). A government organization that operates a nationalized public telecommunications network.

Presentation Layer. Layer 6 of the OSI model. Concerned with data format and display.

Private Branch Exchange (PBX). A telephone exchange on the user's premises. Provides a circuit switching facility for telephones on extension lines within the building and access to the public telephone network.

Private Network. A facility in which the customer leases circuits and, sometimes, switching capacity for the customer's exclusive use. Access may be provided to a public switched telecommunications service.

Protocol.† A formal statement of the procedures that are adopted to ensure communication between two or more functions within the same layer of a hierarchy of functions.

Protocol Data Unit (PDU). * Information that is delivered as a unit between peer entities of a network and may contain control information, address information, or data.

Pseudoternary Coding. A form of digital signaling in which three signal levels are used to encode binary data. In ISDN, the form of pseudoternary is one in which binary one is represented by no line signal and binary zero is represented, alternately, by positive and negative voltage pulses.

Public Data Network (PDN). A packet-switched network that is publicly available to subscribers. Usually, the term connotes government control or national monopoly.

Pulse Code Modulation (PCM). A process in which a signal is sampled, and the magnitude of each sample with respect to a fixed reference is quantized and converted by coding to a digital signal.

Recognized Private Operating Agency (RPOA). A private or government-controlled corporation that provides telecommunications services (e.g., AT&T). RPOAs participate as nonvoting members of CCITT.

Reference Configuration.† A combination of functional groups and reference points that shows possible network arrangements.

Reference Point.† A conceptual point at the conjunction of two non-overlapping functional groupings.

Service Access Point (SAP).   A means of identifying a user of the services of a protocol entity. A protocol entity provides one or more SAPs, for use by higher-level entities.

Session Layer.   Layer 5 of the OSI model. Manages a logical connection (session) between two communicating processes or applications.

Signaling.†   The exchange of information specifically concerned with the establishment and control of connections, and with management, in a telecommunication network.

Sliding-Window Technique.   A method of flow control in which a transmitting station may send numbered protocol data units (PDUs) within a window of numbers. The window changes dynamically to allow additional PDUs to be sent.

Software Defined Network (SDN).   A facility based on a public circuit-switched network that gives the user the appearance of a private network. The network is "software defined" in the sense that the user provides the service supplier with entries to a data base used by the supplier to configure, manage, monitor, and report on the operation of the network.

Space-Division Switching.   A circuit-switching technique in which each connection through the switch takes a physically separate and dedicated path.

Specialized Common Carrier.   In the U.S., a telecommunications common carrier other than AT&T and the Bell Operating Companies, authorized to provide a variety of transmission services.

Spectrum.   Refers to an absolute, contiguous range of frequencies.

Subscriber Loop.   See *Local Loop*.

Synchronous Time-Division Multiplexing.   A method of TDM in which time slots on a shared transmission line are assigned to devices on a fixed, predetermined basis.

TDM Bus Switching.   A form of time-division switching in which time slots are used to transfer data over a shared bus between transmitter and receiver.

Teleaction service.†   Telemetry service. A type of telecommunication service that uses short messages, requiring a very low transmission rate, between the user and the network.

Telecommunication Service.†   That which is offered by an Administration or RPOA to its customers in order to satisfy a specific telecommunications requirement. Bearer service, teleservice, and teleaction service are types of telecommunication service.

Telematics.   User-oriented information transfer services, including teletex, videotex, and facsimile.

Teleservice.†   A type of telecommunication service that provides the complete capability, including terminal equipment functions, for communication between users according to protocols established by agreement between Administrations and/or RPOAs.

Teletex.   A text communications service that provides message preparation and transmission facilities.

Teletext.   A one-way information retrieval service. A fixed number of information pages are repetitively broadcast on unused portions of a TV channel bandwidth. A decoder at the TV set is used to select and display pages.

Time Compression Multiplexing.   A means for providing full-duplex digital data transmission over a single twisted pair. Data are buffered at each end and are sent across the line at approximately double the subscriber data rate, with the two ends taking turns.

Time-Division Multiplexing (TDM).   The division of a transmission facility into multiple channels by allotting the facility to different channels, one at a time.

Time-Division Switching.   A circuit-switching technique in which time slots in a time-multiplexed stream of data are manipulated to pass data from an input to an output.

Time-Multiplexed Switching (TMS). A form of space-division switching in which each input line is a TDM stream. The switching configuration may change for each time slot.

Time-Slot Interchange (TSI). The interchange of time slots within a time-division multiplexed frame.

Transport Layer. Layer 4 of the OSI model. Provides reliable, sequenced transfer of data between endpoints.

User-user protocol.† A protocol that is adopted between two or more users in order to ensure communication between them.

Value-Added Network (VAN). A privately-owned packet-switched network whose services are sold to the public.

Videotex. A two-way information retrieval service accessible to terminals and TV sets equipped with a special decoder. Pages of information at a central resource are retrieved interactively over a switched telephone line connection.

Virtual Circuit. A packet-switching mechanism in which a logical connection (virtual circuit) is established between two stations at the start of transmission. All packets follow the same route, need not carry a complete address, and arrive in sequence.

REFERENCES

ABBO84   Abbot, G. "Digital Space Division: A Technique for Switching High-Speed Data Signals." *IEEE Communications Magazine*, April 1984.

AHUJ83   Ahuja, V. *Design and Analysis of Computer Communication Networks*. New York: McGraw-Hill, 1983.

AMAN86   Amand, J. *A Guide to Packet-Switched, Value-Added Networks*. New York: Macmillan, 1986.

ANDR87   Andrich, W.; Bostelmann, G.; and Weygang, A. "Concept and Realization of the Broadband ISDN." **Electrical Communcation,** No. 1, 1987.

AOYA88   Aoyama, T.; Daumer, W.; and Modena, G., eds. *Special Issue on Voice Coding for Communications. IEEE Journal on Selected Areas in Communications*, February 1988.

APPE86   Appenzeller, H. "Signaling System No. 7 ISDN User Part." *IEEE Journal on Selected Areas in Communications*, May 1986.

ARMB86   Armbruster, H. "Applications of Future Broad-Band Services in the Office and Home." *IEEE Journal on Selected Areas in Communications*, July 1986.

ARMB87   Armbruster, H. "Broadband Communication and Its Realization with Broadband ISDN." *IEEE Communications Magazine*, November 1987.

ASCH86   Aschenbrenner, J. *Open Systems Interconnection*. IBM Systems Journal, Nos. 3/4, 1986.

ATT61   American Telephone and Telegraph Co. *Principles of Electricity Applied to Telephone and Telegraph Work*, 1961.

ATT87   American Telephone and Telegraph Co. *ISDN Planners Guide. AT&T Network Systems Marketing Communications*, 1987.

BARC81   Barcomb, D. Office Automation. Bedford, MA: *Digital Press*, 1981.

BART86   Bartee, T. *Digital Communications*. Indianapolis, In: Sams, 1986.

BAUW87   Bauwens, J., and Prycker, M. "Broadband Experiment Using Asynchronous Time Division Techniques." **Electrical Communication,** No. 1, 1987.

BELL82a   Bell Telephone Laboratories. *Transmission Systems for Communications*. Murray Hill, NJ, 1982.

BELL82b   Bellamy, J. *Digital Telephony*. New York: Wiley, 1982.

BELL84   Bellchanbers, W.; Francis, J.; Hummel, E.; and Nickelson, R. "The International Telecommunication Union and Development of Worldwide Telecommunications." *IEEE Communications Magazine*, May 1984.

BELL86   Bell, P., and Jabbour, K. "Review of Point-to-Point Routing Algorithms." *IEEE Communications Magazine*, January 1986.

BERL87   Berlekamp, E.; Peile, R.; and Pope, S. "The Application of Error Control to Communications." *IEEE Communications Magazine*, April 1987.

BERT87   Bertsekas, D., and Gallager, R. *Data Networks*. Englewood Cliffs, NJ: Prentice-Hall, 1987.

BEVA86   Bevan, M. "Image Processing May Cause Future Problems with Network Loading." Data Communications, March 1986.

BHUS83   Bhusri, G. "Optimum Implementation of Common Channel Signaling in Local Networks." *Proceedings of IEEE INFOCOM 83*, 1983.

BLAC87   Black, U. *Computer Networks: Protocols, Standards, and Interfaces*. Englewood Cliffs, NJ: Prentice-Hall, 1987.

BODS86   Bodson, D., and Randall, N. "Analysis of Group 4 Facsimile Throughput." *IEEE Transactions on Communications*, September 1986.

BROO83   Broomell, G., and Heath, J. "Classification Categories and Historical Development of Circuit Switching Topologies." *ACM Computing Surveys*. June 1983.

BROW86   Browne, T. "Network of the Future." *Proceedings of the IEEE*, September 1986.

BURG83   Burg, F. "Design Considerations for Using the X.25 Packet Layer on Data Terminal Equipment." *Proceedings, IEEE INFOCOM 83*, 1983.

CARL80   Carlson, D. "Bit-Oriented Data Link Control Procedures." *IEEE Transactions on Communications*, April 1980.

CASA87   Casali, F., and Treves, S. "Towards the Integrated Broadband Communication Network." **Electrical Communication,** No. 1, 1987.

CERN84   Cerni, D. *Standards in Process: Foundations and Profiles of ISDN and OSI Studies. National Telecommunications and Information Administration, Report 84-170*, December 1984.

CHEN87   Chen, P. "How to Make the Most of ISDN's New LAPD Protocol." *Data Communications*, August 1987.

CHOU85   Chou, W., ed. *Computer Communications*, Volume II: *Systems and Applications*. Englewood Cliffs, NJ: Prentice-Hall, 1985

COCH85   Cochrane, J.; Falconer, W.; Mummert, V.; and Strich, W. "Latest Network Trends." *IEEE Communications Magazine*, October 1985.

COLL83   Collie, B. "Looking at the ISDN Interfaces: Issues and Answers." *Data Communications*, June 1983.

COOK84   Cooke, R. "Intercity Limits: Looking Ahead to All-Digital Networks and No Bottlenecks." *Data Communications*, March 1984.

COOL87   Cooley, K.; Goodman, M.; Kerner, H.; and Simmons, D. "Wideband Virtual Networks." *Telecommunications*, February 1987.

CUNN84   Cunningham, I. "Electronic Mail Standards to Get Rubber-Stamped and Go Worldwide." *Data Communications*, May 1984.

CUNN85   Cunningham, I., and Kerr, I. "New Electronic Mail Standards." *Telecommunications*, July 1985.

DAVI73   Davies, D., and Barber, D. *Communication Networks for Computers*. New York: Wiley, 1973.

DECI82 Decina, M. "Progress Toward User Access Arrangements in Integrated Services Digital Networks." *IEEE Transactions on Communications*, September 1982.

DECI86a Decina, M.; Gifford, W.; Potter, R.; and Robrock, A. *Special Issue on Integrated Services Digital Network: Recommendations and Field Trials. IEEE Journal on Selected Areas in Communications*, May 1986.

DECI86b Decina, M.; Gifford, W.; Potter, R.; and Robrock, A. *Special Issue on Integrated Services Digital Network: Technology and Implementations. IEEE Journal on Selected Areas in Communications*, November 1986.

DEUT86 Deutsch, D. "Electronic Mail Systems." In [BART86].

DHAS86 Dhas, C., and Konangi, U. "X.25: An Interface to Public Packet Networks." *IEEE Communications Magazine*, September 1986.

DONO86 Donohoe, D.; Johannessen, G.; and Stone, R. "Realization of a Signaling System No. 7 Network for AT&T." *IEEE Journal on Selected Areas in Communications*, November 1986.

DORR83 Dorros, I. "Telephone Nets Go Digital." *IEEE Spectrum*, April 1983.

DUC85 Duc, N., and Chew, E. "ISDN Protocol Architecture." *IEEE Communications Magazine*, March 1985.

ERDE86 Erdelyi, B., and Batista, J. "Implementation and Verification of X.25 Packet Data Networks." *Proceedings, Fifth Annual International Phoenix Conference on Computers and Communications*, March 1986.

ERIK86 Eriksen, W. "The How and Where of Switched 56-kbit/s Service." *Data Communications*, August 1986.

FALC82 Falconer, D. "Adaptive Reference Echo Cancellation." *IEEE Transactions on Communications*, September 1982.

FALE87 Falek, J., and Johnston, M. "Standards Makers Cementing ISDN Subnetwork Layers." *Data Communications*, October 1987.

FOLT81 Folts, H. "Coming of Age: A Long-Awaited Standard for Heterogeneous Nets." *Data Communications*, January 1981.

FRAN84 Frank, C. "Legal and Policy Ramifications of the Emerging Integrated Services Digital Network." *Journal of Telecommunication Networks*, Spring 1984.

FREE80 Freeman, R. *Telecommunication System Engineering.* New York: Wiley, 1980.

FREE85 Freeman, R. *Telecommunications Engineering.* New York: Wiley, 1985.

GAGG87 Gaggioni, H. "The Evolution of Video Technologies." *IEEE Communications Magazine*, November 1987.

GALL68 Gallager, R. *Information Theory and Reliable Communication.* New York: Wiley, 1968.

GAWD86 Gawdun, M. "Virtual Private Networks." *Telecommunications*, April 1986.

GERL80 Gerla, M., and Kleinrock, L. "Flow Control: A Comparative Survey." *IEEE Transactions on Communications*, April 1980.

GERL81 Gerla, M. "Routing and Flow Control." In [KUO81].

GERL84 Gerla, M. "Controlling Routes, Traffic Rates, and Buffer Allocation in Packet Networks." *IEEE Communications Magazine*, November 1984.

GERW84 Gerwen, P.; Verhoeckx, N.; and Claasen, T. "Design Considerations for a 144 kbit/s Digital Transmission Unit for the Local Telephone Network." *IEEE Journal on Selected Areas in Communications*, March 1984.

GIFF86 Gifford, W. "ISDN User-Network Interfaces." *IEEE Journal on Selected Areas in Communications*, May 1986.

GILH87 Gilhooly, D. "Towards the Intelligent Network." *Telecommunications*, December 1987.

GLEN86 Glen, D. Networks, *Signaling, and Switching for Post-Divestiture and the ISDN. National Telecommunications and Information Administration Report 86-191*, February 1986.

GREE77 Greene, W., and Pooch, U. "A Review of Classification Schemes for Computer Communication Networks." *Computer*, November 1977.

GREE87 Green, P., and Godard, D. "Prospects and Design Choices for Integrated Private Networks." **IBM Systems Journal**, No. 1 1987.

GRIF87 Griffiths, G., and Stones, C. "The Tea-Leaf Reader Algorithm: An Efficient Implementation of CRC-16 and CRC-32." *Communications of the ACM, July* 1987.

HARI86 Haring, J. "The Political Economy of Telecommunications Regulation." *Proceedings of the IEEE*, September 1986.

HARR86 Harrington, E.; Cipriano, G.; and Micheroni, V. "Public Switched 56-kbps Networks." *Telecommunications*, March 1986.

HASK81 Haskell, B., and Steele, R. "Audio and Video Bit-Rate Reduction." *Proceedings of the IEEE*, February 1981.

HASK87 Haskell, B.; Pearson, D.; and Yamamoto, H., eds. *Low Bit-Rate Coding of Moving Images. Special issue of IEEE Journal on Selected Areas in Communications*, August 1987.

HELM82 Helmrich, H., and Bartuska, P. "Teletex: More than a Speedy Alternative to Aging Telex." *Data Communications*, February 1982.

HIRS85 Hirschheim, R. *Office Automation.* Reading, MA: Addison-Wesley, 1985.

HOBE83 Hoberecht, W. "A Layered Network Protocol for Packet Voice and Data Integration." *IEEE Journal on Selected Areas in Communications*, December 1983.

HODG87 Hodges, P. "Three Decades by the Numbers." *Datamation*, September 15, 1987.

HOLM83 Holmes, E. "A Closer Look at AT&T's New High-Speed Digital Services." *Data Communications*, July 1983.

HORA84 Horak, W. "Concepts of the Document Interchange Protocol for the Telematic Services CCITT Draft Recommendation S.A." **Computer Networks**, 8, 1984.

HORA85 Horak, W. "Office Document Architecture and Office Document Interchange Formats: Current Status of International Standardization." *Computer*, October 1985.

HSIE84a Hsieh,W., and Gitman, I. "Routing Strategies in Computer Networks." *Computer*, June 1984.

HSIE84b Hsieh, W., and Gitman, I. "How to Prevent Congestion in Computer Networks." *Data Communications*, June 1984.

HUI87 Hui, J. and Arthurs, E. "A Broadband Packet Switch for Integrated Transport." *IEEE Journal on Selected Areas in Communications*, October 1987.

HUMM85 Hummel, E. "The CCITT." *IEEE Communications Magazine*, January 1985.

HURL87 Hurley, B.; Seid, C.; and Sewell, W. "A Survey of Dynamic Routing Methods for Circuit-Switched Traffic." *IEEE Communications Magazine*, September 1987.

INOS79 Inose, H. *An Introduction to Digital Integrated Communications Systems.* University of Tokyo Press, 1979.

ISO84 *International Organization for Standardization. Basic Reference Model for Open Systems Interconnection.* ISO 7498, 1984.

JAYA84 Jayant, N., and Noll, P. *Digital Coding of Waveforms.* Englewood Cliffs, NJ: Prentice-Hall, 1984.

JAYA86 Jayant, N. "Coding Speech at Low Bit Rates." *IEEE Spectrum*, August 1986.

JULI86 Julio, U., and Pellegrini, J. "Layer 1 ISDN Recommendations." *IEEE Journal on Selected Areas in Communications*, May 1986.

KADE81 Kaderali, F., and Weston, J. "Digital Subscriber Loops." **Electrical Communication**, Vol. 56, No. 1 1981.

KAHL86 Kahl, P. "A Review of CCITT Standardization to Date." *IEEE Journal on Selected Areas in Communications*, May 1986.

KANE80 Kaneko, H., and Ishigura, T. "Digital Television Transmission Using Bandwidth Compression Techniques." *IEEE Communications Magazine*, July 1980.

KANO86 Kano, S. "Layers 2 and 3 ISDN Recommendations." *IEEE Journal on Selected Areas in Communications*, May 1986.

KEIS85 Keiser, B., and Strange, E. *Digital Telephony and Network Integration.* New York: Van Nostrand Reinhold, 1985.

KELC83 Kelcourse, F., and Siegel, E. "Switched Digital Capability: An Overview." *IEEE Communications Magazine*, January 1983.

KIM86 Kim, K., and Li, P. "Video Telephone: Gone Today, Here Tomorrow?" *Data Communications*, November 1986.

KIMB75 Kimbleton, S., and Schneider, F. "Computer Communication Networks: Approaches, Objectives, and Performance Considerations." *ACM Computing Surveys*, September 1975.

KLEI76 Kleinrock, L. *Queuing Systems, Vol. II: Computer Applications.* New York: Wiley, 1976.

KLEI78 Kleinrock, L. "Principles and Lessons in Packet Communications." *Proceedings of the IEEE*, November 1978.

KOBA85 Kobayashi, K. "Advances in Facsimile Art." *IEEE Communications Magazine*, February 1985.

KUMM80 Kummede, K., and Rudin, H. "Packet and Circuit Switching: Cost/Performance Boundaries." *Computer Networks*, No. 2, 1980

KUO81 Kuo, F., ed. *Protocols and Techniques for Data Communication Networks.* Englewood Cliffs, NJ: Prentice-Hall, 1981.

LECH86 Lechleider, J. "Loop Transmission Aspects of ISDN Basic Access." *IEEE Journal on Selected Areas in Communications*, November 1986.

LEE86 Lee, E. "A BOC Explains Where the Bits Went." *Data Communications*, June 1986.

LIN84 Lin, S.; Costello, D.; and Miller, M. "Automatic Repeat-Request Error-Control Schemes." *IEEE Communications Magazine*, December 1984.

LIN88 Lin, N., and Tzeng, C. "Full-Duplex Data Over Local Loops." *IEEE Communications Magazine*, February 1988.

LUET86 Luetchford, J. "CCITT Recommendations on the ISDN: A Review." *IEEE Journal on Selected Areas in Communications*, May 1986.

MARI79 Marill, T. "Why the Telephone Is on Its Way Out and Electronic Mail is on Its Way In." *Datamation*, August 1979.

MART73 Martin, J. *Security, Accuracy, and Privacy in Computer Systems.* Englewood Cliffs, NJ: Prentice-Hall, 1973.

MART81 Martin, J. *Computer Networks and Distributed Processing.* Englewood Cliffs, NJ: Prentice-Hall, 1981.

MARU83 Maruyama, K., and Shorter, D. "Dynamic Route Selection Algorithms for Session-Based Communication Networks." *Computer Communication Review*, April 1983.

MCNA88 McNamara, J. *Technical Aspects of Data Communication*, Third Edition. Bedford, MA: Digital Press, 1988.

MCQU80 McQuillan, J.; Richer, L.; and Rosen, E. "The New Routing Algorithm for the ARPANET." *IEEE Transactions on Communications*, May 1980.

MCQU85 McQuillan, J. and Herman, J. "Problems and Opportunities in Advanced Data Net Architectures." *Data Communications*, November 1985.

MESS84a Messerschmitt, D. "Echo Cancellation in Speech and Data Transmission." *IEEE Journal on Selected Areas in Communications*, March 1984.

MESS84b Messerschmitt, D. *Special Issue on Applications of Digital Signal Processing in Communications. IEEE Journal on Selected Areas in Communications*, March 1984.

MESS86 Messerschmitt, D. "Design Issues in the ISDN U-Interface Transceiver." *IEEE Journal on Selected Areas in Communications*, November 1986.

MINZ87 Minzer, S. "Toward an International Broadband ISDN Standard." *Telecommunications*, October 1987.

MIYA75 Miyahura, H.; Hasegawa, T.; and Teshigawara, Y. "A Comparative Evaluation of Switching Methods in Computer Communication Networks." *Proceedings, International Communications Conference*, 1975.

MOOR83 Moore, D. "Teletex A Worldwide Link Among Office Systems for Electronic Document Exchange." **IBM Systems Journal,** Nos. 1/2, 1983.

MULL87 Muller, N. "ADPCM Offers Practical Method for Doubling T1 Capacity." *Data Communications*, February 1987.

MURA87 Murakami, H.; Matsumoto, S.; Hatori, Y.; and Yamamoto, H. "15/30 Mbit/s Universal Digital TV Codec Using a Median Adaptive Predictive Coding Method." *IEEE Transactions on Communications*, June 1987.

NEME85 Nemeth, K. "Principles of the Document Interchange Protocol for CCITT Telematic Services." *IEEE Communications Magazine*, March 1985.

NETR80 Netravali, A., and Limb, J. "Picture Coding: A Review." *Proceedings of the IEEE*, March 1980.

NETR88 Netravati, A., and Haskell, B. *Digital Pictures: Representation and Compression*. New York: Plenum, 1988.

NOJI86 Nojima, S.; Hashimoto, M.; Fuduka, H.; and Tsutsui, E. "High Speed Packet Switching Network for Multi-Media Information." *Proceedings, Computer Networking Symposium*, November 1986.

NOJI87 Nojima, S.; Tsutsui, E.; Fuduka, H.; and Hashimoto, M. "Integrated Services Packet Network Using Bus Matrix Switch." *IEEE Journal on Selected Areas in Communications*, October 1987.

NSPA79 National Standards Policy Advisory Committee. National Policy on Standards for the United States. 1979. Reprinted in [CERN84].

OHNS86 Ohnsorge, H., ed. Special Issue on Broad-Band Communications Systems. *IEEE Journal on Selected Areas in Communications*, July 1986.

PAND87 Pandhi, S. "The Universal Data Connection." *IEEE Spectrum*, July 1987.

PERE83 Perez, A. "Byte-wise CRC Calculations." *IEEE Micro*, June 1983.

PETE61 Peterson, W., and Brown, D. "Cyclic Codes for Error Detection." *Proceedings of the IRE*, January 1961.

PHEL86 Phelan, J. "Signaling System 7." *Telecommunications*, September 1986.

POPE84 Pope, A. "Encoding CCITT Presentation Transfer Syntax." *Computer Communication Review*, October 1984.

POTT77 Potter, R. "Electronic Mail." *Science*, March 19, 1977.

POTT85   Potter, R. "ISDN Protocol and Architecture Models." *Computer Networks and ISDN Systems*, No. 10, 1985.

POUZ81   Pouzin, L. "Methods, Tools, and Observations on Flow Control in Packet-Switched Data Networks." *IEEE Transactions on Communications*, April 1981.

PRAT80   Pratt, W., et al. "Combined Symbol Matching Facsimile Data Compression Systems." *Proceedings of the IEEE*, July 1980.

QUAR86   Quarterman, J. and Hoskins, J. "Notable Computer Networks." *Communications of the ACM*, October 1986.

RAAC84   Raack, G.; Sable, E.; and Stewart, R. "Customer Control of Network Services." *IEEE Communications Magazine*, October 1984.

RAHN88   Rahnnema, M., "Smart Trunk Scheduling Strategies for Future Integrated Services Packet-Switched Networks." *IEEE Communications Magazine*, February 1988.

REY83   Rey, R., editor, *Engineering and Operations in the Bell System*, Second Edition. Murray Hill, NJ: AT&T Bell Laboratories, 1983.

RIND79   Rinde, J., and Caisse, A. "Passive Flow Control Techniques for Distributed Networks." *Proceedings, IRIA Flow Control and Computer Networks Conference*, 1979.

ROBE78   Roberts, L. "The Evolution of Packet Switching." *Proceedings of the IEEE*, November 1978.

ROBI84   Robin, G. "Customer Installations for the ISDN." *IEEE Communications Magazine*, April 1984.

ROBI86   Robinson, R. "Digital Voice Compression." *Telecommunications*, February 1986.

ROEH85   Roehr, W. "Inside SS No. 7: A Detailed Look at ISDN's Signaling System Plan." *Data Communications*, October 1985.

RONA87   Ronayne, J. *The Integrated Services Digital Network: From Concept to Application*. London: Pitman, 1987.

ROSN82   Rosner, R. *Packet Switching: Tomorrow's Communications Today*. Belmont, CA: Lifetime Learning, 1982.

RUFF87   Ruffalo, D. "Understanding T1 Basics: Primer Offers Picture of Networking Future." *Data Communications*, March 1987.

RUMS86   Rumsey, D. "Support of Existing Data Interfaces by the ISDN." *IEEE Journal on Selected Areas in Communications*, May 1986.

RUTK82   Rutkowski, A., and Marcus, M. "The Integrated Services Digital Network: Developments and Regulatory Issues." *Computer Communication Review*, July/October 1982.

RUTK85   Rutkowski, A. *Integrated Services Digital Networks*. Dedham, MA: Artech House, 1985.

RYAN87   Ryan, D. "Making Sense of Today's Image Communications Alternatives." *Data Communications*, April 1987.

SABR84   Sabri, S. and Prasada, B. "Coding of Broadcast TV Signals for Transmission Over Satellite Channels." *IEEE Transactions on Communications*, December 1984.

SAND80   Sanders, R. "Effects of Switching Technologies on Network Delay." *Data Communications*, April 1980.

SAZE87   Sazegari, S. "Network Architects Plan Broadening of Future ISDN," *Data Communications*, July 1987.

SCAC86   Scace, E. "Integrated Services Digital Networks." In [BART86].

SCHL86   Schlanger, G. "An Overview of Signaling System No. 7." *IEEE Journal on Selected Areas in Communications*, May 1986.

SCHU87   Schutt, T; Staton, J.; and Racke, W. "Message-Handling Systems Based on the CCITT X.400 Recommendations." **IBM Systems Journal,** No. 3, 1987.

SCHW77   Schwartz, M. *Computer-Communication Network Design and Analysis.* Englewood Cliffs, NJ: Prentice-Hall, 1977.

SCHW80   Schwartz, M. and Stern, T. "Routing Techniques Used in Computer Communication Networks." *IEEE Transactions on Communications*, April 1980.

SHNE84   Shneiderman, B. "Response Time and Display Rate in Human Performance with Computers." *Computing Surveys*, September 1984.

SILV87   Silver, D., and Williamson, J. "Data-Compression Chip Eases Document-Processing Design." *Computer Design*, November 15, 1987.

SIRB85   Sirbu, M., and Zwimpfer, L. "Standards Setting for Computer Communication: The Case of X.25." *IEEE Communications Magazine*, March 1985.

STAL86   Stallings, W. "Here is One Way to Get a Close Estimate of a Data Link's Efficiency." *Data Communications*, October 1986.

STAL87a   Stallings, W. *Computer Organization and Architecture*, New York: Macmillan, 1987.

STAL87b   Stallings, W. *Handbook of Computer-Communications Standards, Volume I: The Open Systems Interconnection (OSI) Model and OSI-related Standards.* New York: Macmillan, 1987

STAL87c   Stallings, W. *Computer Communications: Architectures, Protocols, and Standards, Second Edition.* Washington, DC: IEEE Computer Society Press, 1987.

STAL88a   Stallings, W. *Data and Computer Communications, Second Edition.* New York: Macmillan, 1988.

STAL88b   Stallings, W. *Integrated Services Digital Networks (ISDN).* Washington, DC: IEEE Computer Society Press, 1988.

STAL90   Stallings, W. *Business Data Communications.* New York: Macmillan, 1990.

STEN86   Stenger, L. "Digital Coding of TV Signals For ISDN-B Applications." *IEEE Journal on Selected Areas in Communications*, July 1986.

STUC85   Stuck, B. and Arthurs, E. *A Computer Communications Network Performance Primer.* Englewood Cliffs, NJ: Prentice-Hall, 1985.

SUGI88   Sugimoto, M.; Taniguchi, M.; Yokoi, S.; and Hata, H. "Videotex: Advancing to Higher Bandwidth." *IEEE Communications Magazine*, February 1988.

SZEC86   Szechenyi, K.; Zapf, F.; and Sallaerts, D. "Integrated Full Digital U-Interface Circuit for ISDN Subscriber Loops." *IEEE Journal on Selected Areas in Communications*, November 1986.

TAKE87   Takeuchi, T.; Yamaguchi, T.; Niwa, H.; Suzuki, H.; and Hayano, S. "Synchronous Composite Packet Switching A Switching Architecture for Broadband ISDN." *IEEE Journal on Selected Areas in Communications*, October 1987.

TANE81   Tanebaum, A. *Computer Networks.* Englewood Cliffs, NJ: Prentice-Hall, 1981.

TAO84   Tao, Y.; Kolwicz,D.; Gritton, C.; and Duttweiler, D. "A Cascadable VLSI Echo Canceller." *IEEE Journal on Selected Areas in Communications*, March 1984.

THAD81   Thadhani, A. "Interactive User Productivity." **IBM Systems Journal,** No. 4, 1981.

TURN86   Turner, J. "Design of an Integrated Services Packet Network." *IEEE Journal on Selected Areas in Communications*, November 1986.

TYME81 Tymes, L. "Routing and Flow Control in TYMENET." *IEEE Transactions on Communications*, April 1981.

VAUG59 Vaughan, H. "Research Model for Time Separation Integrated Communication." *Bell System Technical Journal*, July 1959.

VOEL86 Voelcker, J. "Helping Computers Communicate." *IEEE Spectrum*, March 1986.

WEIN87 Weinstein, S. "Telecommunications in the Coming Decades." *IEEE Spectrum*, November 1987.

WHIT87 White, P.; Hui, J.; Decina, M.; and Yatsuboshi, R. *Special Issue on Switching Systems for Broadband Networks. IEEE Journal on Selected Areas in Communications*, October 1987.

WOOD85 Wood, D. "Computer Networks." In [CHOU85].

WYND82 Wyndrum, R., ed. *Special Issue on Subscriber Loops. IEEE Transactions on Communications*, September 1982.

YASU80 Yasuda, Y. "Overview of Digital Facsimile Coding Techniques in Japan." *Proceedings of the IEEE*, July 1980.

YUM87 Yum, T., and Schwartz, M. "Comparison of Routing Procedures for Circuit-Switched Traffic in Nonhierarchical Networks." *IEEE Transactions on Communications*, May 1987.

INDEX

College Division
Macmillan Publishing Company
Front & Brown Streets
Riverside, NJ 08075

ORDER FORM

Ship To:
(Please print or type)

Name _____

Co. _____

Address _____

_____

City _____ St _____ Zip _____

Bill To:
(If different from shipping address)

Name _____

Co. _____

Address _____

_____

City _____ St _____ Zip _____

Mail your order to the above address or call 800-548-9939 (in New Jersey call 609-461-6500) or Fax 609-461-9265

Shipping Method **(select one)**
_____ UPS Ground _____ 2nd Day Air _____ Book Rate

Payment Method **(select one)**	
_____ Check	_____ Visa
_____ Bill Me	_____ MasterCard

_____
Authorized Signature

_____   _____
Card Number   Exp Date

(continued)

TEAR OUT THIS PAGE TO ORDER OTHER TITLES BY WILLIAM STALLINGS:

SEQ.	QTY.	ISBN NO.	TITLE	PRICE	TOTAL
1	_____	002-415491-1	Computer Organization & Architecture 2/e	$55.00	_____
2	_____	002-415451-2	Data and Computer Communications 2/e	59.00	_____
3	_____	002-415531-4	Local Networks 3/e	40.00	_____
4	_____	002-415431-8	Business Data Communications	43.00	_____
5	_____	002-415471-7	ISDN	48.00	_____

PSR-PSL 350-3500 Offer #33705   FC# 1433

Handbooks of Computer Communications Standards: (Available through Howard Sams & Co.)

6	_____	0-672-22697-9	Volume 1, The Open Systems Interconnection (OSI) Model and OSI-Related Standards, 2/e	34.95	_____
7	_____	0-672-22698-7	Volume 2, Local Area Network Standards, 2/e	34.95	_____
8	_____	0-672-22696-0	Volume 3, The TCP/IP Protocol Suite, 2/e	34.95	_____

GRAND TOTAL _____

A small shipping charge will be added. Prices subject to change without prior notification.

TRSHTS;0368A   JMM   10:22   11-06-89   P0001   U1   C1954   0008

LIST OF ACRONYMS

ARQ	Automatic Repeat Request
B8ZS	Bipolar with 8-Zeros Substitution
BISDN	Broadband ISDN
BOC	Bell Operating Companies
CCITT	International Telegraph and Telephone Consultative Committee
CRC	Cyclic Redundancy Check
DCE	Data Circuit-Terminating Equipment
DTE	Data Terminal Equipment
DNHR	Dynamic Nonhierarchical Routing
FCS	Frame Check Sequence
FDM	Frequency-Division Multiplexing
HDB3	High-Density Bipolar — 3 zeros
HDLC	High-level Data Link Control
IDN	Integrated Digital Network
ISDN	Integrated Services Digital Network
ISO	International Organization for Standardization
ISUP	ISDN User Part
LAN	Local Area Network